Yours truly
P. H. Fisher

Ætat 92.

Notes and Recollections

of

Stroud

By

Paul Hawkins Fisher

ALAN SUTTON
1986

Alan Sutton Publishing Limited
30 Brunswick Road
Gloucester
GL1 1JJ

Copyright © in introduction 1975 N.M. Herbert

First published 1871
This edition first published 1891
Reprinted with new introduction 1975
Reprinted 1986

ISBN 0 86299 316 4

Printed in Great Britain
By the Guernsey Press Co. Ltd.
Guernsey C.I.

Notes and Recollections of Stroud.

◆

INTRODUCTION

In the year 1871 the people of Stroud were conducted on a tour of their town by one of its oldest inhabitants. At many of the houses he stopped to tell them something of former occupants and at several corners of the old town he recalled buildings and other features that had long since vanished. The temptation to tell once again his favourite stories of amusing incidents and personalities was not resisted, and his reminiscences sometimes took him so far from his place in the itinerary that his hearers began to wonder if they would ever complete it. But they listened with interest and were tolerant of his digressions, for their guide, Paul Hawkins Fisher, was over 90 years old and he spoke of a time of which many of them had no memory—when their town was much smaller and more introspective in character, its people less educated and more superstitious, its streets unpaved and unlit, and its link with the outside world by coach and carrier's wagon along ill-made roads.

The tour was of course made only in the pages of *Notes and Recollections of Stroud*, though the nonagenarian author, whose 'unimpaired faculties, light and sprightly step, and animated conversational powers were those of a man five-and-twenty years younger',[1] could no doubt still have conducted it in person. He was born at Stroud in 1779[2] into a family of fairly prosperous tradesmen. His father Benjamin Fisher, a currier, came to settle in the town from Gloucester in 1763, the year that he married Margaret White, daughter of a Newent tanner.[3] They had eleven children, all but two of them boys. Paul was the seventh son. Most of his older brothers went into trade in Stroud or neighbouring towns, two as curriers, another as a grocer, and another as a maltster,[4] Paul, who completed his

1 *Stroud Journal Jubilee Supplement* (1904).
2 Details of the Fisher family are from the Stroud and Newent parish registers (in Gloucestershire Records Office), a monument in Stroud parish church and tombstone in Holy Trinity churchyard, and pedigrees which Major C. A. Fisher, of Lasborough Manor, kindly allowed me to see.
3 Gloucester Diocesan Registry wills 1784/108; *Notes and Recollections* (1891 edn.), 13.
4 Glos. R. O., D 44A/37.

education at the College School, Gloucester,[1] became an attorney at Stroud, forming a partnership with a younger brother Samuel.[2] He was probably well established in his profession by 1809 when he bought one of the larger houses of the town, the Castle,[3] his home until his death in 1873.

Fisher's first wife Janet Travers, apparently the daughter of a director of the East India Company, died young, and he married secondly, in 1824, Anne Colborne of an old-established Stroud family; her father had been rector of Syde parish[4] and her grandfather a Stroud attorney. Fisher and Anne had three sons, of whom the eldest, Charles Hawkins, became an authority on falconry. Perhaps by his marriages as much as by success in his profession Fisher became fairly prosperous; before 1838 he bought a considerable estate in Newent,[5] his mother's parish, and in 1845 he became the owner of one of the large Woodchester cloth-mills on which he had held a mortgage.[6]

An attorney in a small town was involved in local affairs at all levels, his work ranging from estate business for local landowners to poor-law litigation for the parish. It was a profession that, almost as much as that of clergyman or surgeon, gave a detailed knowledge of the workings of the town. Fisher was not one of those who, like the banker Joseph Grazebrook or the brewer Joseph Watts, stand out in the history of the changes and improvements in Stroud at the period; nevertheless he played a modest role in public affairs, acting for example as a trustee of one of the town charities,[7] as secretary of the Stroud Institution founded in 1835,[8] and as a member of the committee of the Stroud Hospital.[9] He gained a respected position in the town, which was enhanced as his longevity made him something of a survivor from another age. When the parish church was rebuilt in 1866 he was chosen, with the millowner and former M.P., W. H. Stanton, to lay the foundation stone.[10]

Fisher acquired a reputation for his knowledge of the town's past and this, coupled with the literary ambitions manifested earlier in prologues for amateur theatricals and in

1 *Stroud Jnl.*, Fisher's 'Reminiscences', no. xix.
2 *Pigot's Directory* (1822–3), 63.
3 Glos. R. O., D 1842/T2.
4 Hockaday Abstracts (Gloucester Library), volume cccxxxviii.
5 Glos. R. O., P 225/SD 1; D 1842/E 2.
6 Ibid. D 44A/59.
7 Ibid. D 914/22.
8 *Notes and Recollections*, 170.
9 *Stroud Jnl.* 11 Oct. 1873 (obituary of P.H.F.). He gave the proceeds from *Notes and Recollections* to the hospital.
10 *Notes and Recollections*, 309.

the editing of a periodical miscellany called the *Gloucestershire Repository*,[1] led to his writings on Stroud. Between 1860 and 1865 he wrote for the *Stroud Journal*, under the style of 'An Old Inhabitant', a long series of articles entitled 'Reminiscences of Stroud and its Vicinity'. These articles, with some minor alterations and some additional material,[2] were later formed into *Notes and Recollections of Stroud, Gloucestershire*, published in 1871. Fisher made some revisions to the book before his death and a second edition, with some notes added by his son Charles, appeared in 1891.

Although popularly known as 'Fisher's History of Stroud', the book, as its correct title implies, is something other than the conventional Victorian town history. It concerns itself mainly with the period of the author's lifetime and is based very largely on his own reminiscences. This is particularly true of the early chapters in which Fisher perambulates the town, recalling incidents and personalities and detailing the changes he had seen; the method is haphazard and discursive but we gain from these chapters a comprehensive picture of the town, an evocation of its character, and, by the way, much concrete information about such things as coach-services, banks, and charity schools. The later chapters dealing with particular topics, generally adopt a more conventional historical approach and are less entertaining though still valuable. Fisher made careful use of such documentary evidence as was then available for the more ancient history of the town and he is difficult to fault on the score of accuracy; his profession, of course, made him familiar with many of the documentary sources.

But it is his own recollections that I think set the book above most contemporary town histories. So often their authors lost sight of the real history of the town and its people, occupying themselves instead with disquisitions on half-understood matters of remote antiquity or in establishing links, however ephemeral, between their town and notable events in national history. Fisher was content to record matters which the average Victorian antiquary would have regarded as too mundane for his attention but which are the substance of a town's history.

Much that he tells us is, of course, recoverable from the other sources—happily, many and varied—that survive for the history of Stroud in the late 18th and earlier 19th centuries;

1 Ibid. 38–9, 139.
2 Mr. G. T. St. J. Sanders kindly allowed me to see his set of cuttings of the *Stroud Jnl.* articles. Fisher's own set and his copy of the 1871 edition of the book, both with his MS. revisions, are *penes* Major Fisher.

but without his book we would lack much of that eye-witness detail that gives an extra dimension to the story, enlivening the facts and making them more immediate to us. To take two tiny examples, the picture he retails to us of the grass growing in the mill courtyards during the mid-1780s slump in the cloth trade, and—epitomizing the bad roads for which the region was notorious before the 19th century—his information that a loaded wagon took a whole day going and returning between Stroud and Chalford.

He also breathes life into some of the people of the period, the local notables who feature in contemporary documents performing their public roles but betraying little of their individual personalities. We have a more human picture of the magistrate Henry Burgh, Thomas Hughes the surgeon, and the two active curates of Stroud, Ellis and Williams. Fisher's brief mention of the bacchanalian triumvirate of Wyatt, Griffin, and Hawker, whom other surviving references clothe only in a bland respectability, makes us wish his good nature had allowed less reticence about the more disreputable of his contemporaries. We might, for example, have had a lively sketch of the notorious spendthrift Paul Wathen, for Fisher's detailed account of Wathen's alterations to Lypiatt Park suggest he was a regular visitor there, perhaps on business matters. Apart from the notables, Fisher has preserved for us some of the humbler townspeople, those of whom we would otherwise have probably never heard. The deftly-drawn portraits of people like Daniel Bloxsome the linen-draper, Adamson the aspiring Beau Brummel, and the self-appointed scholar Jemmy Wyndowe, convey something of the flavour of small-town life.

It is natural that in assessing the value of Fisher's book in 1975 I should lay much greater stress on the information it provides for the period of his own lifetime than on the information he collected for the history of Stroud in earlier times. The matter culled from ancient documents by Fisher and other 19th-century local historians is of less value to us today than it was to their contemporaries, because we now have a much wider field of documentary sources available to us than ever the 19th-century writers had; much that was then dispersed and inaccessible is now collected and catalogued in public record repositories. So naturally we value most the books which transmit to us the otherwise irrecoverable eye-witness detail or local tradition, forgetting perhaps that the information about the more distant centuries was of equal or greater interest to the authors' contemporaries. Nevertheless, in Fisher's case, the inclusion of so much of his own recollections must have made his book much more entertaining to his fellow-townsmen. His older readers would have enjoyed being reminded of things they had forgotten, while to his younger readers many of his memories were, in any case, ancient history; not many others alive in 1871 could recall the year 1786 when John Wesley came to preach in the chapel in Acre Street.

The period over which Fisher's memories extended was one of great change for Stroud. Though long the recognized centre for the rich cloth-producing valleys which lay all around it, in the later part of the 18th-century it remained a modest-sized and traditional market town with little to justify any claim to pre-eminence over its immediate neighbours, Painswick and Minchinhampton. Its life focused on the steep, curving High Street beside which stood its parish church, its market-house and market-place, and its various inns, principally the George, so affectionately described by Fisher. Above the High Street were a few narrow streets with modest gabled houses and two nonconformist chapels. It boasted few houses of any pretension for the leading inhabitants of the parish and region, the clothiers, mostly lived outside the town at their fulling-mills along the valleys.

In Fisher's lifetime, however, 'the modern spirit of improvement . . . raised up the old town from her slumber';[1] Stroud was enlarged and transformed into a thriving business and social centre with buildings and institutions befitting the hub of an important industrial area. The year of his birth, 1779, in fact saw two significant events at the start of this process, the opening of the canal link with the Severn and the founding of the first Stroud bank.

Improved communications played a vital part in the process, notably the building of new turnpike roads along the valleys to replace the steep hillside tracks. Two of the new roads, the Cheltenham–Bath road brought through the town in 1800 and the new London road built along the Chalford valley in 1814, were particularly significant in the expansion of the town, causing the development of several new streets down hill from its old centre. The transference of the business of the old George Inn from High Street down to a building on King Street in 1819, recorded by Fisher, pointed to this shift in the town's centre of gravity, and in 1833 a fine public meeting-place, the Subscription Rooms, was opened in the new, lower part of the town. The building of the latter was prompted by the creation under the Reform Act of a parliamentary borough of Stroud, embracing the surrounding

1 *Stroud Jnl.*, Fisher's 'Reminiscences', no. i.

cloth-making parishes. With the expansion of the town came many developments in public services; an improvement Act of 1825 led to the paving of the streets and the provision of gas-lighting. The limited educational resources of the old charity schools were replaced by new National and British schools, and the 19th-century thirst for self-improvement was met by reading-rooms and lecture societies. The non-conformist churches enjoyed a great expansion in numbers and the established church opened the new Holy Trinity in 1839.

Many of these improvements were completed or well under way before the railway came to Stroud in 1845, but that event was no less significant than for other provincial towns, accelerating the pace of change and generating the suburban expansion of the later 19th-century. The beginnings of this, in the Lansdown and Uplands area, were evident by the end of Fisher's life, but he did not see the considerable eastward growth of the town, which was made possible by the sale of the Field estate in 1873, the year of his death.[1]

Fisher has given us a faithful record of most of the changes of his lifetime, though his picture is not comprehensive. In particular those to whom the name Stroud is synonymous with the cloth-making industry may be disappointed to find only incidental references to it. The important changes in that field during his lifetime—the mechanization and rebuilding of the old fulling-mills, the sufferings of the handloom weavers, and the introduction of new types of industry to the area—affected most directly the valleys and the outlying hamlets and were outside his main preoccupation, the changes in the town itself.

One of the most obvious features of *Notes and Recollections* is the author's enjoyment in recalling the sights of his early years—the coachman's dexterity as he guided his vehicle through the narrow streets, the tradesmen gossiping in the evenings at the Golden Heart, or the favourite rural walks that had vanished under new roads and houses. The disappearance of so much that he had known prompted the old man to nostalgia and some simple philosophy but not to rancour; he accepted most of the changes as necessary improvements. The changes that another hundred years have brought to Stroud would, if he could see the town today, give ample scope for Fisher's philosophizing. But, having experienced so much change in his own lifetime, he would perhaps be only mildly disconcerted by the absence of old landmarks, to find Mr. Watts's brewery vanished, the New George Hotel

1 The story of the development of Stroud was continued, more prosaically, by John Libby in his *Twenty Years History of Stroud* (Stroud, 1890).

gone the way of the old, and John Cole's house, like its
ornamental garden, now 'only a vision in the mind's eye.'[1] A
modest man, he would probably express more surprise at the
value we still place on *Notes and Recollections of Stroud* as an
evocation of the town's past.

N. M. Herbert, 1975.

---

1 *Notes and Recollections*, 130.

Notes and Recollections of Stroud.

CHAPTER I.

THE COTTESWOLDS — THE VALE OF STONEHOUSE — STROUD, AND
THE FIVE VALLEYS — THE VALE OF SEVERN VIEWED FROM
THE COTTESWOLDS — CHANGES IN THE COUNTRY DURING
LONG INTERVALS OF TIME.

THE Cotteswolds, which form the eastern side of the county of Gloucester and one of its natural divisions, slope gently back into the levels of Oxfordshire and Wiltshire ; but are raised into a mountainous range of irregular elevation on those sides which bound the valleys below.

The portion of the range extending from Haresfield Hill downward, overlooks the vale of Gloucester and the river Severn. This vale is sometimes divided by writers into the vales of Gloucester and Berkeley, from the names of those places, as if there were two separate valleys, whereas it is only one, and its more appropriate name would be the Valley of the Severn.

The western face of the southern range has numerous headlands and capes projecting into this valley, forming some beautiful bays—in one of which Dursley is nestled : but it has no inlet of any considerable extent, except near its upper end ; and there, at Sandford's Knoll, (which is a bold projection, connected with Frocester hill by the lofty Buckholt wood,) this inlet breaks into the range, which, however, reappears at Doverow hill, about two miles distant on the opposite side, and proceeds thence, about the same distance, to the upper extremity of Haresfield hill.

This inlet divides the northern from the southern Cotteswolds. It is about two miles wide at its entrance, and two miles deep, but contracts as it advances. It is bounded on the south by the lofty ridges of Longwood and Selsley Hill, on the north by Doverow hill, (which is part of the southern slope of Randwick hill,) and by Whiteshill and the other high land reaching to Stroud. The hills on its southern side rise more abruptly than those on the north ; and being higher, of greater extent, and maintaining a continuous varying line from Sandford's Knoll, they surpass the latter both in grandeur and beauty ; but on both sides the junction of their bases with the vale land is everywhere gentle and gradual.

This has been called the vale of Stonehouse, from the pleasant village of that name which lies near its entrance, under the western slope of Doverow hill ; and, passing eastward into the mass of the Cotteswolds, is the approach to various tortuous, gorge-like valleys, in which—and fed by whose streams—is the Stroud clothing district, commonly known to the upper Cotteswoldians by the name of The Bottoms.

Stroud stands at the head of this inlet, and near it begin those tortuous, gorge-like valleys ; each of which, (as it winds upward into the mass of the hills,) breaks into numerous smaller lateral valleys, and into combs, dells, and glens, having their own local names and peculiarities, and all being " beautiful exceedingly." The number of the main valleys is five, known, at their respective entrances, as the vales of Cuckold's brook ;[1] Painswick ; Slad and Steanbridge ; Stroud and Chalford ; Rodborough, Woodchester, and Nailsworth ; each having its appropriate stream of water and tributary feeders, falling into the river Froom at and a little below Stroud. The hills which separate these valleys from one another, are spurs of the Cotteswolds projecting into the Inlet at its eastern extremity ; and are Whiteshill, Wickeridge hill, Stroud hill, and the towering eminence of Rodborough hill, crowned with the conspicuous building called The Fort,—all stretching upward, until they attain an equal height in the summit or table land of the range.

The great valley of the Severn, with its wide expanse of gleaming water, backed by the Forest of Dean and the

---

[1] Cuckold, as a name, is a corruption of Coxwold

distant Welsh hills, presents, from the heights of Frocester and Randwick, such a magnificent picture as is probably unrivalled in England : whilst the Inlet, or Stonehouse valley, when viewed from the hills on either side, furnishes a most interesting prospect of churches, mansions, manufactories, woods, meadows, the river Froom, and the Stroud Navigation,—with numerous villages and cottages reposing on the sides and in the hollows of the hills,—suggesting altogether ideas of great activity, opulence, and social comfort. Each of the gorge-like valleys of this district, will well repay the lover of the picturesque for his trouble in exploring it, howsoever often it may be visited : but neither tongue nor pen can give an adequate idea of their peculiar and varied beauties.

In minds of a curious and imaginative cast, there may arise, as there has arisen in mine, a longing desire to behold, not only the present aspect of this region, but to see in the mind's eye, what may be conceived as its appearance in past historic and pre-historic times. And, as astronomy has long since given us ideas of incalculable distance and illimitable space, so geology has made us familiar with the vast epochs and un-numbered ages required for the stupendous violent agencies and slower operations which have been at work in the earth, before it acquired its present condition of comparative tranquility, positive beauty, and grandeur. In pursuance of this desire, we may ask, what was its state and appearance in some of those remote periods?

If we look at the western boundary of the Cotteswolds, with its bold capes and headlands, it may be compared to a long line of sea-cliffs ; and it requires only a little imagination to picture it as an actual coast bordering a wide inland strait, having for its western shore the hills of the Forest of Dean, and the steeper chain of the Malverns. Sir Roderick I. Murchison has shown the high probability that at one, and not a remote geological period, (but since the country had acquired its present conformation), it formed a gulf of the sea, separating England from Wales, and that the entire region had been subsequently elevated. This elevation, and the consequent retiring of the waters, was probably gradual, from the fact that plants which affect marine situations are found in Worcestershire, up to which the waters may have once flowed : and a spectator, viewing the present low region from the outward

line of the Cotteswold range, may trace the ancient
boundaries of the gulf, and at once perceive how large a
portion of the vale would be again submerged, were a
subsidence of the whole to take place to the extent of only
a hundred feet. In that case the lateral vale of Stonehouse
would once more form an inlet of the sea, and the sites of
Gloucester and Tewkesbury be again beneath the level of
the water of the gulf.

And now, (following the example of Dr. Mantell), we
may imagine some higher Intelligence from another sphere,
describing a small part of the physical changes which
(from the inductions of geology) he may be supposed to
have witnessed,—and that we hear him say :—Countless
ages before man was created I visited this region, and I
beheld only a vast solitary ocean, in restless activity spread
around me. Its waters teemed with nautili, ammonites, and
other cephalopoda, with innumerable fishes, ichthyosauri,
plesiosauri, and other marine reptiles, of races now extinct.

Thousands of centuries rolled by, when I returned, and
lo ! dry land appeared ; and I saw in the rivers and marshes
the beaver and hippopotamus, and the rhinoceros and
elephant roaming in the plains : but between one elevated
range and another, there lay a gulf of the old ocean, whose
mighty waves dashed against its shores ; and, into this
inlet, its gorges and fiords, the waters of the gulf flowed,
and the tide repeated its diurnal action.

Another vast epoch passed, and I came again to the
scene of my former contemplations ; the mighty forms I
left there had disappeared, the entire region had been
further elevated, the waters of the gulf had retired, and in
its place appeared a beautiful and fertile valley, with a
silvery river flowing down it. Herds of deer, with horses
and kine, were to be seen in the plain ; and swine and
wolves roamed in the woods and forests. I also beheld
human beings clad in the skins of animals, and armed with
clubs and spears, who had formed habitations in caves,
constructed hut-circles for shelter, inclosed pasture for
cattle, and were endeavouring to cultivate the ground.

A thousand years more elapsed, when again I visited the
country. The Romans were then in the land, as its masters,
and had built cities, fortresses, and villas ; had established
entrenched camps on the hills which overlooked the great
valley and its tributaries ; and their legionaries were passing
from one encampment to another, and marching through

the land on their grand military roads from station to station, in ceaseless vigilance.

Fifteen centuries more passed away, when I returned, and beheld the broad smiling Severn valley,—its gleaming waters bearing white sails ;[1] and the lateral inlet and its branches, with canals, railways, manufactories, towns, and villages ; its teeming population, and energetic life,— all speaking unmistakably of a high state of civilization and prosperity ; and forming an integral part of the great English nation, which has so important an interest in the progress and welfare of mankind, to which it has so largely contributed. And I perceived many of its intelligent inhabitants searching the rocks and quarries, the detritus, gravel beds, and caves of past ages, for the fossil organic remains of the former world ; gathering together the bones and other vestiges of the beings who had lived and died long, long since, but whose very forms had now disappeared from the face of the earth ; and endeavouring, by arranging these natural memorials, to trace the succession of events that had preceded the history of their race.

[1] Standing on Stroud hill I have seen, with my naked eye, a fleet of vessels sailing in the sunshine up the Severn on the flood tide ; being a distance of nine miles.

CHAPTER II.

THE parish of Stroud lies in the hundred of Bisley, in
the county of Gloucester, on the lower slope of the
interior part of the Cotteswold range, where it forms the
eastern end of the inlet before mentioned. It is divided
into two parts, by an intervening tongue of land belonging
to Painswick, which runs down to the river Froom, between
the streams called the Slade on the east, and the Painswick
water on the west,—the former falling into the Froom at
Wallbridge, and the latter at Lodgemore, where they are
about three-hundred-and-fifty yards apart. Both these
portions of the parish are separated from the parishes of
Minchinhampton and Rodborough by the Froom on the
south ; another portion is bounded by the parish of Bisley
on the east ;[1] and another is separated from Randwick on
the west, by the rivulet which falls into the Froom below
Cuckold's brook, from the valley of that name.

Froom, or Froome, is probably derived from the British
word, *ffrom*, rapid. It rises at Climperwell, in the parish of
Brimpsfield, where, Mr. Rudder says, " It is known by its
right name " ; and, after a circuitous route of about fourteen
miles, reaches Stroud, near which place it receives its
principal affluents, and falls into the Severn at Framilode,
about eight miles below. In its course it gives name to
Frampton Mansell, a hamlet of Saperton ; Froom-mill,
and Froom-hall in Stroud ; Froombridge ; Frampton, which

1 The division between the parishes of Bisley and Stroud is no where
marked by such a natural boundary as the stream, rising near Lypiatt, passing
down Toadsmore Bottom, through Bourne, and then falling into the Froom,
would have been, if it had been made a boundary line through its whole
length. But on setting out the Chapelry of Stroud in the Composition of
1304,—for which see Chapter xl., and Appendix B,—it was deemed proper
to give it the whole vill of Bourne, "*tota villata de Bourne*," whereby it
acquired a portion of Bourne, (about thirty-five acres in extent), lying on the
Bisley side of the stream. And thus it has come to pass that only the upper
part of the stream remains a boundary between the parishes, while its lower
course lies within the parish of Stroud.

signifies the town on the Froom, but is generally called Frampton-on-Severn, to distinguish it from Frampton, near Bristol ; and Framilode, which means the exit or emptying of the Froom;—all tending to prove that Froom is its proper name.[2]

It has, however, been erroneously called by other names. Even our county historian, Sir Robert Atkyns, who resided at Saperton, about seven miles above Stroud, and had a large estate there, through which the river flows, calls it "the river Stroud,"[3] and "the Stroud river from the name of this place."[4] Moreover, in an Act of Parliament, 3 Geo. II, 1727, for making it navigable from the Severn, at or near Framilode, to Wallbridge, near the town of Stroud, it is called "the river Stroudwater." This latter name is, indeed, only another term for the "Stroud river ; " but, as used in the Act, it becomes a distinctive name, and the Undertaking is still officially known as "The Stroudwater Navigation," by virtue of the Act, 16 Geo. III, 1775, under which it was completed as an independent canal.

The parish contains 3810 acres [5] of diversified hill and valley. The high ground, being a light, stony soil, is chiefly in tillage ; and many of the declivities are still clothed with remains of the ornamental beech woods which largely abounded in former days.

Domesday-book does not mention this place ; for when that record was completed (A.D. 1087,) it was part of the parish and manor of Bisley, and did not become a distinct parish until the year 1360. Even then, the division between them was so ill-defined that, in some title deeds of so late a date as 1773, the land conveyed is described as "situated in Stroud or Bisley, or one of them."

Sir Robert Atkyns says that Stroud "is so called from *Strogd*, which in the Saxon language signifies scattered, from their houses lying dispersed at a distance." But it may have obtained the derived name from its divided condition, rather than because of its scattered houses.

Mr. Rudder says :—"The first mention I have found of the name is in a composition between the rectors of the church of Bisley and the inhabitants of *La Stroud*, dated

2 *Vide* Rudder's History, p. 452.

3 *Vide* Atkyns' History, second edition, 1768, p. 237.

4 *Ibid*, p. 368.

5 *Vide* Census, A.D. 1861.

1304." This is correct, as to the date of the document, but incorrect as to the name of the place mentioned in it, which is not La Stroud, but *Strode;* and the inhabitants are called "*habitatores capellæ de Strode.*"[6]

In reference to the origin of the name, he says :—" Some persons have taken Stroud and Strand for synonymous expressions ;[7] and it seems not improbable that this place obtained its name from the houses which were first built here, standing on the *strand* or bank of the river Froom." [8] But no part of the town stands, or perhaps ever stood, on the strand or bank of this river ; the nearest houses being separated from it by Mansel's mead, a considerable tract of low ground which was probably a swamp in ancient times : and it was not until the value of the river, as a motive power, began to be perceived, that clothing-mills and dwelling-houses were erected on its banks at any place ; for the roads to all the mills lead down a steep descent from the highway on the hill side, and generally terminate at each mill.

Mr. Rudge assigns the same origin to the name as Mr. Rudder ; and says—" The greatest objection to Atkyns's etymology is the improbability of applying a Saxon word at so late a period after the Norman Conquest as 1304, when the name was first mentioned in a Composition between the rectors of Bisley, and La Stroud." [9] To this it may be replied, that the name in that instrument is not a Saxon word, but the derivative *Strode :* and the place must have been known as a scattered or divided portion of the parish of Bisley by that very name long before the Composition was made.

About the year 1539, John Bygge died, seised of a messuage, two fulling mills, sundry land, wood, &c., "called Brymscombe in *Strod* and Minchinhampton," Esc. 30, H. VIII ;[10] and about the year 1642, Lord Windsor is said

---

6 A copy of the original Composition, which is in Latin, will be given hereafter. It will be perceived that *capella*, the chapel, is here used in the sense of our English word chapelry.

7 Probably this has reference to Camden, who, in his Remains, article Surnames, says :—"*Stroad, Stroud ;* as some doe thinke, the same with *Strand.*"

8 Rudder, p. 710.

9 Rudge's History of the County of Gloucester, v. 1, p. 326.

10 Cited by the Rev. T. D. Fosbrooke in his History of Gloucestershire, 4to, v. 1, p. 338-9.

to have died, seised, among other manors, of *Strowed*, &c. ;
Esc. 17, Car. : [11] so that the name of this place may be
traced from the Saxon *Strogd*, thus :—Strode, Strod,
Strowed, [12] Stroud.

The appellation of Stroudwater has been sometimes given
to the town, as well as to the river ; but I have not met
with any deed of conveyance, either ancient or modern,
drawn by a gentleman of the legal profession, wherein the
town or parish has been so called. We may therefore conclude that Stroudwater was never regarded as its real or
legal name ; and may congratulate ourselves that, at length,
the river and the town are universally called by their right
names—the Froom, and Stroud, respectively : or, if "Stroudwater" still lingers in the memory of a few old persons, it
is only as the faint echo of a sound which has passed away,
to return no more. Time the destroyer, is also Time the
restorer.

11 Fosbrooke. v. I, p. 378-9.

12 Here it occurs in the form of a well-known English word, of the same
meaning as the original Saxon.

CHAPTER III.

THE town of Stroud stands on the lower declivity of the
hill of that name, in latitude 51° 44′ 21″ north and
is about ten miles south from Gloucester, four west from
Bisley, and the same distance north from Minchinhampton.
It has a market on Fridays, and two annual fairs—on the
10th of May, and 21st of August. The May fair was
formerly held on the 12th; but was changed to the 10th,
early in the present century, in order to prevent its
interfering with a fair held at Stow-on-the-Wold on the
first of those days. The August fair was formerly held on
the 10th, that being the feast-day of St. Laurence, to whom
the parish church was dedicated, and it is still regarded as
the parish feast-day; but the fair was changed to the 21st
of August, and is called the cattle-fair, in distinction from
the pleasure-fair of May.

In the origin of Stroud, as in that of other towns, the
first houses were probably erected at the junction of the
highways or tracts in the locality. The chief of these
comes from the outlying portion of the parish called
Pakenhill tithing, across the intervening piece of land
belonging to Painswick; when, passing the Slade stream at
Badbrook, it enters the residue of the parish, and runs
straight up the steep central chine of Stroud hill, on
its way to Bisley. From this central ridge the hill sides
descend rapidly, and in some places very rapidly, to the
bottoms of the adjacent valleys—the southern slope going
down to the Froom in the Stroud valley, and the northern
slope down to the stream in the Slad valley; and both widen
out as those valleys ascend.

On the lower rise of this main road, about one hundred yards above Badbrook, it is joined on the south by the highway from Rodborough; and probably this was a favourable point for its first cluster of houses. Accordingly, here begins the main street of the town—the High-street. At the top of High-street is an open space called The Cross; from which, in continuation of the road to Bisley, runs Silver-street, the steepest of our streets, having its termination at a place called Town's-end.

From the Cross, another road branches up to the right, on the steep slope of the hill side, and proceeds along its southern face in the direction of Bowbridge and Thrupp. Up the ascent of this latter road from the Cross, runs what is now called Nelson-street, that being a modern name for an old street, of which I do not remember the former, nor indeed that it had any. From the Town's-end before mentioned, is a road leading out of the Bisley road down to the top of Nelson-street; and by this way loaded carriages pass to and from High-street more easily than they could by the steep declivity of Silver-street. This road was lately called Chapel-street, from the Wesleyan chapel which adjoins it; but its older name—by which also it is still known—was Acre-edge, (since changed by authority to Acre-street,) shewing that, originally, it was a mere high-way by the side of a piece of land called the Acre. And, as Town's-end indicates a termination of the houses in that direction at some former period, it may be concluded that the road which unites it with Nelson-street was once the upper or eastern boundary of the town.

In continuation of Silver-street from Town's-end, on the Bisley road, is Parliament-street; and from the top of Nelson-street, on the highway to Bowbridge, are Castle-street and Lower-street, extending to Snow's-hill or The Pumphouses. On the southern side of this line, overlooking the beautiful valley, is the dwelling-house called The Castle. It has a narrow lane on each side,—one of which leads down to the Brickhouse and Capel's mill, and the other to Arundel's mill, both on the river Froom, but no farther. These are examples of the steep roads from the hill-side highways to the river Froom, to which we have before alluded. The old part of the Castle was built by Simon and Jane Chadwell, A.D. 1610; it was newly fronted by Charles Freebury, about 1789; and has been much enlarged and improved by its present owner. It is not

known when, or why, it acquired its name ; but there is a
tradesman's token of the time of King Charles II, having
" Henry Allen, of the," as its obverse, and " Castel in
Stroud," as its reverse.[1]

Between Parliament-street on the north, and Lower-street
on the south, are two streets nearly parallel with them,—
one of which was called Meeting-street, but is now called
Chapel-street, from the Independent Chapel near its upper
end ; and the other is called Middle-street ; both standing
on a piece of land anciently called the Seven Acres. From
the top of Chapel-street proceeds Wood-street, (which has
houses only on its western side,) at a right angle, up to the
north, where it joins the Bisley road above Parliament-
street.

At the upper end of Middle-street stands Whitehall, built
on part of a piece of land formerly called Square Acre. It
is pleasantly situated, by reason of its proximity to the
Fields and the breezy hill-tops rising beyond them, to
which, and to the once pretty valley called Horns, it has an
easy access.

From the end of Lower-street, a road runs at a right
angle to the north ; which, passing the Pumphouses and
Whitehall, proceeds up the hill until, at a place called (in
old deeds) Nounsell's Cross, it joins and crosses the Bisley
road. The road from Whitehall to Nounsell's Cross, was
formerly called Bittern's Ditch, and Hollow-lane ; and, in
the writer's young days, it was both narrow and deep, lying
below the level of the adjoining Fields, whereby it deserved
its appellations. It has since been widened and otherwise
repaired ; and, by connecting Lower-street with Nounsell's
Cross, has become a second eastern boundary of the town,
and has received the name of Trinity-road.

Not one of the old streets was laid out in a regular form,
or on a pre-arranged plan ; but each house, or block of
houses, was erected according to the convenience or fancy
of the owner : consequently they were irregular in their
lines and frontages, one house coming more forward than
another, and all standing on the original inequalities in the
surface. Moreover, the streets are generally so narrow, that
not one of those above the Cross has a footpath on both
sides ; nor could two carriages everywhere pass one another.

1 Mentioned by John Delafield Phelps, Esq., of Chavenage House, in his
Collectanea Gloucestriensis, 1842.

Besides these inconveniences, Chapel, Middle, and Lower streets range along the southern slope of the hill, on which they stand, and had many of the houses on their south sides several feet below the roads and the houses on their northern sides, of which some examples yet exist.

An aged person[2] told me that when he rode up the High-street, on coming to reside here in 1763, he seemed to be in a hollow way, with houses on its banks : and such, from its situation, it must necessarily have been, and would still be, by the dragging of loaded carriages and the rushing of floods of rain-water down its steep roadway, unless it were kept in order by constant repairs. Even within my own recollection, Nelson-street was very narrow, the high ground on its north side intruding into it : and the first improve-ment of the town was the widening of this street, by the cutting down and removing part of the bank on its upper side, and constructing walls to support the foundations of two or three buildings that were endangered by the opera-tion, as may yet be seen. This was effected at the sugges-tion, and under the direction, of the Rev. Joseph Colborne.

In the year 1776, Middle-street was in a very bad con-dition, being (as the accusation ran) " dangerous and unsafe for His Majesty's subjects travelling to and from the said town of Stroud." And, as it led up to Whitehall, where stood at that time the most important houses in the upper part of the town, their owner exerted himself to get the inconvenience remedied. Notices were given by him to all the house-owners and others on its north side, where is the only footpath, to do the necessary repairs, on pain of being indicted for neglect. The result was the reparation of the street ; and, until a comparatively late period, posts and rails stood before the chief houses in Whitehall and Middle-street, as fences between the one footpath and the carriage-way.

Besides some small courts, and passages to houses behind streets, in this old part of the town, there are a few inhabited winding alleys, so narrow as not to exceed the width of the footpaths, on the old lines of which they stand. They are called *Churs;* and are generally ill-kept.[3] But there is one

[2 This was the old author's father.]

3 In Newcastle-on-Tyne there are several narrow streets or lanes called " *Chares* " ; and it is said that at the local Assizes some years since, one of the witnesses in a criminal trial swore that " *he saw three men come out of the foot of a chare, eating a brick.*" The judge cautioned the jury not to pay any

narrow passage, sometimes called a *Chur*, which has always been known to me as the *Tween-walls*. It leads from the top of Middle-street up to the chapel in Meeting-street; and being straight, clean, and used only as a footpath, does not deserve the ill-favoured name of *Chur*. Moreover, it lies between two lofty garden-walls, and is the abode of an Echo which children delight to waken by running down it, clattering with their feet.

About twenty-five yards below this passage in Middle-street, stands the house in which our celebrated townsman, John Canton, "an ingenious natural philosopher," was born and resided, working with his father, a broadcloth weaver, until he was seventeen years of age. I well remember the "upright stone dial," which his biographers mention as computed by him, and carved with his pocket-knife,—an extraordinary performance of his juvenile days,—when it stood against the front of the house. About the year 1815 it was removed by the late Mr. Stephen Price, an ingenious machine-maker and engineer of Acre-edge, and placed on the south angle of one of his large and busy workshops, where it stood until they were taken down in 1865. The dial is now in the possession of Mr. Canton's great-grandson, Mr. Edwin Canton, an eminent surgeon of London. It was Mr. John Canton who calculated the latitude of the town.[4]

Lower down, on the south side of this street, is an old house—an example of the original irregularity of the front lines and levels of the streets. It stands eleven feet back from the frontage of the adjoining houses; and its lower floor was once five feet below the present roadway. It still bears, as the date of its erection, "1686," in large figures, with some quaint devices, which were wrought into its plastered front nearly two hundred years ago. Both the adjoining houses were on the same level, and still continue so, as to their back floors. In 1768, the adjoining house on the east was newly fronted by Mr. Ezekiel King, one of the early followers and friends of the Rev. John Wesley, the celebrated founder of the Society of Wesleyan Methodists; and there Mr. King entertained him when he visited Stroud on his itinerating rounds. On such occasions Mr. Wesley

---

regard to the man's evidence, as he must be insane. A little explanation by the foreman, however, satisfied his lordship that the original statement was correct. A small brick-shaped loaf or roll is there called "a brick."

4 Rudder, 711.

rose at five o'clock in the morning to conduct the early prayers at the Round-house, as his chapel in Acre-edge was then called. It is even now remembered by that name, having been, originally, a small octagonal building of equal sides. On one of Mr. Wesley's visits, about the year 1786, the writer, then but a little boy, heard him preach ; and remembers his reproving some women of his congregation for their excessive snuff-taking in the chapel.

Matthew Lamburn, a baker, who occupied the lowest house in Middle-street at that time, was the first person who introduced here, and let for hire, the now old-fashioned post-chaises.

CHAPTER IV.

NELSON STREET — JAMES WYNDOWE — THE KNAPP — REV. WILLIAM
JOHNS — HIS CHARITIES AND LIBRARY — SILVER STREET —
WHITEHART PUBLIC ROOM — THE CROSS.

IN proceeding on our way to notice various other parts
of the town, and the memories connected with them,
we must pause on the south side of Nelson-street, at a small
house which belonged to James Wyndowe, a shoemaker,
in which he resided for many years, and died about A.D.
1855, in the 90th year of his age. He was familiarly called
Jemmy Wyndowe; and was an original character, with a
large stock of old remembrances, and of a pompous carriage.
From his habit of collecting and retailing public matters,
he acquired the name of "the walking newspaper." He
affected an air of independence and superior intelligence,
with the use in conversation of words which were often of
his own coining. He would talk of the twelve signs of the
Zodiac; and when once challenged to tell their names, he
replied loftily—"There's *Harris*, the bull; *Sagtarus*, the
archer; *Jem-and-I*, the twins; and—and—all the rest of
them."[1] He was a tradesman of the longest standing in
the town, an honest man, and connected by birth with a
very respectable old family near Gloucester. He was the
first person who appeared in the streets here with an
umbrella, to the surprise and amusement of the boys and
girls.[2]

Opposite Wyndowe's house, on the high ground that
forms the north side of this street, is a property called The
Knapp, which signifies a knoll or projection in a hill. It
was bequeathed in 1720, by the Rev. William Johns, a
former incumbent of Stroud, upon trust, that in case of the

1 He seems to have confounded *Aries* (which he calls Harris) with *Taurus*.

2 He brought it from Bristol, where umbrellas had been introduced about
1780.

death of his grandson, Henry Adderly, without issue, (which occurred in 1760,) the rent should be applied to the payment of "twenty shillings yearly, and every year, to the treasurer of the Charity Society at Stroud, if it continues, for teaching poor children; and ten shillings yearly for keeping in repair the pump at the Cross; and also ten shillings yearly for him that shall ring the bell at eight at night and four in the morning; and also twenty shillings yearly to him whom the parishioners may appoint for keeping in repair the clock and chimes." Adding—"As for my books, my will is, that if the feoffees of the parish will, in six months after my decease, provide a convenient place in the Market-house at Stroud, that they shall be placed there as a public library, to which purpose I give them for public use, and freely bequeath them; and him who keeps the school for the time being, I would have to be the library-keeper, and appoint and bequeath to that library-keeper twenty shillings yearly out of my aforesaid house at the Knapp. And, if there be any surplus of rent out of my house, I will that it be for the putting poor children apprentice."

Mr. Johns died in 1721, having been for thirty-three years a faithful minister of this place. It was he who first established a Charity school in this parish, which may explain the somewhat doubting expression in his will—"if it continues." I have unexpectedly met with the following contemporary notice of this early school: "Stroud, Gloucestershire.—Fifty poor children taught, to which is subscribed £22 per annum; they are provided with Bibles, and have received a gift of £6."[3] Sunday-schools had not then been introduced. The ringing of "the bell at eight at night"—(curfew time, but no longer the *couvre-feu* of

3 This appears in a pamphlet containing "An account of the Charity Schools existing in and about London, in the year 1705, and some Charities of the like nature in other parts of the Kingdom;" London, printed by John Browning, in Bartholomew Close, near West Smithfield, 1705, pp. 16. This pamphlet is appended to a charity sermon preached at the parish church of St. Sepulchre, May 31st, 1705, by Dean Stanhope; London, printed for S. Keeble, 1705, 4to., pp. 28. It may not be uninteresting as regards the general history of Charity Schools, to learn from this "Account" that the schools of the thirty-eight parishes in and about London, therein mentioned, contained only 2,237 children, (boys, 1,462; girls, 775.) These were educated at the annual cost of about £2,242 "in voluntary subscriptions," and £1,071 "in collections at sermons." The schools had been established nine years. From such a small beginning arose those great results—great, but still inadequate— which we now behold.

William the Conqueror)—"and four in the morning," may be regarded as another version of Poor Richard's valuable maxim—

" Early to bed, and early to rise,
Makes a man healthy, wealthy, and wise,"

daily promulgated in a universal language. As for the chimes, I have often stood and listened with pleasure to their slow melody of the Easter hymn ; and it may be hoped that future generations will hear and feel the effect of the same solemn sounds. With respect to Mr. Johns's books, it is not known whether the feoffees provided "a convenient place" for them in the Market-house ; but all the books were subsequently removed to the attic of one of the houses of the feoffees, in the centre of High-street, where they were lying scattered on the floor, in great confusion, in the year 1792. The house was then occupied by Mr. Samuel Jenner, a bookseller, who had succeeded Mr. Bond, and it has ever since been a bookseller's shop. As a schoolboy fond of books, I was permitted to rummage among them ; but soon after they all disappeared, and probably found their way, as waste paper, to the huckster's shop or the paper mill, as thousands of valuable books have done, to the regret of collectors. With respect to the trust for "the putting poor children apprentice,"—although that was named as Mr. Johns's last object, and with the doubtful remark, " if there be any surplus rent,"—it will be gratifying to know that it became the largest and the most useful of his charities, and that one hundred and twenty-five poor boys were put apprentice between A.D. 1814 and 1860. Mr. Johns's trust-property was for many years known as the New George, being a public-house of that name, but previously called the Horse Shoes. In 1860 it consisted of three private houses with large gardens ; and passed from the trustees by sale, under the authority of the Charity Commissioners,—the purchase-money remaining as a fund for the original purposes.

In carrying out the trust for apprenticing poor boys, it was found that the old plan of apprenticeship was no longer practicable among artisans ; youths being unwilling to be placed under the constant tuition and supervision of their masters, and masters not less unwilling to board and lodge their apprentices for a term of years. So that it became the practice for the apprentice-fee to be paid to the master, for merely instructing his apprentice during the usual working hours ; and for him to pay the apprentice for his labour, a weekly stipend, varying with his age and ability,—the apprentice being boarded and lodged by his parent or himself, during the stipulated time.

From the Knapp to the bottom of the north side of Nelson-street, the houses, &c., belong to the Charity feoffees. One of them was formerly The Red Lion public-house, though commonly called The Red Cat. It had a rampant flame-coloured figure on its signboard, as much like a cat as a lion ; and the painter had omitted to write under it the old formula, " This is a lion." The corner house below it, formerly known as the Minister's house, has its chief front in the Cross ; and, together with the adjoining house, which also belongs to the feoffees and extends to Silver-street, forms the upper or eastern side of the Cross, over which these two houses look down High-street.

The space in Silver-street, for about sixty yards upward, is, in old title deeds, called Hocker-hill, but has long been better known as Tower-hill. It is the first rise in the acclivity of the street, and has a respectable old house of that name near its brow. Higher up in the same street, on its southern side, is Dyer's-court ; and there, tradition says, the early Nonconformists of Stroud held their first assemblies.

The open space of the Cross lies nearly in the centre of the old town ; and it may be conjectured that a stone cross formerly stood there, because there seems no other reason (such as cross roads might be) for its acquiring that appel-lation ; but I have not found any direct authority for the supposition. On the north side of the Cross, immediately below Silver-street, is an old inn called The King's Head ; and on the same side stood another, still older, called The White Hart. The latter is mentioned in a faculty-grant, A.D. 1733, as being then a large Inn belonging to Mr. Robert Brown, an apothecary of the town. About the year 1815, Mr. Joseph Birt, its then owner, took down an old malthouse which stood on the west side of the yard, and erected on its site some buildings, including a large room for public meetings. For many years, this room occa-sionally resounded with addresses from advocates of various benevolent, religious, and political objects. Here, on the 18th and 19th days of April, 1827, was held a bazaar, or fancy fair, in aid of the funds of the National Charity Schools of the parish, which was so successful, that out of the sum raised, £150, 3 per cent. consols was purchased and placed in trust for that object.   Here also, about the year 1831-2, meetings were held in favour of slave-emancipation, at which several important disputations were carried on with Mr. Peter Borthwick, a paid advocate of negro-slavery, hired by the West India planters to give lectures on their side of the question.   This man was subsequently brought into Parliament to advocate the same cause ; but neither what he was, nor what he said, commanded any attention in the House of Commons.   In a short time after the great battle of almost fifty years was won ; the mighty voice of justice and humanity prevailed ; and, with the payment of twenty millions sterling to the planters, the emancipation of the slaves in our colonies was accomplished.[4]   Birt's room, as this place was called, was next used for the meeting of farmers and corn-dealers on market days.   The yard in which it stands was for several years called Leadenhall Market, and its name was affixed to the wall near its entrance ; so that a passer-by might regard it either as a mockery of its metropolitan namesake, or a backward reading of Virgil's "*parvis componere magna*," according to his fancy.

Near the end of the year 1861, both this and the old sign of the antlered White Hart were taken down, part of the extensive buildings Converted into dwelling-houses, and the large room into a corn-exchange ; and in 1862 the whole was named Exchange Buildings.

About the year 1786 a bull was baited in the open space of the Cross, immediately below the entrance of Silver-street.   The animal was fastened by a rope to an iron ring in a large stone imbedded in the ground ; but the rope was not long, as the place did not admit of his taking a great circuit in moving round, nor were any large or very fierce dogs set on him ; and it is pleasant to record that this was the last, as it is hoped it was the only exhibition of the kind in Stroud.

The Cross has been used from time immemorial, for public open-air meetings, on festive and other occasions.   Here May-poles have been set up, adorned with ribbons and garlands of flowers, and men and women have danced round them.   Here sheep and oxen have been roasted and eaten, and barrels of beer have been broached and drunk.   Here

4 The Bill for the abolition of Slavery, passed 28th August, 1833.

multitudes have shouted for victories won, for peace restored, and other great public and local causes of rejoicing ; and I suspect "the great bull *feast*," alluded to in "The Razor-grinder's Dream,"5 was one of the festive meetings. Here, too, wild beasts are exhibited in caravans at fairs, and tamer animals are penned and sold on market days. Here the "Cheap John" of modern times, with his wonderful volubility and sustained vociferation in selling his wares, far outdoes the mountebank and jack-pudding of old times. And, in this place as on a stage, have been acted the various businesses, the follies, and the other strange doings of many past generations,—the register of which cannot be found in any *earthly* book, wheresoever else it may be recorded.

5 One of the old satirical poems, hereinafter referred to.

CHAPTER V.

AMONG the various exhibitions at the Cross was one
of a man exposed in the pillory. His name was
Benjamin Evans, of the Box, near Minchinhampton, who,
having acquired considerable repute as a cunning man and
soothsayer, had for several years imposed on ignorant and
superstitious people, wishing to know their fortunes, or to
trace stolen property; all which they believed he could
certainly reveal. He professed to "rule the planets"; and
I have met with some whose nativities were cast by him
when they were children, at their parents' request; but, as
one of them told me, his prognostics of her fortunate
marriage and numerous progeny had entirely failed. For
each horoscope Evans charged a shilling; and, having no
lawful calling, he continued to live as well as he might, and
as long as he could, on the public credulity. In the year
1814 he was summoned before the magistrates at Stroud,
by a young man named Hall, of Mackhouse, near Lower
Lypiatt in this parish, from whom he had obtained several
sums of money under a promise of finding out the thief who
had broken open his box and stolen its contents. This he
of course failed to do; though as often as Hall called on
him for the information, he said he was "getting nearer
him," (the thief): but, as often, demanded more money, by
way of *refresher*—as lawyers call the fee paid to a barrister
in the course of a long suit, in addition to that given at first
with his brief. Evans was sent to Gloucester gaol to take
his trial; and being found guilty at the next assizes, he was
sentenced to undergo a year's imprisonment; and, once in
each quarter of the year, to be exposed in the pillory at

Stroud on a market day "by the space of one hour."[1]   The
sentence was carried out ; and, the pillory (a large heavy
frame-work of timber) having been brought from Gloucester,
he was pilloried three several times : first, in January, 1815,
at the Cross, near where the old Blind House once stood ;
the second time in the old pig-market, in the centre of
High-street ; and lastly, in front of the King's Arms Inn,
now The Royal George Hotel.   On the first occasion, that
arch mischief maker of the town, "Charley Brown," began
to pelt him with refuse from the shop of his mother Betty
Brown, a tripe-seller and huckster near the place, but his
proceedings were immediately stayed by George Mynett,
the sheriff's officer, who interfered, and prevented any such
addition to the sentence, which was that of mere exposure
in the pillory.   He was, however, plentifully assailed with
wordy wit and coarse jests ; to which he replied with such
smart and cheerful humour, as much amused and mollified
the populace.[2]

Benjamin Evans was not the only person in Stroud and
its vicinity who pretended to "occult and crafty science,"
as the Act calls it ; nor was young Hall the only believer
in it.   For I have been told how two young ladies, bosom
friends, and belles of the town in olden time, determined to
pay a visit to *the cunning woman of Silver-street*, and have
their fortunes told, as some of their young companions had
already done ;—how they disguised themselves in clothes
borrowed of their servants, and, one dark night, made their
way to her cottage ; how they found her crouched before a
scanty hearth-fire, with a gaunt black cat by her side ;—
how she greeted them with—"I know what you are come
for ;" and how, after sundry cabalistic words and signs, she
proceeded, by a dingy pack of cards, and by inspecting the
sediment of some tea, which she had directed them to pour
out, each for herself, in a tea-cup,[3] to tell their fortunes—
much to the satisfaction of one, but more to the consternation of the other ; how the night-wind, rising suddenly,

1 This prosecution was under Statute 9 Geo. II., c. 5, s. 4, which contains
a curious list of such offences, with the punishments to be awarded.

2 The punishment of the pillory was abrogated by an Act of June 30th,
1837 ; being one of the batch of Acts passed in the first year of the reign of
Queen Victoria, by which many judicial and social improvements were effected.
Fortune-telling is now classed with swindling ; and persons pretending for hire
and gain to a knowledge of the occult sciences, and to expound the secrets of
time to come, are deemed rogues and vagabonds, and may be punished with
imprisonment and hard labour.

3 This is called "cup-tossing" in Ireland.

shook the hut, and howled round the door, as if something
unearthly wanted to come in ;—and how, when the old
crone heard it, she made signs to the two friends with
mysterious earnestness, and said—" Return to the place
where you came from, with all speed—for the spirits are
abroad " ;—as if, like the " monk of St. Mary's aisle," she
had been a pupil of the dread wizard Michael Scott himself,
and

> "   knew, by the streamers that shot so bright,
>   That spirits were riding the northern light ; "4

and how the young ladies crept out into the murky night,
and made their way home, in the greatest alarm and terror.
Perhaps the old woman knew who they were ; but this I
could not ascertain, although my informant had heard the
adventure from her mother,5 who was one of them.

I remember, too, when one *Edith Lewis*, better known as
old *Idleehous*, (into which her name had been barbarized,)
was a professor of the black art in this town.   But *Sarah
Creed*, who lived in a low thatched hut in the Leazes, behind
the north side of Parliament-street, was the most celebrated
fortune-teller of the day, and the most frequently consulted
of all her contemporary pretenders to that character.   She
professed to tell fortunes by palmistry,—that is, by observ-
ing the lines and marks in the inner surface of the hand
and fingers ; and to trace stolen goods, or the thief who
stole them, by more secret arts, practised in private.

In more modern times, as many persons yet remember,
Philip Wood, son of a respectable clothier of Painswick, set
himself up as an adept in astrology and the occult sciences.
He lived in the house next below the Greyhound Inn, on
the right hand side of the road from High-street to Badbrook.   There he set up a large sign-board, having " Philip
Wood, astrologer," &c., &c., in large letters, in the centre ;
with a representation of the sun and moon on one side, and
the seven stars on the other, by way of supporters to his
name and pretensions.   Thence, he sent forth handbills,
and inserted advertisements in the newspapers, announcing
that he was prepared by his art to answer, and was ready
to be consulted on, all questions of secrecy, doubt, and
difficulty ; to cast nativities ; to reveal future events ; discover lost property, &c. : and he often boasted of the

4 *Vide* Scott's Lay of the Last Minstrel, canto 2, stanza 8.

[5 My grandmother.—C.H.F.]

numerous letters received, inclosing large fees from persons at a distance, who applied for his help in such matters. For some time he succeeded well : but the stars played him false, his success declined, and he died at Whiteshill, in this parish, A.D. 1855, without having discovered the grand elixir, or the philosopher's stone.

> "Fortunes he told of other folk,
> No star revealed his own."

Even the veritable prophet *Zadkiel* himself, the writer of the well-known almanac of that name, claims a place in our list of local soothsayers ; for he was once an inhabitant of Sheepscomb, in the parish of Painswick. He was that Lieutenant Richard J. Morrison of the Royal Navy,[6] who came to reside at Sheepscomb House in the year 1842 ; where he remained until 1845, and there composed "Zadkiel's Almanac," which he had commenced several years before.

Previously to his arrival, this house had the reputation of being haunted ; or, as it has been stated to me, was " a place where spiritual forces made themselves apparent " ; and it is said that even Morrison, when he lived there, " appears to have been subject to their influence." How- ever that may have been,—and though the person who had the care of the house while it was unoccupied, had the most assured belief in the appearance of sights, and the hearing of sounds there, which could not have been the result of human or material agencies,—I have been told that such "spiritual manifestations" ceased in Sheepscomb House when Morrison left it.

From this it has been inferred (how logically we need not stop to inquire) that Zadkiel, the magician and astrologer, having mastered the spirits, and subjected them to his control, carried them away with him as his servants, vassals, and familiars, to the new scene of his occult operations.

Zadkiel's next scene of action was in London, and his almanac obtained a large circulation. Its reputation was increased by Alderman Humphreys calling attention from the magisterial bench to one of Zadkiel's predictions for 1861, "which had a kind of hazy coincidence" with the lamented death of the Prince Consort.[7]

---

6 Navy List, Seniority 1815.

7 His Royal Highness Prince Albert of Saxe-Coburg and Gotha, husband of Queen Victoria, died at Windsor, December 14th, 1861.

The following story belongs to a part of the district I am endeavouring to illustrate, and may be regarded as a rare page in the history of fortune-telling.

In September, 1810, a party of gipsies pitched their tents in the old blind lane called Green-street lane, leading from Stonehouse to Westrip, to wait for the approaching Stonehouse fair. Before the making of the turnpike road down the valley, a hundred years ago, this narrow winding, miry lane, was a common highway. One of the gipsies, a very aged woman, was a noted fortune-teller; and many foolish young persons from the villages near came to her to have their fortunes told. At this time, one Samuel A——, in the employ of a cloth manufacturer, had stolen a quantity of apples from farmer D——'s orchard, and had secreted them in an oak chest, which usually contained (and ought then to have contained) soap, for fulling cloth, in the stock-mill of his master. In the afternoon of Sunday, the next day, Samuel, and his sweetheart Nancy H——, made their way to the gipsies, for the purpose of having their fortunes told, as others had done; and halted at a stile which led from the open fields to the tents in the lane. The old Sibyl and her handsome grand-daughter were basking in the sun before one of the tents, and the rest of the party before another, as Samuel and his friend rested against the stile. The old crone no sooner perceived them than, in a slow solemn voice, she cried, "Come hither, Samuel, Samuel; I have been waiting for you these many years!" Samuel was sceptical as to the real power of any one to reveal coming events; but, like many others, he had the weakness to desire some knowledge of his own future; and was especially awed on hearing himself called by name in that manner—for neither of them had even seen the other before. Samuel's fear was increased when the gipsy, in a commanding tone, called on him to leave his companion and follow her into the tent. She told him she could read his past life as well as his future; and, after mentioning some things that had actually happened to him, she added "There is an old oak chest—broad, long, and deep—in a place you well know, filled with the *fruit* of your dishonest labour last night; farmer D—— has already missed the 'moonshines,' and before twenty-four hours he will be on the thief's track." She then seriously adjured him never to rob or steal again. Having said this and received her fee, she bade him retire, which he did—nothing loth. The old woman then summoned Nancy into the tent; and, after telling her some few facts in her little history, said "You will soon be married to a young man," whom she minutely described, as she could well do; and "you will be very happy, and will become the mother of many children"; all which, in process of time, really came to pass.   Samuel and Nancy left the gipsy camp together; but each in a different state of mind.   Samuel kept his own secret ; and early the next morning emptied the contents of the oak chest into the mill-stream, down which the apples were floating when the sun arose.   Samuel's fears had been excited, his conscience alarmed, and his moral sense quickened ; so that he repented sincerely, and became an honest man.   As soon as he had provided and comfortably furnished a cottage, he married the Nancy of the story, with whom he lived happily, in credit and respectability, several years, and was in due time surrounded by the "many children" promised by the gipsy.   Often and often in after life, did Samuel A—— think of the scene in the Green-street lane tent ; but never without thankfulness for its happy results.

About twenty years afterward the key to this enigma was found.   Two middle aged men, taking a walk in the fields, came to the place in Green-street lane where the gipsies had encamped in 1810; and this, calling to the mind of one of them the circumstances just related, he said— "At that time I occupied the mill at ——, and Samuel A—— was my millman.   I discovered his theft, by finding the old oak chest full of apples, instead of soap for fulling my cloth, which ought to have been there, but had been removed ; and I knew they were farmer D——'s apples from their being such as only grew in his orchard, which had been robbed the night before.   Further, I had overheard Nancy H—— tell one of her companions that the gipsies were come to Green-street lane ; and she and Samuel were going there to have their fortunes told on that Sunday afternoon.   Immediately I repaired to the gipsy camp, and told the old woman what had occurred, at about what time she might expect two visitors, (both of whom I described,) and gave her a few particulars about each of them.   She thanked me for the information, which she well knew how to turn to account, and promised to give Samuel the good advice I suggested.   I gave her some silver to secure the performance of the promise, and departed."   The sequel of the story has been already told.

We might well desire that pure and intelligent agencies were, always and everywhere, at work to arouse, instruct, and guide the moral faculties in man ; and that he, always and everywhere, was obedient to their teaching. Nevertheless, moralists have not disdained the aid of inferior means, —even such as the old gipsy of Green-street lane,—to bring about the same beneficent end.

CHAPTER VI.

TOWN PUMP — BLIND HOUSE — STOCKS — ORIGIN OF WATER SUPPLY
TO THE TOWN — GAINEY'S WELL — HEMLOCK'S WELL, AND
NANNY CROKER.

NEAR the centre of "The Cross" is a deep well of
water, in which formerly stood the public pump.
Before the writer's time it had ceased to be used; but the
small rectangular stone building by which it was enclosed,
(the well being covered), had become a temporary receptacle
for criminals, under the name of the Blind House, having a
room in the roof called the Guard-house, which was entered
from without by a ladder. Behind it stood the Stocks,
where drunken men were "laid by the heels," to recover
their own sobriety, and be a warning to others to preserve
theirs. But the Stocks are gone; for we have been taught
to regard them as an unsuitable punishment in this fastidious
age; and drunkenness has increased to such a degree, as to
have become an enormous social evil, and the parent of
many other evils. This building was taken down in 1811;
and the materials were used in the construction of a lock-
up house in the Shambles, which was afterward removed to
Nelson-street, under its original name of Blind House.

In 1839 an attempt was made by the Improvement
Commissioners to restore the old well to the public use.
With this object it was deepened, and an iron pump set up
in it, at a considerable expense. But it soon appeared that
the water could not be raised by the machinery employed,
without a more than ordinary expenditure of muscular
strength; and, when obtained, it was not sufficiently pure
for drinking. On these accounts the pump remained useless until 1866, when it was converted, by some benevolent
individuals, into a modern public drinking fountain.

It has not been exactly ascertained when the original
pump ceased to be used; but probably its failure suggested

the bringing in a regular and more considerable supply of pure water to the town. The first attempt to effect that desirable object was made by Mr. Richard Arundel, who, in 1744, obtained from Thomas Stephens, Esq., lord of the manor, the grant of a power to lay down pipes for that purpose.

Mr. Arundel's scheme was unsuccessful; and it is not known what was his plan, what he had done towards it, or what caused his failure; except so far as is obscurely hinted in two old satirical poems—"The Razor-grinder's Dream," and "The Speech of the Fakeer of Gotham."

About the year 1769, however, the desired object was effected by Mr. Benjamin Grazebrook, an enterprising tradesman of the town, who, at his own cost, and as a private enterprise, constructed a large round basin, which he named *The Reservoir*, behind the gardens of the houses then known as The White Hart Inn ; and, by means of leaden pipes, conducted water into it from the spring called Gainey's Well, which rises in a hollow of Gainey's Leaze, on the northern side of Stroud-hill. From this reservoir Mr. Grazebrook and his successors distributed, by pipes, a daily supply of water to such of the houses below the Cross as required it, at an annual payment per house. Mr. Grazebrook is the person alluded to under the pseudonyme of "*Glass*," by the rhyming satirist of that day, in the second of the poems alluded to,—which was written in burlesque celebration of the public rejoicings on opening The Reservoir. It says :—

> "What Ar——ll[1] fail'd with wooden pipes and bread[2]
> To do, is now perform'd with tubes of lead.
>
> *   *   *   *   *   *   *   *   *
>
> May Gotham's glorious name remain on high,
> And *Glass*, th' immortal artist, never die."

The Reservoir, and the water from Gainey's Well, with other water collected from various springs which rise in Kilmister's estate belonging to Dr. W. H. Paine, situated near the top of Stroud-hill, became the property of a Company in 1835, and by them were both the upper and lower

---

[1] Arundel, which is the name intended, is vernacularly pronounced Arn-del, as two syllables.

[2] Perhaps this suggests that he used kneaded bread to close the cracks in the wooden pipes.

parts of the town supplied with water ; but in the year
1864, the whole concern passed by sale from the Water
Company to the Local Board of Health, for the supply of
the inhabitants, and for general sanitary purposes.

After all, the water in this neighbourhood, though perhaps
sufficient, is not abundant. The dip of the strata of the
Cotteswolds is from the north-west to the south-east—the
direction of the valley of the Thames—which, consequently,
receives the larger supply of the Cotteswold water-shed ;
whilst Stroud and the other smaller valleys receive from
this source only what flows from the scarp or western face
of the hills, into which those gorge-like valleys run. This
is equally true of the whole Severn valley, so far as its
supply is derived from the Cotteswolds. The range is
composed of an upper stratum of porous stone, in oolite
rocks, resting on impervious lias-clay ; and the rain-fall of
the district gushes out from the sides of the hills at the
junction, in the form of springs. The pervious or percolating
character of the stratum, is occasioned by the divisions
between its solid beds ; from the fissures and fractures of
the freestone rocks, caused by the shrinking of the soft
deposit of which they were composed, in the process of
drying. Examples of this may be seen in the large Conygar
quarries, belonging to Richard Wyatt, Esq., beyond the
Cemetery, on Stroud-hill, where numerous fossil crustacean
remains may be found. These fissures are in some places
large and cavernous ; and it is said that, about the year
1840, one Charles Nichols, a stone mason, put a ferret into
a hole in these rocks, in pursuit of a rabbit : the ferret did
not return ; but on the next, or second day after, it was
seen to come out of the earth on the wooden spout of a
spring, called Hemlock's Well, a quarter of a mile in a
direct line from the hole in the rocks which it had entered.
Hemlock's Well is a public spring of water, flowing out of
the south side, as Gainey's Well does out of the north side
of Stroud-hill; both of them from the same causes, and both
being on nearly the same level at the junction of the lias
clay with the porous oolite rocks. But the springs in
Kilmister's farm rise from beneath the upper oolite rocks, at
their junction with a clay bed of the fullers-earth formation.

Hemlock's Well lies on the east side of the private road
before mentioned as leading down from Lower-street, near
the Castle, to Arundel's mill ; and is much resorted to for
its clear, cool water, by the inhabitants of that part of the

town.   It probably took its name from plants of the common
hemlock, *(conium maculatum,)* which grew near it, and are
found on the rocky eminences of the neighbourhood.   This
spring formerly poured out a considerable stream of water,
which is now somewhat diminished ; and this, it is understood, was caused by a labourer at the quarry which was
(for a temporary purpose) opened above the spring.   Coming
down unexpectedly to its covering stone, he imprudently
raised and displaced it.[3]

About sixty yards farther down in the hill side, is an old
stone cistern which was formerly supplied from the same
source, and was called Nanny Croker's Well.   Tradition
says a person of that name hanged herself on a tree which
grew near this cistern, but is silent as to the wrongs or
sorrows which led to the fatal act.   Time, with stern justice,
leaves behind him the memory of human crimes written on
the doer's names ; but carries away the record of their griefs
and suffering, and drops it into Oblivion's pool.

[3 So changed are all things earthly, that for several years past the abundant
water of this fine spring is permanently contaminated and is unfit for drinking.—C.H.F.]

CHAPTER VII.

PROCEEDING from the Cross down the south side of High-street, we come to a narrow lane called the Swan-lane, or the Back-lane,—for it is known by both these names. It obtained the first name from an old Inn called the Swan, which, having its front lower down in High-street, extended back to this lane, where stood its stable and stable-yard. It is now converted into a dwelling-house and shop. This lane at first takes a curved westerly direction as far as the site of the stable, about forty yards from its commencement; and then, becoming still narrower, it passes in a southerly direction behind the new Swan stables, down to what was known as the Swan grounds, and Capel's orchard, before the making of the Stroud and Chalford turnpike road.

Old Peter Mason lived in the upper part of this lane in my boyhood. He was the last of our barbers who used the old fashioned pewter basin, with a piece cut out of the rim, by which it was fitted to his customers' necks while they were being shaved. In this basin, when adjusted, he made the lather, and laid it on the beard with his two forefingers, preparatory to using the razor; and, when he had finished the operation, he folded up his napkin, tucked the basin under his left arm, and walked away to shave some other customer.

About forty yards below the Swan-lane, in High-street, the George Inn formerly stood; having its entrance through a gateway under a chamber in the street front. On the right-hand side was the inhabited part of the Inn, and on the left, (within the yard,) were the domestic offices. An assembly-room crossed over the whole south end of the yard; and the way into it, as also to other chambers, was by a wide outside staircase. A gateway under the assembly-room led to the stables and stable-yard beyond; and both ends of the inner yard were closed at night, by large doors.

A public footpath led from the Swan-lane across the stable-yard of the George, and proceeded thence nearly in

the direction of the present John-street and Russell-street.
It passed by a field called Great Shurmer on its left hand,
and on its right by gardens, near where the Baptist Chapel
now stands, and where once stood Mr. Jenner's aviary of
rare and beautiful birds ; and then, rounding Freebury's
orchard, it entered the road from King-street to Wallbridge,
near houses formerly called Saint Briavels, which now form
the north-west corner of Russell-street.   There was not
then, as there now is, a public carriage way across the
George Inn stable yard, but there was access from thence
for carriages, by the Back-lane, into High-street.   And thus
it happened that the writer, in his boyhood, saw a pair-
horse stage-coach of the day, which had come from the
George yard, standing at the acute turning from the Back-
lane into High-street, before proceeding down it on its
journey ; while the driver fired off a blunderbuss, ostenta-
tiously announcing to the people of Stroud that he was
provided with fire-arms, as a protection against highway-
men, if any should be encountered on the road.   This coach
was one of those old " Diligences " of which we have all
read.   Its wide driving-seat and front boot, as also the
boot behind, rested on its carriage or bed, and not on
springs, as in a modern stage coach.   They were, moreover,
of a very primitive and rude construction ; and were not
much less inconvenient and disagreeable, as seats for the
coachman and outside passengers, than a common cart or
wagon.   The boot behind the body of the coach, wherein
luggage was stowed, and whereon outside passengers sat,
was usually made of strong, coarse, wicker-work covered
with leather, from which it obtained the name of the basket;
as in the Irishman's humorous song, (in a farce by O'Keefe,
I think,) which runs thus—

> "If the *coach* goes at nine,
> Pray, what time goes the *basket?*"

I have met with a mention of both the George Inn and
the Swan, in a conveyance of June 7th, 1654, by John
Arundel to John Bond of the close lying on the south-west
side of the town of Stroud, called Great Shurmers, containing ten acres, "with a way leading from the street through
the court of a house called the *Swan*,[1] and through the

[1] This was a public way at the time referred to, and for some years after
I remember Dr. Snowden, when he resided at the Brick House, coming from
Capel's orchard, mentioned early in this chapter, into the Back-lane, and
thence through the Swan court into High-street, on his way to the church, on
Sundays.

backside belonging to the house called the *George;* which premises, with other lands, were purchased by Richard Arundel, grandfather of the said John, of one John Huckvale and Cuthbert his son, and were theretofore reputed to belong unto a certain ancient messuage in the parish of Stroud called *Huckvale's Place.*" This ancient messuage will be identified hereafter.[2] The George Inn, with Great Shurmer and other adjoining lands, was sold by Dr. John Paul, of Rodborough, in the year 1771, to William Turner, who occupied it as an Inn. Upon his insolvency, it was bought by Mr. Jasper Winnett, of Old Meeting-street, on whose death it came, by devise, to his three daughters—Elizabeth, wife of the Rev. William Harris; Susan, wife of Mr. Solomon Hopson ; and Priscilla, wife of Mr. Charles Kendrick ; and from them it passed, by sale, to Mr. Edward Humpage, surgeon of Nelson-street.

In the writer's youth and early manhood, this Inn was well conducted by Mrs. Driver, Mr. and Mrs. Manning, and Mr. and Mrs. Wall, in succession, and was much frequented. But, since 1819, it has been abandoned as an Inn ; the chamber and the assembly-room over the gateways have been taken down, considerable alterations have been made in the adjoining houses, and the sites of the Inn yards are now a part of Union-street, which leads down to the London-road. This is a great accommodation to the town, especially to the inhabitants of High-street, from which it proceeds. These alterations were effected by Mr. Thomas Wall, who purchased the property about the year 1813 ; and on the right hand of the entrance to this new street may yet be seen, blocked up in the wall, a long flat arch, which formerly led to the bar, the front parlour, and other principal parts of the old Inn, but which are now a dwelling-house, with a shop fronting to High-street. The public business of the George Inn, when abandoned there, was transferred by Mr. Wall to the house at the old end of King-street, which he rebuilt, and changed its name of the King's Arms into The Royal George Hotel. The whole of its frontage looks down Rowcroft, and, in all respects, it is most advantageously situated. A new Inn, called the Swan, was established about the same time, on the left-hand side of Union-street, occupying part of the site of the old George and the stables belonging to it.

[2 It has long been known as "The Field."]

We cannot take leave of the old George without remembering that it was for many years the principal hostelry of the town—a most important place in days of yore. There the magistrates, and the various societies of the day, held their meetings ; there balls, assemblies, and public and private convivial gatherings, brought together troops of pleasant people ; and there many a *bon vivant* caroused, and many a weary traveller rested.   It was, indeed, one of those comfortable houses of entertainment in which a man at once found himself at home ; and the existence of which, widely scattered throughout the land, gave rise to the popular phrase which Falstaff has immortalized—

"Shall I not take mine ease in mine inn ?"

Every age has its own modes of providing for its necessities.   An old man may be permitted to look back with complacent partiality on the scenes which accompanied his youth.   But the *laudator temporis acti* must beware how he intrudes on the living of the existing generation any depreciative estimate of the present time, in comparison with the past.   In such a case he will too surely be regarded like the mummy at the old Egyptian banquet, who, from his niche, frowned reproof on his posterity at their joyous feast ; and was, in his turn, regarded as the representative of obsolete institutions and manners.

CHAPTER VIII.

ABOUT seventeen yards below Union-street is a narrow
passage, (a public footway,) that formerly led from
High-street to Freebury's orchard, but now leads to a lane
that was taken out of it.

In the year 1855 this lane acquired the quaintly significant name of Threadneedle-street, from a large factory
established there by Messrs. Holloway Brothers, for making
clothes by the then newly-invented patent sewing machines.

Freebury's orchard lay behind part of High-street, as
the lane now does, forming the southern boundary of the
gardens of the houses there. Freebury was the name of
its former owner; and, in his time, the Rev. John Wesley
once preached there in the open air to a large congregation;
Freebury, his wife, and her relatives being favourers of the
religious movement in which that celebrated divine bore
so large a part. This orchard was afterwards known as
Kendrick's; for, on Freebury's death, it came, by devise, to
his nephew, Charles Freebury Kendrick, whose son disposed
of it in building lots.

Immediately below the narrow passage above mentioned
is a house which formerly belonged to a Mr. Aldridge, one
of an ancient, long resident, family of that name; and was
a private dwelling-house until about the year 1803. It has
a handsome stone front of the Ionic order; but its appearance is much injured by a modern glazed shop-front, which
now fills the whole of the lower part of the building. In
1817 it was occupied by Mr. F. Vigurs, a stationer and
printer; and in that year he printed and published a
pamphlet of fifty-six duodecimo pages, entitled "The
Chronicles, and the Lamentations of Gotham: to which are
added John, a model for Volunteer Captains; The address
of Captain Hollings to the Loyal Stroud Volunteers, and

other Historical Documents, illustrative of the character of the Gothamites." This was a collection of such old poetical prose, and other pieces relating to Stroud,—under the depreciatory name of Gotham,—as could then be found ; and it contained, moreover, the song which has for many years past, been sung annually at the installation of the mock mayor of Randwick, in that village, on the Monday after Low Sunday.¹ Mention has already been made of two of these pieces, "The Razor-grinder's Dream," and "The Speech of the Fakeer of Gotham ;" and perhaps we may read of others in reference to events hereafter to be noticed.

Another of the pieces, entitled " The British Merlin," is a poetical translation, in 126 lines, of a Latin poem of 93 lines, which was first printed on a folio half sheet, and circulated in the year 1731. It was intended to ridicule, as an absurdly ambitious project, the plan for making the " Stroudwater navigable from the Severn to Wallbridge," which was then first attempted. The author's name is not known ; but when, in 1776, the plan was renewed, and a third Act of Parliament was obtained, under which the Stroudwater navigation was ultimately completed, one Nathaniel Elliott, of Oxford, (who had previously lived in Stroud,) wrote and published " A Prophecy of Merlin, a Heroic Poem," in 277 lines (London, 1776, 4to., pp. 22.) It purported to be a translation, and was indeed a new translation, of the above-mentioned Latin poem, which Elliott appended ; but it comprised, also, a considerable addition to the original satire, prompted by his intimate acquaintance with Stroud.²

At Mr. Vigurs's office, was printed and published, in the year 1817, a fortnightly Journal, (as its prospectus

---

1 The ceremonials, the mayor's duties and privileges, with the rude proceedings of the lowest of the people on this day of revel, would be "more honoured in the breach than the observance." The history and supposed origin of *Randwick's Wap* (as it is more respectfully called, a name suggestive, perhaps, of *Wapenshaw*) would supply some interesting particulars, if such a senseless custom could deserve to have them preserved.

2 Mr. Elliott was generally known as a character, and was noted for his talents, his ready wit, and his many avocations. Some of these last are enumerated in the following lines which were circulated in Oxford A.D. 1790, as the production of one of his offended school-boys :—

> Nathaniel Elliott liveth here,
> Poet, Coroner, and Auctioneer,
> He teacheth boys to read and spell,
> And mendeth old shoes very well.

announced,) under the title of "The Gloucestershire Repository, or Literary and Political Miscellany ; comprising original communications in prose and verse, select extracts, &c., &c." It was projected by a few young friends who, with casual contributors, supplied its original articles. The first number appeared on the 10th of January, 1817, and its twenty-sixth and last on December 26th of the same year, making an octavo volume of 512 pages. Its publication was then suspended until 1821, when a second series was undertaken, and issued monthly from the press of Mr. G. Skey, who had succeeded Mr. Vigurs. The first number is dated July 2nd, 1821 ; and it closed with No. 10, on the 19th of April, 1822 ; making a second octavo volume of 360 pages. The difficulty, if not the impossibility, of carrying on a provincial periodical for any considerable time has been experienced wherever attempted ; and it may be imagined how arduous were the editor's duties in conducting and providing supplies for The Gloucestershire Repository, unaided by any paid writers. One individual alone, (the present writer,)[3] contributed, in original articles, a fifth part of the first volume and half of the second, including the two serial papers entitled "The Reflector," and "A three weeks' tour into Wales" ; of both which a few copies were struck off for distribution among his friends. A perfect copy of the two volumes is rarely to be met with ; but there is an interleaved one yet remaining, in which are mentioned the names of most of the authors, of whom three only were living in 1871.

The next house below Mr. Vigurs' was, in the writer's boyhood and for many years afterward, occupied by Mr. Tanner, linen draper ; and, on his decease, by Mr. Thomas Mills, whose quaint, pleasant humour will be remembered by those of his contemporaries who survive. The year 1820 was that of the persecution (as it was called) of Queen Caroline, the wife of King George the Fourth, who sought by "A Bill of Pains and Penalties" to be divorced from her. Upon this occasion, addresses of sympathy were presented to Her Majesty from almost all parts of the kingdom ; and, among the rest, one from Stroud and its neighbourhood. It was very numerously signed ; and with its four columns of signatures, was exhibited unrolled, from an upper window of Mr. Mills's house, whence it reached far down the street. Thomas Mills was, at that time, the head

[3 Who was also the laborious editor thereof.]—C.H.F.

official of the neighbourhood, being the High Constable of
the hundred of Bisley; and was accordingly deputed to
present the Address to the Queen at Brandenburgh House,
Hammersmith, where she resided.   On his return he gave
a humorous report of his proceedings.   Among other things,
he told us that at the same audience several other addresses
were presented; one being from the Spitalfields, whose
deputation was composed of men of diminutive stature and
mean appearance, whom he contrasted disadvantageously
with his own tall and portly figure.   He also told us that
while he was reading the Address he dropped one of his
gloves, which the Queen perceived, and after he had retired
she directed the glove to be picked up and restored; and
that, when the attendant asked to whom the glove should
be given, Her Majesty replied—" Take it to the tallest and
handsomest man in the room—he it was, who dropped it;"
and that a gentleman in waiting brought the glove to *him*.
He did not say who heard the Queen give the direction;
nor did we ask him, having been accustomed to listen to
other strange tales of his adventures without any ques-
tioning.4

4 The unpopularity of the King made the public regard this proceeding
against the Queen with great dissatisfaction; and, as a judicial question, it
was considered impossible for him to obtain a divorce for her supposed
infidelity to him, by reason of his own infidelity to her.   At a dinner at
Cashiobury, Lord Essex's, at this time, the conversation turned on Queen
Caroline.   A gentleman present mentioned a reply made by a Quaker, who,
being asked what the Society of Friends thought of the Queen while this dis-
graceful business was going on—" We are of opinion," said he, "that she is
not good enough for our Queen, but too good for our King."—*Autobiographical
Recollections of C. R. Leslie, R.A.*, *8vo, London*, 1860, *vol.* i, *p.* 146.

CHAPTER IX.

JOHN MILES AND THE BLACK-BOY — MISS JENNER — CHANDLER THE ARTIST.

WE now come to that place on the south side of High-street, where stood the house in which John Miles, a watchmaker, formerly lived. It was taken down in 1871, soon after this book was published; and its site now forms the entrance to the new street called Kendrick-street. This street, after crossing Threadneedle-street, the square of the Subscription-Rooms, and George-street, enters Russell-street. It was opened in 1872; and is a valuable addition to the communications of High-street with the comparatively modern parts of the town.

On the front of the house alluded to, John Miles set up a clock, having a large dial-face, and the figure of a negro-boy with a bell before him, on which he sounded the hours with a club. This, it is believed, was the greatest noise, actual or metaphorical, the watchmaker ever made in the world. But he boasted of vast mechanical abilities; and told the writer, then a youth, that he possessed the secret of perpetual motion: and, when standing with him at his door, he pointed to a heavily-laden timber-carriage, with a long team of horses passing down the street, and said he could construct a machine that would take up the carriage. timber, and horses, throw them into the air, and turn them round for ever and ever! As may be supposed, this foolish boast had an effect on the writer's mind contrary to what was intended; for it convinced him that Miles was ignorant both of the proper objects of mechanical science, and of the laws of matter and motion which regulate and determine its power.

After John Miles's death, the clock and bell, with the figure of the negro-child, which had acquired the name of the Black-boy, were removed to the front of the Duke of

York public-house, in Nelson-street, where they remained several years. But, on the erection of the National school at the entrance of Castle-street, in the year 1844, the clock and Black-boy, with his club and bell, were bought by subscription, and set up against that building. There the Boy has stood ever since, doing the duty of turning his head, lifting his club, and striking the hours of day and night as often as they come round ; and there, it is hoped, he will for many years continue to perform his useful automatic exercises. But it has thereby come to pass, that the identity, if not the very existence of the school, has been well-nigh lost in that of the Black-boy himself ; inasmuch as a little girl being asked, "What school do you go to?" replied, "Please, ma'am, I go to the *Black-Boy*" ; and this is the answer that all the children would give to the same question —"Please, ma'am, I go to the *Black-Boy*." Indeed, it has been whispered that some high and grave authorities, whose duties often lead them to the *Black-Boy*, call the school by the same name, to the great dismay of the purists in nomenclature, who prefer its more accurate appellation of The National school in Castle-street.

A little lower than John Miles's house, in High-street, there was, just before the beginning of 1800, an old house —now handsomely re-built—belonging to the feoffees of Stroud, in which Miss Jenner lived, and, together with the post-office, kept a boarding-school. At the annual fairs she was accustomed to dress her young ladies in white, and range them, tier above tier, before the large window of her house ; thus at the same time advertising her school, and enabling the young people to see a little of "the fun of the fair."[1]

In the same house John Westbrook Chandler, an artist of considerable abilities, had apartments. There he resided for several years, and painted numerous portraits, many of which are of great merit, as may yet be seen here and there in the neighbourhood. He was—perhaps he had become—a man of strange moods, and was a poet and musician as well as a painter ; but the muses who preside over those arts have not always been propitious to the lofty aspirations of their votaries. It was said by a correspondent of the Apollo Magazine, in June, 1823, under the

[1 Miss Jenner was a sister of Samuel Jenner, bookseller, mentioned pp. 18 and 34.]

signature *J.D.*, (when giving a short account of Chandler after his death,) that the "romantic singularity," and the other irregularities in his conduct, there glanced at, were caused by a disappointment in love. However that may have been, he was a very proud man, who would have felt acutely any ill-success in pursuit of the divinity he worshipped, whether metaphorical or mortal. In May, 1800, before he came to Stroud, he had published "Sir Hubert, a heroic ballad, a tale of the baronial age," comprised in a thousand four-line stanzas, ballad measure, dedicated to the Earl of Warwick, whom he addressed as—

> "My kind preceptor, guide,
> My patron and my friend."

His other poetical works were—(on the authority of "J.D.")—the lyric beginning

> "Adieu, my native land, adieu"

and, (on the authority of a friend,) the song of "The Beggar Girl," which became a favourite with the public, and of which the following is the first stanza,—

> "Over the mountain and over the moor,
> Hungry and barefoot I wander forlorn;
> My father is dead, and my mother is poor,—
> And she weeps for the days that will never return."

followed, as was every other stanza, by the refrain,—

> "Pity kind gentlefolk, friends of humanity;
> Cold blows the wind, and the night's coming on;
> Give me some food for my mother for charity;
> Give me some food, and I will be gone."

I have two portraits and two landscapes by his hand. One of the portraits is himself when a young man. The other is Merilla, a gypsy, apparently twenty-five years old. She died "gypsy" at Norwood, where she had been known in her quasi regal state by a person to whom I showed the portrait in 1855. It is a fine characteristic head; and was painted when Chandler retired for a short time from Stroud, to lodge at a farmhouse above Steanbridge, near a camp of his gypsy friends which had been pitched near Bulls-cross.[2]

[2 As a matter of fact, it is painted on one of the gypsy towels, (honestly acquired or not) stretched on four sticks cut from a hedge, and done at one sitting.]

One of the latest portraits he painted here, was in June 1809, being that of a young lady, taken after death, and representing her as asleep on a grassy bank, with her bonnet and a wild flower lying by her side. The latter was a Forget-me-not—a fitting emblem of herself, a flower plucked which could not be revived, yet would not be forgotten.3 A few years after he quitted Stroud there appeared in the obituary of Phillips' Monthly Magazine a notice that he had died in neglect and extreme indigence. Alas! for the wayward, gifted man who, in a life of disappointed hopes, does not seek help from the Mighty Mediciner who alone can

> "minister to a mind diseas'd ;
> Pluck from the memory a rooted sorrow ;
> Raze out the written troubles of the brain ;
> And, with some sweet oblivious antidote,
> Cleanse the stuff'd bosom of the perilous stuff
> Which weighs upon the heart."4

[3 She was a daughter of Mr. Paul Wathen.]
4 Macbeth, Act v., Scene 3.

CHAPTER X.

THE shop-floor of the house next below that in which
Miss Jenner lived, was then and still is, so high above
the street as to be reached by four steep steps. At the end
of the last century it was tenanted by Charles Reinger an
ironmonger, and has continued from that time to the present, in the hands of one of the same trade.

The three next houses require more special notice, from
a circumstance which occurred about the year 1779. The
first house was the bank of Messrs. Hollings and Co., the
floor of which, though somewhat elevated above the street,
was then on the ground, without any cellar under it. This
house was entered from the street through a passage at one
side, running parallel with the front room, (wherein the
business of the bank was transacted,) and with the wall of
the house below; and both the passage and the bank-room
were laid with paving stones. The latter house belonged
to a Mrs. Bond, but was then uninhabited; and had a cellar
whose ceiling was on a level with the floor of the bank.
The third house was then in the possession of one Pegler,
a hair-dresser.

A young man, a stranger, then lodged with Pegler, keeping two riding-horses for his own use. He made himself
agreeable to the youths of Stroud by his strength and
dexterity in the popular games of the period. His name
was Spear; but, instead of being called by it, he was generally known and spoken of by the simple designation of
"Mister." Some suspicions and rumours soon arose about
him, from, (amongst other things) the fact of his riding out
at night; his having been seen coming home very early in
the morning, with his horse tired and travel-stained; and
his occasional secret absence for two or three days.

At this time one Dennis Day resided with his father in a
public-house called The Marlborough head, on the opposite
side of the street; and he, coming home in the middle of
the night and waiting to be admitted, heard a noise in the

cellar of the empty house, which attracted his attention. On crossing over softly and listening, he thought some one was digging, and removing rubbish from the wall which separated the cellar from the foundation of the Bank. In the morning he mentioned to his father what he had heard, and it was communicated to Mr. Hollings, who, gaining access to the cellar of the empty house, found a quantity of faggots screening a hole which had been tunnelled through the wall and partly under the passage, with the apparent intention of getting beneath the floor of the bank room, and breaking into it. The discovery was kept secret, but the nightly progress of the tunnelling was noticed, until it had reached so far that the work of another night would have made an entry practicable. Mr. Hollings then stationed his clerk, Edward Haines, and two or three other men, in the bank, as watchers in the dark, for the purpose of seizing the operator on his expected entrance : and, while they were watching, a paving-stone of the floor was slowly upheaved,— when, the impatience of the clerk getting the better of his prudence, he suddenly cried out "There he is!" and rushed forward; but, having thereby given the alarm, the stone fell back in its place again, and the intended burglar escaped by the way he came. The baffled robber was Spear, who had availed himself of his residence with Pegler to work at night in the cellar of the vacant house for the purpose of breaking into and robbing the bank.

Pursuit being made after him, he was traced to the house of his father, a blacksmith, near Salisbury; and it was said that the constables found him concealed behind his father's forge, in a building the hastily-constructed appearance of which excited their suspicions. He was committed to Gloucester gaol, and there remained awaiting his trial ; but was removed by *habeas corpus* to Salisbury, on a charge of shooting the guard in an attempt to rob the Salisbury mail, on which a conviction was more likely to be obtained. On being removed from Gloucester, and told that the guard —(whom he thought he had killed and who knew him)— was alive, Spear foresaw his fate and exclaimed, "Then I shall be hanged"; and, so it proved : he was tried, found guilty, and executed. As Pegler was supposed to have been implicated in some of his misdoings, especially in his attempt on the Bank, or in succouring and harbouring him as a rogue and vagabond, he, too, was committed to prison, and being tried at Gloucester was found guilty. He was

sentenced to twelve months' confinement, and to be branded
in the hand. I cannot state the precise legal offence on
which he was arraigned, but such was the sentence : and
he was accordingly branded publicly in the old Booth-hall
at Gloucester ; but died before the term of his imprisonment expired. He was the last person in this county who
underwent the punishment of branding.

To proceed,—the house formerly standing on the site of
that which is now the north-east angle of Bedford-street,
belonged to Edward Keene, a carpenter, who subsequently
rebuilt it, and it is now a handsome shop. The site of
part of Bedford-street was, in Keene's time, only a private
passage to his workshops, which lay at the back of his
house. Prior, however, to Keene's death, those workshops
were often fitted up for theatrical representations. There a
company of comedians under Watson the Cheltenham
manager performed ; and there Richer, the great rope-
dancer of the day, exhibited his agility on the tight-rope.
Early in 1808, one Beverley had a company of comedians
here. Among them was Edmund Kean, then a young
man self-conscious of the great powers with which he afterward delighted the world,—ambitious, but as yet undis-
tinguished. Being displeased with Beverley for depriving
him of the opportunity of playing Hamlet for his benefit, he
abruptly left the company and joined another at Leaming-
ton ; but soon returned to marry Miss Mary Chambres,[1] a
member of the Stroud company, who lodged in the house
of Mr. and Mrs. Thornton, at the end of what is now called
Church-street. The ceremony was performed in our parish
church, July 17th, 1808. From this time Kean's reputation
as an actor grew so rapidly that, within six years he had
attained the highest distinction in his profession on the
metropolitan stage ; and his abilities were appreciated by
the élite of society.[2] It is pleasing to add that about the
year 1832, when Mr. and Mrs. Thornton had removed to

1 In a "Life of Edmund Kean," published in 1833, this lady's name is
spelled "Chambers" ; but, in the parish register, she wrote her name as it is
given in the text ; and so did her sister Susan who was one of the subscribing
witnesses.

[2 The following notice of him is extracted from " The Recollections of a
long life," by Lord Broughton, (John Cam Hobhouse,) vol. i., p. 761. " On
December 14, 1814, I dined at Mr. Kennaird's with him [Kean] and Lord
Byron ; and on that occasion he [Kean] mentioned that at Stroud, in Gloucestershire, one night he acted Shylock, danced on the tight-rope, sang a song
called 'The Storm,' sparred with Mendoza, and then acted Three-fingered

the Duke of York public-house in Nelson-street, a gentleman paid them a visit, announcing himself as Mr. Charles Kean, son of Edmund Kean, who had come in performance of a promise made to his mother, formerly Miss Chambres, that he would wait on them with the assurance of her regard, and her continued remembrance of their kindness before her marriage. This courteous act was in full harmony with the characters both of mother and son.

Returning to Edward Keene's workshops :—they were a playhouse so late as 1839, and were so called in a published map of that date. Further, when the carpenter had given place to the comedian and the rope-dancer, and they in turn had made their exit, the building was for three or four years used as a place of worship by the Primitive Methodists. It afterward became the magistrates' office ; and now comprises an attorney's offices, and the cellars of a wine merchant.

About nine yards from the bottom of High-street was the residence of one Chappel, a blacksmith and farrier, commonly known as *Doctor* Chappel, while the resident physician of the town was termed plain *Mister* Snowden. Before the front of this house stood a large open shed in which horses were shoed ; and behind this shed were his forge and smithy, under the apartments of the house. This unsightly mass of buildings was taken down about the year 1808, and two respectable dwelling-houses with shops were erected on the site, one of which was immediately tenanted by Messrs. Martin, Mills, and Wilson, as their bank.

Jack. Kean also told us, that there, one night, he forgot his part, and repeated the Allegro of Milton, without being detected by the audience. He gave us admirable imitations of Incledon, of Kemble, of Sinclair, and Master Betty. He concluded the amusement of the evening by dressing up his hand with a napkin and painting it with cork so as to look like a man, and dancing a hornpipe with two fingers, imitating at the same time a bassoon so wonderfully, that we looked round to see if there was not some one playing that instrument in the room with us. I should not think these matters worthy of record, if Kean had not been by far the greatest actor I had ever seen."]

CHAPTER XI.

DANIEL BLOXSOME — MR. NAYLER — SIR GEORGE NAYLER.

WE now return to the top of High-street, and proceed down its north side. Here we find two large buildings of nearly similar architecture and contemporary date, separated from one another by two old houses. Each of these buildings comprised more than one house, having their ground-floors on the same level ; but, the street being on a declivity, the lower entrance door of each group was formerly reached by several stone steps, with iron rails on each side. The upper building is divided into two houses, the lower of which was, at the beginning of the present century, occupied by Daniel Bloxsome, a linen draper, a neat little man with prominent eyes, and a voice which partook of the "childish treble." His second wife and her maiden sister, who lived with her, were tall, portly women. They were called his two wives, from their almost insepar-able companionship, and the similarity of their rich dresses. When Mr. Bloxsome sold any goods, he dismissed his customers with the somewhat equivocal compliment—"You are welcome." He might often be seen standing on the steps of his doorway, with an air of self-satisfaction, attired in a many-curled powdered wig, dress-coat and vest, knee breeches and buckles, speckled stockings on his short thin legs, and square-toed shoes with large shining buckles ; and when he took a walk he appeared with a cocked hat, and a cane, and often with a nosegay. It would be well if all men's small affectations were redeemed by the honest and kindly qualities of "little Dannie Bloxsome." He died in 1808, aged 72. His wife, who survived him and her sister many years, was always noted for great natural shrewdness; the effect of which was heightened by her use of the broad dialect of the neighbourhood.

The lower of the two buildings has been occupied as one house and shop for several years past; but at the time referred to it consisted of three separate houses and shops, in the lowest of which Mr. Nayler, an apothecary and one of the coroners of the county, once lived. He died in 1780; some years after which his family left the town.

Mr. Nayler's son Richard settled at Gloucester, where he became a celebrated surgeon of the County Infirmary. His son George was, when young, a clever artist. Amongst other things he painted a small full-length portrait of my eldest brother, with his gun and favourite spaniel dog. It was a work of considerable merit, for the fidelity of the likeness and for its colouring and rich impasto: and I remember a small saddle, painted by him, which for many years appeared in the shop window of one Willis, a saddler, in High-street, as a symbol of his trade. George Nayler had a great predilection for heraldry. In the year 1792 he published, anonymously, by subscription, " A collection of the Coats of Arms borne by the nobility and gentry of the county of Gloucester ; " being, as he admitted, chiefly a compilation from Atkyns and Rudder. The engraved title page is embellished with a vignette, representing the figure of Time leaning on a shield, bearing the ancient arms of the city of Gloucester ; and above is a winged figure of Fame pointing to the Cathedral in the back ground. The book was published by J. Good, New Bond-street, London. George Nayler was appointed Blanc Coursier Herald and Genealogist of the Order of the Bath, in September, 1792 ; Blue Mantle Pursuivant, December, 1793 ; York Herald, 15th March, 1794 ; was created Clarencieux King at Arms, 10th May, 1820 ; and Garter Principal King at Arms, 10th May, 1821. He was elected F.S.A., 27th March, 1794 ; Knighted, 25th November, 1813;—(could the young aspirant, who rose so high and so fast, have desired anything more ?) —and died SIR GEORGE NAYLER, KNIGHT, GARTER PRINCIPAL KING AT ARMS, AND F.S.A., 28th October, 1831. He left a wife and four daughters.

CHAPTER XII.

THE house in which the family of the Naylers had lived was, in the years 1820 and 1821, occupied by Joshua Holder, a tailor, one of whose journeymen was Benjamin Parsons, afterward so well known as the Rev. Benjamin Parsons, minister of Ebley Chapel.

Mr. Parsons was born at Nibley, in this county, in 1797, of pious parents, and was residing with them in the toll-house of a turnpike gate, in the parish of Kingscote, when his father died. Benjamin was at that time only six years of age. About two months before his father's death he was seized with a fever, from sitting on the damp ground, which caused a paralysis of his left leg, and a lameness that continued through life. His general health was at all times feeble. He was apprenticed to one Reynolds, a tailor, of Frampton-on-Severn, where, as he told a shop-mate at Holder's, his lameness was increased by jumping out of his bed-room window, in a fright, caused by a dream of being attacked by serpents. While he worked for Holder, he was a constant student of biblical and of such secular learning as was accessible to him ; the Bible, or his book of "exercises," (as he called his first Latin book,) being always by his side on the shop-board, so that he could read as opportunity served. He was a regular attendant at Divine worship on Sundays ; and his wonderful memory enabled him to repeat to his shop-mates on Monday mornings the substance, and often the very words, of considerable portions of the sermons he had heard on the previous day. In his frequent disputes, too, with them, he gave proofs of his propensity for discussion, and the caustic and persistent manner of conducting it, which so strongly characterised him in after-life. While he was in Stroud he lodged with good Isaac Grimes in Church-street. From thence he went to Cheshunt College, to be educated and trained for the ministry in Lady Huntingdon's connexion. In August, 1826, he was appointed Minister of Ebley Chapel, then under Lady Huntingdon's trust ; and

there, for some time, he officiated, reading the Church-of-
England service in a surplice, as his predecessors had done,
in conformity with the general practice of ministers of that
denomination. At length Mr. Parsons relinquished the use
of the surplice and Common Prayer Book ; and, having
fully identified himself with the Nonconformist body, he
became "more properly classed with the Independent
dissenters."[1]

The populous hamlet of Ebley being at a considerable
distance from the churches of Stonehouse and Randwick—
in both of which parishes it is situated,—a new church was
opened there in the spring of A.D. 1837, which had been
built by the subscriptions of members of the Establishment.
Its incumbent, the Rev. J. G. Uwins, was appointed in
1841, and—in personal harmony with Mr. Parsons,—with
quiet, earnest, and untiring activity in his clerical duties,
and in educating the children of the poor, he kept and still
keeps "the noiseless tenor of" his "way."[2]

Mr. Parsons was a man of great natural abilities and
strength of character, uniting a mind of unquestionable
individuality with ample courage to display and defend its
peculiarities.   During the twenty-eight years of his residence
at Ebley, (where he died in 1855,) he was not only a
laborious and faithful pastor of his flock, but he prominently
filled the public eye and ear, with his agitation of nearly all
the social, political, and economical questions of the day,
including polemics, and with his strenuous advocacy of the
views he entertained concerning them.

His labour in preparing, delivering, and travelling to
deliver, (often in distant places,) his numerous speeches,
lectures, and orations, and in writing and publishing his
various letters, addresses, pamphlets, and larger works on
the subjects of his controversies, was prodigious ; for, as his
biographer admits, "he intermeddled with all subjects and
affairs."[3]   But of all his great exertions, perhaps the part
he took in advocating the Temperance movement, gave
him, as it gave his friends, the highest satisfaction.   He was
a teetotaller for the last twenty years of his life.

In his public speeches he generally found his way to the
minds and hearts of his auditory, especially of those whom
he most delighted to address ; for he was always plain,
pungent, and argumentative, and never tamed down or

1 Life, p. 390.
[2 And does so still, in 1890.]
3 *Ib.*, p. 172.

weakened his harangues by elegance or refinement. In opposing persons or things obnoxious to him, his manner was bold, undaunted, scornful, and derisive ; his matter was satirical and bitter , and he employed unsparingly "his terrible power of sarcasm."4 " Some of his opinions were extreme, and he had an odd and unceremonious way of expressing them."5 He sometimes advanced startling paradoxes, as if for the pleasure of dexterously explaining them away. His complexion was dark, his features irregular but very flexible, his voice powerful ; and, when excited in speaking, his eyes, flashing from beneath his large, black, scowling eyebrows, gave fearful effect to his fierce denunciations.

Mr. Parsons was not without his faults and errors. Even among his dissenting brethren there were those who, (as was delicately said by one of them,) "could not see 'eye to eye' with him." Nevertheless all who knew him will acknowledge that he was a really sincere man, and always aimed at truth and right. But then—all his ideas, and all the convictions of his ardent mind, seemed to him to possess those characteristics, and now and then they ran away with him.

Mr. Uwins and Mr. Parsons had learned highly to respect each other : and the many kind visits of Mr. Uwins to Mr. Parsons in his last long and painful illness, were regarded by him as among the most valued attentions of his christian friends.

To any sketch of Mr. Parsons should be added, as his biographer has done, that in his private relations, in his family, and by his fire-side, he was a bright example of genuine tenderness, patience, and affection ; and that his memory is held in the greatest esteem in Ebley, where he taught and acted, lived and died.

An ample and interesting biography of him, under the title of " The Earnest Minister," was written by his friend Mr. Paxton Hood.6 Some persons think it savors somewhat of hero worship. Perhaps it does.7 It is the fault of biography. But let us remember how seldom it is that a biographer has a subject so well deserving a high measure of commendation as Benjamin Parsons.

4 Life, p. 176.

5 *Ib.*, p. 391.

6 London, pp. 511. 1856.

7 Life, pp. 177, 286.

CHAPTER XIII.

WE now come to Church-street, which leads from the
north side of High-street, at a right angle. It is
narrow,—the first half of its length being of the average
width of only nine feet, including the paved footway. The
second house on the right hand is the Lamb Inn, on which
account it was, for many years, appropriately called Lamb-
lane.

When James Wakefield was in possession of this Inn,
from 1824 to 1836, the four-horse London mail-coaches
started from it in the evening and returned to it the next
morning, daily, performing each journey in twelve hours.

As this Inn had not sufficient stables and yards to accommodate the coaches and horses, they were kept at the Swan
Inn, Union-street ; and, in consequence of the narrowness
of Church-street, the coaches were taken to its farther end
and turned round, before they started in the evening, and
on their arrival in the morning. The dexterity of the
coachmen was often admired, when, in driving from the
Inn-door on their outward journeys, and turning at a right
angle down High-street, the leaders entered Union-street
at another right angle on the opposite side, before the hind
part of the coach had well cleared Church-street ; and *vice
versa* on its return.

The two houses at the end of this street are low and old,
and belong to the trustees of Webb's charity. Thomas
Webb, of the Hill, by his will, dated the 4th of November,
1642, gave ten pounds a-year out of his lands at Huccle-
cott, "toward the maintenance of a good schoolmaster at
Stroud." Item, his house in Stroud, "over against the
churchyard, to be employed in charitable uses." Item,
twenty pounds a-year for ever out of his lands at Huccklecott, "for the breeding up of four poor children, to be kept

at school until they should be able to be put out apprentice." Also two rooms in his house, and four pounds a-year for ever, to be paid unto two honest poor widows, "to keep four poor children," to be paid out of his lands at Huccklecott. Further, six pounds a-year out of the same lands "for the reparation of the house, and apparelling of the poor children, and such uses as his overseer and executor should see good."

The house was subsequently divided into two. In the year 1825, the first of them, (which had become two dwellings,) was occupied by the two poor widows,—the dames or mistresses—one of whom had the care of four boys under this charity, and the other the care of two boys under Wyndowe's charity, which will be next mentioned. The other house, then also in two, was let to yearly tenants; the income of the charity being £54 1s., and its expenditure £61.[1] Some short time after the inadequacy of the funds caused the trustees to reduce the number of the boys to two, and of the dames to one.

Wyndowe's charity was founded by Henry Wyndowe, of Lypiatt Hall, formerly of Churchdown, in this county, who, by his will, dated the 13th of December, 1734, devised to three persons therein named, and their heirs, certain messuages and lands in the parish of Stroud, in the occupation of William Neale and Elizabeth Yates; upon trust, out of the rents and profits, to pay yearly five pounds to the schoolmaster, who should be entitled to the ten pounds given by Mr. Webb, as before mentioned, "on condition that he should teach to read and write and cast accounts two poor boys of the parish of Stroud, to be nominated by his trustees, the survivors or survivor of them, their heirs and assigns for ever;" and four pounds to the two women who, from time to time, should be employed and paid out of Webb's charity, "upon condition that such poor women should take care of and provide the provisions, washing and mending their clothes, and all other necessaries for the said poor boys." And upon further trust to apply and dispose of the remaining part of the said rents and profits, "for the maintenance and clothing, and for the placing of the said two boys apprentice, as the said trustees should see fit." By a codicil to this will, dated the 17th of June,

1 See Further Report of the Commissioners for inquiring concerning Charities, 1825.

1744, the testator gave the said hereditaments to the same
three trustees and two other persons, (five in all ;) and he
provided that the survivor of them should convey the
premises to the use of himself, and such other persons and
their heirs, as he should think proper, upon the like trusts.
The last renewal of trustees was by deed of December,
1848, when the trust property was conveyed to the use of
Robert Gordon, William Capel,[2] and Joseph Watts Hallewell,
of whom the last two are yet living.   The trust property
consists of a small farm, chiefly arable, containing about
twenty-eight acres, situated at Far Thrupp.   Besides a
farm-house, it formerly comprised two cottages, which have
long since fallen down.   The rent is £35 a-year, and a sum
of £322 7s. 10d., the produce of accumulations, has been
invested in the Three per cent. Consols, on account of this
charity.   The funds were somewhat in excess of the
ordinary expenditure, when the Charity Commissioners of
1820, in their report of July 2nd, 1825, said :—" As this
charity was evidently intended to be in aid of Webb's
charity, it is proposed to supply the deficiency which we
have already noticed in our account of that charity, out of
the surplus funds of that of Henry Wyndowe."   Perhaps,
however, it was not found legal, or expedient, to follow out
the proposal alluded to, for nothing was done respecting it.

The young subjects of both these charities are nominated
for two years, and are newly clothed once in each year.
The whole of their clothing was, until long within my
memory, made of red cloth, on which account they are
popularly called the Red Boys ; but now their coats and
waistcoats only are of that color.   The boys belonging to
Wyndowe's charity are apprenticed from its own funds ;
but the boys of Webb's charity, not being so provided for,
have generally been selected by the trustees of the Rev.
William Johns' charity, and with other boys of the parish,
have been put apprentice from their funds.

The Red Boys of both the charities were boarded at the
dame's house, and educated by the schoolmaster in the
Market-house, until the year 1865.   But then, the master
being deprived of his school by alterations made in the
Market-house, and the last appointed dame being dead,
the several trustees deemed it expedient to send the boys
for education to the National Boys'-School of the parish ;

[2 Mr Capel died in 1883.—C.H.F.]

OF STROUD, GLOUCESTERSHIRE.   57

paying its schoolmaster a salary for their special instruction,
and the parents of the boys for boarding them at home.
This arrangement was sanctioned by the Charity Commissioners, and admits of the accumulation of a fund for
repairs, &c. The old schoolmaster, John Selby Howell,
died in June, 1867, after filling his office for forty-eight
years.3

Immediately beyond Webb's charity-houses, the road
turns suddenly to the right for about twenty yards, and
then as suddenly to the left, down to Little Mill in the
Slad valley. From below this turn, the road is a private
carriage-way to the mill, and was the only one, until the
making of the Lightpill and Birdlip turnpike-road up the
valley, in 1801.

At the first turn of the road beyond Webb's charity
houses are some buildings used as a brewery ; and there,
about the year 1779, a theatre was fitted up by the manager
of the Bath theatrical company. This was between the
unaccountable dismissal of Mrs. Siddons from Drury-lane
Theatre, and her successful re-appearance there.   She was
then one of the Bath company ; and here she exhibited her
wonderful and her maturing histrionic powers.   She was in
the twenty-fourth year of her age, and the sixth of her
married life. She lodged in the house of Mrs. Romieu,
who kept a ladies' school near the top of Nelson-street ;
and I heard an old lady, who had been a parlour-boarder
in the school at the time, speak of Mrs. Siddons' quiet and
domestic habits. In her after life, I saw this celebrated—
perhaps this greatest—actress, in several of her favourite
characters, including Lady Macbeth ; and I regard the recollection of her as among my treasured memories.   Her
noble face and figure,—her fine voice,—her perfect concep-
tion of, and complete identification with, the characters she
represented,—fully entitled her to the honour of being the
subject of that sublime personification of the Tragic Muse,
which Sir Joshua Reynolds painted, in the very attitude
she first assumed when sitting for her portrait.

Across the road at its first turning, stands a large old
house, having its south gable fronting Church-street. It
was built in 1633-5, by the same Thomas Webb who gave

[3 He was also Parish Clerk for most of that time. Both those charities
have been recently suppressed by the Charity Commissioners, and their revenues appropriated to the new "Marling School."—C.H.F.]

the two houses near it, to charitable uses as before mentioned.   It was called "the house behind the church" in a
deed of 1775, and by that name alone it was known until
a few years since : it now belongs to W. H. Paine, Esq.,
M.D.,4 and is called Rodney House. Its western front is in
a garden, whence there are pleasant views into and across
the valley below.   Many years ago it was the residence of
Mr. Robert Hughes, a clothier, whose manufactory was at
Little Mill ; and in his time there was a noted highwayman
and burglar, named William Crew, whose sister was a
servant in the house.   She was much esteemed by her
mistress ; but it was suspected that, moved by sisterly
affection, she had once or twice secreted her brother there,
when he was in danger of arrest.   As for Crew himself,—I
was told by an old gentleman who happened to be detained
one night at an Inn in Northleach, in the upper part of the
county, that he saw Crew, who (as it afterward appeared)
was then fleeing from justice, enter the common-room, and
stand there in deep abstraction, biting the ends of his
fingers until they bled.5   Verily, Satan is a hard master !

[4 Dr Paine died in 1890.]

   5 William Crew was a native of Wotton-under-Edge, in this county.   He
was hanged at Gloucester, April 21st, 1786, with his two companions, John
Chapman and William Matthews, for burglary in the house of Mrs. Fowles,
of Huntley, near Gloucester, on the 30th November, 1785.   There were five
other men hanged with them ; at which time the place of execution was in a
meadow near Over bridge, about a mile from Gloucester.   A narrative of
Crew's life, &c., was published in the same year, entitled "The Progress of
Vice, exemplified in the life of William Crew," &c.

OLD MARKET HOUSE

CHAPTER XIV.

THE HOUSES OF THE CHARITY FEOFFEES — THE SHAMBLES — MARKET HOUSE — TOWN HALL.

RETURNING from Church-street into High-street, and continuing our downward route, we have to notice three of its houses. The first was formerly occupied by Samuel Jenner, who was succeeded by J. P. Brisley, and he by John Elliott, all booksellers and stationers; in whose successive occupations it has been for more than eighty years. It extends backward a considerable length; and, with the back of the Market-house and the churchyard beyond, forms the whole west side of Church-street. The second house was heretofore tenanted by James Winchcombe, next by —— Morris, afterward by John Sims, and then by Charles Sutton, all mercers; and by them it was collectively held one hundred years. The first house was newly fronted in Jenner's time, and the second was wholly rebuilt A.D. 1846.

The third house was once united to the second by some of its upper rooms, which extended over a narrow entrance into the Shambles, and thence to the Church. Those upper rooms were taken down, and the way beneath them was made wider, at the request of the inhabitants of Highstreet, when the second house was rebuilt; and thereby a considerable improvement was effected.

Beyond the third house, and in a continuous line with it, are two others. One of them is the old public-house so long known as the Butcher's Arms, but which is now called the Corn Hall Hotel, from the handsome building contiguous to it, which was lately erected by the Charity Feoffees for the accommodation of farmers and dealers in corn. The Corn Hall is forty-six feet long, by twenty-two feet wide, and twenty feet high; and, with the Inn and its offices, extends to the churchyard.

These five several houses, with the Corn Hall, the Market-house, and their appurtenances, now form three sides of a quadrangle, of which the churchyard is the fourth side, inclosing an open space, thirty-six yards long, by an average width of thirteen yards.

This open space was formerly called the Pitching, from having been laid with that kind of stonework. It was the general market-place of the town, especially for butchers, who brought meat from the country for sale on Fridays ; and on that account it acquired the name, which it still bears, of the Shambles.

Here the Rev. John Wesley preached his first sermon at Stroud, standing on a butcher's block, which made a pulpit as convenient as many others, hastily raised elsewhere for that celebrated man, in the early days of his itinerant ministrations.

In 1847 stationary stalls were erected there for the butchers, and the whole space was paved. It has two entrances,—one from High-street, the other from Church-street, at the south end of the Market-house ; but it has gradually ceased to be much frequented by butchers or other traders.

The several premises before mentioned are generally supposed to be the plot, or part of the plot, of ground anciently called Pridie's Hay, or Pridie's Hay Acre ; and now constitute the most valuable portion of the trust property of the persons popularly called the Feoffees.[1]

The Market-house is a lofty stone-built edifice of venerable aspect, standing on the east side of the Shambles, and is noticeable for the peculiar architectural appearance of its front. I have not been able to ascertain the exact date of its erection ; but, by a deed of October 10th, in the thirty-sixth year of Queen Elizabeth, (A.D., 1594,) Richard Freeme, and other "feoffees of the lands belonging to the parish of Stroud," and Richard Arundell and Richard Price, "churchwardens of the same parish," leased to John Throckmorton and Thomas Clissold, "all that messuage and house; with the appurtenances then newly erected and builded, near the utter [outer] churchyard of Stroud, with

1 Their early predecessors were invested with the fee, or feoff, of the property, by the delivery of corporeal possession,—livery of seizin. The written instrument was called a Feoffment, and the invested persons Feoffees. The Trusts on which they hold the property will appear elsewhere.

a parcel of ground thereunto adjoining," for the term of thirty-one years, under the yearly rent of one penny; and by deed of August the 18th, 1609, John Throckmorton underleased the same premises to Edward Hall, by the description of "one messuage, with the *Market-house*, and all the shops, ground, and Market-place, situate in Stroud aforesaid," for the term of thirteen years, under the yearly rent of ten pounds.

From the description in the lease, identified by that in the underlease, it may be supposed to have been erected a little before the year 1594; and, from the long term and nominal rent, that it was built, chiefly if not wholly, at the cost of Mr. Throckmorton, who had become possessed of the manor and estate of Upper Lypiatt in the year 1581.[2]

The Market-house is fifty feet long, by twenty-five feet six inches wide. Its front stands on four low arches, springing from a semi-octagonal pilaster at each end, and from the three intervening octangular pillars. Its north end rests on a flat arch, eleven feet wide. The height of the pillars is six feet ten inches; from the ground to the centre of the arches is nine feet, and the intercolumniation is eight feet three inches. The diameter of the shafts is one foot eight inches; the lofty wall they support is two feet three inches thick, and is perpendicular with the projection of their basis and capitals. In the front wall, beneath its huge centre gable, is a fine pulpit-shaped bay-window, fourteen feet wide and eleven feet high, having stone mullions with transoms. It projects boldly forward over the two middle arches and the central pillar from which they spring, and is flanked by two windows, each eight feet two inches wide, by seven feet high, with mullions and transoms. Above the bay-window is a four-light window; and over that, (beneath the apex of the gable,) is a three-light window,—all ranging with the face of the wall.

2 The particulars of this lease and sub-lease are obtained from the Answer of John and Thomas Stephens, filed in the Chancery suit, commenced in 1737 by Bond against Gardner and others, which will be related hereafter. Therein they also say that the residue of the term of 31 years was, by deed of July 6th, 1610, assigned by Throckmorton to their ancestor, Thomas Stephens, to whom he sold Upper Lypiatt; and that the lease, with the counter-part of the under-lease to Hall, were then in the possession of John Stephens with his other title deeds. The property so assigned is expressly called "my lease of Stroud Market-house," in the will of Thomas Stephens, the ancestor.

We have alluded to the peculiar architectural appearance of the front of this building.   On a careful inspection of it, we discovered that, originally, it had not any projecting member, except the bay-window; and that the present ornamental parts were subsequently added, in order to strengthen the edifice.   It appears that the large bay-window and centre gable had deflected forward, and the arch in the north end had been fractured—the former, probably, by the weight of the window and gable on the supporting pillars, and the latter by its almost unresisted outward pressure.   Under these circumstances, a buttress was built against the north-west angle, as an additional resistance to the outward thrust on the pier;[3] and the architect provided a remedy for the other defects in the following manner.   First, he designed the erection of a semi-circular arch of small dimensions, within each of the two old central arches, and abutting on their outer imposts. These were to be only four feet six inches wide by six feet nine inches high, but were to be as deep as the thickness of the superincumbent wall, with plain soffits: and the spaces left between the new and old arches and the central pillar from which each springs, were to be filled in, so as to unite the smaller arches with the original structure, as integral parts of it.   By this means, the inner semi-diameters of the two pillars would be inclosed and masked by the outward imposts of the new ones; and the centre pillar would be enlarged, so as to become a wide massive pier. Next, he designed to erect a stone screen one foot two inches thick, and five feet two inches wide at the bottom, with its base advanced two feet two inches before the new work, in order to cover and conceal it.   After rising as high as the imposts of the new arches, this screen was to expand over them by several lateral projections, resting on bold carved brackets; the whole surmounted by a simple, bold cornice, carrying a blocking to be built into the base of the overhanging bay-window, and be its support.   Lastly, in order to give ornamentation and an air of lightness to the screen, the architect designed two disengaged Ionic columns, advanced on the projecting base, immediately before the centre of the screen,—their shafts to be six feet

3 Part of this buttress was removed, when the modern building for the use of the judge and officers of the County Court was erected in 1851; which building seems to have the effect of a flying buttress, in place of the old one.

two inches high, with a lower diameter of eight inches. These columns were to support entablatures in the shape of beam-ends, (their original type) which, being let into the wall behind, should give to it their quantum of additional strength.

All this was successfully effected ; and, being built into, and incorporated with the front wall, it became a powerful buttress to the endangered edifice. At the same time, its object was so disguised, that it looks like a light and happy freak of fancy in the original architect himself, and part of his first design. The two columns had supported grotesque faces, but these, having gone to decay, were restored by the churchwardens of the day, who were obnoxious to the rude boys of the town. The restored faces being more ugly than their predecessors, the boys called them Chambers and Barter ; whereupon those officers removed them, and substituted the present plain stones resembling inverted brackets.

The date of this ornamental buttress-work is not known ; but, in the year 1698, a lease of the Market-house was granted by the feoffees, Thomas Stephens and others, to the Rev. William Johns, the minister, for twenty-one years, from the 29th of September in that year, " in consideration of his repairing the Market-house," without the reservation of any rent. Although I have not found any special information on the subject, it seems highly probable that *this* was the "repairing of the Market-house" referred to in the lease. It appears from the feoffees' account book, that they were frequently in want of funds for reparations, and that they granted leases for years, to tenants, on fines paid, in order to raise them ; as also, that Mr. Johns, who was a public-spirited man, several times repaired the trust property, and advanced money, which was subsequently repaid. Moreover, it does not appear that any money-rent was received for the Market-house, after granting the lease to Mr. Johns, until 1720, when its term had expired. Besides the repairs before-mentioned, it was found necessary, in 1728, "to screw up the Market-house": and this was effected by passing an oaken beam, secured by iron-work, through the back and front walls, as a tie ; and then, by means of irons from the beam through the south wall, that wall was also "screwed up."4

[4 The whole building, which since the old author's death had again become unsafe, has since been very suitably strengthened and restored.—C.H.F.]

To the ground floor of the Market-house butter-women and dealers in poultry, fruit, and vegetables from the country, formerly resorted on market-days, to sell their various commodities; and there, on other days, were deposited their benches, with the butchers' blocks and moveable stalls, used on Fridays; the arches being then closed with open-work iron gates. The tenants of the Butchers' Arms Inn always had the charge of the fittings of the Market-place, and the collection of the tolls.

From within the southernmost arch of the ground floor a wide stone staircase led to the first floor, and thence a wooden staircase to the rooms above. A part of the floor underneath the staircase was anciently converted into a strong room, for the temporary confinement of culprits; having an oaken door, with massive iron fastenings.

On the first floor was a room, thirty-six feet long, by twenty feet eight inches wide, and twelve feet three inches high, besides a small closet-like room at its south-west end. It was lighted by the large bay-window, and its two side windows. At its upper end was a raised platform, with a balustrade in front, having three steps at each end, and seeming coeval, or nearly so, with the original structure. This room was, no doubt, intended for public meetings; but, at the time of my earliest recollection, it was, and for many years had been, a school-room entirely fitted up with cross desks and benches, where the Red Boys and others were instructed.

Above the school was another room, thirty-seven feet long by twenty-one feet eight inches wide, and eight feet high; and, above that, another, wholly in the roof of the building, its floor being four feet above the wall-plate on which the ends of the rafters rested. Both the upper rooms were occupied for several years by Mr. Robert Hughes, clothier. In one of them he worked spinning-jennies, soon after their introduction; the other was his wool-loft. About the year 1816 or 1817 the Red Boys' school was removed from the first to the room above it; and the old school was repaired and fitted up for the use of the Magistrates of the district, and for the general convenience of the inhabitants of the town and neighbourhood, at the cost of nearly £50, which was raised by subscription.

From this time the Market-house—or rather the large room on its first floor—has been called the Town Hall. Here the Commissioners met to administer the Stroud

Improvement Act, while it continued in force; and here assemble, on the first Tuesday in every month, the members of the Local Board of Health, which succeeded it under the Public Health Act, (11th Vict., c. 62, 31st August, 1843,) since it was made applicable to this parish by the Order of 1856. In this room, also, the Justices of the Peace have their weekly petty sessions on Fridays; and the Judge of the County Court holds his monthly sittings for the district. Here, too, are held such vestry meetings of the parish as may be adjourned from the vestry room, for want of space there; and generally, with the consent of the feoffees, it is open for all meetings on matters of interest to the inhabitants.

In the latter end of the year 1865, it was found necessary to make large and substantial repairs to this edifice without delay; and the feoffees took the opportunity of altering the interior of the building. Accordingly, they entirely removed the second and third floors, together with the staircases, and all the interior fittings; they took down the weak south wall, and re-built it from the foundation; they then secured the roof and the four walls, by passing iron rods, well tied, through the building from east to west, and from north to south, at the level of the removed second floor; and they made an open-work ceiling,—the principals springing from four corbels at the same level, and reaching to the roof. By these means the Town Hall has been improved, and now includes the whole interior area of the building above the ground floor, measuring forty-six feet long, by twenty feet six inches wide, and twenty-two feet high, and is well ventilated and fitted up with all necessary conveniences for its varied uses.

The entrance to the Town Hall is now by an inclosed door in the new-built south wall, under a large window; the door being approached from the outside by a double flight of stone steps,—one from Church-street, and the other from the Shambles. The alterations were effected at the cost of £300; and the Market-house and County Court offices, &c., now yield a considerable annual income.

CHAPTER XV.

IT is not known at what time the first floor of the
Market-house was set apart by the feoffees for a
school, or when it was fitted up so suitably for one of a
better class. But we may presume that it was done with
a view to "the maintenance of a good schoolmaster at
Stroud," and teaching the Red-boys "to read, write, and
cast accounts," as was intended by Mr. Webb and Mr.
Wyndowe in their charities before-mentioned. Accordingly, the masters of the school, for the time being, have
been paid annually the fifteen pounds bequeathed for those
purposes.

With respect to the school-masters, I have met with the
name of "a Mr. Davis," residing at Stroud, in the year
1726, who was, probably, one of them. He is honorably
mentioned in the biography of John Canton, our eminent
townsman, of whom it is stated that he "was placed, when
young, under the care of Mr. Davis, a very able mathe-
matician, with whom, before he attained the age of nine
years, he had gone through both vulgar and decimal
arithmetic. He then proceeded to the mathematics, and
particularly to algebra and astronomy, wherein he made a
considerable progress."

In the year 1736, Daniel Shatford, parish clerk, was the
schoolmaster, and taught the Red-boys, with his other
pupils, in the schoolroom, which he rented of the feoffees,
at two pounds per annum, for that purpose.[1]

Many years afterward, Samuel Purnell was the master
of the Market-house school. He resided in one of the

---

[1] The feoffees allowed Shatford to retain to himself this rent, for his salary
as parish clerk.

"houses behind the church"; and, besides teaching the Red-boys, had, for several years, a very good school of boarders and day-scholars. Among the latter were sons of the most respectable inhabitants of the town ; and, among the former, juvenile branches of the Kingscotes of Kingscote, the Hawkers of Woodchester, and other neighbouring gentry.

One of these was John Alexander Ball, whose family had been long settled at Stonehouse Court, and were Lords of the Manor of Stonehouse. On one occasion, soon after an execution of felons at Gloucester, the boys took it into their heads to play at hanging, in the Shambles ; and prevailed on Ball, who was a bold and daring lad, to submit to the dangerous experiment. He was accordingly suspended and the other boys regarded his struggles as a clever acting of his part: even his younger brother, who was one of them, said "our Aleck likes it,—he wont speak." Providentially, at this critical moment, an older boy came by, who, seeing Ball's condition, cut him down. That boy was afterward Mr. Thomas Holbrow, of Badbrook House, who related the circumstance to me; and said that Ball when cut down was black in the face. The lad who had been suspended, became in after life Sir J. A. Ball, Bart., Rear-Admiral of the White Squadron, and Port-Admiral and Governor of Malta. He was made a Post-Captain in 1783, before he was twenty-six years of age. He commanded the "Alexander," of seventy-four guns and 590 men, in Lord Nelson's victorious engagement with the French fleet, under Admiral Brueys, in Aboukir Bay, August the 1st, 1798 ; and was promoted to a flag in 1805. He died at Malta, October the 20th, 1809, aged 52, and was buried there in a fort, close to the remains of Sir Ralph Abercrombie, who fell in the battle of Alexandria, soon after Nelson's victory. Before the battle of the Nile, as Nelson's was called, the Vanguard, one of his squadron, had sustained great damage from a sudden storm in the Gulf of Lyons ; and Captain Ball was directed to take her in tow, and carry her into St. Pietras, Sardinia. Nelson, apprehensive that the attempt might endanger both vessels, subsequently ordered him to cast off ; but Captain Ball, possessing a spirit like his commander's, replied—he was confident he could save the Vanguard, and by God's help he would do so, and he did it. Previously, there had been a coolness between these two brave seamen ; but, from that

time, Nelson became sensible of the extraordinary merit of
Captain Ball, and a sincere friendship subsisted between
them for the remainder of their lives.

Mr. Purnell's successor in the Market-house school was
John Hyde, a thin, spare man, of pompous speech, manner,
and mode of walking ; which was said, of old, to be after
the true pedagogic fashion, whether natural or acquired.
He was sometimes so violent in reproving and chastising
his pupils, as to provoke their resistance and open rebellion ;
but at other times he exhibited feelings of great tenderness ;
and it is only just toward a good man, to suppose that his
harshness to his scholars, as well as to others, might have
been partly owing to the constant irritation of a wounded
spirit,—labouring under the straightened circumstances of
an unavailingly laborious life.   His school was composed
of day-scholars, and a few boarders.   Of the latter we will
mention one, in order to give a specimen of Hyde's humour,
and his rhyming talent, of which last he was proud.   This
boy was the illegitimate son of Justice Henry Wyatt, of
Farm Hill, after whose death in 1784, there was considerable delay in the settlement of his pecuniary affairs ; and
this will explain some expressions in the following receipt
given by Hyde in 1785, for money received on account of
the lad's board and instruction.   The receipt ran thus :—

> " Received of Stroud Bank, this first day of October,
> One thousand seven hundred, and forty twice over,
> With five added more,—pounds exact twenty three,
> Of true British coin, as below you may see ;
> In part for young Wyatt's tuition and board :
> (I've waited too long for the same on my word,)
> And for shoes, hats, and breeches, with trifles beside,
> If my name must appear to't, here take it,—
> £23.   JOHN HYDE,"

As for Justice Wyatt himself, he had been one of a noted
Triumvirate, some of whose wild bacchanalian and other
irregularities are still floating in memory among us.   His
name appeared, with those of his two boon companions, in
a contemporary satirical poem, describing a special visit
which he of the cloven foot—ycleped Satan—once paid to
his friends in this neighbourhood.   It told how he made
his first call on Justice Thomas Gryffin, of Gryffin's Mill,[2]
whence, resuming his flight, he visited Captain Hawker at

2 The third mill above Bowbridge, on the river Froom.

Rodborough Fort ; [3] and then alighted at Farm Hill, to talk over past transactions with old Justice Wyatt. [4]

John Hyde resided in his own house near the upper part of Middle-street, until his death. His successor in the school was John Mosely, who occupied the house near Little Mill ; and, besides instructing the Red-boys, had pupils who boarded with him. He was followed by Edward Wall, Benjamin Franklin, and John Selby Howell in succession.[5]

---

3 This building was erected by Mr. George Hawker, (generally called Captain Hawker,) in 1761, upon a piece of common land, granted to him by the Lord of the Manor, on a lease for lives. Here he resided several years. On his death in 1787, it came, by devise, to his son Joseph Hawker, who sold it in the same year to Mr. James Dallaway, who died there ; and it was purchased by Mr. Joseph Grazebrook in 1791. The Fort has the architectural appearance which its name imports ; and its flag has floated, and its three cannons have been fired, on occasions of public and local rejoicing, for many years past. It was rebuilt in 1871, by Mr. Alexander Holcombe, its then owner.

It stands on a bold eminence, from which are very varied and extensive views of the Stroud vale on the right, Woodchester on the left, Stonehouse, the Severn, and Dean Forest in front ; and, beyond all, the lofty Sugar-Loaf Mountain, near. Abergavenny, may be distinctly seen, low in the western horizon, in the light of a quiet summer evening, or when clothed with snow or ice in winter. It is, itself, a conspicuous object from almost every point in the surrounding neighbourhood.

4 Farm Hill is an eminence above the village of Pakenhill. Its modern mansion stands on the site of the old house, where Justice Wyatt lived and died.

5 The resignation of his office by this last master, his death, and the new arrangements made for keeping, and teaching the Red-boys, have been already mentioned. See pp. 56, 57.

CHAPTER XVI.

SAMUEL SPENCER — MR. JAMES WITHEY — FIFTH OF NOVEMBER
RIOT.

THE second house below the entrance to the Shambles
from High-street is a handsome building, erected
about the year 1782, in lieu of an old house which projected
into the street several feet farther that the present large
door-steps, and even beyond the advanced foot-pavement.
It belonged to William Knight, of Gannicox, generally called
Banker Knight, from having been a banker in London. On
his monument in the late parish church was a medallion,
sculptured in white marble, representing his profile in the
bushy wig of that day. The first tenant of the new house
was Samuel Spencer, a grocer, who had previously carried
on his business in the large balconied house on the south
side of the Cross ; and, after his death, it was occupied, in
succession, by Messrs. Joseph Watts, Thomas Mills, James
Withey, and his son William Henry Withey, who is its
present owner.

I remember seeing, with juvenile admiration, Mr. Spencer's
handsome widow, walking in the fields slowly and majestic-
ally, as became a discreet matron,—with a tall, slender,
ebony staff, tipped with an ivory crook. This she handled
daintily, and with the semblance of its being a support :
but, the next time I saw her taking a walk, she had discarded her ebony staff for the supporting arm of a stalwart
suitor. She was married to the Reverend George Wilkins,
September the 2nd, 1793.

In the year 1816 Mr. James Withey purchased this
house, and was residing there in 1824 ; at which time he
was High-constable for the Hundred of Bisley. Until that
year, the discovery of the Gunpowder Plot of 1605 had
been celebrated at the Cross on every returning fifth of
November, by a bonfire and fireworks ; and sometimes by
rolling flaming pitch and tar barrels down High-street, to

the great annoyance and terror of the inhabitants. At length, it was thought desirable to put an end to such dangerous proceedings ; and, in 1823, an effort towards that object was made, which failed through the opposition of the rabble. Toward the end of 1824 it was resolved, at a meeting of the inhabitants, to make another attempt to abate the nuisance, without depriving the populace of their annual rejoicing. With this view, a piece of ground, where Trinity Church now stands, was hired for the approaching fifth of November, and money was subscribed to provide fuel for a large bonfire. On November the 2nd, in that year, hand-bills were distributed, containing a notice from the magistrates' clerk to that effect, and warning people against making the old demonstrations of the day, at the Cross, or elsewhere in the town. Four wagon loads of wood were purchased, and hauled to the place provided, and a huge fire was kindled there on the evening of the fifth. It was soon perceived that the rabble, who had assembled in unusually large numbers, were dissatisfied, and bent on mischief. They provided themselves with bludgeons from the reserved firewood ; and, when the fire was getting low, they removed the residue of the wood to the Cross, where they made a new bonfire, bringing to it whatever other fuel they could collect, in order to increase the display.

The High-constable, with the petty constables, tithing-men, tradesmen and others, whom he had charged to aid in keeping the peace, repaired to the Cross. There they expostulated with the assembled multitude, and endeavoured to extinguish the fire, but in vain. A violent riot ensued, and when any ringleader was taken into custody, he was immediately rescued by his companions. Mr. Charles Sutton was wounded in the head by a cudgel, and Joseph Horton, a constable, was beaten so severely that it was necessary to carry him home. The riot proceeded to such a height, that the High-constable, with his assistants and supporters, were at length obliged to retire, and leave the mob masters of the town. About eleven o'clock at night they procured a tar-barrel, which they ignited and sent rolling down the street, and, when it fell to pieces, they scattered the burning brands. They then proceeded to the High-constable's house, and assailed it with stones and other missiles, breaking the windows, damaging the doors and window frames, and endangering the inmates. It was nearly three o'clock in the morning before the crowd dispersed, and left the town in quiet. The assault on Mr. Withey's house was made in revenge for the active part he had taken in the matter. Without delay, information was laid against some of the chief rioters, who, being apprehended and taken before Henry Burgh, Esq., J.P., were bound over to appear at the next general quarter sessions of the peace, to answer for their misconduct. Accordingly, at the Easter sessions of 1825, eleven of them were prosecuted for "a riot, and obstructing the peace officers in their duty"; and, being found guilty, several of the most violent were sentenced to three months' imprisonment. Two of the ringleaders were Charles Brown and Charles Stanley; the former of whom was the chief instigator of, and actor in, most of the mischief-making and depredations for several years, both before and after this; and was feared as the secret enemy of all who had given him offence. Since that time, not any fifth-of-November bonfires have been kindled at the Cross, nor any flaming pitch-barrels rolled down High-street. Even the number of bonfires formerly seen on the neighbouring hills at this anniversary, has gradually diminished, and it is hoped that, before long, its celebration will cease altogether, and be remembered only among the things that were.

CHAPTER XVII.

MR. Thomas Hughes commenced his medical practice as early as 1770, at the feoffees' house, in High-street, immediately below the entrance to the Shambles. Thence he removed to the house beyond Mr. Withey's; and finally, to the next, both of which he had purchased and rebuilt; and in the last he died, May the 13th, 1813. In my boyhood, Mr. Hughes always appeared in the old medical costume, which was not laid aside until near the end of the last century; namely, a broad-brimmed hat, a wig with three rolls of curls, square-toed shoes with large buckles, and a gold-headed cane. Thus attired, and having an austere countenance and deliberate walk, he impressed my young mind with great awe. In person he was heavy; in manners somewhat uncouth and abrupt; in character, hard, stern, and tenacious of his sentiments; but just, independent, and self-reliant. He was a diligent student, especially in the literature of his profession. He kept a common-place book, in the form of loose sheets of folded paper, wherein he entered notices of his reading, and extracts from the books he perused. At a meeting of his brother practitioners, where an interesting surgical case came under discussion, he was able, (in addition to two others cited as the only two known), to mention a third reported case of the same kind, and at length he came to be called the Medical Dictionary. He learned Greek after he was fifty years of age, in order to read the New Testament in the original, and had prepared a Harmony of the Gospels for publication,—when his design was superseded by the appearance, in 1803, of Warner's *Diatessaron.*

In 1804, when Mr. Hughes was nearly sixty years of age, his patriotism led him to join the Longtree, Bisley,

and Whitstone Troop of Volunteer Cavalry, commanded
by Henry Burgh, Esq.   On that occasion he discarded his
large hat, wig, and square-toed shoes, and thenceforward
wore his own short-cut grey hair.   Equipped with cavalry
boots, sabre, and a helmet, with an artificial regulation pig-
tail hanging from within the hinder part of it, he joined
the ranks on his old horse, and regularly attended drill and
exercise.   After his military services expired, his old charger
grew so fat and heavy, by rest and much feeding, that his
movements became slow, like those of his master, whom he
carried at only a foot-pace, as if even ambling was a motion
too undignified for him.   So that it might have been said
of him, as of a certain other celebrated steed,—

" He was well stay'd, and in his gait,
Preserv'd a grave majestic state."[1]

Even boys in the road have walked by the side of the
horse and his rider, in giggling admiration of the "great
fat beast of a horse," and their mutual suitableness.   Once,
however, Mr. Hughes had especial cause for congratulation
on the slowness of his steed ; having arrived safely at
Alkerton—more than six miles from Stroud—without the
linch-pins having been put into the axletrees of his gig
wheels, before he left home.

I remember William Dowman, a poor half-witted man
of the town, well known for his mixed character of fool
and humorist, whom Mr. Hughes, about the year 1806,
charitably employed as a domestic servant, in the hope of
fitting him for that line of life.   On one occasion, when
Mr. and Mrs. Hughes had been to a winter evening party,
Dowman came to light them home.   It was in the days of
large glass lanterns, when, as yet, High-street was innocent
of still larger gas-lamps.   Dowman carried the lantern
behind, instead of before, them ; and, when ordered by Mr.
Hughes to go forward, he replied,—" Master, if *you* don't
know manners, *I* do ; and it shan't be said of me, as how
I walked before my master and mistress."   When Mr.
Hughes found his experiment on Dowman [2] was a failure,
and dismissed him from his service, he was employed as a

1 Hudibras, c. 1, p. 1. 1, 427-8.

2 The decay of the family of Doleman, ancient mill-owners in the Tithing
of Lower Lypiatt, may be traced by the gradual corruption of its name in
some old parish registers, thus—Doleman, Dolman, Dowman, Doman.

labourer in the dye-houses at Badbrook, where he sometimes made sport for the friends of his new master, the fun
of which he, perhaps, enjoyed as much as they. Indeed,
I suspect that he was, in some degree, "ambitious for a
motley coat,"[3] and the license which belonged to that livery.
The last vision of Mr. Hughes that remains in my mind
is, as he appeared in the street before his house, mounted
on his fat slow-paced horse, ready to start on a summer
excursion ; having his cavalry cloak strapped to his large
military saddle, and his white leather sword-belt buckled
round his waist, from which was suspended an umbrella,
where whilom had hung his no less peaceful sabre. This
is an example of the manner in which he carried out his
plans, quite independently of all conventionalities, and the
opinions of both the great and small world around him.[4]

The part of High-street in which Mr. Hughes' houses
stood, was, until a few years since, called the Pig-market ;
for there the inhabitants on both sides of the way were
accustomed, on market days, to set up before their houses,
pens made of hurdles, to which pigs were brought for sale.
To this offensive inconvenience they submitted, for the
poor remuneration of sixpence per day for the use of a
pen. At those times, the high road was so much narrowed
that two carriages could not pass each other.

While the pig-market was held there, Mr. Saunders, an
attorney residing at Lower Grange, a short distance from
the town, had a fancy to fatten pigs for sale, which he did
on an extensive scale, and taught them to come to their
food at the sound of a bell. Thus it happened, when he
had sent a score of pigs to be sold, and they had been
safely penned, that Arthur Hewlett, the town crier, rang
his bell preparatory to making some public announcement ;
and the pigs, unable to distinguish one bell from another,
no sooner heard Hewlett's, than they all leaped over the
hurdles, and scampered home to the Grange, in expectation
of their food,—leaving the pigs of other dealers, as well as
the dealers themselves, astonished at the unexpected movement.

3 As you like it. Act ii, sc. vii. l. 393.

4 Mr. Hughes' valuable services to the Dispensary will appear in the
account of that Institution.

Mr. Saunders inserted in the agricultural publications of the day favourable accounts of his proceedings ; and, in particular, the discovery of a valuable economical food for pigs, namely, an infusion of hay in boiling water, which his sceptical neighbours called hay tea.   But, at length, he found to his cost that, with his mode of managing and feeding pigs,—at least those of the breed then known,— they paid less for what they ate than any other animals.

Soon after the passing of the Stroud Improvement Act, A.D. 1825, the market for pigs was removed from this part of High-street to the Cross.

CHAPTER XVIII.

THE MARLBOROUGH HEAD INN — ELECTION OF LORD JOHN RUSSELL.

MR. Hughes' house now belongs to Mr. Gay, chemist, whose predecessors in the same business were Mr. Jones, Mr. Durden, and Mr. Randall.[1] Immediately below, are the house and shop of Messrs. Mills, Brothers, and Co., grocers, which were erected by the father of Messrs. Mills, about the year 1795, on the site of a Blacksmith's shop, and was occupied by him until his death in 1827. It is the lowest house in the old Pig-market; but, unlike the others, the pavement and side of the street in its front were always kept free for access to the shop.

The succeeding house was an old Inn called The Marlborough Head, indicating its existence so far back as Queen Anne's reign; and one of its former landlords was the father of Dennis Day, before mentioned in connection with Spear's attempt to rob the Bank.[2] The front parlour projected nine feet beyond the front of Mr. Mills' house; and, as it had a window looking southward across, and another, eastward, up the street, it was a favorite resort of the tradesmen of the town, wherein to hear, tell, and discuss, the local and general news of the day. The projection of this room made the highway before it permanently narrower than even the Pig-market on Fridays, the house being separated from the road by only a row of stones, barely fourteen inches wide. Thus it happened that, about the year 1828, as Mr. Henry Newman was conversing with a lady in the street, under the wall of the Inn parlour, a wagon which had one of its hind wheels chained, to retard its pace, came down unperceived by them. It slipped and swerved to their side, dashing them against the wall so violently, that blood gushed from Mr. Newman's ears. The lady was not seriously hurt; and, the wagon being stopped by the wall, they were able to crouch down into the hollow made by the sloping wheel, and so escaped.

[1 At present (1890) to Mr Coley]
2 See page 46.

On the opposite side, (and on both sides of the way a little lower down,) the pavement was so narrow as to need the defence of posts and chains.   But that was remedied in 1836, when the front parlour of the Inn was taken down, and its whole face rebuilt, at the distance of only nine inches in advance of Messrs. Mills' shop.   At the same time, the fronts of several houses below were removed back, and made to range with it.   All this was effected at the cost of about £800, which was raised by subscription.

At the General Election of Representatives in Parliament for the Borough of Stroud, in January, 1835, Colonel Fox was chosen in the place of W. H. Hyett, Esq., who had resigned.   In the month of May following, Lord John Russell, (who had been unsuccessful as a candidate for Devonshire, and whose presence, as a member of the Government, was needed in the House of Commons,) was elected for Stroud in the room of Colonel Fox, who had vacated his seat to make way for him.   The old Inn belonged to Mr. Joseph Watts, of Stratford House ; well known for his friendly qualities, and for the quiet, yet powerful, influence he so long and deservedly exercised in our political movements ; and on this occasion he changed the name of the Inn from Marlborough Head to Bedford Arms.   At the same time, the former passage to Keene's workshops, which lay opposite to it, was dignified with the name of Bedford-street, and one of the new streets was called Russell-street, all in compliment to Lord John Russell, that distinguished member of his noble family.   The Bedford Arms Inn has since followed the fate of the Marlborough Head, and lost its name.   In the year 1854 it was bought by Messrs. Mills, Brothers, & Co., and ceased to be a public-house, the ground floor now forming a part of their establishment, and the upper rooms being used as a School of Art.

Lord John Russell subsequently purchased Hill House Estate, formerly the seat of Sir George Onesiphorus Paul, Bart., and changed its name from Hill House to Rodborough Manor.   In the year 1861 he was created Earl Russell of Kingston Russell, Dorsetshire, and Viscount Amberley of Amberley, Gloucestershire.[3]

3 Amberley is a hamlet in a large tract of common of pasture of the same name, in the parish of Hampton.   It is an ecclesiastical district, having a church and parsonage house, built and endowed by the late David Ricardo, Esq., of Gatcombe, in 1836.   Its first incumbent was the Rev. R. E. Blackwell. The present incumbent is the Rev. W. Bryan-Brown.   Amberley adjoins the parish of Rodborough.

CHAPTER XIX.

JOHN HOLLINGS — LOYAL STROUD VOLUNTEERS — LODGEMORE
VOLUNTEERS — THE SEVERN, AND THE KING STANLEY RIFLE
CORPS — THEIR MILITARY AND LEGAL CONTESTS.

THE lowest house on the north side of High-street is a
handsome brick building, having a row of lime trees
within the iron railing of the front court ; but, in my boyhood, a row of trees stood on the outside of the court,
having had their branches so much cut and trimmed, that
they had grown into masses of knotted open-work. It
belongs to the Gloucestershire Banking Company,[1] who
conduct their business in the adjoining offices, and requires
some further notice, on account of its old associations.

It is said to have been built by one Alderley, a baker of
the town. He had a friend who was a brick-maker, of
whom he asked permission to take from his store, bricks
wherewith to build an oven. Permission was granted, and
from time to time the baker took all the bricks required in
raising his whole house. From this large use of the licence
given, the public called it Alderley's *Oven*, which it retained
for a considerable time. When anyone ascended its staircase in haste the house shook, indicating that its walls were
slightly built, and that the unconscionable baker had taken
from his friend, "good easy man," only the quantity of
bricks that just sufficed to erect so large an oven.

This house formerly belonged, for her life, to Mrs. Doctor
Jones, (as she was called,) the widow of a physician of the
town. The reversion belonged to Mr. John Hollings, who
then resided on Tower Hill ; and he, making very frequent
and tender inquiries after the old lady's health, she interpreted them into a too eager anxiety for her death. Upon
one such occasion she bade his messenger to carry back
her reply, in the quaint words of the distich—

"The age of a man is three-score years and ten ;
But the age of a woman is—the Lord knows when."

[1 Now the Capital & Counties Banking Company.]

At length Mr. Hollings became possessed of the property, and, in my youth, its grounds and gardens were laid out so tastefully, as with their stately trees, shady walks, well-stocked aviary, and beautiful flowers, to give me a very lively idea of those *plaisaunces* which belonged to great mansions in olden times.

It comprised the whole space between the church and the brook in the valley below ; for the road through Lansdown had not then been made. One day, in the spring of the year, Mrs. Hollings being in the kitchen garden of the house, dropped a valuable diamond ring, which was after-wards found by her cook, on a carrot she was preparing to be boiled for dinner. The ring had fallen on ground newly sown with carrot seeds, one of which, in growing up, had thrust its feathery top through the ring, and so preserved it for discovery, and, eventually, for a return to its owner.

Mr. Hollings was a retired mercer and banker, a justice of the peace for the county, and was appointed Captain Commandant of the Loyal Stroud Volunteers in the year 1798, when the threat of invasion by Napoleon the First had so roused the patriotism of the nation, that 450,000 volunteers were speedily raised, armed, and trained, for its defence.

The commissioned officers of this corps were John Hollings, Captain ; William Tanner and John Saunders, Lieutenants ; and Thomas Holbrow, Ensign. There were four sergeants, four corporals, and eighty-four privates ; besides two drummers, two fifers, and a drum-major. The band consisted of six clarionets, one bassoon, one serpent, first and second French-horns, one triangle, and one double-drum. The Rev. Joseph Colborne, A.M., of Stroud, Rector of Side, was the Chaplain, and Edward Thornton the Surgeon.

The uniform of the corps consisted of a jacket of scarlet broad-cloth, with blue cuffs and collar, waistcoat and breeches of white kerseymere, white cotton stockings, and black cloth gaiters. The cap was somewhat helmet-shaped, and the arms of the privates were a musket and bayonet, which, with the drums, were supplied by the Government.

The Countess of Berkeley presented the Colour [2] to the Corps, at a grand review on Hampton Common, September the 19th, 1799 ; on which occasion Mr. Hollings made an

---

2 There was but *one*.

address, which has come down to us, having been printed for some other reason than its eloquence as a military oration.

The Flag was of a deep purple colour, having the Royal Arms in the centre, and the Union Jack in the upper corner near the staff, with the motto "Si Deus est nobis, quis contra nos," and "Loyal Stroud Volunteers" below in scrolls. At the return of peace with France in 1802, the services of the Corps were dispensed with, and the arms, &c., were returned.

When the Captain died the flag was deposited with Lieutenant Tanner, from whom it came to Thomas Mills, his successor in business, an old member of the corps ; and was, (A.D. 1867,) in possession of William Mills, his nephew.

On the formation of the second battalion of the Gloucestershire Rifle Volunteers, in 1860, its two Stroud companies, the fifth and sixth, assembled on Hampton Common, July the 31st, in that year, when the old flag was brought forward, and once more floated in the breezes of that high region, supported by William Franklin and William Purcell, the only members of the old corps then living. Franklin had played the clarionet, and Purcell the triangle, in the band. The former was still a fine stout man, in the 85th year of his age, and the latter, who was in his 75th year, showed me, with evident satisfaction, his little smart military jacket.

Mr. Hollings' name appeared in several poetical and prose compositions of the day ; in all of which he was represented unfavourably, according to the usual practice of adversaries and writers of satire.

They may be found in Vigurs' collection ; and all the allusions and the names there given in initial letters and asterisks might yet be explained, if the petty squabbles of that day were of sufficient present interest to repay the trouble of deciphering them.

One of these pieces, entitled "John a Model," was written by Mr. Joseph Lewis, of Brimscomb, and contains the following couplet, in allusion to Mr. Hollings' alleged arrogance toward the members of his corps,—

> "Tis all a weigh-jolt, John, depend upon't,
> The lower they go down, the more you mount."

It is transcribed here chiefly for the purpose of adding that "*weigh-jolt*" is one of our provincialisms, and means a see-saw. The syllable "weigh" expresses the resemblance of its motion to that of a balance, and "jolt" the effect of the motion on the riders, when either end of the plank they sit on comes to the ground.

It is said of Mr. Hollings that, to some one who had angrily expressed the hope of living to see him safe under ground, he replied—" *That you never shall.*" Accordingly, when he died in 1805, his coffin was not literally *interred ;* but was placed above the ground, within a pyramidal tomb raised over it, in Stroud churchyard.

The mention of the Loyal Stroud Volunteers of 1798 suggests a notice of other contemporary volunteer corps in the neighbourhood. One of these was the Lodgemore Volunteers ; so called from the place of residence of their Commander, Captain George Hawker. Of this corps I remember but little more than that it was sometimes called "The Awkward Squad,"—provincially pronounced *Hawker'd Squad.* Of this name the kind-hearted Captain was well aware, and always heard it with his usual smile of genial humour. There were, likewise, two rifle corps. One of these, the Severn Rifle Corps, consisting of three companies, numbering 180 men, was under the command of Major Samuel Wathen, of Newhouse, in this parish ; and the other, called the King Stanley Riflemen, was commanded by Captain Nathaniel Peach Wathen, of Stanley House, in this county. The uniform of the former was a bottle-green jacket and pantaloons, with black velvet cuffs and collar, a black velvet stock, a helmeted cap with upright blue feather, black leather cross belts and pouch, with horn powder-flask, a short rifle, and sword ; and the uniform, &c., of the latter corps very much resembled it.

On the 19th of April, 1804, there was a shooting match on Broad-barrow Green between these two corps, which led to unpleasant consequences. It had been agreed that ten men of each corps should fire 30 shots at 150 yards, and 30 at 200 yards distance, and that the unsuccessful one should give the winners a dinner at the King's Arms Inn (now the George Hotel) in Stroud. At the trial of skill the Stanley riflemen, (all of whom, except one, fired standing) put into the target 11 shots at 150, and two at 200 yards ; and the Severn riflemen, (who lay down and fired, resting their rifles on their caps) put in 16 shots at 150, and 7 at 200 yards ; the latter being, of course, the victors. Modern riflemen may well smile at the target practice of that day.

The twenty sharp-shooters, and a few others of each corps, with their respective officers, dined at the King's Arms, at the expense of the officers of the Stanley riflemen ; the dinner passing off with great hilarity and satisfaction to all present. A somewhat incorrect report of the day's proceedings, and especially of one of the toasts given after dinner, was written by James Burden, a private in the Severn rifle corps, and appeared in the next *Gloucester Herald*. 2 This report gave such offence to the Stanley riflemen that, after several unsuccessful attempts to prevail on Burden to publish an apology for the obnoxious report, he was challenged to fight a duel with Joseph Cam, a private of that corps.

Upon this, Burden moved the Court of King's Bench for a rule to show cause why a Criminal information should not be filed against Captain N. P. Wathen, Joseph Cam, and Lieutenant Henry Perry, 3 for a conspiracy to provoke him to fight a duel, in breach of the peace, &c.

A rule was granted, and on June the 16th, 1804, it was argued by Garrow and Wigley, on the part of the defendants, and by Erskine, on the part of the prosecutor,—before Ellenborough, C.J., and Le Blanc and Lawrence, J.J.,—and was made absolute. A Criminal imformation was accordingly filed against Wathen, Cam, and Perry, which was set down for hearing at the Spring Assizes for Gloucestershire, in 1805. A verdict of acquittal was entered by consent, the matter having been left to the arbitration of Milles and Dauncey, two leading barristers of the Oxford Circuit, who made their award during the same assizes ; in which they certified their opinion—"That the publication in the *Gloucester Herald* was not intended to convey any imputation or reflection upon the whole or upon any member of the King Stanley riflemen, and that the consequences which followed such publication arose entirely from misapprehension"; concluding with—"We are therefore of opinion, under such circumstances, that further explanation is unnecessary." Thus a foolish affair was terminated ; though at the cost to the defendants of nearly five hundred pounds.

2 This newspaper was discontinued a few years afterward.
3 Mr. Perry resided at the Field, near Stroud.

CHAPTER XX.

BROAD-BARROW GREEN.

THE story of the Rifle Contest has been told : let us now take a view of Broad-barrow Green, where it occurred. It has a history and memories of its own, entitling it to a separate notice.

The chief characteristic implied in its name has, however, been lost ; for, in a few years after the event referred to, the open Green was enclosed, and is now under cultivation; so that it is no longer free of access to the lovers of healthy exercise, or of grand and varied scenery.

Nevertheless, I can shew it to you as it was in its former state, having a picture of it in my mind, painted there some sixty years ago, the lines of which are yet strong, and its tints only a little faded, in the mean time.

Broad-barrow Green is a tract of nearly level land on the Cotteswolds, lying within the angle or junction of the northern and western ranges. Haresfield Hill is the name by which the bold buttress-like projection which forms the angle is known to the dwellers in the great valley below ; but, by the Cotteswoldians, it is called, indiscriminately, Ring Hill, Beacon Hill, Beacon Tump, and Standish Beacon. The hill is 715 feet above the level of the sea ; and, straight up its western face, from the vale to its summit, runs the line between the parishes of Standish and Haresfield ; the latter, however, overlaps the top, and comprehends Broad-barrow Green within its limits.

This place is situated beyond the outlying portion of the parish of Stroud called Pakenhill tithing, and about three miles from the town itself. It belongs to J. D. T. Niblett, Esq., of Haresfield Court, the Lord of the Manor, whose father inclosed it, under an Act of Parliament, [1] about the year 1820.

---

[1] 52 Geo. III., cap. 22.

In its former state, it was an open common of fine turf,
—tempting to the feet for its carpet-like surface, to the
health-seeker for its bracing air, and to the poetic and
picture-loving eye for the glorious and suggestive views
that lie below, and in the distance beyond it.   It was
accessible to the public ; and, in my youth, foot-races, trials
of strength, and games, were held there, by the merry men
and boys of Stroud and other parts of the clothing district.
Here, too, were occasional horse and donkey races ; and an
aged tree, called the Starting Beech, is yet standing, in
which have been hung up saddles and bridles, as prizes for
the winners.

With respect to its name, both Atkyns and Rudder call
it Broadbridge-green, although there is not any bridge
there, or anything to suggest the idea of one, even to the
imagination.   Rudge says it is called Broad Ridge, or
Broad-barrow Green, and Fosbrooke calls it only Broad-
ridge.

It is really a ridge of the Cotteswolds, formed, on one
side, by the escarpment of the northern range, and, in part,
on the other side, by the bay-like hollow in the western
range, where Standish Park is embosomed: moreover, there
are upon it several ancient artificial mounds or barrows.
Hence it is called both Broad-ridge Green and Broad-barrow
Green, more frequently the latter, which is commonly pronounced Brodbro' Green. [2]

Besides the artificial mounds, a high bank and ditch, the
remains of an entrenchment, crosses the plain at a short
distance from its western end.   This long mound is called
The Bulwarks ; and it was against its green slope that, in
1804, the targets were raised, on which the two rival corps
—The Severn, and The Stanley Rifles—expended their
ammunition, with such very moderate results, when compared with the superior target-practice of modern riflemen.

The western portion of The Green was a camp, of which
The Bulwarks formed the eastern boundary, dividing and
defending it from the other part of The Green.   It was,
probably, an ancient British work, and is of such extent as
might have contained a whole community of that period.
But, the Romans have been there, and seem to have re-
stricted their occupation of it, (as a defensive camp for their

[2] The epithet " Broad," in all its names, is appropriate, whether it be
taken to mean wide, or clear, or open.

more compact military body,) to the extreme western end. This they converted into a smaller and complete entrenchment, the vallum of which enclosed the whole summit of Standish Beacon, called also Ring Hill, probably from the shape of the Camp that crowns it.   This was effected by raising a lofty bank, and scarping the rock, nearly midway between the two extremities of the original work ; and now the road from The Green passes through the hollow between the separate portions, as it winds down to the village of Haresfield.   Ring Hill Camp is, in shape, almost a parallelogram, and must have been nearly impregnable, except on the narrow western side ; and there it was defended by several strong banks and ditches on the sloping edge of the hill.

To the westward of the lofty bank are two entrances opposite one another, and about one hundred and twenty yards apart.

This Camp was probably one of the long chain of outposts, established by the Romans to overlook the Severn ; and lies between that on Painswick Hill on the northern range, and Uley Bury on the western.   It can be seen from Uley Bury, and from Painswick and Bredon Hills ; on which last was another of those military stations.   Some few years since an earthen pot, containing between two and three thousand Roman small brass coins, ranging in date from A.D. 292, to A.D. 392, was ploughed up within the vallum, near its eastern entrance.   The pot, with its contents, is in the possession of Mr. Niblett.   Several bronze *fibulæ*, (one washed with silver,) have also been found here; and there are the remains of a Roman villa, in Harescomb, at Stock-end, (the wooded end of the parish,) beautifully situated below the northern ridge of Broad-barrow Green. Other people, however, may have occupied these entrenchments since the time of the Romans.

Within the western part of the inclosure is the site of the Beacon, the fires of which may in time past have given warning to the inhabitants of the surrounding district of the approach of an enemy ; and hence the hill derived one of its names.   From this place the abrupt hill-side, which is the western defence of the inclosure, exhibits itself in a large mass of hard, bare rock,—standing, perhaps, as it stood for unnumbered ages after the whole Severn valley rose out of the ancient sea ; and having, from that period, presented its bold perpendicular face, like a mighty wall, to

the vale, and to the storms which have beat upon it.   Here,
in the inaccessible fissures between its layers, the jackdaws
of many generations have made their nests ; and from it I
watched them taking their noisy, circling flights in the air,
far below my feet.

The eastward side of Broad-barrow Green joins the rest
of the northern range, which, falling back into the high
ground above Painswick, Stroud, and Hampton, unites with
the mass of the Cotteswolds.

Having leisure to look around us, we advance to the
edge of the western scarp ; and there, on the right hand, we
see its line stretching away eastward beyond Cheltenham,
to Broadway Hill ; broken, at intervals, by the bold pro-
montories of rock, which thrust themselves forward into the
valley, with its varying vertical and horizontal outlines,
gradually rising in altitude almost to its extremity,—Cleeve
Hill being 1080 feet above the sea.   Looking westward, we
see in the near middle ground the City of Gloucester (the
Caer Glow—the fair city—of the Britons, and the Glevum
of the Romans,) reposing under it in a thin canopy of smoke,
in the loveliest of vales.   There the unrivalled tower of its
Cathedral rises grandly and solemnly, a most commanding
and interesting object. 3

In the distance, the eye is invited to that old town and
venerable Abbey, where lies "the field by Tewkesbury,"—
that bloody field which, without a name, has been immortalized by Shakspeare in his Dream of Clarence. 4

Beyond this, observe that thin lance of sunlight which
leads the eye to the place where Worcester lies, calling to
mind the battle there between Charles II. and Cromwell,
which for many years proved so disastrous to the fortunes
of the King.   It is said that the tidal waters of the Severn
have been known to rise so high, as to be felt at Worcester
Bridge.   Here, turning a little to the left, the beautiful
range of the Malvern Hills, through all its length, lies
before us, rising from the level plain in solitary grandeur,
with its graceful outline and undulating surface, enveloped
in its soft, grey haze ; its highest point being 1313 feet
above the Severn.   So it lay, but not so lovely, when, for

3 It has been said that this tower is worthy of being put under a glass
case ; and that its exquisite proportions, and its fine open-work pinnacles, are
seen to the best advantage by moonlight.

4 Richard III., A. 1., Sc. 4.

innumerable ages, it was an island in the midst of an inland sea. Methinks the view is marred by the intrusive white houses on the hill side : I wish they could be withdrawn into the shade, until we have taken our fill of the beautiful vision. Those eminences in the distant back ground are the mountains of Wales.

Let us now turn to the westward,—and there, in the middle ground, lies the broad reach of the Severn below Hock Crib, gleaming in the sunshine ; and on its surface are the trading vessels, with their white sails, passing up the river with the flowing tide, for the tide is up. Here also is the pretty, rounded Barrow Hill, which hides the river whilst it takes its horse-shoe sweep of seven miles round it, and beyond is the Forest of Dean, with its fine woods and dales, its rich seams of coal and other mineral wealth.

And now, withdrawing our attention from special objects, we take a rapid glance over all the vale below us, on the east, north, and west ; and we see it studded with villages, churches, mansions, parks, woods, farmhouses, orchards, meadows, and corn fields,—all of surpassing loveliness and interest ; and suggesting ideas of material wealth, social comfort, and general advancement, such as not any former age could have witnessed.

Before we take leave of Broad-barrow Green, however, I will mention an adventure of one of my elder brothers, who spent a whole winter's night there. He had been to an entertainment at Haresfield, and, returning in the evening, had reached the summit of the hill, entering on the Green at nightfall. There was not any well-defined road over it, but only footpaths, and the tracks of horses and wheels on the turf. In the darkness he lost the right direction, and wandered round and round, coming more than once to places he had already passed ; but always being unable to find the gate he sought, leading into the road through the wood, down to the hamlet of Whiteshill, until the morning light disclosed it to him.

Nor must I omit the following anecdote of the sagacity of a fox, which was witnessed there, as told me by the late Miss Dimock, of Stonehouse. Her father was a clothier residing at Bridge-end, in the Stonehouse valley, near the village of that name ; and a workman at his factory, who lived at Harescombe, passed across the Green to and from his work, daily. Early one morning, as he was on his way, he there saw in the obscure light, some animal stealing along, and apparently with a heavy load. His curiosity being excited, he followed, and soon perceived that it was a fox carrying a goose toward the wood which crowns the hill above Standish Park. He saw the fox attempt several times to leap over the wall into the wood, with the goose in his mouth, but its weight as often pulled him back. He then placed the goose close to the wall, leaped on it, and, stretching himself forward, tried to reach his prey as it lay on the ground. In this, too, he failed. But the wall was what is called a dry wall, and built of rough unhewn stones without mortar ; and the fox leaped down, and after a short seeming deliberation, seized the head of the goose, and thrust its long bill into a crevice of the wall, as high up in it as he could reach ; then, mounting again, he drew it from the wall, dragged the goose over into the wood, and was gone.

CHAPTER XXI.

HENRY BURGH, ESQ. — BADBROOK — IMPROVEMENT OF THE
GLOUCESTER-ROAD INTO STROUD.

AGAIN I find myself at the bottom of High-street, and
have to add to my account of the large brick house
there, that, after Mr. Hollings' death, it was purchased by
Mr. Charles Newman, an Attorney, and became his professional residence. He, and his son Henry Newman,
were, in succession, for several years Clerks of the Magistrates for the Stroud division of the county; their chairman
being Henry Burgh, Esq., who claims a place in my notes,
as he holds a large one in my remembrance.

Mr. Burgh was born at Shipton Moigne, in this county,
September 13th, 1759. He was educated at Winchester
College-school; and in November, 1776, became an articled
clerk to John Colborne, an Attorney of Whitehall, who had
succeeded to the professional practice of his uncle, John
Heart. Mr. Burgh commenced his business as an Attorney,
at Stroud, and continued it successfully for several years
there and at the Grange, now known as the Upper Grange,
by way of distinction from the house he built, and called
Lower Grange.

After relinquishing his profession to his partner, Mr. John
Saunders, he became a Justice of the Peace in 1802. He
was the chief, (and I may say the most active,) magistrate
in the neighbourhood, for about forty-six years; during the
early part of which time frequent and alarming disturbances
broke out amongst the cloth-working and agricultural populations of the district.

He was also a Deputy Lieutenant of the county; and
was Captain of the Longtree, Bisley, and Whitstone troop
of Volunteer Cavalry, numbering about seventy troopers,
when it was re-organised on the breaking out of the French
war in 1802.

From his past professional experience, his great acquaintance with people and their affairs, and the extensive period of his magisterial life, Mr. Burgh had become the depository of more general information, relating to the men and things of this neighbourhood, than any other living person ; all which his retentive memory enabled him to reproduce when called for. He had lived in the five reigns of George the Second, Third, and Fourth, William the Fourth, and Victoria. He knew five generations of the Colborne family; and when I asked him where he thought I might find the baptismal register of one of its aged members, he replied "It must be in some parish not far off ; for I heard the old lady "—the person referred to—" say she had not been ten miles from Stroud in all her life."

It seems that this untravelled lady, who nearly attained the age of ninety years, had been contented with a distant view of the Severn and Gloucester from the neighbouring hills—if, indeed, she had seen them from anywhere.

Mr. Burgh was a great wit, and very satirical. He had a quick perception of the ridiculous ; with the disposition to enjoy, and a ready power to caricature and expose, whatever was strange or absurd in habit, character, or manners. It is even now remembered how largely and unsparingly he indulged in the exercise of this particular talent. He, however, could always distinguish the quality of the company present ; and he well knew when a gentleman ought to remember that he was a gentleman, though, sometimes, he might have seemed to forget it.

The following is an example of his ever-ready humour. A tailor, who had nearly completed the building of a house in Union-street, invited him to inspect its arrangements. "This," said he, on entering one room, "is to be my cutting-out shop; and," pointing to another, "this will be my kitchen"; "and this," shewing a third room, "is to be my bedroom. Can you give me a good name for the house?" "Yes:" replied Mr. Burgh, "Call it Snip-Snap-Snorum." [1]

Mr. Burgh once owned the estate of Stanley Park, where he resided for some years. He had good features, with keen grey eyes, and was somewhat below the middle height, well made, and of gentlemanly appearance. He lived to become the senior magistrate of the county. He died at

[1] Snip-Snap-Snorum is a round game of cards, played with counters and a pool. For which, see Notes and Queries, 3rd series, v. 11, pp. 331-379, A.D. 1862, in answer to my *Query*.

Spillman's Court, Rodborough, February 9th, 1848, in the eighty-ninth year of his age.

Immediately below the large brick house before mentioned, is Lansdown, into which, in a line from King-street across the bottom of High-street, enters a road leading to the Parsonage House, erected there in 1837. This road is now becoming a street ; and it would be a public benefit if it were continued in the same direction into the Slad-road, near Little Mill. This was proposed long ago, and is actually indicated on a map of the town, published by John Wood in 1835, and, in this age of progress, it may yet be carried out. [2]

Meanwhile Dr. Paine, to whom Lansdown belongs, has extended the road from the Parsonage House—but at a right angle with it—down to and across the brook into the Slad-road, which it enters midway between Badbrook and Little Mill. He has opened and dedicated both these roads to the public, and thereby supplied a very valuable means of communication between the town and the Slad valley.

At the bottom of High-street begins the road down to Badbrook, situated on the river Slade, which rises above Steanbridge, and passes this place on its way to the Froom. This river derives its name from the Saxon, ꝑleb, a long flat strip of ground, a valley,—and is commonly called Slad ; so is the valley through which it runs, its northern side, situated in the parish of Painswick, being distinguished as Painswick Slad, and its southern side, in the parish of Stroud, as Stroud Slad.

The name of Badbrook has an evident connection with the river on which it stands, though I have not been able to discover its origin. As there is not any injurious quality or other obnoxious tendency in the water itself, to justify the epithet "bad," I can only suggest that, at some past time, an untoward accident happened there, which called forth an exclamation—"What a *bad* brook," and furnished a name for this special locality.

At Badbrook is a house with an ancient mill, out of which William Hawker and his wife, by deed of January the 8th, 1676, granted an annuity of six pounds, viz.—to the minister yearly for ever £2 10s. ; and to the poor, and putting out apprentices, yearly £3 10s. This annuity is regularly paid, and duly applied.

[2 This has long since *been* carried out, and very thoroughly, the new road entering the Slad-road far beyond Little Mill. The Lansdown end of this road is already much built on.]

Above the mill, on the west side of the road, and nearly on a level with the stream, was a cluster of very old cottages, formerly one large house, where, in my early days, lived Mr. Window, a dyer, generally called " Bustle " Window, from some peculiarity in his manner.   He was an early follower of the Rev. John Wesley, and occasionally conducted the religious services at the Round House, in Acre-edge.   Mr. Window's dye-houses lay on both sides of the road, and were subsequently rebuilt on an extended scale by Mr. Thomas Holbrow, under whose management a large dyeing business was carried on there for several years.

For the convenience of the new dye-houses, the Slade was there diverted from its original course ; so that a strip of Stroud parish, (measuring about one hundred and thirty yards in length, by about twenty-four in width,) now lies on the north side of the river ; but its boundary line is defined by incised marks in the walls of some adjoining buildings.   The road here is a principal, and was formerly the only, approach to Stroud from Gloucester, by way of Painswick.   At that time it passed by a ford through the river, for horses and carriages, and by stepping stones laid in its shallow bed, for foot passengers.   The ascent to the town was very steep, being a gradient of about one foot in eight, and the ascent to Beeches Green, on the Painswick side of the river, was on a still greater inclination.

Here, in the year 1784, an improvement was made by the erection of a narrow stone bridge across the brook, for horses and carriages ; and, a little later, a narrow wooden bridge, with a single hand rail, superseded the stepping stones.   Nevertheless several accidents happened by the overturning of carriages into the water, in attempting to enter on the bridge in the dark, and by reason of the steepness of the descent to it.   In the year 1794 Badbrook House was built by Mr. Holbrow, on the left ascent to Beeches Green, and there he resided until his death in 1833. There are some few persons yet living who may remember his kind hospitality and good temper ; as well as the fine eagle which stood chained to its perch near the entrance door, and his white setter dog Bacchus, that was everywhere. Mr. Robert Hodges also built, on the lower right ascent to the same place, a house, up to the front door of which was a flight of eight or nine stone steps.   It is now the Police Station of the district.

In June, 1801, an Act of Parliament was passed for making a turnpike-road from Lightpill, on the Bath-road, to Birdlip. [3] This road enters Stroud on its western side, near Wallbridge,—thus making the communication with Woodchester about two miles shorter than it was before ; and it leaves Stroud at Badbrook, on its eastern side, whence—under the name of Slad-road—it proceeds toward Birdlip.

Until that time, the only public way up Slad valley was a footpath ; but, as it passed through pleasant fields and was well kept, it was a favorite walk with the inhabitants. Now the turnpike-road supplies to Little Mill, New Mills, and places beyond, a convenient access for horses and carriages, much shorter and more level than by the roads which previously led to them. [4]

On a Sunday in September, 1798, after a warm and dry summer, a great torrent of water suddenly rushed down Slad valley, during the afternoon service. Its volume was so great as to raise the stream at Badbrook high above the bridge, and to detain persons who had to return from the church to their homes on the other side, until it had sufficiently subsided. The cause of this flood was said to have been a waterspout, which broke over the high ground above Steanbridge, Stroud, and Minchinhampton ; and thereby, not only this valley, but also the Stroud and Woodchester valleys were inundated, and several mills above and below Stroud sustained great inconvenience and damage. Even Kingstanley meadows were overflowed, and remained impassable for many days. [5]

In the year 1817 an Act of Parliament was passed for making a turnpike-road from Stroud to Gloucester, by way of Pitchcomb. One of its chief objects was the improvement of the approach to Stroud through Badbrook, across the hill called Beeches Green, by cutting a new road over it at a lower level than the old one, and by raising the road in the valley. All this was satisfactorily accomplished,— one part of the hill being lowered about thirteen feet of

3 39th and 40th Geo. III., c. 43.

4 The carriage-road from Badbrook to Little Mill—distant only about 400 yards—was up High-street, along Church-street, and thence down the private road mentioned in page 57. The horse-road from Badbrook to New Mills was up the town to Nounsell's Cross, along Somer-street, (now spelt " Summer "- street,) and down a private way through the fields.

5 " A very heavy rain fall " occurred September 2nd, 1750, which caused a similar high flood and damage throughout the same district. See *Gentleman's Magazine* for that year.

vertical height, and the road below being raised to a level with the entrance into Mr. Hodges' house, instead of being seven feet below it, as it was before.

While these alterations were in progress, Daniel Clift, a Stroud and Gloucester carrier, was killed in returning home at night, by falling with his horse and cart from the old road into the deep cutting intended for the new one.

There is, on Beeches Green, an ancient house, long well known as the successive residence of the Rev. W. Ellis, his widow, and Mr. Robert Hughes. [6] It is called "The Green"; and the old highway passed it on the same level, separated by only a narrow strip of ground; but, by cutting down the hill, the new road passes it a little farther off, and on a lower level, so that it is now approached by an ascent of several yards. It belongs to Mr. J. A. Morton Ball.

The improvement made by the new road on the Painswick side of the river Slade seems to have moved the people of Stroud to improve the old road on their side of it. Accordingly, they immediately widened the bridge, and raised the road ; and, soon after they had obtained the Stroud Improvement Act, [7] they again raised both the bridge and the road, and made the elevated footway up to King-street. By this means the previous steepness of the ascent to the town was considerably relieved.

In 1840 the large British School, near Badbrook, was built by subscription ; having its entrance from Slad-road, across the brook, which was arched over for that purpose. Since that time the dye-houses have been taken down, and their sites covered with houses ; [8] and the whole road, from the brook up to Lansdown and King-street, is called Gloucester-street.

Until the year 1867 the cluster of old cottages where Mr. Window, the dyer, once lived, together with the Chequers' Inn, at the north-west corner of King-street, and all the intervening property, belonged to Thomas Mills Goodlake, Esq., grandson of Mr. Yarnton Mills. It was part of certain hereditaments, lying dispersedly in the parishes of Bisley and Stroud, called Coventry land from the Earls of Coventry, who had been its former owners for

6 This Mr. Robert Hughes was the nephew of Mrs. Ellis's first husband Robert Hughes, clothier, and of Thomas Hughes, surgeon, both mentioned before. In 1849 he bequeathed £200 to the Stroud Charity Schools.

7 6th Geo. IV., c. 5.

[8 One of which is used for many public purposes, and is called Badbrook Hall.]

a long time. In that year it became, from the brook upward, the property of Sebastian Stewart Dickinson, Esq., by an exchange with Mr. Goodlake, who obtained from Mr. Dickinson a small farm at Througham Slad, in the tithing of Througham, (generally called Druffham,) in the parish of Bisley ; which, in order to mark the distinction, has been named the Chequers' farm.

Before the end of the year 1867 Mr. Dickinson had taken down the Chequers' Inn and the old cottages ; and the foundations of several houses were laid, and other arrangements were made for completing that whole side of Gloucester-street, and for improving the entrance into it from King-street. In excavating the foundations for the new houses on the site of the Chequers' Inn, several old lime-kilns were discovered below the former surface of the ground. They were rather less than the ordinary size ; and at the bottoms of them small quantities of lime and charcoal were found, indicating that they had been worked before fossil coal was used in this district.

CHAPTER XXII.

STROUD NEWSPAPERS — DUEL BETWEEN LIEUTENANT HEAZLE AND
LIEUTENANT DELMONT.

AGAIN we come to the bottom of High-street; and
turning to the south, enter King-street which lies,
as before stated, on the road to Wallbridge and Rodborough.
The first house in King-street, and the last house in
High-street, is one original structure, its form being that
of a rounded centre with wings, which incline to the lines
of those streets. It belonged to the late Benjamin Bucknall;
and there he carried on his business of a bookseller, printer,
&c., for about thirty-seven years, having his shop-front
toward King-street. Here was printed and published the
first newspaper of the town, under the name of *The Monthly
Observer*, being a small quarto of four pages. It was begun
in 1848, under the management of his son S. G. Bucknall;
and was carried on until its name was changed to *The Free
Press*, in 1850. It then appeared as a weekly paper of four
folio pages, but was discontinued in 1856.

In the month of May, 1854, Mr. F. W. Harmer another
bookseller and printer, commenced the publication of *The
Stroud Journal*, a Saturday's weekly paper of eight folio
pages. On Mr. Harmer's removal with his family to
Canada, in 1858, this paper came into the hands of its present
proprietors; under whose management it has preserved the
public favor, and attained a large circulation. On Saturday
the 2nd of November 1867, was issued the first number of
another newspaper, called *The Stroud News and Gloucestershire Advertizer*, of which the same may be said.

We pause at the third and fourth houses on the east side of King-street, for they call to mind a melancholy event, which greatly excited the public sympathy in the year 1807. These houses were then one, in the occupation of Mrs. Hyde[1] In that year, and for many years before and after it, England was engaged in the long and arduous war with France, which terminated only after the battle of Waterloo, in 1815 : and as a necessity of the war, several recruiting parties, with their respective commissioned and non-commissioned officers, were stationed here to raise recruits for the army. The number of men raised in Stroud was very large, parties of twenty or thirty young men going from the town at one time, on their way to the depôts of their respective regiments. England had never before witnessed such drumming and fifing for recruits. In 1805 the military forces of the United Kingdom amounted to nearly 700,000 men.

Among the recruiting officers were Captain Robert Candler,[2] of the 50th Regiment ; Captain William Barry, of the Plymouth division of Royal Marines ; Lieutenant Benjamin Heazle, of the 3rd Regiment, or Old Buffs ; Lieutenant Joseph Francis Delmont, of the 82nd, and Lieutenant John Sargeaunt of the 61st Regiment. There were nine such officers, here, at the least, Captain Candler being the senior.

Delmont was a good looking man, with an open agreeable countenance, twenty-two years of age. Heazle was a native of Bandon, near Cork Ireland ; a tall strong-built man, of a swarthy complexion, about twenty-eight years of age. Sargeaunt was a well-made handsome man, with a pleasant address, about twenty-six years old, and a native of Newnham, in this County. Delmont lodged at Mrs. Hyde's house, and Heazle at the (Old) George Inn, High-street.

After their dinner, on the afternoon of Friday, the 14th of August, 1807, Heazle and Delmont took a walk together

---

1 She was the widow of Frank Hyde, once the well-known owner and driver of the Stroud and Bristol coach.

2 Captain Candler resided four or five years with his wife in Middle-street, and was held in great respect. He fell at the storming of Fort Napoleon, before Almarez in Spain, May the 19th, 1812 ; and was honorably mentioned by General Hill, to whose division his regiment belonged. "The only officer slain in the actual assault was Captain Candler, a brave man, who fell while leading the grenadiers of the 50th, on the ramparts of Fort Napoleon." See Napier's Peninsular War, v. 19.

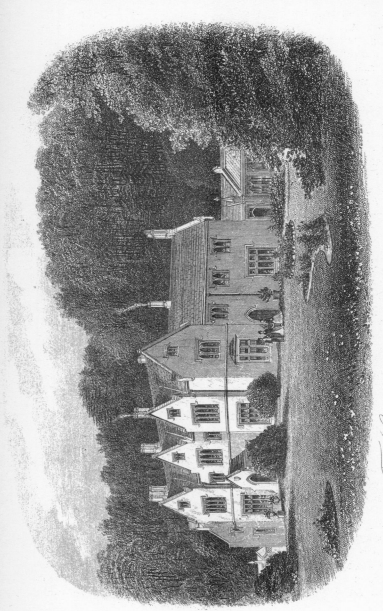

The Grove. (rebuilt by William Capel. 1845)

into the country. They were then on good terms with each other ; but, in the course of their walk, Delmont made some remark which displeased Heazle, though it was understood not to have had any direct personal reference to him. Heazle, however demanded an apology for it, which Delmont refused to give, having, as he afterward said, resolved never to make an apology. On mentioning this resolution, however, after the duel, he added, "but on the present occasion I meant to have done it." The reluctance to apologise was no doubt founded on the idea that doing so was unbecoming a soldier. In consequence of the refusal, Heazle demanded satisfaction ; and then the young men agreed to settle the difference by a duel to take place the same evening.

At that time Sargeaunt was one of a dinner-party at the Lower Grange, the residence of Mr. George Wathen ; and, on returning from their walk, Delmont sent for Sargeaunt to come to them. On his arrival, they acquainted him with what had occurred, and asked him to accompany them to the field declaring that, if he refused, they would go there alone. Upon this, and after an ineffectual attempt to reconcile them, Sargeaunt, unwisely and unfortunately, acquiesced : and he and Heazle immediately went into the town to procure pistols, powder, and ball, while Delmont loitered about in the neighbourhood of the Grange, awaiting their return.

The Grange stands on the western edge of a small dell, which, running up from the Slad valley into the body of Wickeridge hill, terminates near the Grove, the residence of William Capel, Esq.; and the road from Beeches Green to the Grange, becomes, in passing that place, a steep, hollow lane, leading down and across the dell, on its way up the south side of the hill. The field selected for the duel, lies in this dell, about 120 yards above the place where the lane crosses it ; and part of the road, which passes by a fish-pond to it, (but not the field itself,) is visible from the back windows of the Grange.

It appears that there was much delay in procuring pistols, &c. About six o'clock Heazle called on Mr. Jenner, bookseller, wishing to borrow a pair of duelling pistols, which he represented were wanted to shoot at a mark for a wager ; but Jenner had none. About the same time Sargeaunt went to Thomas Howell, landlord of the Green Dragon Inn, King-street, who was a blacksmith.—and

inquired if he had any pistols. Howell replied that he had
one, which he showed him, and he, saying it was too large,
went away without it. It was a horse-pistol that had belonged to one of the volunteer cavalry, and is said to have
been foul and rusty. Sargeaunt then went to Jenner, and
asked him for a pair of pistols, as Heazle had already done.
This was about seven o'clock : when, being disappointed
there and at some other places he returned to Howell, and
said the pistol he had shown him would do, if he could
get the fellow to it ; for they were going to shoot at a mark
for a dinner and wine, which if he won, should be had at
Howell's house. Upon this, Howell sent William Hewlett,
his journeyman, to procure another pistol ; which he did,
by borrowing one from Partridge a confectioner, who lived
at the upper corner of the lane now called Bedford-street.
This pistol was similar to the other, but was clean and in
better condition. Hewlett brought it to Sargeaunt, who
asked him whether he had any powder and ball, to which
he replied "no"; and then Howell's son handed his father's
pistol to Sargeaunt, upon whose continued request for bul-
lets, Mrs. Howell bade her daughter go to a drawer upstairs
and fetch one ; which she did and brought it to him. At
his further request she went up again, and returned with
another bullet, being the only one she could find. He then
said, "I'll make these do," and immediately left the house
in great haste. During some part of this time, Heazle and
Delmont were seen sitting on a low wall near Badbrook
House, playing with a dog, waiting for Sargeaunt ; and
perhaps intending thereby to divert attention from the serious purpose on which they were intent.

Hewlett's curiosity having been excited, he followed
Sargeaunt from Howell's house, but soon lost sight of him.
He afterward saw him come from the Grange entrance-
court, go down the lane and there join Heazle and Delmont;
when all three, (Sargeaunt being in regimentals, and the
others in plain clothes,) proceeded to the ground. One
George Bryant, a labourer, was going to mow barley in the
adjoining field ; and he, seeing three gentlemen come into
that retired place, ran down and looked at them over the
intervening hedge; when one of the party asked him roughly
what he wanted there, and bade him mind his own business, or they would shoot him.

In about ten minutes after they had entered the field, the
report of a pistol-shot was heard by Bryant and Hewlett,

and also at the Grange.   Heazle and Sargeaunt ran from
the ground in great consternation.   Heazle went towards
Stroud ; and, on his way down the steep path from the
Grange to Badbrook, he met Mr. Sweeting, surgeon, (whose
attendance had been previously requested,) and told him he
was coming to fetch him, for that he had shot "poor
Delmont" ; and desired he would go to him with all speed.
Heazle was afterward seen to go into the yard of the White
Hart Inn, where his sergeant was billeted, probably to
direct him what to do under the circumstances ; and was
seen no more at Stroud.   It is understood that he set out
on foot, and walked up the towing-path of the Thames and
Severn canal, on his way to Cirencester and London.

Sargeaunt had run to the Grange, where the report of
the pistol had been heard, causing the greatest anxiety ;
and, having told Mr. Wathen what had happened, hastened back to the field.   There Mr. Sweeting found him near
its entrance, supporting Delmont, who was on the ground,
bleeding profusely from a wound in his left side.   A ball
had passed through his body ; and Mr. Sweeting on pro-
bing the wound in the chest, at once declared its dangerous
character.

Assistance was soon at hand; and a scallet 3 was procured
from Badbrook dyehouse, on which covered with cushions
obtained from the Grange, Delmont was removed to his
lodgings.   On the way, he asked Mr. Sweeting,—"Did I
fire my pistol or not ? "   Sweeting answered, " Yes, I believe
you did."   But Hewlett who was assisting to carry him,
interposed and said, "No, you did not ; I heard only one
report " ;   whereon Delmont exclaimed, " Thank God, I did
not ! "

Sargeaunt returned to the Grange, sent for his clothes-
chest, (which was taken to him by Howell,) took off his
regimentals, put on plain clothes; and, at nightfall, departed

---

3 *Scallet* is the provincial name for a kind of hand-barrow, used by dyers in
removing wet cloth from their vats.   I have not met with it in any writing.
But it is obviously derived from *scala*, a ladder : a short ladder having been,
probably, the original, as it was a convenient form for the implement.   In its
modern shape, however, the spars or rails which compose its open-work bed
or carriage, are laid longitudinally, not horizontally.   Hand-barrow is a genuine
old English word.   Among the quaint riddles entitled " the Demaundes Joyous,"
Wynkyn de Worde, 1511, is this Demaunde.   "When antecryst is come into
this worlde, what thynge shall be hardest to hym to knowe?" R.   "A hande
barrowe, for of that he shall not knowe whiche ende shall goo before."

from his friends with such a stony look of desolation, as one of the dinner party who saw it, could never forget. He rode on horseback to Cirencester, and so escaped.

When Delmont reached his lodgings, he expressed a conviction that the wound was mortal, and earnestly requested that the Rev. John Williams, the officiating minister of the parish, should be sent for. On his arrival, Delmont desired to partake of the Holy Communion, which after conversing with him, Mr. Williams administered. He remained there all that night; and failed not in the most assiduous pastoral attention to him until his death.

On an examination of the wounds by the surgeons, (for all the medical gentlemen of the town gave, and continued to give, Mr. Sweeting their assistance,) it was found that a ball had entered his left side, and passed through his body, coming out at the chest; and had also wounded his left arm.

This discovery caused great surprise, and a difficulty in understanding how it could have happened, unless he was left-handed, and had stood in a corresponding position, with the left side to his antagonist.

On being questioned, he said they were placed back to back, and directed to advance six paces; then to turn round and fire: but that he was shot before he had completed his sixth pace, and before he had turned round to receive his adversary's fire.

On being asked by Mr. Williams the cause of the unhappy affair, he replied that, in their walk, he had made use of some jocular remarks, which Lieutenant Heazle had taken too seriously: but the pride of his heart would not allow him to make an apology. He likewise expressed his great concern as to the effect of the news on his father and mother, who had already lost an elder son in a duel at Malta. The same evening he said to his friend Captain Barry— "Barry, I was shot in the act of turning round; I forgive him, and may God also forgive him." On the next morning, Saturday the 15th, he gave the same account of it: and, on Captain Barry's asking him whether he was left-handed, he replied that he was not; adding,—" Barry I'll tell you how it was. We were placed back to back, and ordered to take six paces each, and then to fire. The word 'fire' was not given. I was shot in the back: or at least I think so": and such was indeed the fact. He further said he did not wish Sargeaunt should be punished.

On Sunday the 16th, Sargeaunt made his appearance in

London, at the house of Lieutenant Delmont's father, in Duke-street, Westminster ; to whom he introduced himself by saying—" I am the most distressed man in the world ; I am a military officer and shall lose my commission; I am without any pecuniary resources." On being asked what was the cause, he said—" Sir, you have a son in the army. He has been engaged in an unfortunate duel, in which I was the second, and the only second" : and in answer to an inquiry whether he could not have accommodated matters, he said he had done all he could. Sargeaunt then left the house, promising to come again ; but (of course) he did not.

In the chamber where Delmont lay, there was a print of General Wolfe, hanging on the wall, with whose history and character he had made himself familiar : and, seeing his nurse, Elizabeth Mennie, looking at it, he said—"Ah! I shall not die on a bed of honour, as he did. I was not prepared to receive the shot of my adversary ;—I had not turned round." Delmont lingered until the following Tuesday, and then expired. It was said that the nurse had given him a lotion which was intended for bathing the wounds,— instead of the draught which he ought to have taken ; and that the remedies administered to get rid of it, or to neutralize its effects, produced a new internal hemorrhage, which probably accelerated his death a few hours. His father arrived too late to see him alive.

On the next day, Wednesday, the 19th, a coroner's inquest was held on the body ; when the jury, (of whom Mr. Richard Rickards, of Farm Hill, was foreman,) after hearing evidence of the facts, and the opinion of the medical gentlemen that Lieutenant Delmont had died from the wound in the chest, gave a verdict of wilful murder against Heazle and Sargeaunt.

Mr. Sweeting took me with him to the chamber of death ; and raising the stiffened corpse on its right side, showed the place where the bullet entered. There was the dark, dull, round spot in the fair white body, from which all the stains of blood had been washed ; and I was fain to hope that the soul, too, had been washed in the "fountain opened for sin and for uncleanness."[4]

His funeral took place on Friday the 21st, attended by his brother and a military friend as chief mourners, and by

4 Zechariah XIII. 1.

several gentlemen of the neighbourhood, who had paid kind attentions to him. The pall was borne by six military officers, his accoutrements being laid on the coffin; and a great crowd of spectators assembled to witness the ceremony.

On the following Sunday, the Rev. John Williams preached a funeral sermon on the pernicious vice of duelling, from the text, Romans XII. 19; in which he detailed some particulars of the deceased, and of conversations with him. It was published by Mr. Jenner; and so great was the general excitement, that a second edition of it was called for in a few days.

The parish officers put advertisements into the *Hue and Cry*, and in the provincial newspapers, describing the persons, dress, &c., of the two culprits; and offering a reward of £20 for the apprehension of either of them.

The attorney of the parish officers was, moreover, prepared to prosecute them at the then next County Assizes, in case they should appear there, (as it was possible they might do,) to take their trials under the verdict of the coroner's inquest: but they came not. Thenceforward their names ceased to appear in the army list.

As to the pistols, the rusty one which was borrowed of Howell, had been allotted to Delmont; and was discharged after the duel though not without difficulty. The other was forfeited as a deodand, [5] to Mr. Thomas Croome, lord of the manor of Painswick, in which the fatal field is situated; and it is now in the hands of his grandson, Thomas Myers Croome, lord of the same manor.

It was said that Heazle died in the West Indies soon after his escape. Sargeaunt retired to America, from whence, after some years, he came once to England, in secret, to see his aged father whose only son he was; and then he returned to his melancholy exile where he died, just as his friends were hoping to obtain his pardon.

On a flat stone, near the south-west corner of the burial ground of the parish church, is the following inscription,—" Here lie the remains of Lieutenant Joseph Francis Delmont, of His Majesty's 82nd Regiment, born 25th

---

5 A *deodand* was either a forfeiture of, or the price of, or a fine for, the chattel by which a homicide was caused, as awarded at the Coroner's inquest. It originally belonged to the Crown, but last to the lord of the manor in which the homicide happened. It was abolished by act 9th and 10th Vic., cap. 60, from September the 1st, 1846.

November, 1785, died 18th August, 1807." This memorial says but little more than do the words of James Montgomery's poem, *The Common Lot :*—

> "Once in the flight of ages past
> There lived a man."

But I have told the story ; in which you may read how the precept "Avenge not yourselves," in the text of Mr. Williams' sermon, was violated ; and how fearfully was verified, in the fate of these three young men, the awful declaration that follows it—"Vengeance is mine ; I will repay, saith the Lord."

CHAPTER XXIII.

IN the early part of the present century, the property in King-street adjoining the house in which Lieutenant Delmont died, belonged to Mr. Sweeting. It consisted of the dwelling-house where he resided until his death in January, 1839; and of its lawn, elevated about four feet above the street and enclosed by a high wall. Beyond this was the house formerly of John Pegler, glazier, on the site of which the shop of Mr. T. N. Clarke, draper, has been erected. And, next to this the, four or five houses that were subsequently built where stood the warehouses and dwelling-houses of Charles Freebury, and, afterwards of C. F. Kendrick: all which stand five feet farther back from the street than did Mr. Sweeting's house and lawn.

After Mr Sweeting's death, his property was sold by his grandson, Charles G. Miles, to Mr. Goddard in 1843; and, by him, in 1853, to Mr. Benjamin Bucknall, who sold the dwelling-house to Miss Farr. The latter being about to rebuild what she had purchased, and the former having determined to erect two houses on the site of the lawn, advantage was taken of this to widen the street; and arrangements were made with both of them for that purpose.

Miss Farr took down the front of her dwelling-house, and built two good shops, one of which she occupied; and Mr. Bucknall built two other houses with shop fronts, on the space retained by him,—all of them being at the distance of five feet from the former line of the street, and the fronts of the first three houses of the street.

This improvement was made in the year 1855, by the payment of £157 to Miss Farr, and £20 to Mr. Bucknall; £60 of which was contributed by the Commissioners of the (old) Improvement Act, and the rest from a public subscription raised on the occasion. By these means, a length of seventy-eight feet of this street was widened five feet ; so that the whole of it is now of a respectable breadth, except opposite its first three houses. It was confidently expected that those houses would have been put back simultaneously with the others—to complete the improvement of the street; but difficulties arose and prevented it. Its desirableness, however, is so great, and its necessity so much felt every day,—(for here is the entrance to the street, and its narrowest and most crowded part,)—that it is hoped the public endeavours will not cease until this improvement be effected. [1]

The Chequers' Inn, which until 1867, formed the opposite corner of King-street, had for its sign a chequered square, resembling a chess-board. It had been occupied by members of the same family for several generations, the last of whom was the William Purcell, before mentioned as one of the two survivors of the old Stroud volunteers. His maternal grandmother was born there ; and the writer remembers her son, William Purcell, as its landlord in 1787. He was succeeded by his widow, and their sons, Henry, John, and William, in succession, until 1862.

The house that adjoined the Chequers, was the Golden Heart Inn, which, in my youth was kept by William Pritchard ; and, after his death, by his widow and his son Samuel in succession ; during which time it was a favourite place of resort for the tradesmen of the town. Here, in the evenings, especially on market days, they smoked and tippled, whilst they chatted over the local news, and discussed general politics : for all men were politicians at the time alluded to, when the great, startling, and rapidly changing events of the first French Revolution were being transacted.

From this Inn a four-horse, six-inside stage-coach between Stroud and London started, when I was a boy, and for several years after. It was known as Masters' coach, from a family of that name living at Cirencester, who were part-proprietors, and horsed it a few stages from Stroud. In 1795 it started from the Belle Sauvage, Ludgate Hill, London, at three o'clock in the morning, and arrived in Stroud about ten the same night. But in 1805 its London Inn and time of starting had been changed ; for it then left Stroud at eleven o'clock in the morning on Sundays, Tuesdays, and Thursdays, and reached the Bull and Mouth, [2] Aldersgate-street, the next morning at ten o'clock ; starting on its return

[1 In 1890, it is still as desirable, and as far off, as ever.]

2 The sign of this Inn was the figure of a bull, and an open human mouth. But the Bull and Mouth was a corruption of the original name and sign of

at three in the afternoon on the alternate days, and arriving at Stroud at eleven the next morning. Until that year, the driving box of the coach and the luggage-boot beneath it, rested bodily on the front part of the carriage: and who-ever, now living, has sat there with Dan Sellars the coachman, during the journey, will remember this ; for he cannot have forgotten the incessant shaking, jolts, and jerks which he encountered by the way. But in 1806 an improvement took place ; and the coachman's seat was made to rest on springs, as did the body of the coach.

The mention of the old six-inside coach, however presents an opportunity for jotting down a few notices about coaches.

The London Gazette, from Monday, August the 17th to Thursday, August the 30th, 1696, contained the following advertisement: "Cirencester stage-coach goeth out every Monday, Wednesday, and Friday, from the Bell Sauvage Inn, Ludgate Hill, to the King's Head, Cirencester, in Gloucestershire, or any part of the road, in two days ; and returns from thence on the same days to London." Chamberlayne in his *"Present State of Great Britain,"* 1718, mentions " flying coaches," which made sometimes 70, 80, and 100 miles " in a day from London,"—as to Southampton, Bury, *Cirencester*, Norwich, &c.

In February, 1770, there was a stage-coach from Stroud to London and back twice in each week ; which started early in the morning, and reached London in the evening of the next day. It went by way of Oxford ; which route it followed for many years, and put up at the Bull Inn, Holborn.

In the summer months, when the roads were in their best condition, it was a "flying coach," and made the journey in somewhat less time ; but in the winter months, it was a two-day coach ; as will be seen by the following advertisement, copied from the *Gloucester Journal* of January the 15th, 1770,[3] " The proprietors of the Stroud-water coach beg leave to inform their friends and the public in general, That the coaches left off flying on Saturday, the 14th of October last; and on Monday, the 16th, began going in two days : will set out from Stroud and London, every Monday and Friday

Boulogne Mouth or *Harbour :* at a time when England possessed that town and others in France. This Inn has been taken down ; and part of the General Post-office, St Martin's-le-Grand, now stands on the site of it.

3 In the same copy of the Journal appeared a notice that "the Gloucester coach began the two-day stage on Monday the 9th of October, during the winter." It went to London and back three times a week.

at six in the morning ; meet at the Bear Inn, Oxford ; and return from thence both for Stroud and London, every Tuesday and Saturday." 4

This coach left Oxford early in the morning, even in summer ; as I learn by a letter of June, 1772, from an attorney of Stroud, who, having arranged to call on a student at one of the Colleges in Oxford, on business, as he passed through by the coach to London, afterward reported that it " passed through the town too early in the morning, so that he had no opportunity of calling on him."

In another letter of the same year, its writer speaks of this coach as "the Stroud Machine" ; not as its proper or technical name, but only as a term then applied to stage coaches. 5 This designation of them is now obsolete, though it still gives a name to the class of horses used in omnibuses, such horses being called machiners ; and perhaps the bathing machines used at marine watering places derived their name from their box-like enclosures having been, originally, mounted on carriages and wheels of dilapidated coaches. An early instance of a stage-coach being called a machine, occurs in Anstie's Bath Guide, in 1767 ; where in Letter XIII, are the following lines:—

> " E'en tho' I'd the honour of sitting between
> My Lady STUFF-DAMASK and PEGGY-MOREEN,—
> Who both flew to *Bath* in the *London* Machine."

In 1780 a coach called a *Diligence* came from Gloucester to Stroud every Friday, being market day,—and returned in the afternoon. In May, 1781, the stage-coach set out from Stroud in the evening, and arrived in London the next evening, at the Belle Sauvage,. to which Inn it then ran ; being a journey of nearly twenty-four hours.

Until 1807, Masters' old coach was the only one that ran between Stroud and London. But, in May in that year, a Company was formed for raising £4,000 in £10 shares, and setting up a new London coach. It consisted of 210 subscribers, residing chiefly in Stroud and the surrounding clothing districts ; including Uley, Dursley, and Wotton-under-Edge ; and on the 1st of June, the *Union* four-horse six-inside coach began its first journey from Stroud to London.

---

4 Even so late as 1820 "a two-day coach from the Plough Inn, Cheltenham at half-past ten in the morning, arrives at the Angel and Star Inn, Oxford, to dine and sleep, and proceeds next morning at eight to London."

[5 Carriages of all sorts are still called Machines in Scotland, occasionally.]

It started from the King's Arms Inn, now known as the George Hotel; and continued to run Sunday, Tuesday and Thursday in each week; to the Angel Inn, Angel Street, London, and to return on the next days; performing the journey in about nineteen hours.

One of the new coaches was on a novel construction designed to obviate danger by the falling off or breaking down of a wheel; and was patented as the "safety coach." With this object the luggage was not to be laid on the top, but to be stowed in a huge receptacle under the dicky, and beneath the body of the coach, reaching down to within about eighteen inches of the road-way; and having four small stationary wheels, ready to receive and support the coach and enable it to proceed slowly, in case such an accident should occur. The patentee was, doubtless, desirous of proving its practical safety, and this was accordingly effected; for, soon after it began to run, I was sitting on the front of the coach one night on a journey to Town, and suddenly, found the part of it whereon I sat, sink down; but the shock was slight, and we moved on for a short space, without damage or any inconvenience. One of the fore-wheels had fallen off. It was not discovered at the time, by what agency this had been effected, though I surmised it, and the wheel being sought for and found, was re-adjusted, and we proceeded on our way. This patent coach, however, was so ugly in shape, and so heavy in draught, by its unusual weight and resistance to the wind, that it was soon exchanged for one of another construction.

From its large number of proprietors, the *Union* coach was expected to be a flourishing concern: but it was conducted by a committee of the subscribers, who, for the most part, had businesses of their own, and but little knowledge of coach-matters: and these, with other causes, (such as the reduction of fares, to meet the opposition of the old coach, —the want of a constant and vigilant superintendence, and the lavish, if not dishonest, expenditure by some of the *employés*,) produced their natural results, in a speedy embarrassment. Before the expiration of a year it had become impossible to liquidate its debts, though additional calls of £5 and £6 each were made on the subscribers, by the vote of a general meeting; which also decided that the coach should be given up on the 17th of June, 1808.

Under these circumstances a new Company was formed, with a smaller proprietary, for raising another £4,000 in shares of £50 each.   This Company purchased the coaches, horses, &c., belonging to the old one ; and, commencing on the 17th of June, 1808, continued to run the *New Union Coach*, until, before the end of another year, it too, became inextricably embarrassed; and found it expedient to dissolve the partnership in July, 1809.

It appears that about £7000 had been sunk by both those concerns in the course of two years.   But this did not terminate their troubles ; for some of the prominent individuals amongst them were sued, both in Chancery and at Common Law, for debts, and for damages arising from accidents, which they were finally obliged to liquidate out of their own private means.

Masters' old coach having triumphed in the contest, continued to run for several years afterward ; and, on its discontinuance, was followed by others carrying only four inside passengers ; their speed and accommodation being also increased.   Thus, in 1820, the day-coach left the George Hotel at seven o'clock in the morning daily, and reached London about the same hour in the evening ; starting and arriving on the return journey at the corresponding hours of the next day.   At the same time Richard Miller and Co's four-horse night coach, the *True Briton*, (which had been started in 1817,) was running from the George Hotel at five o'clock in the afternoon, reaching London at eight the next morning, and making its return journey to Stroud at similar hours.

This coach ceased on Miller's insolvency in 1823 :[6] when Mr. Cox, of Chalford, started a four-horse night coach called the *Safety Briton*, to run between that place and London ; with a pair-horse branch coach to Stroud and Gloucester.

Both these ceased in about twelve months ; and then Messrs. Wakefield, Hayward and Co., set up the four-horse Royal Mail coach, which set out from Stroud at seven o'clock in the evening and arrived at the Bull and Mouth, London, at the same hour the next morning ; and returning from town at eight in the evening, reached Stroud at that hour the following morning.   It ran first from the Lamb Inn, Church Street ; and then from the George Hotel, after Wakefield removed there from the Lamb, in 1836.

6 This enterprising man — barge-master, coal-merchant, banker, coach proprietor, and auctioneer—became at length, for a short time a pauper inmate of the Union poor-house at Stroud.

The *True Briton* coach had a pair-horse branch coach, which ran between Chalford and Wotton-under-Edge, through Hampton, Nailsworth, Horsley and Dursley; and another between Stroud and Gloucester. After 1815 all the London coaches ran through Chalford and up Cowcomb Hill, by the new road made in that year; and not, as previously, up the steep Rodborough Lane and Hill.

Besides London coaches, there was in 1806 and for several years before and after, a three-horse coach which ran between Stroud and Bristol. It belonged, at first, to Frank Hyde, and afterward to John Evans, who had acquired the *sobriquet* of Sober John; not because of any unusual abstinence from liquor, but for his stolid look and slow movements. It started at eight o'clock in the morning three days in the week, from under the wall of Mr. Sweeting's garden, nearly opposite the stable-yard of the Golden Heart; and, going down Rowcroft at a walking pace, contrived to arrive at Bristol, distant thirty-two miles, in the evening! In like manner, it occupied the whole of the next day in returning. This coach passed through Hampton, Tetbury, and Didmarton; at which latter place it stopped an hour, whilst the passengers dined. But this hour was sometimes extended to two or three: for a Mr. Ward, who was a frequent passenger, could detain the coach, whilst he and his boon companions loitered over a previously-ordered choice dinner, pipes and ale, or a game at bowls: and he was accustomed to send back Sober John to "take another glass of brandy-and-water," if he came too soon for them and announced— "Gentlemen, the coach is ready." But, if Sober John's was not a "flying coach," we have had Tanner and Baylis' "flying wagons"; which conveyed cloth, wool, and general merchandise between Stroud and London, in about the same number of hours as that in which Sober John took his passengers to Bristol and brought them back again.

Before John Evans' death, a light four-horse coach called the *Dart*, was established between Stroud and Bristol, through Nailsworth, Horsley, and Wotton-under-Edge. It left this town at seven o'clock in the morning, and returned in the evening, having allowed a stay of five hours at Bristol. Ben Pearce first drove it, then William Moody for thirteen years, and John Williams for eleven. It continued to run for more than thirty years; during the latter part of which it carried the mail-bags to and from Bristol.

In 1828, an omnibus ran from Stroud to Gloucester three days in each week, and to Cheltenham the other three days, conducted by J. Bradford, who afterward set up a light coach,[5] which ran daily between Stroud and Cheltenham. And in 1836, he and James Bishop, ran, each, a daily coach between those places ; but, by mutual agreement, one of them drove to Gloucester the days on which the other went to Cheltenham, and *vice versa;* which arrangement continued for several years. At the same time, a four-horse coach to and from Bath and Cheltenham, by way of Painswick, passed through the town daily.

Meanwhile, stage coach travelling had attained its highest perfection. For, hard, smooth, macadamized roads, elegantly built coaches, blood horses, clean, bright harness, superior coachmen and guards, with a speed of ten miles an hour now generally prevailed ; so that men rejoiced in this as the golden age of travelling. Even peers of the realm had "handled the ribbons"[6] on the mail-coach box between London and Brighton : and having donned the coat, hat, and manners of the driver, accepted his fees from the passengers, with suppressed smiles of enjoyment.

But the iron age of railways at length commenced, to the dismay of coachmasters, landlords of way-side inns, and posting houses. The Bristol and Gloucester,—now a part of the Midland Railway,—drove the Bath and Bristol coaches off the road. Then the Great Western Railway,—as fast as it was opened from London to Maidenhead, Swindon, and Cirencester, in succession,—shortened the journey of the London coaches, which drove only to those places respectively ; and there, depositing their passengers for London, returned with those for Stroud.

This continued until the opening of the Great Western Railway to Stroud, on the 14th of May, 1845 ; soon after which our coaches ceased running. Then came, to startle us from our propriety, the huge iron horse,—with his eyes of fire, his breath of flame, and his long white mane of steam,—snorting, shrieking, roaring, and seeming to swallow the ground as it flashes through our beautiful valleys, at the speed of thirty miles an hour. We have thus acquired

5 Its builder was Hill, and it was the first stage-coach built in Stroud.

6 " Ribbons" was a slang term for the reins of a team of coach horses.

greater rapidity and perhaps greater safety, 7 in travelling than formerly. But there are many who continue to regret the loss of their pleasant journeys on a well appointed coach, through the invigorating air and magnificent scenery of our picturesque neighbourhood.

7 On the question of comparative safety, the following inconclusive observation was once made by a coachman to a passenger, when sitting on a coach box with him;—" When you meet with an accident by a stage-coach—*there* you are ; but if on a railway—*where* are you ? " Excellent reasoner !

CHAPTER XXIV.

J. ADAMSON — THE GOLDEN HEART — THE REV. GEORGE WHITE-
FIELD — HIS ONLY AUTHENTIC PORTRAIT — RODBOROUGH
TABERNACLE.

IT has been already stated that the Golden Heart Inn
was, (in the stirring days of the first French Revolution,
when Samuel Pritchard was its landlord), a favorite place
of resort for the tradesmen of the town.

At the same time, one J. Adamson, who was a resident
in the house, made his frequent appearance among them
in the common room ; and him we cannot dismiss without
some further mention.

Adamson was a poor man, in destitute circumstances,
but of an educated and cultivated mind.   On the former of
these accounts he was kindly welcomed by the company,
and partook of their liquor, &c. ; and on the latter he was
regarded as an authority, and became sometimes the arbiter
or moderator in their various political and other discussions.
He had come into the neighbourhood a young man, as clerk
to the Thames and Severn Canal Company at Brimscomb
port, with a good salary : but he was indolent, and of expensive habits ; and often appeared abroad in top-boots and
spurs, with a riding whip in his hand, although he did not
ride on horseback.   On being dismissed from his employment, he was occasionally engaged to make up tradesmen's
books and accounts : but the natural consequences of his
inaptitude for steady application soon followed ; and, step
by step, he fell into difficulties, neglect, and poverty.   During
his descent, however, he acquired a residence in the Golden
Heart ; first as a lodger, and eventually, (for all other resources failed him), as the occupant of a humble bed-room
there ; in which he lived on the sufferance of the landlord,
and on the alms-like food and broken victuals of the Inn.

In this poor chamber, and without making any effort to improve his condition, Adamson remained several years; spending his time chiefly in bed, in order to economise the wear of his old and scant clothing, to hide his poverty, and somewhat to mitigate the feelings of hunger. It was from this room that he often emerged in the evening, and appeared among the tradesmen of the town in their smoking room; occupying, for his brief hour, a half-regal chair, as before stated. In this condition he remained a long while, kept alive by occasional eleemosynary help. During this period I, then a youth, knew him; and once dined with him at a table, to which he had been invited, in consideration of his former position, and his then pressing want. He appeared there clean, upright in figure, and well-mannered; with shining black shoes and large metal buckles, as had been the fashion; in an old, ill-fitting, thread-bare coat and vest, —well brushed, however; and with, perhaps, a shirt, though it was not visible. But it could not fail to be remarked that he ate his food with such an appetite as only a half-famished man might have been expected to do. Time went by, his poverty continued, his misery deepened; and at length he passed out of life, neglected and forgotten,— no one seemed to know when, where, or how. However, the fact was, that having been at length deprived of his bed at the Golden Heart, he spent nearly a year in wandering about, and sleeping wherever he could find shelter,—even in barns, sheds, and under hay ricks. In the extremity of his condition, and in the last stage of disease and misery, he found his way to a bed of straw, in a warehouse of the Thames and Severn Canal wharf below the town, where he had once resided as manager for the Company.

Here he was fed and cleaned by Mrs. Gurner, the wife of the then resident manager; and then removed to the poor-house of the town, where he died in a few days. He was buried with a pauper's funeral, on a gloomy, rainy night, in the corner of the parish church-yard, opposite the belfry door of the steeple. This narrative is the only memorial of his resting place, and of the man himself; who left behind him (as hundreds had done before) a lesson on the evils of wasted talents, indolent habits, and neglected opportunities, —to be read, and read in vain, by the young men of generation after generation.

The Golden Heart Inn was rebuilt about the year 1810, on a higher level than where it formerly stood; so that, from its front door, the foot pavement declined rapidly, as it rounded the Chequers to join the road down to Badbrook. And, although its front is only twenty-six feet wide, it had, (behind it and the next three houses,) ample yards, stable-room, and gardens, besides a piece of pasture ground called the Bowling Green, which was occasionally used for open-air meetings, and as the Sheep Market on Fair-days. The carriage entrance to all these, (and indeed the only entrance from the street,) was at the end of those three houses.

It is noticeable of the Bowling Green, that the Rev. George Whitefield, [1] the Apostle of Calvinistic Methodism, preached there to a large congregation, in the early days of his evangelical ministrations, soon after his first return from America, and from his Welsh tour. During the first twenty-three days of April, 1739, he conducted twenty-four religious services, and preached twenty-four sermons, chiefly in the open air, in addition to the labor of travelling for that purpose in Wales and Gloucestershire. Among those services, he preached "on Friday," the 20th of April, "at Chalford,"—"on Saturday morning, in the *Bowling-green*, Stroud,"—in the afternoon "at Painswick"; and the same night "in the Booth Hall, Gloucester, to about 3,000 or 4,000 each time: and on Sunday afternoon, (although raining) to a very crowded audience in Stonehouse church-yard." [2] Tradition says that, on this last occasion, he stood and preached on the stone stairs that were against the south wall of the old church. [3]

Mr. Whitefield had a fine, clear, powerful voice, which enabled him to be heard by a congregation of 20,000 persons, in the open air. That grand voice was often lifted up in the cause of his Divine Master, and for the good of his fellow men, in the neighbourhood of Stroud, and on

---

1 In the biographies of him, and in his published sermons, his name is spelled White-field; but at Gloucester, his native place, and generally elsewhere, it is pronounced as if it were written Whit-field.

2 See the *Gloucester Journal* of April the 24th, 1739, in which was a full statement of the various services and journeys alluded to. But even this large amount of clerical labor was exceeded by that of the true-hearted enthusiast Edward Irving, formerly of the National Scotch Church, London, during his visit to Ireland, in September and October, 1830. A detailed account of it, given in his wife's letter to her sister at the time, concluded thus—"Edward preached thirteen times in eight days." *Life of Edward Irving*, by Mrs. Oliphant, 8vo., London, 1842.

3 These stone steps led to a gallery within the church: they were removed when the church was re-built in 1854.

Hampton Common, where a grassy mound on which he stood and preached is still called Whitefield's tump. When I was a boy, old farmer Cox, of Fennels, used to tell that as he was passing Nounsell's Cross at the top of the town, in returning home one evening from the market, he distinctly heard Mr. Whitefield preaching to a large congregation, in a field on the opposite—the Painswick—side of the Slad valley which lay between them. This field is now covered with houses and gardens.

Mr. Trigge, who was elected coroner of this district of the county in 1793, and resided at Cuckold's Brook as a practising surgeon for many years, was said to be the nearest living relative of Mr. Whitefield. He possessed the portrait from which all the engravings of Mr. Whitefield's likeness have been professedly taken ;—representing him in his well-known attitude of stretched-out hands, raised higher than his head, in the act of addressing a congregation. This portrait, which was painted by N. Hone, was not valuable as a work of art, though, probably, it was a good likeness. The figure was nearly of life-size. Subsequently, Mr. Trigge parted with it ; and it was said to have been taken to America, (where Mr. Whitefield's memory is held in great veneration,) instead of being retained, (as it ought to have been,) in his native county, or at least in his native land. Our National Portrait Gallery has thus, probably, lost the only original representation on canvas that exists of one of the most remarkable men of all ages.

Here, in connection with the name of Whitefield, a notice of Rodborough Tabernacle may not be inappropriate ; as he was mainly instrumental, (with "Thomas Adams, gentleman, of Rodborough, preacher of the gospel,") in raising the religious society, whose successors still assemble there. Mr. Adams built a chapel near his dwelling-house, [4] and preached in it until his death, August the 10th, 1770 ; after which, by a deed dated in 1771,—"the meeting-house, tabernacle, or place of religious worship, and dwelling-house" were, under the direction of his will, conveyed to trustees for the use of "a society of persons who profess themselves to be of the Calvinistic principles, professed and upheld by the late Rev. George Whitefield"—who had died the previous year in America—"and according to the doctrines of the articles of the Established Church, who

4 It is now the minister's house belonging to the chapel.

are called Methodists, for assembling together for the preaching and hearing the word of God, and for the residence of a minister of such society." It was thereby also provided, that, when the trustees should be reduced to five, the members of the society should nominate other persons to fill up the vacancies in the original number.

In this last particular, which was Mr. Whitefield's usual arrangement, it will be perceived how much he differed, in the organisation of his societies, from the Rev. John Wesley, all whose chapels are vested in trustees for the Wesleyan governing body called the Conference, which also appoints their ministers.

In its early days the religious services at Rodborough Tabernacle were conducted by occasional supplies of various popular preachers in the same connexion, from London and elsewhere. But, for many years past, there has been a stated resident minister, chosen by the members of the society. In this way it has gradually assumed the character of a Congregational church, as many other societies of Calvinistic Methodists have done. In the chapel is still preserved the chair in which Mr. Whitefield used to sit, when he came there on his ministerial visits.

In the year 1836 the then existing chapel was taken down, and a handsome and much larger edifice was erected in its place, which now forms a conspicuous object from a distance in the great valley below. It is about a mile and a quarter from Stroud, in a fine situation on the western side of Rodborough Hill, where,—standing on the verge of the hollow in which Stringer's estate lies, and which it overlooks,—the eye commands a view nearly unrivalled in variety and beauty.

It has been a favorite place of worship from its earliest days. I knew Mr. Thomas Loveday, an aged gentleman of Painswick, who, in his youth, lived at Frampton-on-Severn, from whence he was accustomed to walk to Rodborough Tabernacle (a distance of more than seven miles) every Sunday morning, to attend the religious services there, and to return in the evening. "The word of the Lord was precious in those days";[5] precious by reason of its scarceness,—precious for its value to an awakened mind. His mortal remains now repose in the burial ground of the chapel.

5 1 Samuel III. 1.

It was said by one of competent judgment, after the experience of a long life,—" I believe the church of the Tabernacle, from its commencement and for many years after, contained a number of the most devoted servants of God which this country ever produced." Men of such a community would be distinguished for conscientious diligence and integrity in all their concerns and duties : and the late Mr. Joseph Watts once said to me, "The best servants I ever had were Rodborough Tabernacle men."

Two of these men were Edward Dicks and William Gurner. The former was the elder of the two ; but both of them were employed in some department of the brewery, when Mr. Watts joined it, and both died in his service,— Dicks after a total service of thirty, and Gurner after above forty years, as Mr. Watts' confidential clerk.

Dicks was in good pecuniary circumstances. He had been in trade as a shoemaker, living at St. Briavels, a cluster of houses where now stands the north-west corner of Russell-street ; and there he used to entertain, as his guests, the various ministers who came to officiate as "occasional supplies " at the Tabernacle in its early days.

In September, 1866, several "Centenary Services" were held there, in celebration of its original erection in 1766. The particulars of those services, with a history of the place, are given in "A Memorial of Non-conformity," published on the occasion.

CHAPTER XXV.

ROYAL GEORGE HOTEL—MICHAEL BALLARD, AND VISIT OF PRINCE
FREDERICK TO CIRENCESTER — VISIT OF KING GEORGE III.
TO STROUD.

BEYOND the Golden Heart is the Green Dragon Inn,
an old house requiring a total renovation, to bring it
in keeping with the recent improvements of the street.
Following that are four good houses, with shops. The two
first were erected in 1866 by Mr. Dickinson ; and the others
in 1862 by Mr. Hewlett, on the garden ground which, for
many years, stood between the street and his father's old
house and workshops.

Adjoining the last is the Royal George Hotel, which has
a frontage of thirty yards to the street, and a west-front of
twelve yards, looking down the road to Rowcroft.   Formerly
this house was a portion of the estates of the family of
Halliday.   In the year 1795 it became the property of
Thomas Gardner, a Stroud and Bristol carrier, who followed
his business there until 1801, when it became the King's
Arms Inn.   It retained that name until, being purchased
by Mr. Thomas Wall, in 1818, and much enlarged and
improved, he removed to it from the George Inn, High-
street, and changed its name to the Royal George Hotel.
From him it passed to Mrs. Mary Pearce, who subsequently
married Mr. Richard Parker ; and by them it was ably
conducted for several years, as an Inn and posting-house.
In 1836 it was sold to J. E. Wakefield, of the Lamb Inn,
who soon after removed thither ; and, in 1852, it became
the property of William Ellis.   It is—perhaps I should
now say it was—the last house on that side of the street ;
and well situated for being the principal Inn of the town.
It has long been conducted by the Bradford family.

Previously to its occupation by Thomas Gardner as before mentioned, this house, with its large stables and warehouses, belonged to Daniel Ballard, an extensive common carrier, whose ancestor, Michael Ballard, gave occasion for a chapter in the satirical history of Stroud, which may not be without interest to the reader.

In the year 1750 King George the Second paid a visit to his German dominions ; and, during his absence from England, his son Frederick, then Prince of Wales, (father of King George the Third), made a short excursion into Gloucestershire, with his princess, their daughter,[1] and a large retinue ; when they became the guests of Lord Bathurst, at Cirencester. While there, the Prince was waited on by the nobility and gentry of the county ; and thence he made several short excursions. Upon this occasion Michael Ballard, in his great zeal for the honor of his native town, and with a desire to exhibit as well as to magnify his own importance, went to Cirencester to invite the Prince to pay a visit to Stroud ; and returned home fondly believing that he had actually obtained his promise to do so.

One of the Prince's visits was to Lord Ducie, at Spring Park, Woodchester, on which occasion his Lordship shewed him the clothing manufactory at Southfield mill, belonging to Mr. (afterward Sir) Onesiphorus Paul. Michael Ballard expected the Prince to "call at Stroud" during this visit ; and, hearing of his arrival there, he went to escort him to the town ; but in this Michael was disappointed, and returned from his bootless errand in great dudgeon.

On the 18th of July, 1750, Lord Bathurst escorted the Prince and his party to Whitminster House, in this county, the seat of Richard Owen Cambridge, Esq. They were rowed in Mr. Cambridge's boats down the river Froom, which ran through his grounds, to its confluence with the Severn at Framilode, and thence to "the Venetian barge," fitted up for the occasion. This vessel was moored in a beautiful reach of the river, and there they dined. After a short sail, the Prince and his party returned to Cirencester in the evening ; but, although they approached so near Stroud as to pass up and down Rodborough Hill, they did not condescend "to call" there, either in going or returning.

1 This daughter became Duchess of Brunswick, and mother of Queen Caroline, the wife of King George the Fourth. Prince Frederick died in the following year, 1751.

The story of the sayings and doings of Michael Ballard and some of his townsfolks, in their delighted expectation of a Royal visit, and in their chagrin at its failure, is humorously, though with the license of a satirist, set forth in a publication which appeared soon after, under the title of—

THE CHRONICLES, 1750.

" 1. It happened in these days, that the K——g of the *Lili——ans* took a journey into the country, even to the land of his nativity, and in which his forefathers were rulers of the people.

" 2. And while he sojourned there, his eldest son said unto himself, My father is a man stricken in years, and his days few on the earth ; therefore will I now shew myself to the people, that I may find favour in their sight.

" 3. So he made ready, and took with him his wife, and his little ones, with the chosen men of the land that ministered to him ; and he came to the dwelling-house of one of the rulers of the people.

" 4. And he abode there many days ; and he visited the groves, and the pleasant places, and the villages, and what his heart sought after, that did he.

" 5. And the inhabitants of the country went in great numbers to see the K——g's Son ; for they said one to another, Surely this is the man that will reign over us.

" 6. But the inhabitants of *Gotham* 2 exceeded those of the other places in the numbers of their people, and of their horses and wagons ; for they had determined to exceed all others in their duty to the K——g's Son.

" 7. And there was among them a man whose name was *Michael ;* a man of great boldness and assurance, though of little understanding : And he went also to see the K——g's Son, that if possible he might speak with him.

" 8. And when he came to him, he saluted him on this wise,—' May it please thy honor's worship, I am a Gothamite ; and all the inhabitants of the place, and those round about us, are thy friends ; I would, therefore, that thou wouldst come amongst us, and shew thyself unto us.'

" 9. He said, moreover,—' I have stable room sufficient for thee, and for thy horses, and for those that are with thee :

" 10. And thou mayest breakfast with me and my wife ; and eat of the buttered loaves which we will cause to be well buttered for thee, and drink of the tea which we will prepare of the best for thee : And whatsoever thy servant is possessed of, is at thy command.'

" 11. And the K——g's Son said unto Michael, ' What is thy trade or occupation ; or, what art thou, that thou seekest to entertain the K——g's Son ? '

2 By this term Stroud was meant. *Gotham* is a kind of *nomen generale*, applied contemptuously to any locality where stupid blunders and vulgar vanities are assumed to be the ordinary characteristics of the inhabitants. The original " Gothamites " were said to have mistaken the reflection of the moon's face on a sheet of water for a cheese, and to have attempted to draw it out with a rake. (One piece of poetry affirms the instrument used to have been a casting net.)

"These be the men, who when the moon,
    Bright in a crystal river shone,
  Threw casting nets, as subtly at her
    To catch, and drag her, out of the water.'

"12. And he said unto him, I am a '*London Wagoner.*' Then the K——g's Son turned to his wife, and to the people, with a smiling countenance, and bade his charioteer drive on.

"13. Now when Michael saw the K——g's Son look with a cheerful countenance, he said within himself, Surely I am in favor with the K——g's Son, and my request is granted unto me.

"14. So he returned to Gotham, and told the men of Gotham that the K——g's Son would call on them : then they rejoiced, and were exceeding glad at the tidings Michael the Gothamite had brought.

"15. And they said one to another, Behold the tidings Michael hath brought unto us ! and the K——g's Son calleth on us ! Surely we shall be chief in favour with the K——g's Son, and be honored with his presence above all that are round about us.

"16. And there had been lately in the country a man whose name was C——s : and he was a man of valour, and he had warred against the K——g : For he said, These nations are the inheritance of my father.

"17. Now the men of Gotham had commissioned together, and said, We will set up the image of C——s the K——g's enemy, and we will burn it before the face of the K——g's Son, when he cometh amongst us ; and it will please him well.

"18. And in a few days the K——g's Son journeyed to the land of the Gothamites, to the dwelling-place of one of the great men of the country.

"19. And, when Michael the Gothamite heard thereof, he made haste and followed him even to the great man's house.

"20. And he said to the servants of the house, Get ye unto the K——g's Son, and say unto him, that his servant Michael would fain speak with him.

"21. But the servants were sore afraid of their lord, and told not the words that Michael had said unto them.

"22. Then was Michael angry, and went to the apartment where the K——g's Son was ; and would have shewn himself to him, but the steward of the lord's house would not suffer him.

"23. Now while Michael was at the great man's house, behold all the men of Gotham had adorned their houses, and their streets, and their highways, and their churches, with the workmanship of their own hands.

"24. And they had made garlands of silver of their own, and what they had borrowed of their neighbours ; and they had hung up their spoons, and their papdishes, and whatever they had valuable ; that the K——g's Son might behold the riches of their land.

"25. Now when the time was nigh at hand that they expected the K——g's Son, they sent a chosen messenger out of the tribe of the *Tuckers*, to be a guide to him by the way ; for they said, Surely the K——g's Son hath need of a guide.

"26. And they sent musicians with instruments of music to play before him, and singers and dancers ; and nothing but joy and gladness appeared in the faces of the men of Gotham.

"27. But when the musicians, and the singers and dancers returned, and told the men of Gotham, 'Lo ! ye have done foolishly, and the K——g's Son calleth not on you !' then were they cut to the heart ; for it grieved them greatly.

"28. And they said among themselves, Behold the K——g's Son calleth not on us ; and the men of Gotham are grown weak in his sight : therefore we will not have this man to reign over us :

"29. But we will chuse the man we have lately rejected, even C——s : and we will set him up, for he is of a most honorable house.

"30. So they set up the ensigns and banners of C——s; even of the colour of those he showed in the day of battle, when he fought against the King.

"31. And they took the image of C——s, and arrayed it with raiment like to the raiment of the K——g's Son, and said, 'Now will we consume this image of the K——g's Son, as we would have consumed the image of C——s.'

"32. And when they would have burnt the image of the K——g's Son, lo ! the elders of the people distributed forty pieces of silver amongst the people : So was their anger stayed.

And the rest of the acts of the *Gothamites*, and the rivers they digged, and the numbers of the King's enemies they slew, and their customs and their manners, behold, are they not written in the book of the *Razor-Grinder's Dream* ?" 3

Since then, other satirical pieces have appeared here, written in the same style. Of these, the last—and perhaps the most popular—was issued a few days after the election, in December, 1867, of Mr. Henry Selfe Page Winterbotham to represent the borough of Stroud, in Parliament, in the place of Mr. Scrope, who had resigned, after holding the seat for nearly thirty-three years. It was entitled "Chronicles of Gotham," and consisted of ninety-four verses, in twelve chapters, printed on four small folio pages.

But the annals of Stroud are not without the record of a Royal visit. On Thursday, August the 14th, 1788, His Majesty King George the Third, with his Royal Consort, Queen Charlotte and the three eldest Princesses, having spent some weeks at Cheltenham, for the benefit of the King's health, passed through Stroud on their way from Cheltenham, to see the clothing manufactory of Mr. Obadiah Paul at Woodchester mill.

Upon this occasion great crowds assembled to welcome the Royal party ; and flags and triumphal arches were erected,—the chief arch being thrown across the road at the Chequers, where they entered the town from Badbrook. The King made his progress on horseback,—the Queen and Princesses being in open carriages,—escorted by the influential persons of the neighbourhood. His Majesty wore a blue coat, with a scarlet collar—the Windsor uniform,— and a cocked hat, with which he acknowledged the salutations of the people ; and, when he raised his hand for that purpose, a rent was visible under the arm of his Majesty's coat.

3 The *Razor-Grinder's Dream* had already told (among other things) how "Gotham's sons," the rabble of Stroud, had behaved at the proclamation of peace, made there upon the defeat of Prince Charles Stuart,—(commonly called the Pretender,) at the battle of Culloden, in April, 1745.

The route from Stroud was by way of Wallbridge, where the Royal party visited the junction of the Thames and Severn Canal with the Stroudwater Navigation, and witnessed the passage of a barge through the lock there, from the former to the latter canal.

The usual road from Wallbridge to Woodchester was steep and circuitous ; and, as the King's coming had been previously announced, a temporary way was made for him through the grounds of Spilman's Court, and Stringers. It entered the former a little above the house called Mowmead; and, (crossing the highway that leads from the village of Rodborough to Dudbridge,) it passed through the latter, and came out into the Bath turnpike road, near Lightpill mill. It lay nearly in the direction of the present turnpike road, subsequently made between those two places. By this route the cavalcade went and returned ; and, from that day, the space between the east end of the Chequers and the west end of the George Hotel, has been called *King*-street, in honor of his Majesty's passing over it.

Great preparations were made by Mr. Paul at Grigshoot House to receive the Royal party, and to shew them the manufactory, machinery, &c.

They breakfasted at Hill-house, the seat of Sir George Onesiphorus Paul, Bart. ; and were afterward entertained by the Right Honorable Francis Lord Ducie, at Spring Park. [5]

It may not be uninteresting to add that Woodchester mill, visited by the King in 1788, stands on the same stream, and next below Southfield mill, which Prince Frederick, his father, had visited in 1750, as previously stated.[6]

[5] This visit was recorded by the Rev. William Ellis, at the time, in the parish Register of Stroud.

[6] It was, for many years, the property of the old author himself.

CHAPTER XXVI.

WE have now traced—and in some measure described —the town, as it stood, up to the last ten years of the eighteenth century. At that period there were not any houses between the south-end of King-street and the Brewery, except Rowcroft House.

Immediately below the Brewery a narrow lane ran diagonally from the road there, down to Maggot's Bridge ; across which was a public footpath into the parish of Painswick.

The Slade stream, after leaving Badbrook where it is last mentioned, drives the wheels of Badbrook mill. It then passes under Maggot's Bridge, and falls into—or rather flows through—the lower level of the Thames and Severn Canal, and thence into the pond of the grist mill below. Seventy yards farther on, it falls into the river Froom, just below Wallbridge clothing mill ; and thus continues to be the boundary between the parish of Painswick, and the home-division of the parish of Stroud.

Wallbridge, with its two mills, is a small vicinage at the junction of those rivers ; and was anciently quite separated from Stroud, though it may now be said to be one of its suburbs. It is situated in the three parishes of Stroud, Painswick, and Rodborough ; and probably derived its name from the bridge over the river having been built of stone,—a wall-bridge. The road between it and Stroud is on a considerable descent ; and was formerly so narrow that, when a wagon was about to pass from one to the other, a person went forward to see that no carriage was coming in the opposite direction. But, about the year 1825, it was made of its present ample width, by the Commissioners of the (old) Improvement Act, and by the proprietors of the Thames and Severn Canal.

In my youth, the road at Wallbridge passed between some of the houses and the river Froom, where it bounds the garden of Mr. Smith's mill ; in which there was a row of fine yew trees, clipped into the shape of pillars, joined to each other by intervening arches. These trees were pleasant to look upon, as the remains of a fashion which, even then, was passing away ; but, having been long since suffered to grow wild and untrimmed, they have lost their old-fashioned interest ; and, moreover, they are no longer visible from the road ; which was diverted from the brook to the other side of the houses, by the Commissioners named in an Act passed for the renewal of the Turnpike Trust.

The story of a barbarous murder committed many years ago at Spilman's Court, near this place, has been preserved by occasional mention of it, with some very revolting details. But these may have been mere additions to the fact that a servant of the family, the cook, was murdered one Sunday morning, while the rest of the household were at church, and on their return home her body was found lying on the hearth before the kitchen fire.

The last mill on the Slade stream, with the adjoining house and other property, formerly belonged to Mr. Cole, who rebuilt the dwelling-house in 1714. This house stands at the bottom of the declivity from Stroud. Its entrance door had originally three steps up to it, but is now approached by three steps down to it,—the road which passes it having been elevated in 1825, in order to relieve the descent from above. Mr. Cole appears to have had a love for the ornamental, perhaps greater than for the useful. He set up over the door of his mill a very graceful statue of a child ; and he adorned the house and garden with figures of heathen gods, goddesses, and other ornamental objects,—such as vases, urns, &c.

At the upper angle of the garden, pointing toward the town, he erected a small, elegant, summer-house, in ex-quisite taste as to its proportions, and the architectural disposition and enrichment of its parts. It was embellished with eagles and other figures carved in stone, and was surmounted by a handsome weather-cock. Its interior was adorned with pictures of the four seasons, and other subjects. It was fitted up rather sumptuously ; being furnished with oriental china ornaments, together with a tea service for the rural entertainment of friends,—all arranged in elegant open buffets, and in closed cupboards with the painted and gilded panels.

This choice building, with its variegated holly tree, and the elegantly wrought iron gate leading from the garden to the road, was an object of general attraction. Its cost was £400 ; and, as a young lady said, "it seemed that Mr. Cole intended his garden and summer-house for a mythological paradise." Among other mythic personages therein, was one which old Kit Webb, the gardener, [1] said was "Venus the god of war ; and a fine looking fellow he be." In company with Venus, (or Mars if it were he,) were cupids, posture-making and seeming to fly, and eagles, doves, &c., all appearing to be on amicable terms with each other. The garden also contained quaintly-clipped yew hedges, and a fine oak tree,—remarkable for the length, straightness, and smoothness of its trunk, and for the perfect shape and fulness of its large round head.

By the cutting of the Thames and Severn Canal through this property above the dye-houses, in 1785, the garden was not only diminished in size, but what remained of it was cut off from the house. A communication, however, was made between the separate parts, by a pretty wooden Chinese bridge which projected from the side of the brick bridge over the canal ; and the remnant of the garden, with its summer-house, was bounded by the road on the southeast, and by the narrow lane down to Maggot's Bridge on the north.

The property came to Mr. Peter Watts, a dyer, by marriage with Mr. Cole's daughter Diana ; and there he lived and died. From him it came by devise to several of his children, of whom Richard, George, Edward, Susan, and Elizabeth, resided there for many years.

The brothers Watts had considerable musical taste and talents, playing well on the violoncello ; and in their music room a club of amateur performers, vocal and instrumental, held their periodical meetings. Thither parties of friends were occasionally invited to partake of the musical feast. But alas ! the music room has disappeared ; while some few members of the club are yet living, to regret that with the

---

[1] This man pretended to a complete knowledge of botany. On one occasion, Mr. Burgh shewed him a sprig of the common heath he had brought from Wales, in an empty hair-powder bag. It smelled of the perfume of the powder ; and when Mr. Burgh asked him what plant it was,—"That" (said Webb without any hesitation) "is a sweet-scented Indi-Chinese Arbor Vitæ."

last strains of music which resounded there, some of the most agreeable reunions of the neighbourhood ceased for ever.

We must not omit to mention the fate of some of the garden images. Several years ago, an insane gentleman escaped from his keepers, and came to the George Hotel, where he spent the night. In wandering out early the next morning, he espied the figures; and making his way to them, he proceeded to demolish "the idols," as he called them, with his staff, with true iconoclastic zeal and vigour. This, however, was perceived by one of the Messrs. Watts, who kept the despoiler in conversation on the theological view of the matter, until, further assistance being procured, he was removed to the George Hotel, and finally restored to his friends.

But, in 1826, this titled "paradise" underwent a more complete destruction, by the making of the new "Stroud and Cainscross" turnpike road; [2] which required the enlargement of the narrow lane as its entrance; and, in consequence, the summer-house was taken down, the shapely oak felled, and the upper part of the ground thrown into the road. Utility triumphed over beauty.

The whole is now only a vision in the mind's eye of the writer, and the few (if any) others who remember its former state; though the shape of the acute angle on which the summer-house stood may yet be traced, in the diagonal direction which carriages take in passing from the town to Maggot's Bridge.

The grist mill, house, and other premises below the canal, became, by purchase in 1850, the property of Mr. John Biddell; and the whole residue of the garden, from the canal upward, is now covered with a large malt-house, erected by Mr. Joseph Watts, in connection with the brewery that stands on the opposite side of the road.

2 Under Act 6, Geo. IV., c. 22.

CHAPTER XXVII.

MAGGOT'S Bridge was, in my young days, a narrow wooden structure for foot passengers. The pathway over it entered the parish of Painswick, and led through the fields to Cuckhold's Brook, a hamlet situated on the small stream of that name, where it is crossed by the highway between Pakenhill and Cainscross.

My earliest recollection of this bridge is connected with the balloon ascent of Mr. Sadler, of Oxford, from Wallbridge Wharf, in the year 1785. He was one of our earliest aeronauts, and the announcement of his intended ascent attracted a vast number of persons to witness it ; so that the wharf being too small to accommodate them, the neighbouring eminences and houses on both sides of the valley were covered with the assembled multitudes. I was then six years old, and remember being carried astride on a man's shoulders, to witness the proceedings, from the place where now stands the entrance lodge of the house called Far Hill, which commands a good view of the wharf below.

At that time there were not, as there are now, gasworks, from which ready-made inflammable gas might be conducted to the balloon : but the gas was made in casks containing small pieces of iron with diluted vitriolic acid ; and thence, as it evolved, it was conducted by pipes into the balloon, round which the casks were ranged. This was a tedious process ; and when the day was far advanced and the spectators had become impatient, Sadler sent up a small pilot balloon to ascertain the direction of the wind, and commenced his ascent before the balloon was sufficiently filled. Under these circumstances, the altitude he attained was not great, and his aerial journey was short; for he descended near King Stanley, about three miles off, in a field called Ireland. Perhaps it may be thought a somewhat curious fact, that the next balloon which ascended here some years after, fell in a field near Stonehouse, called Scotland.

That part of the parish of Painswick which is entered from Maggot's Bridge is the tongue of land before mentioned,[1] into which the body of Wickeridge Hill is contracted, as it slopes down to the river Froom in the main valley, and by its intervention divides the home part of Stroud from its outlying tithing of Pakenhill.

On entering that parish, there is, on the right, an ancient mansion called The Hill, pleasantly situated on the ridge of this lower eminence of Wickeridge Hill. From its south front the eye looks over the river Slade to Stroud, and from its north front into the valley beneath Whiteshill. It was formerly the inheritance and residence of the old family of Webb de Hill; and was built, or nearly rebuilt, in the year 1634, by Thomas Webb, the donor of "Webb's Charity" before mentioned. This appears by the date, with his initials and monogram, carved on the lintel of the fine old porch in the northern front. It was he who, about the same time, erected "the house behind the church," now belonging to Dr. Paine, at a small distance from the Charity houses. His successor, "John Webb de Hill," died in 1715, aged 61 years, as might have been read on an altar tomb, which once stood against the south wall of the old parish church, on the left hand side of the chancel door.

The last resident owner of this property, of the name of Webb,—and I believe the last male representative of that branch of the family,—was Samuel Webb, who lived there as late as 1801. He became possessed of it in 1777, as devisee of his father John Webb, who took of Sara Webb in 1727; but this, with his other wealth, to the amount of £30,000, had all passed away from him before his death. He sold The Hill Estate to Mr. Thomas Holbrow, of Badbrook House, in the year 1800. Late in life he married a Miss Munden, and went to reside on a farm at Huntley in this county, which he rented in partnership with his wife's brother; and there he became so reduced in his pecuniary circumstances as to be obliged to relinquish it. Coming to

1 See p. 6.

Stroud, he took lodgings in High-street, and fell into such extreme indigence as to require parochial relief: and then, in 1816, he—the last Webb de Hill—an aged man, was passed as a pauper to Huntley, where, (according to the then existing poor laws,) he had acquired a settlement by renting; and was delivered to the overseer of that parish, at the same farm house in which he himself had resided.

Many years ago, there was another ancient house near the south front of The Hill. It was the older of the two, and was taken down within my memory: but near its site the remnant of a very old elm, (consisting of a small portion of its hollowed trunk,) still bears, on its few branches, a scanty leafage in summer time. It is the only living thing that was contemporary with Thomas Webb who rebuilt the mansion; and there it stands in its decay, like a veteran sentinel, keeping ward over the buried memories of its past ages. The avenue of trees that leads up to The Hill was planted in 1786.

At a short distance from this place, on a lower slope of the same tongue of land, is the house called Far Hill, from which there is a full view of the Rodborough Hill side of the valley, with the Fort on its brow. It was erected by Mr. Benjamin Grazebrook, and occupied by his son Joseph until he died, October the 30th, 1843, in the ninety-second year of his age. The way to it passes under some fine tall elms, which remind me that, when I was a lad, I shot an arrow at a rook perched in one of them, for which Mr. Grazebrook reproved me; and further, they call to mind a feat of strength, not unworthy of mention, in relation to them.

In the year 1802, Lodgemore mill, which had been destroyed by fire, was being rebuilt;[2] and the masons employed were accustomed to resort, at their dinner hours, to the Anchor Inn near it, on the sloping side of the valley, immediately opposite Far Hill. Two of these men were William Franklin and his younger brother Fream Franklin. The latter was a very fine, handsome man, twenty-two years of age, six feet three inches high, and of great muscular strength. His masons' axe was two pounds heavier than that used by a man of ordinary strength; and when he was twenty years old he, with one hand, lifted from the ground

2 It was burnt down a second time in 1807; and again September 14, 1871, when it belonged to Mr. Strachan.

eight half-hundred weights chained together.   On more than one occasion, when in the yard of the Anchor Inn, he threw a stone across the valley and the tops of the elms at Far Hill,—being a distance of 115 yards to the foot of the trees, over which the stone mounted in its flight to the field beyond.   Among other feats of this kind, he threw a stone over the church steeple, which is ninety feet high, both when standing in the Shambles, and when he had one foot against the base of the tower.   On another occasion, when standing in the Castle-street, he threw a stone almost to the river Froom which bounds Mansell's mead in the valley below, a distance of 250 yards : and Richard Ayers, who was present and saw the direction of the stone toward a tree in the copse beyond, ran down the steep lane by The Castle, into the mead, and returned bringing the identical stone with him.   Fream Franklin lost his life by a strange accident in 1805, when 25 years of age : he stumbled when walking down hill, with a stake as a staff ; and falling forward, the pointed end of the stake pierced through one of his eyes into his brain.

To resume—formerly, the foot path from Maggot's Bridge, (after passing the avenue to The Hill,) entered the grounds belonging to Far Hill, near its present lodge gate ; then, running under the tall elms, it skirted the northern wall of the house in its rapid descent to the deep dell, through which runs the Painswick stream.   There it crossed the water on another narrow wooden foot bridge, and again entered the parish of Stroud, by an equally rapid ascent to the house called Gannicox, on its way to Cuckhold's Brook.   At the bridge in the dell was a small copse ; and this, with the rookery in Gannicox's pleasure grounds, which overhung the high quick hedge of the pathway, made it a very pleasant, shady retreat, and a favourite walk in summer time.   It was said, in those days, that the dell was haunted, and so it may have been ; for there the lover waited for his mistress in the soft twilight, and the coward trembled at the spectre raised by his own fears in the dark.

At that time, the only carriage way to The Hill was from the high road over Beeches Green, near the house called Cooper's Hill,—where it enters its own grounds.[3] In like manner, the carriage drive to Gannicox was across

---

3 A deep cutting of the Great Western Railway, which passes near the back of the house, deprived it of this communication.

fields from the Stroud and Pakenhill road, where it entered by a gate, the stone jambs of which are, from their great size, called Hercules' pillars. In the year 1826, however, a turnpike road from Stroud to Cainscross, by way of Maggot's Bridge, was made, which passes by the ascent to The Hill, the entrance lodge of Far Hill, and Gannicox; and thus furnishes a convenient access to each of those places. This road is a great public accommodation, being much shorter and more level than the old one by way of Pakenhill. It passes over Maggot's Bridge thirteen feet six inches above the river Slade; at the viaduct over the little dell and the Painswick stream, it is eighteen feet six inches above them; and nearly the same height above Cuckold's Brook, which it crosses before it enters Cainscross. It also supplies a good substitute for the old foot-path through the dell, which, thenceforward ceasing to be used, was thrown into the adjoining ground; and the pleasant shady copse was cut down.

For some years there were toll-gates on this road, and on that from Stroud and Pakenhill to Cainscross; but they have been removed, and the roads are now repaired at the expense of the respective parishes through which they pass.

CHAPTER XXVIII.

STROUD BREWERY — EDWARD WILKINS THE POET — MR. JOSEPH WATTS.

THE Stroud Brewery was established toward the end of the last century, by Mr. Peter Leversage, of Middle Lypiatt. He was soon joined by Mr. Grazebrook and Mr. Burgh, under the firm of Leversage, Grazebrook, and Burgh. Mr. Burgh retired from the partnership about the year 1799, and Mr. Grazebrook in 1804. Mr. Leversage then took Mr. Joseph Watts into the business, which was carried on for fourteen years, in the names of Leversage and Watts; but under the active and successful management of Mr. Watts alone. Early in that period Mr. Leversage died, leaving his son Peter, a minor, his representative in the Brewery. On the 5th day of January, 1819, Mr. Watts became its sole proprietor, and continued to conduct it for thirty-six more years, during which time it became a prosperous concern.

Among the inferior persons who were hangers-on about the Brewery, during this latter period, was Edward Wilkins (commonly called Teddy Wilkins,) who thought himself a poet, and wrote quires of poor verses under that delusion. His greatest work, as he esteemed it, in that line, was entitled "Stroud Brewery, A new poem in praise of good beer, &c." It consisted of eighty-four stanzas, each of four lines,—all in celebration of the huge brewery casks and their contents, the brewery servants, the horses, and the wagons laden with their thirst-assuaging, or (it may have been) thirst-provoking burdens. The following four lines were reported to be "of his own composing"; and, if genuine, they certainly were (from the bold metaphor and the physiological fact they contain) a lofty poetical flight :—

> "When going, one day, to my employ,
> I met a wagon load of joy :—
> It made me thirsty to see't—for why,—
> It came from Watts's Brewery."

He seemed to have taken upon himself the office of Poet Laureate of the Brewery; and it was surmised that the strong beer, which he drank to excess, was both the source of his inspiration and the wages of his Laureateship. His beery performances were at their highest about the year 1820, as was also his poetic reputation. He died at Rodborough in 1825, from the effects of hard drinking.

Among other persons of the same class was Tom Blades, an idle, sottish fellow of the town. It was said of him that he met Mr. Watts returning home from the church one Sunday morning, and that, touching his hat with one hand, he held out the other in the act of begging; that Mr. Watts gave him sixpence to get rid of him, upon which Blades said, with an arch leer,—"Thank you, Sir,—it will soon come back to you again," and slunk into the first public-house to which he came, as a step toward the accomplishment of the prediction.

Mr. Watts had a calm and composed manner, with an untiring perseverance in the pursuit of any object on which he set his mind. He was kind and charitable, and in the course of his long life deservedly obtained a high position in the public estimation. He was so influential as to become the acknowledged head of the Whig interest in the borough, and the neighbouring parts of the county: and his Brewery counting-house, where he was to be seen almost daily, has often witnessed the presence of high and distinguished personages, friends and acquaintances, in political or other consultations, or familiar conversation. Thus for many years he filled a large space in the political and social history of the neighbourhood.

He died at Stratford House, October the 17th, 1855, aged eighty-four years; and was buried on the 25th in Stroud church-yard. The funeral procession was joined by a long train of persons who had assembled to testify their respect for his memory. At their head was Earl (then Lord John) Russell, who had come from London for the purpose of being present.

Mr. Watts bequeathed the Brewery, with much other property, including Stratford House and Estate, to Joseph Watts Hallewell, one of his grandsons.

The Brewery was carried on by the partnership firm of Messrs. Watts Hallewell, Biddell, and Stanton; under whose management it became one of the largest establishments of the kind in this part of the kingdom, and is now "The Stroud Brewery Company Limited."

CHAPTER XXIX.

WE are now about to enter on the more modern parts
of the town,—namely, the additions successively
made to its old area, as already described.

Toward the latter end of the last century the growing
prosperity of the clothing trade, and the consequent increase
of the local population, created a great demand for dwelling-
houses for all classes of persons.

At that time, a piece of land called Rowcroft, containing
about six acres, lay between the King's Arms Inn—now the
Royal George Hotel—(or rather between the large open
space belonging to its west front)—and the Brewery ;
having the road on the south, and the river Slade on the
north. [1] It was the property of William Tanner. He sold
the upper part of it, (containing 3A. 2R. 2P.,) to Edward
Thornton, surgeon, who, in the year 1795, erected on it
Rowcroft House.

This, and the other parts of the field, were subsequently
further divided by sales. In 1801 Mr. Joseph Grazebrook
built two dwelling-houses at its lower end ; and, soon after,
two others, at some distance up toward Rowcroft House ;
and into one of those first built he removed his banking
business. Thus was commenced the line of buildings
which, extending up the whole road-frontage of the field,
was (at first) called Rowcroft, from the name of the field
itself.

In a few years after, Charles Harrison, a speculator in
house-building, filled up the space between Mr. Grazebrook's
two blocks of houses, by the erection of five others of a

---

[1] Alice Hampton died seized of a messuage called Rowcroft in the 8th
year of King Henry VIII.

similar kind ; and these, with some additions made at the upper end, completed the line to which the name of Rowcroft is now more exclusively confined.   This line comprises about three-fourths of the whole distance, and has a paved footpath between it and the road, and garden ground down to the river Slade behind.

In the year 1799, Peter Playne, of Downfield, built two houses in his orchard on the other side of the road, opposite the upper part of Rowcroft ; and Arthur Robinson, who afterward purchased it, erected an adjoining house, which extended to St. Briavels.

All the houses in Rowcroft were tenanted as soon as ready for occupation : an early inhabitant of one of them being Mrs. Brydges, widow of the Rev. Edward Tymewell Brydges, of the Kentish family of that name.   She was fond of dramatic representation ; and for two seasons gave private theatricals, for the entertainment of her friends. Her front and back sitting rooms were divided by folding doors : and, these being thrown open, one was made the stage, and the other "the house," where sat the spectators. Captain Brew, of the Queen's Bays, then on the recruiting service here, was one of Mrs. Brydges' most efficient amateur actors : and the following prologue, written for the occasion by the author of these pages, was spoken at the opening of the second theatrical season,—that of 1810 :—

PROLOGUE.

When first in elder times the Stage began
Mankind to picture, as a school for man,
In rude bold lines which filled his soul with awe,
Himself pourtray'd, the half-barbarian saw ;
Learnt to despise, then hate, what he had been ;
And rose corrected by the mimic scene.
    Thence downward to these later times, the Stage
Hath been the faithful mirror of the age ;
Reflecting back upon its thousand eyes,
The ever-shifting follies as they rise.
" When Learning's triumph o'er her barb'rous foes
Rear'd England's stage, immortal Shakspeare rose ;
Each change of many-color'd life he drew,
Exhausted worlds and then imagin'd new.
Existence saw him spurn her bounded reign,
And panting Time toil'd after him in vain ;
His pow'rful strokes presiding Truth impress'd,
And unresisted Passion storm'd the breast."

2 The author borrowed these eight fine lines on Shakspeare from Dr. Johnson's prologue, spoken by his friend Garrick, at the opening of Drury-lane Theatre in 1747.

Here, too, our Milton, with a master's hand,
Instructing Innocence and Truth to stand,
Weav'd the wild web of Comus round the fair,
To paint the world's and life's delusive snare ;
Then broke the spell—o'erthrew the enchanter's throne—
To hold us by a magic of his own.
E'en on such boards as these, the scene he drew ;
Actors, spectators, all—he lov'd, he knew ;
And taught the noble, gen'rous, young, and fair,
In Virtue's cause the private Stage to rear.
    And whilst the mighty masters of the mind
Continue here to lead and guide mankind ;—
Teach us what various passions lurk within
The mind, and urge from thoughts of sin, to sin :
Recording that the good alone are blest,
Denying to the guilty conscience rest ;
Whilst they, with thoughts that truth and love inspire,
Warm and dissolve and set the heart on fire ;
Still shall the Stage, frequented and approv'd
By Virtue's friends, be honor'd and belov'd.
    But come not ye, whose cynic length of face
No smile for conq'ring Love did ever grace ;
Who, spell-bound by the dull Lethean draught,
Have ne'er at Pistol or at Falstaff laugh'd ;
Whose stony hearts have not a single tear
To dew the corse of daughter-murder'd Lear :
O, come not hither ! the immortal bard
Looks not to *you* for his deserv'd reward.
    But ye, who human life delighted view
In scenic show, and half believe it true ;
Who, as ye trace the mazy story, find
Alternate hope and fear possess the mind ;
And, by the strong illusion fetter'd, give
Your souls, our captives, in the scene to live ;
Who hang suspended in the dubious fray,
And fear lest cruel Richard win the day ;
Ye who rejoice when murd'rous villains fall,
And weep when bloody tyrants states enthrall ;
View with amaze how to the foulest deeds
Of blood, from crime to crime ambition leads ;
Makes woman's breasts exchange " their milk for gall,"
And Macbeth's blade in Duncan's bosom fall ;
Come ! the ingenuous smile, th' ingenuous tear
Which ye bestow, shall Poets, Actors cheer ;
Proud of their labours, labours not in vain,
If *your*, and *your*, and *your* applause we gain.

In 1845 the houses in Rowcroft were considerably reduced in value, and their eligibility, as residences, was much
affected, by the Great Western Railway, which, after, leaving
its Stroud station, is carried across the road on a black,
plain-looking viaduct. In order to make room for the
railway to pass onward, the first two houses in the row
were taken down ; and, to admit the passing of carriages
under the viaduct, the whole road beneath it and in front

of Rowcroft was excavated, to the depth of six feet at the lowest part, with a gradual ascent to its upper end.

In consequence of this alteration, carriages could not any longer be drawn up before the houses ; and they became, and now are, accessible only from either end of the pavement in their front, which is protected by iron rails from the deep road below. Besides this, it became necessary to build a high, blank wall, as a support of the opposite bank, and to be the fence of the Station : and thus the entrance to the town, at this place, has been greatly disfigured by the ugly railway bridge, and the dirty hollow way that passes under it.

The space between the George Hotel and Rowcroft was left for many years as a void piece of ground belonging to the Hotel; but, in the year 1831, Mr. Parker erected a large building at a right angle with the Hotel, having its front toward the street. He called it The Victoria Rooms, and intended it for public meetings, balls, exhibitions, lectures, &c. It had, on its first floor, a room fifty-eight feet long by forty-three feet wide ; and, along its front, a temporary hustings was erected in 1832, whence the first candidates for the representation of the borough in Parliament were nominated, and the result of the poll declared. There, too, were set up the hustings, on the contested election in 1859, as well as on other intermediate and later elections. Victoria Rooms did not succeed as a pecuniary speculation, in consequence of the superior accommodation and success of the Stroud Subscription Rooms ; and they were subsequently converted into two dwelling-houses with shops.

About 1853 Mr. Dangerfield built a house and shop at the west end of these Rooms, that is, between them and Rowcroft House ; and thus completed the line of continuous houses on the north side of the road from the George Hotel to the railway bridge. In 1856 Mr. Ellis added to the Hotel the Masonic Hall, for (amongst other uses) the accommodation of the Sherborne Lodge of the old fraternity of Freemasons, whose meetings were held there.

As to Rowcroft House,—it was sold in 1806 by Mr. Thornton to Mr. W. W. Darke, and by him, in 1812, to B. H. Brown, M.D., who occupied it until his removal from the town. In 1844 his representatives sold it to Mr. George Edwards, who disposed of it in 1859 to the County of Gloucester Banking Company.

The first bank established in the town, of which I have found any mention, was the "Stroud Bank" of Mr. James Dallaway, who took Mr. Hollings into partnership. On Mr. Dallaway's decease, in 1787, Mr. Benjamin Grazebrook joined Mr. Hollings. On the withdrawal of the latter, about 1798, the business was carried on by Messrs. Benjamin and Joseph Grazebrook ; and, for many years afterward, by Mr. Joseph Grazebrook alone. It then became the bank of Messrs. Grazebrook and Wathen, and, subsequently, of Messrs. Grazebrook, Wathen, and Hawkins.

In 1809 the bank of Messrs. Martin, Mills, and Wilson was opened near the lower end of the south side of High-street as before mentioned, and was discontinued in 1825.

On January 1st, 1830, the bank of Grazebrook and Co. passed into the hands of Messrs. Watts, Wyatt, Hallewell, and Wason ; and they, in 1838, transferred it to the County of Gloucester Joint-stock Banking Company, as their Stroud Branch. When their house in Rowcroft was taken down in 1845 to make way for the passing of the railway across its site, the banking business was removed to the upper-most house in the same row; and, subsequently, to Rowcroft House, where it is carried on by them as the successors to the original Stroud Bank.

In the year 1834 a branch of the Gloucestershire Joint-stock Banking Company was established in a building erected for the purpose, adjoining their house at the bottom of High-street as before mentioned; and it is now a flourish-ing establishment, being absorbed into the Capital and Counties Bank (Limited).

Of both these joint-stock banks it may be said that they ranked among the most extensive of their kind in the kingdom.

Soon after the commencement of Rowcroft, Mr. Graze-brook erected the Brick-Row, for working people. It con-sists of thirty small houses, which were finished in three years, at the rate of ten in each year. Some attempt has been since made to give it the more imposing name of Ryeleaze Place ; and perhaps, if persevered in, time, which deals so authoritatively with all things, may at length establish it ; though a new name cannot improve the real character of anything. These houses stand, with gardens before them, on part of a piece of pasture ground called Ryeleaze, lying on the south-east side of the road already described as leading from Church-street to Little Mill.

This road has been called by the various names of the Back-lane, the Laggar, and "the lane behind the church": and I am not aware that it has yet acquired any other appellation. This lane, (not being a public but a private carriage road to the mill, and having been seldom used by the mill tenants since the better access to it by the Stroud and Birdlip turnpike road in 1801,) became, and, for many years remained, in a very bad state of repair; notwithstanding one of our National school-rooms was built on the north-west side of it in 1835, and several other houses have been erected near its entrance from Church-street. Lately, however, it seems to have been treated by the Local Board of Health somewhat more as though it were a public road, —in respect at least to Brick-Row; and has been repaired, to a limited extent, at the public expense. If Dr. Paine's new road from the bottom of High-street to the Parsonage, should ever be extended, as a public highway into the Slad road, near Little Mill, as before suggested, it would join this lane, and make it a valuable thoroughfare; when, probably, it would be still further improved and repaired.3 Brick-Row may be said to be the second addition to the old town. It lies on its northern side.

About the year 1805 the third extension of the town was in its early stage of progress—beyond Nounsell's cross,— at the upper, or east end of its old area. And from time to time, houses, chiefly for the working classes, have been built there; until they now extend upward to the foot-path which crosses over the hill from Mount Pleasant. They cover the whole space between that foot-path on the east, the old Bisley road on the south, and the old road to the Slad on the north. The whole is of a triangular shape, having its apex resting on Nounsell's cross, with its base upward, like an inverted pyramid: and, including the last-named road, it comprises an area of about twelve acres. Its northern portion formerly belonged to the family of Sheppard; and the South part to the Arundells of the Field. The old occupation road that passes up the central ridge to the fields beyond, and was formerly a public foot-path toward Fennels and Bisley, is now a narrow street called Middle Hill: and the Slad old road, with its almost continuous houses on both sides, is called Somers-street,—

[3 This great public improvement has long been done, and has caused the growth of a large suburb, called "Lansdowne."]

which name it obtained from a house of that name, lying in a small hollow under the bank, on the left side of its entrance.4   This house was, within the writer's memory, the only one beyond Nounsell's cross on that road; and the Ivy House, near New Lodge,5 the only one on the Bisley road.   The group of houses near the lowest, the western point, is called New Town ; and is so named on Wood's " Plan of Stroud," published in 1835, as also in a map made in 1830, long before the whole space above it had been built upon.

The place which here and elsewhere has been called Nounsell's cross, is, on Wood's plan, called " the Knoll " ; though it has not the characteristics of a knoll, which means a little round hill or mount.   It lies in the direct ascending line of the longitudinal ridge or spine of the hill ; and is somewhat flattened by the travelling on the road across it. But the ridge is so narrow at this place, that a ball might even now be rolled down to the south, on one side of the road ; as it could formerly have been to the north, from the other side.   The sharp edge of the uncovered rock is still visible near it.

The houses on the south side of Middle Hill have a pleasant view of the Stroud valley, and of Rodborough Hill beyond ; and those on the north side have a view of the Slade valley, and Wickeridge Hill ; as well as the upward windings of each, on its way into the mass of the Cotteswolds.

Within the writer's recollection there was a long strip of ground not built upon, between Parliament-street and the old house called Somers' : but this vacant space has since been covered with houses ; and besides these, dwelling-houses have been built in the Leazes, which lie on the northern downward slope of the hill behind Parliament-street and the upper part of Silver-street; and the population of this third addition to the town is very considerable.

It must not be forgotten that, in 1853, Mr. Postlethwaite built a house, which he named Belmont, in the field that lies immediately above the south-east end of the hill.   The Grecian simplicity of its form, with the colonnade along its western front, gives it an air of magnitude : and its elevated situation, commanding extensive views, makes it a healthful and pleasant summer residence.

4 The name of this street is erroneously spelled Summer-street.
[5 Now known as " The Chestnuts."]

CHAPTER XXX.

THE CIRENCESTER AND LONDON OLD ROAD — CHALFORD — CHAL-
FORD CHAPEL — FRIAR BACON'S STUDY — THE OLD ROADS
FROM STROUD TO CIRENCESTER, AND THE NEW TURNPIKE
ROADS.

EVERY one who has frequently travelled through the
valleys and over the hills in the district of which
Stroud is the centre, (especially, if he has explored its
more retired parts,) cannot fail to have remarked that the
old roads which pass along the sides of the hills, upon their
spinal ridges, and across, from one valley to another, form
difficult lines of communication, steep, narrow, and tortuous.

These, on the disuse of pack-horses for the general conveyance of heavy burdens, must have been very inconvenient
for traffic by carriages which succeeded them. At present,
I shall notice those old roads only, which (by operating
either proximately or remotely as causes) led to the fourth
and most important extension of the town; and of this I
shall have to give the particulars hereafter.

In olden times, the highway from Stroud to Cirencester
and London was up High-street, Silver-street, and The
Hill, to Bisley; thence across Oakridge Common, by way
of the dip or hollow called Water-lane, down by Tunley
and Henwood, through the river Froom (which is shallow
at that place) and the Gulf, to Park Corner; and thence
along the whole north side of Oakley Wood and Lord
Bathurst's Park, to Cirencester, which it entered at Cicely
Hill. Indications still exist that this was the general public
road, in a few remaining milestones; one of which stands
on the south side of the road to Bisley, a little beyond the
eastern entrance of Lypiatt Park, and another at Water-
lane on Oakridge Common.

The growing prosperity of Stroud and its neighbourhood required better roads than these ; and in the year 1751, by an Act of 25th Geo. II., powers were granted "for repairing the highway from Cirencester to a house called the Blue Boys,[1] near Minchinhampton,"[2] and from thence over Hampton and Rodborough Commons down the steep north side of the hill, through the village of Rodborough, and on "to the lower part of Stroud." Also : "for repairing the road from Cirencester toward Bisley as far as the bottom of Gulf Hill," on the old highway before mentioned.

The road to the lower part of Stroud was accordingly repaired, and became a turnpike road ; after which, the whole of that through Bisley was disused, as the way from Stroud to Cirencester and London.

From the last clause in the title of the Act, it appears that the woolstaplers of Cirencester were desirous of keeping open their communications with the clothing district of Painswick, by way of the old Bisley-road, on one side ; and with the clothing districts of Stroud, Nailsworth, Woodchester, and Stonehouse, by the new turnpike road over Minchinhampton Common, on the other.

Both these roads lie on the high grounds which bound the Froom valley, from the Gulf down to Stroud,—the old road being on its north, and the turnpike road on its south side. This part of the valley is the most important place in the whole manufacturing district ; being studded with houses, mills, and hamlets, and including Stroud and Chalford with their numerous inhabitants.

Chalford is a large and populous village, about one mile in extent, in a deep narrow part of the valley, which is here called Chalford Bottom ; and is distinguished for its singular form and beauty.

It lies in the parishes of Bisley and Minchinhampton ; but chiefly in the former, owing to its wide level river-strand, and the tendency of the increasing population to extend itself on that side. The principal part of the village is, accordingly, on the hill side of the Bisley portion of the valley ; and, (including the two localities called France

1 This was a small way-side Inn, having for its sign a picture of two Blue Boys standing by a dyeing vat as its supporters. It continued until the year 1866.

2 This town is frequently called by its original name of "Hampton" only, the prefix Minchin (Mynchen, a *nun*, Saxon) being omitted.

Lynch and Chalford Lynch), extending upward, even to the high table-land of the Cotteswold range, of which it is a part. The term Lynch is derived from the Saxon, and signifies a ledge, bank, or projection; and might well have designated the sites on which its first houses were erected The clothing manufacture was brought to this place in early times; and, having been carried on extensively, it created a large and crowded population. The mills are situated on the river Froom; but the dwelling houses are chiefly dispersed in an irregular manner on the hill side; so that, in the approaches to some of them, you "ascend to the lowest story, and descend to the highest." 3

The name Chalford intimates that its first inhabitants settled near a ford on the river; probably on the old high-way from Minchinhampton to Bisley. Mr. Fosbrooke says 4 that "Mr. Archer Blackwell is possessed of a charter dated the last year of Rich. II., which mentions John atte Blackwelle of this place, as of Chalkford:" and I have met with a title deed of 1677, in which it is written Chafford. Even now it is commonly called Cha-ford, the "l" in the first syllable being dropped in its vernacular pronunciation.

Its chief place of religious worship was called Chalford Chapel. It was built by subscription in 1725; and was vested in trustees, to provide a minister to officiate in conformity with the usage of the Church of England; the minister to be supported by subscription. Mrs. Hester Tayloe, (who was called Madam Tayloe in the respectful language of that day, and is still spoken of under the same appellation,) made her will, dated August the 5th, 1778, by which she gave the sum of £853 to trustees, in trust to pay the interest of it "to the minister or clergyman who should perform divine service at the Chapel twice on every Lord's day, viz., prayers according to the Liturgy of the Church of England, and a sermon: that, if the nomination or appointment of a minister to officiate there should at any time thereafter be vested in, or should belong to, the Bishop of the Diocese, or to the Vicar of the parish of Bisley; or in case the said Chapel should be suffered to run into decay, or divine service be discontinued for the space of twelve calendar months, then the said interest should be paid to the minister of the Dissenting Meeting House of France

3 Rudder, p. 289.
4 History, 1. 346.

Lynch. And in case the said Meeting House should run to decay, the said £853, and all interest should be held in trust for her nephew John Roberts and his representatives."

In the year 1841, Chalford Chapel, (the primary object of Mrs. Hester Tayloe's bounty,) was enlarged, and a parsonage house and school room were erected. About the same time, the Chapel was consecrated ; and, a sum of money having been granted as an endowment, it was made a District Church, and placed in the gift of the Archdeacon of Gloucester.5 After this, a belfry, in which six steel bells are hung, was added to it. It is now called Christ Church. The Benefice is worth £150 per annum ; and the Rev. W. de Courcey Ireland, who succeeded the Rev. S. Gompertz, is the present Incumbent.

The "Dissenting Meeting House at France Lynch" (mentioned in Mrs. Tayloe's will) was one of the oldest in the county, belonging to the Nonconformists, and was originally of the Presbyterian denomination; but, like many others, its members afterward adopted the Congregational form of church government.

About the year 1823, being out of repair, it was taken down, and a new building erected at Chalford Lynch, where the congregation now assemble.

There are at Chalford places of worship for the Baptists, Wesleyans, Primitive Methodists, and the (Plymouth) Brethren : and a Chapel of Ease to the Mother Church of Bisley has been built near the old Nonconformists' burial ground at France Lynch.

Sir Robert Atkyns says that Friar Bacon was born at Todgmore (Todesmore or Toadsmoor) Bottom, in the parish of Bisley ; and was educated at St. Mary's Chapel, Chalford. This place now belongs to Mrs. Clutterbuck ; and in it is shewn a room, said to have been Friar Bacon's study. The mill belonging to it is called St. Mary's Mill ; and both are situated on the river Froom, but in the parish of Hampton. Roger Bacon was born in the year 1214, and died in 1284. He was a monk of the Franciscan order, and of such knowledge and learning for the age, that his brother monks called him " doctor mirabilis " or the wonderful doctor ; and his experiments in mathematical, mechanical, and optical science, caused him to be suspected

5 It might be asked—by what legal process was this effected ? and what became of Hester Tayloe's trust legacy ? But Lethe hides in her dark bosom a multitude of rights and wrongs, of which her sluggish waves make no whisper.

OF STROUD, GLOUCESTERSHIRE.

of magic. He anticipated many subsequent inventions,— among which were the materials of gunpowder. His great work, the "Opus Majus," has been published : but many of his writings yet remain in manuscript, which, though in his day they were prodigies of a philosophic mind, and learned labor, would now add but little to the vast discoveries of modern science.

From the base of the abrupt and rocky hill which here forms the Minchinhampton side of the valley, issue numerous small rills of water, called "the hundred springs"; and these, collected within the space of a quarter of a mile into an artificial channel, are of sufficient power to drive the machinery of a small mill; after which they fall into the river Froom. These springs flow from a freestone formation, and are said to have a petrifying quality ; instead of which, they merely cover objects submitted to their action with a coat of calcareous earth. I have seen the water-mill-wheel, over which the brooklet falls, incrusted with a thick, white, stony deposit from the water.

The valley of Chalford increases in beauty as it becomes narrower, in its upward sinuous course above the village, where it is called the Golden Valley. It is, indeed, very beautiful, with its thickets, opening glades, and green dells and dingles ; while, in the autumn, it is all a-glow with the bright golden tints of its beech leaves. Though the wood-man has been there with his axe, and the iron horse with his long white mane and discordant shriek rushes up and down daily, its natural forms and colors are so lovely and various, that it will continue to be "a thing of beauty," and, by pre-eminence, the Golden Valley.

Throughout the whole distance between Stroud and Chalford there are small lateral valleys which break into the main line from both its sides, bringing down their tributary rivulets to the Froom at its bottom. And, as all the old highways ran along the sides of the hills, it will be seen that they were rendered difficult and tedious, as well as longer, by having to pass through those lateral valleys in their way.

Thus—the original road from the lower part of Stroud to Chalford, passed up the town to the end of Lower-street ; and then by The Field, until it approached the sharp western edge of the Valley of Horns ; which caused it to turn down the steep descent to Bowbridge.[6] At this place

6 It is so called from an arched or bowed bridge there, over the river Froom.

it turned sharply up the hill side to Thrupp, at the farther end of which it passed by the north front of New-house; and, after crossing the two roads from Brimscomb up to Quarhouse and the Lypiatts, it descended into and crossed Toadsmore Bottom, at the Bourne: and thence, passing through Blackness, it entered Chalford in the same direction as doth the present footway.

From what has been said, it will appear that this highway was, through its whole length, very inconvenient both to the clothiers who lived near their mills on the stream, and to the general public who travelled it: in fact, it required a whole day for a team of horses to draw a loaded wagon from Stroud to Chalford, and to return; although the distance, (when measured in a straight line along the bottom,) is only four miles to the extreme end of the village. Further, the old road on the opposite (the Rodborough and Minchinhampton) side of the valley, was still steeper, longer, and in all respects more inconvenient, than that just described; and was, indeed, entirely useless as a direct mode of communication between Stroud and Chalford; although its several parts are yet available as roads to and from the various intermediate places.

During this state of things, the turnpike road from Stroud toward Cirencester and London lay along the summit of Rodborough Hill: and, accordingly, the principal common-carriers of wool, cloth and general merchandise, found it convenient to fix their large establishments near the Bear Inn, which lies between the two commons of Hampton and Rodborough.

Those carriers were, in the writer's early days, Niblett, whose stables and warehouses were at the Bear Inn; and Tanner, (afterward Tanner and Baylis,) whose business was carried on at 'The Road.' From these two elevated places there were several ways, more or less steep, down the north side of the hill into the Stroud Valley, and Chalford; and down its south side to Woodchester and Nailsworth; as well as to Stroud, Ebley, and Stonehouse, by the roads which descend its western end.

With respect to the difficulties of these communications up and down the sides of the hill, it will suffice to describe one of them by way of example. That one ran from the old Stroud road at Bowbridge, across the river Froom, up a steep, narrow lane, on the rocky projecting spur of Rodborough Hill, between a cluster of houses called The Court,

and another called The Bannut Trees,[7] to the old highway
leading from Rodborough Butts to Butter-row.[8] Then,
crossing that old highway, it still mounted by the tower-
crowned house called Mount Vernon, until it reached the
summit of the hill, passed over it, and ran down its south
side into the valley of Woodchester.

The ascent of this long lane from Bowbridge to the hill
top was an incline of somewhat more than one in six ; and
it may seem strange that it could ever have been traversed
by horses and carriages. But, notwithstanding this extraordinary steepness, it was much used ; and was indeed the
general (being also the shortest) way from the valley and
the upper end of Stroud, into the Cirencester turnpike road,
to the common-carriers' warehouses, and into the valley on
the other side. I have been on horseback up and down
this road. On one occasion, I met a tilted wagon and
horses belonging to Niblett, the carrier, coming down its
worst part ; and, on another, I was passed at the same place
by a young man riding down at such speed as to put me in
fear for him.

The lane cannot be used any longer by horses and
carriages, but only as a footpath to the houses near it : and
this was brought about by the passing of the Great Western
Railway across its lower end ; and, by making the new
winding turnpike road from Bowbridge up to the Bannut
Trees ; thence round the hollows of the two bay-like-sweeps
in the hill side, and on to the Cirencester turnpike road, a
little before it reaches the Bear Inn. The new winding
road is a good, though somewhat steep, substitute for the
old lane ; and is a great public benefit. It reminds me of
the following circumstance.

On the 3rd of January, 1849, after a fall of sleety rain,
succeeded by an intense frost, the surface of the whole
neighbourhood became one sheet of ice. On this occasion,
the three sons of the writer carried their skates up to the

---

7 *Bannut*, a large nut, and the provincial name for a walnut. This place
obtained its name from the old walnut trees, whose successors are yet standing
there.

8 Both these names—the latter being a slight corruption of Butt-row—
indicate the places where butts were formerly set up against the hill, when the
inhabitants of every parish in England were obliged to practice archery. I
have seen some steel bolts, or arrow heads, which were found in the hill side
near the Butts, on grubbing up the roots of a wood which Mr. Pinfold had
felled there.

Fort on Rodborough Hill, to which they scrambled with difficulty ; and from thence they skated along the hill top into the town of Minchinhampton.   They then skated back to the Bear Inn ; where the writer's youngest son left his brothers, and entering on the new turnpike road at its upper end, skated down, through its various windings, to Bowbridge.

This was, no doubt, a perilous exploit ; for he was obliged to crouch as close to the ground as he could, in order to avoid being precipitated headlong down the hill, by the great velocity of his uncheckable motion, and by the sharpness of the curves.   His position was nearly that of sitting on his heels ; and his action that of sliding on both the skates together, rather than striking out with one after the other : and the descent through the whole distance, from the Bear Inn to Bowbridge, was effected in less than four minutes.

But to return :—For several years the inconvenience of the old Stroud and Chalford road, and the steep ascent of the Cirencester and London turnpike road up Rodborough Hill, had been universally felt ; and a desire as universally prevailed for a remedy.   Accordingly, in 1814, an Act, (the 54th Geo. 3rd, c. 80,) was obtained for making a new road from Stroud, through Bowbridge and Brimscomb, to the Bourne ; and thence through Chalford, to near the seventh milestone on the turnpike road from Cirencester to Stroud. There was opposition to the plan : but the Commissioners named in the Act assembled a large body of laborers, who commenced their operations in the night ; and had levelled all the hedges and other obstructions on a considerable portion of the intended road, before the millowners and landowners arose in the morning ; and before any contracts had been made for the land over which it was to pass.

The entrance of this new road was from Rowcroft, near St. Briavels, over a small strip of Kendrick's Orchard, and private road which led towards the old George Inn, in the High-street.   Its farther course lay through Great and Little Shurmers, and across the way to the old Swan grounds ; then, over Capel's Orchard, by the Brick House, and through the Arundel estate, to Bowbridge ; from whence it proceeded along the valley, through Chalford, and up Cowcomb Hill, until it joined the Cirencester road as directed by the Act.   And thus this invaluable communication, so long desired, was at length effected, and opened to the public in 1815. Thereupon, certain small parts of the old highway up the valley from Bowbridge, ceased to be used, and were thrown into the adjoining lands ; while other parts of it, (particularly that through the Thrupp from end to end,) have been kept open by cuts made from it to the new road.

The following may be mentioned (among others) as instances of the great value of the road to millowners and others on its line. Formerly, the only way for horses and carriages from Rowcroft to the Brick House and Capel's Mill, was up the town to The Castle in Castle-street, and thence down the steep private road on its western side. The distance was 825 yards, whilst that by the level new road is only 605. Besides this, the descent from The Castle to the Brick House and the Mill is on the steep gradient of one in six : nevertheless, carts and wagons passed up and down it ; and the old fashioned vehicles, post-chaises, conveyed the ladies of the Brick House to and from balls and assemblies in the town. Formerly, too, the only carriage road from Rowcroft to Bowbridge was that already described, being a distance of 1760 yards ; whereas by the new and level road it is only 1270 yards. Formerly, the only carriage road from Rowcroft to Stafford's (Mr. Stanton's) Mill was by way of Bowbridge, up to Thrupp, and thence down the original lane to the mill, being a distance of 2718 yards, all up and down hill ; while by the new level road it is only 1765 yards.

Moreover, as all the mills in the valley lie on the level line of the new turnpike road, and experienced similar advantages, another of its consequences followed, in the immediately increased value of all the property in its neighbourhood.

Besides this, and its great advantage to the public in general, as an easy means of communication with the localities to which it leads, the road resulted in the making of the fourth and most important enlargement of our town, which stands on Kendrick's Orchard, the Shurmers, and other places on both sides of the road itself. And to the description of this we now proceed.

CHAPTER XXXI.

THE FOURTH ENLARGEMENT OF THE TOWN — THE STROUD IMPROVEMENT ACT, &c. — THE UPLANDS.

THE new turnpike road, before mentioned, was known by the several names of Chalford-road and London-road, from the direction it took toward both those places. On its east side lay the remaining (the chief) part of Kendrick's Orchard with some gardens, containing about four acres; and on its west side was Great Shurmers, pasture, the property of Edward Humpage.

Whilst the making of this road was in progress, Charles Hodges built a dwelling-house on a plot of ground in Great Shurmers, bought at the rate of five shillings per square yard, which he called Wellington Place: it was the first house of this new part of the town. He subsequently built another, adjoining it, and two more behind them.

The public attention being thus very generally drawn to the new road, and to the eligible building ground through which it passed, numerous other plots of land were soon purchased, and houses were erected in various places.

Besides the turnpike road, another road was marked out through the orchard, in a diagonal line from the George Hotel, until it passed into the former road near the point where the "branch-way" left it: and between those roads was inclosed a triangular portion of the orchard, having the highway from King-street to St. Briavels as its base line and north-westward frontage.

Building operations were then actively prosecuted on both the lines indicated, and on other places in all directions; until the whole area was built upon which now forms the fourth enlargement of the town, and of which the following is a descriptive detail.

UNION STREET.—Extending from High-street, through the old George Inn and the stable-yard of the Swan Inn, down to the London-road. Its opening was effected by Mr. Thomas Wall, after he removed his establishment from High-street to the Royal George Hotel in King-street. [1]

JOHN STREET.—Which stands on the site of "the private road" before mentioned. It branches eastward from the London-road into the west side of Union-street, which it thus connects with George-street and Russell-street; and at its south-east angle is the Register Office, and the Board-room of the Guardians of the Stroud Poor Law Union.

GEORGE STREET.—Being on the diagonal line before mentioned across the orchard, and deriving its name from the George Hotel.

BEDFORD STREET.—Extending from High-street into George-street, over the former private passage-way to Keene's workshops.

THREADNEEDLE STREET.[2]—Leading out of Union-street into Bedford-street. The making of it enabled the owners of some of the houses in High-street to enlarge their small gardens, by pieces of the strip of land cut off from Kendrick's Orchard through which it was made.

RUSSELL STREET.—Which stands on the line of the new turnpike road, from its beginning to a little beyond its junction with the upper end of George-street. The place called St. Briavels is now the south-west corner of this street; and, at a short distance above, is the entrance to the Station of the Great Western Railway, and to the Imperial Hotel. Higher up, and branching from it on the same side, is

BATH TERRACE.—The original lane leading into

BATH PLACE.—Which is a collection of houses and gardens, commenced on Great Shurmers, soon after Hodges began building. When completed, it consisted of thirty-seven houses, exclusive of those which compose the Terrace. But, in the year 1845, the Great Western Railway was carried through it, causing seven of the houses to be taken down, and separating the rest of them from the Terrace. When this was effected, the way—the only way—to and from the remainder of Bath Place, was through the lane

---

1 For which see page 35.

2 For the origin of this street and its name see page 37.

and across the railway on the rails.   This was found to be exceedingly dangerous for the inhabitants and the public, as well as inconvenient for the railway traffic : and, there-upon, in 1846, the Railway Company made an agreement with the owners of the remaining thirty houses to provide for them another road, and to give them a pecuniary com-pensation, for relinquishing their right to use the way across the rails.   The compensation was £558, paid by the Com-pany rateably among the house-owners, being one-fourth part of the whole estimated value of their property ; and a new road was made for them on the south side of the station, commencing below the railway bridge at the bottom of Rowcroft.   Thus Bath Place is now cut off from all communication with Russell-street and the town, except by that circuitous route.

A small portion of the line at this end of Russell-street was at first called Wellington Place, from the name of Hodges's first house ; but now the whole line from its union with Russell-street to the end is called London-road ; which has its several parts, on both its sides, called by their own separate proper names.   Thus, crossing over and com-mencing on its east side, we pass Froom Cottage and the entrance to Union-street, and then we come to

FROOM BUILDINGS.—Consisting of four dwelling-houses, which fill up the space between the last named street and the narrow Swan-lane, before mentioned as passing down from High-street to the Swan grounds and Capel's Orchard.[3]

Beyond this lane, and for about half-way up its east side, is the garden of Mr. Foster, nurseryman and florist, having also another frontage to the London-road.   Part of this garden lies in the Swan grounds ; and the whole of it was excavated by Richard Combs, a builder, for its fine brick-earth, out of which he made bricks, and supplied the large demand for such materials when the building speculations were in progress.   When the brick-earth was exhausted, its site was purchased by Mr. Foster, and converted into this pleasant garden.

After passing this place, we enter on what was formerly Capel's Orchard, where stands

VICTORY TERRACE.—Which consists of a continuous row of houses.   The last of them is a public-house, having for

3 See page 33.

its sign a curious stone sundial, inscribed with the two solemn mottoes—*Tempus fugit* and *Memento mori*. Perhaps it may be well for the house that they are in a learned language ; for they preach a sermon which, if it were understood, might disturb the enjoyment of many persons who go in and out beneath them.

The following is the writer's inscription for an ale-house, suggested by, and imitated from, those mottoes :—

Tempus fugit,—

> Drink while the foam is on the cup :
> Quickly drink it,—drink it up.

Memento mori,—

> But, when the jovial hour is o'er,
> Remember—you must pay the score.

Beyond this public-house is the detached residence of the pastor of the Baptist congregation, with the burial ground belonging to their chapel ; and, at present, this is the last house on the east side of London-road.

Returning now to the west side of London-road, from Russell-street, we begin with Thanet house ; which is followed by

UNION BUILDINGS.—Having at their south-east end a row of houses which range back, at nearly a right angle therewith, and face to the east, with small gardens before them. This property is called

WESTERN BUILDINGS.—Which belong to Henry Thornton ; and, together with the last house in Union Buildings, stands on the westward side of what was formerly, called Little Shurmers. A strip of garden ground, situated eastward of Mr. Thornton's property, forms the residue of the old Swan grounds. It is bounded by the remainder of the narrow lane before mentioned, which, having crossed London-road, runs down to Beard's Wharf, on the upper bank of the Thames and Severn Canal, passing to it under the Railway. Beyond this lane are

ALBERT BUILDINGS.—Another row of houses; and further on is another row, belonging to Mr. William Bishop, who named it

HAVELOCK TERRACE—In memory of the brave christian soldier, Major-General Sir Henry Havelock, K.C.B., who distinguished himself so highly in relieving the siege of Lucknow, the capital of Oude, in the year 1857.[4]

Further, the whole north-westward front of Kendrick's Orchard having been covered with good shops and houses, these, with the opposite side of the road, (already mentioned as part of the original Rowcroft,) became a continuation of King-street, and took its name. This extended street, by its junction with Rowcroft—now especially so called, forms an important part of the town. This, with

LANSDOWN and GLOUCESTER STREET—Both before mentioned, completes the summary of its fourth enlargement.

To the foregoing sketch of the old town, and its several additions, must be subjoined the following notices. In the year 1825 an Act of Parliament, (6th Geo. IV., c. 6), commonly called the Stroud Improvement Act, was obtained "for paving, lighting, watching, regulating, and improving the town": and, under its authority, the streets were paved, and other improvements made in it. In 1833 a "Gas-light and Coke Company" was formed, by which works were erected in a meadow below Lodgemore; and the consent of the proprietors of the Stroudwater Navigation Company having been obtained for laying down main pipes for gas beneath their towing path, the town and the mills, &c., in the neighbourhood, were lighted with gas. The Company now also supplies with gas the valley of Slad, Stroud valley up to Brimscomb, Woodchester, Nailsworth, Minchinhampton and Cainscross; and, in 1864, an Act of Parliament was procured called "the Stroud Gas Act," by which the Gas Company was recognised, and placed under the provisions of the several other Acts incorporated with it. In 1856 a Local Board of Health for the town was established, (limited in its area by the old Improvement Act); and, under the powers, &c., of the several Public Health and Local Government Acts, extensive sanitary arrangements were carried out, and the Water Company's sources of water supply were purchased for the use of the town.

But, while I have been writing of Stroud, as confined within its own parish boundary, it has been making a bold effort toward an enlargement beyond its legal limits. For,

4 General Havelock died from the effect of fatigue and exhaustion, at Dalcoosha Palace, near Lucknow, December 24th, 1857; and was buried the next day at Alum Bagh, four miles from that city.

since 1863, a large number of dwelling-houses, resembling a small town in extent, have been erected in such proximity to it, as to seem, (and in general effect to be,) a suburb, if not an integral part of it. These houses already extend from below the Merry Walks, through Badbrook, for the distance of a mile up the north side of the pleasant Slad valley, in the Stroud-end tithing of the parish of Painswick. They have all the advantages of contiguity to a large town, without being subjected to the burdensome parliamentary and other regulations and imposts of the Stroud Improvement Act, and its Board of Health ; and they have already acquired the name of The Uplands.

Since we mentioned the *quasi* suburb of Stroud, (which had extended through Badbrook, up the north side of the Slad valley, and had acquired the name of "The Uplands,") —it has become a large and populous place, where sanitary and other arrangements are in preparation, for its general convenience and accommodation, and where many of them have been long since, more or less, carried out ; the question of a good water supply alone as yet excepted.

CHAPTER XXXII.

WHEN the borough of Stroud had been constituted
by the passing of the Reform Act in 1832, it was
generally felt that a large and commodious building was
wanted in the town, for public purposes.

Accordingly, a meeting was held on August the 28th in
the same year, at which it was resolved to raise a sum of
money, in shares of £50 each, to supply the deficiency :
and sixty-one shares having been subscribed by fifty-seven
persons, five of those persons were appointed trustees, and
five a building committee.

Until that time a piece of ground near the upper end of
George-street had remained unappropriated. It contained
about 2,000 square yards in extent, and was part of a close
of land "theretofore called Burrough's Leaze and the
Orchard," already mentioned by the more familiar name of
Kendrick's Orchard. It was then called George's Square ;
and was bounded on the east by the yard, garden and
house of Mr. Paul Read ; on the west "by a lane," now
called Bedford-street; on the north "by a lane," since named
Threadneedle-street ; and on the south by George-street,
then called Great George-street. This piece of ground was
purchased by the building committee for the sum of £420,
and was conveyed to trustees, on the part of the shareholders, by a deed of November the 6th, 1832. In this
deed it was declared that the intended building should " be
used as a place or places for public meetings or assemblies,
for all lawful purposes, civil and religious, (except as a
chapel or place of worship,) and as a library and reading
rooms : and for other literary, philosophical and scientific
objects and purposes, as the committee of management, for
the time being, should think fit ; and in consideration of
such payments, by way of rent, hire, &c., as to them should

seem reasonable and proper." The deed contained directions for appointing a treasurer and a managing committee,
to be elected annually; with sundry other clauses and
regulations "for the due and orderly management and
well-being of the concern." Amongst these last, is a clause
for letting all or any part of the building for a term of
years, for selling any part of the land not wanted, with the
consent in writing of the majority of the shareholders; and
for discontinuing the undertaking and disposing of all the
premises, by the direction in writing of three-fourths of the
shareholders. In this deed the rights of the proprietors
were, by the creation of a term of 2,000 years, limited to a
chattel interest in their respective shares, for the greater
convenience of holding and transferring them; and the
reversion in fee was vested in Richard Wyatt, Esq., upon
such trusts as the proprietors should appoint.

Plans for the intended structure were furnished gratuitously by Mr. Bassevi, an eminent London architect:
and the entire building was satisfactorily erected by Charles
Harrison for the sum of £2,500.

In order to facilitate the work when near its completion,
a series of scaffolds, on the plan of a long inclined plane,
were erected for the conveying of stones, mortar, and other
materials up the building. It commenced in Threadneedle-
street, which has its entrance from near the yard of the
Swan Inn. This Inn was much frequented by farmers and
other persons from the country, on market days: and it
happened that one Friday evening farmer William Radcliff,
of Woodchester, mounted his horse in the Inn yard to
return home; but being somewhat under the influence of
liquor, he, (instead of turning in the right direction,) rode
into the lane and to the bottom of the inclined plane, up
which the horse walked, and carried his master to the top
of the building.

His perilous position was seen from below; and, indeed,
he himself became aware of it, and dismounted. It was
thought by those who hastened to his assistance, that even
the horse, if skilfully handled, might have been brought
down unhurt, as well as his master; but Radcliff persisted
in backing the horse, which, under his management, fell
from the scaffold and was killed. He himself came down
in safety, and withal a little sobered. [1]

[1] In allusion to this event, the inclined scaffolding was jocularly called
Radcliff Highway.

The building is a rectangular structure, standing on the north side of the square, and facing George-street ; from which it is distant about twenty yards. It is seventy-five feet long by fifty-seven feet wide ; having a handsome south front, beneath the pediment of which is sculptured in high relief—STROUD SUBSCRIPTION ROOMS.

It contains, on the ground floor, an entrance hall, twenty-eight feet long by seven wide ; and on each side of it a room twenty-eight feet six inches long by twenty-two feet eight inches wide,—all fourteen feet five inches high. It has also a well-lighted inner hall, twenty-five feet long ; and, at each end of it, two other rooms, some of which are occupied by the person who takes care of the place. In the centre of the inner hall is a flight of twelve stone steps, eleven feet wide, between stone balustrades ; and from its landing place proceed two other flights, (each of nineteen steps,) leading up to the east and west entrances of the room above referred to.

The large upper room is seventy feet long, forty-three feet wide, and twenty-three feet high ; and has, at its west end, a raised platform, twenty-six feet long by fourteen feet six inches wide, for the use of speakers at public meetings, and for orchestras at balls and concerts. It has an open gallery, nine feet wide, along the whole of its north side, beneath which are the stairs leading up to the room itself. It is furnished with raised seats, and affords much additional accommodation for spectators and auditors. This room has four large windows in its front wall, and the gallery has two windows in the north wall ; and both together form the entire first floor or upper story. The foundation stone of the edifice was laid on March the 9th, 1833, and it was opened early in the following year ; but it was not properly fitted up until 1837, when thirty-six shareholders advanced five pounds each, without interest, which enabled the managing committee to complete it ; and those advances were repaid by instalments. The building has an imposing appearance, and is a great ornament, as well as a great convenience, to the town.

In 1835 Lieutenant-General Sir Samuel Hawker, one of the Woodchester family of that name, presented to the Rooms a large Landscape painted by himself, representing a scene in Portugal, taken when he was serving there with his regiment in the Peninsular war. And, in December, 1840, a fine, life-size, sitting portrait of the late respected

Joseph Watts, painted by H. P. Briggs, R.A., at the
expense of some of his friends, was also presented, and
suspended over the fire-place at the east end of the large
room. A three-quarter length of the figure was engraved
by E. R. Whitfield for the subscribers to the original portrait.

On April the 1st, 1850, the late Henry George Francis
Moreton, Earl Ducie,—so well known and highly esteemed
in the borough as the Honourable Henry Moreton,—when
he sold Spring Park, and removed from it to his seat at
Tortworth,—presented a magnificent painting, eight feet
one inch long by seven feet five-and-a-half inches high,
and of great value, by Snyders,—representing a wolf
attacked by dogs, whilst standing over a dead roe-deer. Lord
Ducie placed this picture in the hands of seven gentlemen, [2]
upon a written trust to put it up for exhibition in the large
room of the building, so long as it should be open for public
meetings. But if the room should cease to be so used,
then to remove it to some other public place, if any such
should exist in the town ; and in case there should not be
any such place, then to sell it, and apply the proceeds to
the promotion of any object of public or general interest in
the town. He directed the number of trustees to be filled
up, on their being reduced by death to or below three.
These three pictures now adorn the room, on the lower
wall of which they are hung.

After the termination of the Crimean war, Lieutenant-
Colonel Edmund Gilling Hallewell, Assistant Quarter-
master-General of the Army of the East, presented to the
Rooms, in 1855, a twelve pound carronade [3] from Sebastopol; which, properly mounted, and with its appurtenances,
stands on the mantel-shelf of the fire-place, in the same
room, under the portrait of his maternal grandfather, Mr.
Watts. [4]

About the same time Lord Panmure, the Secretary at
War, presented the town with two cannons, other part of
the spoils of Sebastopol; which stand near to George-street,
in front of the building. They were mounted, placed on a

2 Their names are Henry Adams Hyett, (since deceased,) Joseph Watts
Hallewell, Charles Hawkins Fisher, William Stanton, Samuel Stephens
Marling, Rayner Winterbotham, and Arthur John Biddell.

3 A piece of ordnance, so called from having been invented and first made
at the Carron Iron Works, in Scotland.

4 He was the eldest son of Mr. Watts' daughter and only child.

stone-planked platform, and enclosed with iron palisades, at the expense of George Poulett Scrope, Esq., and the Right Honourable Edward Horsman, the representatives of the borough in Parliament.

Our prudent and intelligent neighbours at Nailsworth did not mount the cannon which was presented to them. Perhaps they disdained to erect a trophy which might insult any Russian traveller coming that way, by reminding him of his country's defeat ; or they may have feared to remind themselves of the blood and treasure which the victory cost us ; or they may have put the cannon out of sight, to intimate the great blessing it would be to mankind if all the warlike instruments in the world lay as peaceful and quiet as theirs.

It was not expected that the Subscription Rooms would be a remunerative speculation ; neither has it been such : but, at the annual general meeting of the shareholders in 1851, a dividend of ten shillings per share was directed to be paid.   This, however, was the first and the last pecuniary return yet made to them ; all the rest of their income from it having been expended on taxes, repairs, buildings, furniture, and other requisite outgoings.

In the year 1857 the committee opened the room on the left side of the entrance hall as a public reading room, to which the shareholders have free access ; all other persons being admitted at an annual subscription of £1 1s. each. This room is comfortably fitted up, and is supplied with various daily and other newspapers, periodicals, &c., &c. ; and strangers coming to the town may be admitted to it for the day, by a proprietor or subscriber.

This arrangement gave great satisfaction to the shareholders and the public : so that the original shares thereby acquired a marketable value, and have been freely purchased, with a view to the advantage of this new privilege to a proprietor : and it is so well received by the public, that the payments of subscribers are sufficient to defray the current expenses of the room.   Besides this, there has been erected, at the back of the gallery, a billiard room, twenty-five by twenty-two feet, well lighted and suitably furnished with a billiard table, &c. 5   It is approached from the landing place of the stairs in the inner hall ; and is a great additional attraction.

5 The chief cost of the billiard table was raised by a subscription among the amateurs of the game.

Further, at a meeting of the proprietors held May the 7th, 1868, it was resolved that the committee should make various improvements in the building, including the erection of an additional billiard room, and a large portico, with a balcony over it, accessible from the large upper room ; and this was accordingly done. [6]

So many and various were the occasions on which the rooms have been open to the public,—that, if all that has been done there could be detailed, it would go far to illustrate the social and public habits, tastes, business, amusements and character of the last forty years of this wonderful nineteenth century.   For here balls have called forth the evolutions of the dancer, and concerts delighted the lovers of music ; the juggler, with his sleight of hand, has cheated the senses of the beholder ; and the mesmeriser, the mimic, the "poor player," the auctioneer, and even the Ethiopian serenaders with their banjos, and Dr. Mark's "Little Men" with their kits and small trumpets, have played their parts. Lectures on all kinds of subjects,—social and political, literary, scientific, and philosophical,—have been delivered here.   Charity bazaars and fancy-fairs, tea-meetings, and anniversaries of religious and other societies, political and social dinners, with all sorts of gatherings and assemblies, have been held here ;—together with the numerous other entertainments and exhibitions which, (in their circulation about the country,) have kindly and considerately stopped by the way, to give the good people of Stroud the benefit of their wonderful sayings, doings, and amusing performances.   But these I must leave for the antiquary of some future generation to dig up from the buried materials of the present.

There have been, however, a few public meetings and exhibitions in the rooms, which deserve some special notice, —amongst which are the following.   On April the 3rd and 4th, 1834, before the interior of the large room (then called the assembly room) was completed, a charity bazaar or fancy-fair was held there, for the purpose of raising funds toward the building of a National school for girls.   The Honourable Mrs. Moreton and Mrs. Scrope presided at two of the stalls ; and the hearty assistance and cheerful alacrity

[6 Many other alterations have also been made since the 1st edition of this work was issued, and "The Rooms" have long been the head quarters of the "Stroud Club."]

of Mr. Moreton contributed much to its success ; especially on the last day, when he helped to sell the lots which remained on hand, and the numerous green-house plants presented from his collection at Spring Park. This was the first public meeting at the rooms.   The produce of the fair was £440 : and with that sum ground was purchased, and the building which stands on the west side of the "road behind the church" was erected, under the superintendence of the Rev. W. F. Powell, the incumbent.   It was long occupied as the girls' school-room ; but it became the boys' school, on the removal of the girls to the new building in Castle-street.

On the 19th of May, 1835, Lord John Russell was elected to represent the borough in Parliament, in the room of Colonel Fox, who had resigned his seat, as already mentioned :7 and on that occasion a congratulatory dinner was given to him by the electors.   The dinner was held on the same day; the entire area of the large room being occupied by tables at which were seated 400 persons, and the gallery was filled with ladies who graced the gathering with their presence.   The chairman, Donald Maclean, Esq., of King Stanley, was supported by Lord Ducie, Lord Segrave, the Honourable Henry Moreton, and other influential persons.

In April, 1840, there was a public exhibition during the whole of the Easter week, for the benefit of the Stroud Mechanics' Institute.   It consisted of so many hundred interesting articles, and cases or collections of articles, as well nigh to justify the title page of the printed catalogue, —"Splendid Exhibition of Works of Art and Manufactory, objects of Natural History, Antiquities and Curiosities from every quarter of the globe."   It was made up of rare and valuable specimens, liberally contributed by persons of the neighbourhood, and was very well attended.

Another exhibition, for the benefit of the same Institute was opened there June the 21st, 1841, and was continued for ten days ; closing, July the 2nd, with a horticultural show.   The printed catalogue contained an enumeration of 645 articles, and lots of articles, forming (as was stated in the title page) "A special exhibition of interesting and useful objects, illustrative of the fine arts, experimental philosophy, practical science, archæology, geology, natural history, British and Foreign manufactures, &c."   On this

7 See page 78.

occasion daily lectures were delivered on various popular
subjects :—those on natural history by the Rev. Henry
Griffiths, the gifted minister of the Old Chapel ; and those
on chemistry by Messrs. Haycraft and Randall, and W. H.
Paine ; the last of whom was then a student, but afterward
the respected resident M.D. and physician to the Stroud
General Hospital. [8] Besides these,—the steam engine, the
hydraulic press, and the oxy-hydrogen microscope were
explained, with illustrative examples of their application
and power ; the "fire cloud," and experiments in electricity
were exhibited ; the copper-plate printer, the lace maker,
the wood turner, and other industrial operators plied their
work ; the "invisible girl" conversed with the visitors,
occasionally, morning and evening; and music of the piano-
forte, harp, and organ were additional attractions. It closed
with the floral show. Messrs. William Ferrabee, Edwin
Gyde, John Isackë, and others contributed their valuable
services. The exhibition gave great public satisfaction ;
nevertheless, it was unsuccessful in respect of its pecuniary
object, the expense of getting up and conducting it having
exceeded the receipts : and the consequences were that, for
lack of adequate support and encouragement, the *materiel*,
furniture, curiosities, and philosophical instruments of the
society were sold, and the Mechanics' Institute was broken up.

On May the 14th, 1856, Lord John Russell delivered a
lecture on The Study of History, for the benefit of the
Stroud Mutual Improvement Society. Its announcement
had raised high expectations, and it was attended by a
great number of persons,—the *elite* of the neighbourhood
in station, wealth and intelligence. The lecture was worthy
of such an auditory; and they paid the highest compliment
in their power to the distinguished and gifted lecturer, and
to his excellent address. Reporters of the London papers
attended to take notes of it, which were published in the
London and other newspapers.

On the 29th of the same month a public dinner was held,
to celebrate the termination of the Russian war. On this
occasion the rejoicings were heightened by grateful expectations of the inestimable blessings of peace, in addition to
the joyful feelings of victory achieved in that great contest.

[8 Dr Paine died at his residence Corbett House, Stroud, on June 13th,
1890, to the great grief of all who knew him, and the universal regret of the
neighbourhood, as was abundantly shewn by the large attendance at his funeral
at the Stroud Cemetery on the 19th June.]

And, on September the 17th, 1856, a dinner was given
to the gallant Lieutenant-Colonel Hallewell, on his return
from the Crimea; when the most hearty reception was
given to him that his friends could have desired.

Soon after the erection of the Roman Catholic church
and monastery at Woodchester, the efforts of the Romanists
to propagate their faith and worship in the neighbourhood
naturally excited opposition on the part of the Protestant
community; which shewed itself by a public lecture at
Stroud, and by various communications inserted in the
Stroud Journal. This led Mr. Matthew Bridges, of Chester
Hill House, Woodchester—who had been brought up in
the Church of England, but had gone over to the Church
of Rome—to publish in that journal a challenge, to the
effect that he was ready to maintain in a public disputation
"What the Catholic Church really is—what she believes—
what she teaches—what she practises—and why she does
this, that, or the other"; and suggesting that "suitable
means should be adopted for securing a perfectly equal
attention to each speaker, with order and quietness throughout the investigation." He further indicated certain
"branches of the subject which might be successively
discussed." This challenge was accepted, and a committee
of twelve gentlemen was appointed to make arrangements
for the discussion. After the necessary communications
with Mr. Bridges, three of the subjects which he had named
were fixed on; and ten rules were settled by which the
disputation should be regulated. The subjects were—
"The Rule of Faith for those who believe in the Christian
Religion,"—"The Canon of Scripture,"—"Transubstantiation and the Sacrifice of the Mass." The first three rules
were—"Each opening speech not to be more than one
hour. Each second and third speech not to exceed half an
hour. Each opening address to be considered as a full
statement of the subject under discussion, and the succeeding speeches to be replies."

The discussion was held in the large room on the 21st,
22nd, and 23rd days of October, 1856, between the Rev.
Joseph Baylee, D.D., Principal of St. Aidan's College,
Birkenhead, on the part of the Protestants,—and Mr. Bridges,
on the part of the Roman Catholics. Mr. Edwards, one of
the committee, occupied the chair on each occasion. On
the first day he gave a short statement of how the discussion
originated, and then read the rules; on each succeeding

day he announced the subject to be discussed, and repeated the rules ; and the subjects were taken in the order above mentioned.

These proceedings created great public interest ; and the room was filled each day with attentive and well-conducted hearers. Mr. Bridges opened the discussion, as had been previously arranged, having with him a copy of the Douay Bible ; and Dr. Baylee had a small copy of the authorised English version, and a copy of Father Paul's (Sarpi's) History of the Council of Trent.

On the third day, when the subject of Transubstantiation and the Sacrifice of the Mass was opened by Mr. Bridges, he laid on the table four propositions respecting that subject, and then proceeded with his opening speech. Dr. Baylee, in the progress of his address in reply, said " I asserted that the Church of Rome denied the reality of the humanity of our Lord Jesus Christ, because she declares that a little host which we can hold in our hands is His body, His blood, His soul, and His divinity ; but let me ask any Roman Catholic who is now present, if he were in a storm at sea, and if he had a consecrated host in his ciborium, would he kneel down before that host and say 'Deliver me, for Thou art my God'?9 [A voice—'I would.'] Then you and your God would go together into the deep,—and there is the deliverance of Rome." The voice came from a group of persons behind Dr. Baylee, in the rear of the platform : and those who were near and saw him from whom it proceeded, perceived, by the appearance of his face, that he had not yet learned to wear the true expressionless visor, any more than to preserve the discreet silence, of his Order.

The whole discussion was conducted with learning, ability, and courtesy, on the part of the disputants ; and generally with exemplary good behaviour on the part of the auditors : nor was it inferior in importance to any of the disputations of a similar kind which had been held in other places. The details of this discussion appeared in a verbatim report, which was verified by the disputants, and immediately after printed and published by F. W. Harmer.

9 Isaiah xliv., 17.

CHAPTER XXXIII.

THE STROUD INSTITUTION — OTHER LITERARY AND SCIENTIFIC
SOCIETIES.

ONE of the uses originally intended for the Subscription
Rooms was that of a library and reading room, and
a meeting of the shareholders was held, August the 7th,
1834, on that subject. This led to the formation of an
independent company of thirty subscribers of twenty pounds
each, for the establishment of a library and reading room,
under the name of the Stroud Institution; which general
designation was adopted in order to provide for a possible
future extension of the plan.

The company appointed a committee to carry out their
object; of whom W. H. Hyett, Esq., was named the president, P. H. Fisher the honorary secretary, and Robert
Hughes the treasurer. The committee hired of the proprietors of the Subscription Rooms, their room on the left
side of the entrance hall, with some other rooms for the
accommodation of a resident librarian. The rent was £30
per annum; besides which, the librarian was to take charge
of the other parts of the building for the proprietors. The
committee then purchased, and solicited the gift of, books,
provided book-cases, and suitably furnished the room.
They compiled laws and regulations, both as to the rights
of members themselves, and the terms of admission to the
public; and, on the 1st of July, 1835, it was opened with a
large and well-arranged library, supplied with newspapers
and periodicals. In addition to these, new publications and
the lighter literature of the day were regularly procured
from a London circulating library, and periodically exchanged for others.

Mr. Hyett took an active interest in the Institution, and
gave to it the fine busts of Bacon, Shakspeare, Milton,
Newton, and Locke, which stand on the largest of the book-
cases. The sum of £400 was expended in the purchase of
books; and about 500 volumes were presented by persons

in the neighbourhood, of whom the largest donors were Henry Burgh, W. H. Hyett, and David Ricardo, Esqrs. About thirty others contributed the rest ; except the sixty-seven volumes of the publications of the Record Commissioners, which were received from their secretary, C. P. Cooper, Esq.

An alphabetical catalogue was compiled and published by the honorary secretary, in which the presentation of each book was assigned to the donor by name ; and they were by him numerically labelled, and arranged in their cases.

The printed catalogue comprised about 2,000 volumes of standard works, chiefly in English, in the various departments of literature and science ; to which there were several subsequent additions : and even after the library was closed, the secretary and treasurer accepted and lodged with the other books, a set of the voluminous Journals of each House of Parliament, with statutes, and a miscellaneous collection of Parliamentary books and papers, presented by the late Henry George, Earl Ducie.

By the laws of the Institution, each shareholder was to subscribe 15s. per annum, which would entitle him to the use of the reading room, and the privilege of taking any books from the library for the purpose of perusing them ; which compulsory payment was designed to increase the means of maintaining the establishment.

The library and reading room were open every day, (except Sunday, Christmas Day, and Good Friday,) from nine o'clock, a.m., till ten o'clock, p.m. The terms of admission to the public were moderate : and, among the laws there were well and carefully digested rules and regulations as to taking out and returning the books, the duties of the librarian, and the due regulation and conduct of the whole.

The promoters had hoped they were forming an Institution which would be an honour to the town, and an instructive and entertaining resource to them, and to the inhabitants present and future. But, after some time, they discovered that it did not receive the support anticipated, and the annual expenses so far exceeded its income, that by July, 1837, there was a loss of £64 ; and, by July, 1838, a further loss of £46 out of their remaining capital, besides interest on the original outlay. Under these circumstances, the committee adopted various expedients to secure its continuance. They applied to the managing committee of the Rooms to reduce the rent, which was liberally conceded ; they lessened the librarian's salary, raised the annual payments of the original subscribers, lowered the terms of admission to the public, and made their last call on the original subscriptions.

By these means, the library and reading room was kept open until 1844, when its finances were still falling into arrear ; and four of the shares had been forfeited by default in paying the calls made, and three by voluntary resignation. It then became evident that the Institution could not be kept open any longer by the then proprietary ; and, at a special meeting of its members, on June the 3rd, 1844, it was resolved that the room should be closed on the 1st of July, then next. But, being desirous that the valuable library should be kept entire, and converted into a public permanent library, if possible, they appointed four of their number (including the honorary secretary and treasurer) " to offer the books, &c., to the shareholders of the Subscription Rooms ; or, in case of their refusal, to any private individuals who might wish to purchase them with a view to establish, (and who should establish) a permanent public library in the town, at a sum of £150." These offers were made without producing the desired result : and then it may be said that the Stroud Institution was virtually at an end.

Mr. Brisley and Mr. Bucknall, booksellers, joined to keep open the reading room to subscribers, with newspapers, magazines, &c., which they supplied for nearly two years more, when that arrangement also ceased.

In the year 1857, however, the proprietors of the Subscription Rooms opened the room, in the manner, and with the expected success, already mentioned. From that time, the library of books, filling the east and north sides of the room, remained in their cases, with Bacon, Shakspeare, Milton, Newton, and Locke, guarding, as it were, the treasures of knowledge to which they all had contributed, and over which they stood like sentinels ; whilst they seemed continually to say—" When will some liberal spirits arise, and open this field to the intellectual delvers and diggers in these more than golden mines ? " Hitherto (A.D. 1869) there has not been any response to their appeal ; but, in the yet deferred hope of it, the dispersion of this valuable collection of books has been prevented. There is a cash balance of £33 4s. 7d. remaining in the Stroud branch of the County of Gloucester Bank, to the credit of the Institution, awaiting other contingencies in respect of them. The president and the honorary secretary, with two or three other original members, are all who now remain to represent the Society ; and, of these, four are also share-holders in the Subscription Rooms.[1]

The first attempt to multiply the means of reading in the neighbourhood was by the establishment of a Book Society at Stroud, about the year 1790, conducted jointly by the Rev. William Ellis, the curate, and the Rev. William Harries, the pastor of the Old Meeting. It continued, under successive secretaries, (of whom the writer was one for nearly thirty years,) until about the year 1855 ; and was the parent of many flourishing societies of a similar kind.

Prior to the Stroud Institution, there had been a library and reading room at the house of Mr. Bucknall, but it was discontinued in favour of the new Institution, to which several of its members became subscribers.

At the same time, there was a society for literary and scientific information, called the Mechanics' Institute, in aid of which the two exhibitions before mentioned were held in the large Subscription Rooms. During its existence many interesting public lectures were delivered for its benefit in one of the smaller Subscription Rooms, several of which were given by the Revs. John Burder, Henry Griffiths, and Benjamin Parsons.

After its cessation in 1841, the Mechanics' Reading Society was formed, having a library and reading room in Russell-street. But, in 1842, a dissension arose among its members on a proposal to introduce Paine's Rights of Man, which ended in a separation ; when the seceders formed the Stroud Young Man's Improvement Society, which prohibited the subjects of religion and politics ; whilst the remaining members enlarged their rules, so as to include discussion as well as reading. Both of them existed about a year after their dis-union, and then expired.

[1 The old author did not live to see his wish fulfilled for the establishment of a Free Public Library for Stroud ; but in 1887 (the year of the Queen's Jubilee) a movement was commenced, terminating in the opening of the present handsome and well appointed building in Lansdowne. An excellent account of this and many other additions and alterations in the town and neighbourhood in modern times, may be found in Mr Libby's " Twenty Years' History of Stroud—1870 to 1890."

On August the 27th, 1845, was commenced the Young Man's Mental Improvement Society, which sought its object by "mutual discussions, essays, occasional lectures, the use of a library, and the association of religious thought with their intellectual exercises."

In 1847 was instituted the Stroud Athenæum, which announced its objects somewhat ambitiously, together with the numerous means by which it proposed to effect them. Their original apartments were under the *quondam* Victoria Room near the George Hotel, and afterward in the room itself. Their first president was G. P. Scrope, Esq., M.P., who delivered an inaugural address to the members and the public, in the Victoria Room, on July the 22nd, in the same year. In that address he ably and eloquently advocated the formation of the society, as a means of extending literature, taste, and science among the young;—as his own large attainments, and his love of knowledge, so well enabled him to do. He also gave the society 150 volumes of books, toward the formation of a library. In 1848 it established a cricket class, which was the parent of several cricket clubs ; and also a choral class, which was conducted through "Hullah's course of lessons on vocal harmony : " and on August the 3rd and November the 28th in that year, choral meetings were given in the Subscription Rooms, at which the Gloucester Choral Society attended. It also attempted "to furnish its reading room with a collection illustrative of the natural history of the neighbourhood," and, for that purpose, a few weekly pedestrian excursions were taken by the members. After this, it commenced a collection of stuffed birds ; and they began to dream of "a museum of natural history." Public lectures were also periodically delivered, and in 1850 they founded "a class for the study of the French language." But, in 1852, the number of subscribers was so reduced, that their reading room was closed ; and in 1853 the society followed the fate of its predecessors, and altogether expired. Its decline and dissolution was attributed, chiefly, to a continual controversy among the members about the introduction of a book which advocated certain questionable religious views,—as a former society had been broken up, on a question of politics.

A new society was commenced in November, 1853, under the name of the Mutual Improvement Society ; and one of its features was to be the holding of an annual soirée, accompanied with musical performances. The Choral

Society assisted at the soirées of October the 2nd, 1854, and August the 10th, 1855, as did the short-lived Philharmonic Society, in 1856.

During this time, the society prospered, increasing both in numbers and objects. It provided a reading room, with nearly 400 volumes of books; and classes were arranged for scientific instruction of various kinds, together with discussions, and periodical lectures. In the seasons of 1862-3 a series of lectures was delivered by Dr. Paine, on "animal physiology," to a class of sixty members, by whom they were so highly prized as to command their regular attendance, and to call forth an expression of thanks, in a valuable present to the lecturer. A series of lectures on geology, and another on electricity and galvanism, by Mr. Pullen, F.G.S.; a series on chemistry, by Mr. Vick; and one on the Latin and French languages, by the Rev. W. Wheeler, were also delivered during the same seasons. In those, and in several following years, members of the society were in connection with the "Science and Art Department of the Committee of Council on Education, South Kensington," and were successful in their examinations; having received, among other prizes, two Queen's gold medals.

In 1862, Mr. Scrope, with his accustomed liberality, presented the society with fifty pounds, principally for increasing the library. It had convenient apartments in the Subscription Rooms from 1854 to the latter end of 1863, when it removed to the house in King-street—so long known as the Golden Heart—which had been purchased by Mr. Dickinson and ceased to be an Inn.

It was fitted up with a library and reading room, (supplied with newspapers, &c.,) a lecture room, and coffee and refreshment rooms: and, in order to provide for recreation, (which had become a part of the society's object,) Mr. Dickinson, at his own cost, built and fitted up a large covered skittle alley; to which he afterward added a gymnasium, and re-laid the bowling green; and all these he allowed to be occupied, rent free, for more than two years.

In 1866, the society, then numbering about 200 members, changed its name to Stroud Institute; and, in 1867, removed to apartments in George-street. One of its latest plans was the arrangement of a series of Saturday penny readings, kindly given by persons of the town and neighbourhood, which were well attended. Whatever affords a

cheap means of improvement, as well as a pleasant and
rational substitute for the many questionable modes in
which youth is tempted to occupy its leisure hours, must
have a strong claim on the approval and co-operation of all
who are concerned for the welfare of society.

To the several societies before mentioned must be added
the School of Art, located in a part of the late Bedford
Arms Inn, in High-street. It is in connection with the Art
Department of the Committee of Council on Education,
and was established in the year 1860, by the exertions of
Mr. Dickinson. It has been conducted with considerable
success, and holds a good place among other similar schools
in the country. A few drawings of its students have been
considered worthy of a situation in the permanent collection
of the works of schools of art students, at South Kensington:
and, in the year 1867, one of its artizan students was chosen
a national scholar, with an allowance enabling him to pursue
a course of studies at South Kensington Schools, to qualify
him as an ornamental designer for manufactures.   Miss
R. E. Stanton also obtained the gold medal and the Prince
of Wales' Scholarship, £25 ; and both she and her sisters
obtained the National medal.

In the year 1860, Mr. Dickinson [2] was appointed president
of the Mutual Improvement Society, afterwards called Stroud
Institute, and also secretary of the School of Art ; and to
both he continued to give his pecuniary aid, and his valuable
personal attendance and counsel,—with that liberality and
regard to the improvement and welfare of society for which
he so energetically, and yet so quietly, labours.

[2 This lamented gentleman died in 1878, and will never be forgotten in
Stroud, for whose inhabitants, and their public interests, no man has ever
worked harder, or done more.]

CHAPTER XXXIV.

STROUD DISPENSARY — CASUALTY HOSPITAL — STROUD GENERAL HOSPITAL.

WE now proceed to notice the building which forms the angle of Bedford-street and George-street, in which last is its south front. It was erected in the year 1823 for the old Institution called the Stroud Dispensary.

I have not been able to ascertain the exact year in which the Dispensary was established. The earliest mention of it that I have met with, is in a small and scarce pamphlet by Mr. John Dallaway of Brimscomb, printed at Gloucester in 1755, entitled "A scheme to make the river *Stroudwater* navigable," &c. It occurs toward the end of its dedication to the Right Honorable Lord Ducie Moreton, dated December the 8th in that year, and reads thus,—" I cannot help concluding that, as the laudable scheme, some time since begun in this neighbourhood, for fitting up and supporting a Dispensatory in *Stroud*, was afterward the means of establishing one of the most noble charities (considering its infant state) in *England*, out of *London*—I mean the County Infirmary, I am strongly induced to hope that no less encouragement will be given to a scheme tending to promote the emolument and labour of the poor in a state of health and ability, than has been shown to support and relieve them in their state of sickness and consequent distress."

We learn from this extract, that the County Infirmary (in Gloucester) had been opened before the latter end of 1755 : and that the Stroud Dispensary had been already so long in existence as to have acquired an established reputation. And, if we may not accept Mr. Dallaway's statement literally, and regard the Dispensary as actually "the means" of establishing the Infirmary, we may be sure that it contributed to it, by calling public attention to the gratuitous medical treatment of the poor in sickness : and that at least, it had a precedence in point of time. We must, therefore, regard Mr. Dallaway's remarks as having furnished some very gratifying facts in the history of our Dispensary ; and feel with him that the names of the "many worthy gentlemen who began it, deserve to be transmitted to posterity." It is probable that he knew them all, and that he and Lord Ducie Moreton were of the number ; but their names had not been preserved.

Dating the origin of the Dispensary from 1750, we do not find any materials for its history until 1771 : but then I learn that Samuel Jones, M.D., the resident physician of Stroud, was regarded as the chief promoter in that year, of "a Society for providing gratuitous medical advice, and medicine, for the poor of the town and neighbourhood." He received subscriptions for its support, prescribed for the patients, and kept the accounts ; and Mr. Thomas Hughes was the apothecary, and dispensed the medicines. At a meeting of the subscribers of the Dispensary, held at the Old George Inn, August the 11th, 1783, (Sir George Onesiphorus Paul, Bart., in the chair,) it appeared that in the preceding year the number of patients was 774, of whom 355 were cured, 6 found incurable, 18 had died, and the rest had been relieved, at the expense (in subscriptions) of a little more than £570. At the same meeting, Dr. Jones resigned the care of the patients, on account of his declining health ; and Mr. John Snowden, M.D., a physician then resident in the town, kindly offered his services and was appointed physician to the society. It was also resolved that "the subscribers should meet on the first Tuesday after the first full moon in every year, at twelve o'clock at noon, and dine together at the George Inn ; then to elect a treasurer, receive subscriptions, and transact such other business as should be necessary ;" and "the ordinary" was fixed at 1s. 6d. per head. ¹ Sir G. O. Paul was chosen president. The annual subscription was £1 1s., without any limitation as to the number of patients who might be recommended in respect of it ; and at the annual meeting of January the 28th, 1784, it was

---

1 At that time, dinners were thought necessary accompaniments of such meetings ; though, in this case at a moderate rate. And I well remember that, at an annual dinner several years afterward, the president, Sir G. O. Paul, who always aimed at economy in public matters, fixed the gratuity to the waiters at the dinner, at threepence from each guest.

found necessary to resolve "that no subscriber should recommend more than one patient *per* week for each guinea he might subscribe." Even this limited privilege was found to be too large ; for, on the 6th of May following, it appeared that no less than 560 patients had been admitted during the preceding four months. "An unusual sickness, consequent on the distresses of the poor during the previous winter had induced subscribers to extend their recommendations to numbers so disproportionate to their subscriptions, that the whole money subscribed had been expended, and a considerable debt incurred." It was therefore determined that all further recommendations in respect of that year's subscriptions should be suspended, and that a new subscription for the remainder of the current year should be opened, —which was afterward limited to the recommendation of only six persons for each guinea subscribed. The "distresses" above alluded to were owing to a decline in the clothing manufacture, partly owing to "the American war" ; when, as an aged man told me, grass grew in the courts and doorways of the clothing mills.

At that time the drugs were provided by the society ; and Mr Hughes was paid, for dispensing the medicines, a sum equal to two thirds of the annual subscription— limited, however, to £30 : and, at the General Meeting of February the 16th, 1786, Mr. Hughes attended, and stated that "in consideration of the great value of bark," 2 (medicinally,) "he considered himself as paid in too large a proportion for administering that medicine ; he therefore proposed to deduct £5 from his annual salary." This is an example of the rigid integrity of a "stern" and "just" man. 3

At the same meeting, it was found that the expenses of the society for the previous year had been—for drugs £37 9s., dispensing £30, sundries £12 1s. 2d., room and fires £2 9s.,—total £81 19s. 2d. ; and Messrs. Hollings and Dallaway, of the Stroud Bank, were appointed treasurers to the society. From that time instead of having a new treasurer annually, a member of that firm, (and of the

2 The *Cinchona* of the *materia medica*, which had then recently come into general use in England ; and was found so efficacious as to supersede the more slowly operating medicines previously used in similar cases.

3 See Mr. Hughes' character, p. 73.

respective firms that succeeded it,) has since been their treasurer.

For many years, the patients were received by the physician in a single hired room : first in the house of William Mills for three years ; then in a room at the Lamb Inn, Church-street, for six years ; and in a room adjoining the King's Arms for the next twelve years. During all this time, the poor patients had experienced great inconvenience from exposure to the open air in all weathers, whilst their medicines were being prepared ; the number being so great that the apothecary could not receive them into his own house. And although at a meeting, January the 12th, 1795, it was resolved that a room should be provided for the patients whilst attending the surgeon, or waiting for medicines—this desirable object was not attained until after 1805 ; when ample rooms were rented of Mr. Richard Playne, in the house at St. Briavels, which he had built opposite Rowcroft ; and which bore the name of the Dispensary for many years after.

At the annual meeting, January the 14th, 1799. Mr. Hughes resigned his offices ; and received " the grateful acknowledgments of the subscribers for his humane and successful assistance as a surgeon, and for the fidelity and economy with which he had, during twenty-five years, dispensed the medicines committed to his care, as apothecary to the Dispensary."

On this occasion, Mr Darke who had succeeded to Mr. Hughes' medical practice, was chosen his successor.

In 1816 Mr Darke resigned his office of apothecary and dispenser of medicines ; but continued his services as surgeon to the charity with great assiduity until 1823.

In December, 1821, Sir G. O. Paul, the president, had died ; having attended in his place every annual meeting, from his appointment in 1783, to 1818 inclusively ; and, in 1822, his nephew, Major Robert Snow Paul, was chosen president in his stead.

On the death of Dr. Snowden in 1823, "after thirty-nine years of most valuable attention to the patients of the charity," Dr. (late Mr.) Darke was appointed the physician, and Mr. Jones surgeon to the Dispensary.

The amount of the annual subscriptions varied occasionally, and so did the number of recommendations allowed for each guinea. In the years 1791-2-3, the number of tickets was fixed at five ; in 1801, at six ; in 1810, at seven ;

in 1820, at eight ; and in 1830, at six.   In the ten years
—1790 to 1800—the aggregate number of patients admitted
was 4613 ; and in each of the decades between 1800 and
1830, the numbers differed but little therefrom, and from
each other.

For several years it had been thought desirable to
establish a fund out of the occasional donations, legacies,
&c., made to the charity ; and in May, 1823 the fund
amounted to £786 12s. 10d.   This enabled the society to
carry out the long-desired object of possessing a house of
their own with suitable accommodations for the physician,
surgeon, and patients.   Accordingly they purchased a plot
of land in Kendrick's Orchard, and there in the same year
they erected and furnished a convenient building for the
Dispensary.   This was done at an outlay of £741 11s. 10d.
and it now forms a part of the Stroud General Hospital. 4

The general and appropriate source of the funds of this
charity had always been the annual subscriptions of £1 1s.
each.   But they had been occasionally augmented by donations, legacies, and the appropriation (by magistrates of
the neighbourhood,) of fines or parts of fines, levied as penalties for offences against the laws, and for misdemeanours.
The recorded donations amounted to £73 5s. 7d., and the
legacies to £345.

Amongst the fines levied for offences, we must especially
notice those inflicted on persons found in possession of
embezzled materials used in the clothing manufactory,—
such as wool, yarn, cloth, &c.   From the year 1801 to
1833, both inclusive, sums to the aggregate amount of £520
were handed to the charity out of the penalties levied for
that offence alone.

The embezzlement of clothing materials and the dealing
in them, was commonly called *Slinge-ing;* and the embezzled
materials themselves were called *Slinge.* 5

[4 The New Hospital, near Trinity Church, was not erected until 1874, the
old author having died in 1873.   The foundation or memorial stone was laid
by Lord Sherborne, Provincial Grand Master of the Freemasons of Gloucestershire on the 28th May, 1874.   The building was completed at a cost of between
£6000 and £7000, all of which has been defrayed by public and private
benevolence.   The endowment fund of the institution now closely approaches
£10000.   A full account of this admirable charity will be found in " Libby's
Twenty Years' History of Stroud—1870 to 1890," previously mentioned in
1890.   The institution had outgrown its abode, and additions were commenced,
to cost nearly £2000, the whole of which sum was readily provided by benefactors, and public help and subscriptions.

5 In these words the letter " g " is sounded like " j."

This offence was very prevalent in the writer's youth : for then most of the manufacturing operations were done in the houses of the operatives, to whom wool and yarn were entrusted for carding, spinning weaving, &c. And there, as also in the mills themselves, great facilities were afforded for secreting, purloining, and withholding parts of those materials,—of which constant advantage was taken ; and by which the clothiers suffered great losses.   The number of embezzlers and dealers in slinge was also great : and they found ready purchasers in the numerous small clothiers then existing, who worked up the slinge with new materials into inferior cloth.   At that time, stealthy figures might be met in the twilight, crossing Hampton Common from valley to valley ; and in all parts of the district, from one cottage to another : and the lines, or tracks of white stones, which are yet seen on the green turf of the common, are pointed out as having been dropped there, at short intervals from one another, to guide the slinge-dealers on their nightly expeditions.

Of these, William Niblett was most notorious.   His last place of residence here was in Middle-street ; and being a tall, spare man, he was popularly called Long Niblett. So large were his transactions, that he was once fined £120 as a single penalty ; of which the treasurer of the Dispensary received £30.   This man was at last found guilty of forgery, at the Gloucester Assizes, and condemned to be hanged.   But the sentence was commuted to transportation for life, on the intercession (it was said) of some magistrates, who thereby purchased Niblett's disclosure of the particulars of his trade, and a large list of the names and abodes of his fellow slinge-ers, in all parts of the neighbourhood, which he gave before he was shipped for Botany Bay.

The writer once possessed the original paper containing the list, &c., in the handwriting of Sir G. O. Paul, as it was taken down by him from Niblett's dictation.

This offence however is almost (if not wholly,) discontinued.   The introduction of machinery, by which so many of the clothing processes are now performed ; the use of steam-power ; the erection of large manufactories, where almost all the operations are concentrated, and whereby a more complete supervision and control over the operatives is effected ; together with the adoption of stringent regulations,—has made the offence very difficult, if not well nigh impossible.

In 1834, Dr. Darke resigned his office of physician, and "the deep sense of the benefits which the charity had derived from his valuable gratuitous services" was feelingly expressed to him, on the part of the subscribers. His connection with the establishment as apothecary, surgeon, and physician had extended over a period of thirty-five years : and at a meeting, October the 10th in the same year, Dr. Cargill was chosen physician in Dr. Darke's stead.

In the year 1833 there had arisen a strong desire to establish a Hospital for the reception of persons who might meet with accidental injuries, requiring immediate surgical aid ; in order to avoid exposing them to the painful and dangerous journey to the Infirmary at Gloucester.

A goodly list of donations and annual subscriptions having been obtained, a meeting of the subscribers was held at the Town Hall, December 12, 1833 ; when it was thought desirable that a Casualty Hospital should be formed in union with the Dispensary ; and a committee was appointed to apply to the friends of the Dispensary on the subject. This latter society named a committee to meet them : and, after mutual consultations, the proposition was agreed to, and it was resolved to enlarge the Dispensary, so as to afford accommodation for the intended Hospital ; and the trustees of the funds of the Dispensary were authorised to advance the requisite monies for that purpose.

In 1835 that object was effected by the erection of the stone edifice which adjoins and communicates with the brick building previously known as the Dispensary.   This was done at the cost of £308 7s. ; of which sum, £227 8s., (the produce of the Dispensary funds,) formed a part ; and the remaining £80 19s., with a further sum of £39 6s. subsequently expended, was discharged out of monies collected in the parish and neighbouring churches, in dissenting chapels, and from private donations.

The Casualty ward being furnished, Mr. Washbourn appointed surgeon, and a nurse provided,—it was opened September 19, 1836.   It had been agreed that the funds, subscriptions, and accounts of both Charities should be kept separate, but that in all other respects they should be one and the same.   An annual rent of £16 was made payable to the Dispensary for the use of the Casualty ward.

From that time a general meeting of the subscribers to both societies was held once a year ; at which business was transacted, and reports were made of the proceedings and accounts of each division of the Institution, for the previous year ; which reports were printed and circulated. And, at the first meeting of the United Establishment, held May 17, 1837, it appeared that, in the Dispensary department, 408 patients had been relieved in the previous year—at the cost of 5s. 7½d. for each: and, in the Casualty department, of the twenty one in-patients admitted in the preceding eight months, twelve had been discharged cured (three after amputation), three had died, one remained in charge, and two as out-patients ; and that, of the fourteen out-patients, twelve had been discharged cured, and two remained on the books.

It was then thought desirable to provide a separate permanent fund toward the maintenance of the Casualty Hospital. And at a special meeting of the subscribers, (then called governors), held November 8, 1837, it appeared that £170 had been already received for that object: of which £20 was given by Dr. Darke £100 by Lord John Russell, M.P., and £50 by Mr. Scrope, M.P. ; and four persons were named as trustees of the fund.

On June 6th, 1838, Dr. Wilmot was appointed to assist Dr. Cargill, in consequence of his declining health ; and, before the end of August following, Dr. Cargill had died. He was a young physician of great promise, and much respected.

On December 27, 1839, Dr. Gooch was chosen physician in the room of Dr. Wilmot, who had retired.

At the annual meeting, May 19, 1841, it appeared that, in the Dispensary department, the expenditure had exceeded the income ; and that only four tickets were to be allowed for each next guinea subscription. It further appeared that the permanent fund of the Casualty Hospital amounted to £478 18s. 1d. ; of which £72 16s. had been lately contributed by the survivors of the Longtree, Bisley, and Whitstone Troop of Yeomanry Cavalry,—being the balance of the Troop's accounts remaining in their hands. At the same time the Right Honourable Earl Ducie was requested to accept the office of President of the united Institution.

At the Quarterly meeting of the Committee, November, 16, 1841, the Nurse reported that David Franks, a Hospital patient who had been cured and discharged by the medical officers, had refused to leave the Hospital, and had doggedly continued there several days; and that his friends, who had been applied to, were not disposed to assist in his removal. It seemed that the ample dietary of the Hospital, and the quiet idleness of sitting on his bed, and going to and from the window which looked into the street, was more to his taste than his former out-of-door life. The Committee, however, discovered a remedy for his new malady: they directed the nurse not to supply him with any food after his next morning's breakfast. This was told him, with a hint of a more stringent application if needful; and so after the next day's early meal, the lazy drone departed.

The General meeting of May, 1842, was the last that was held at the George Inn, pursuant to the resolution to that effect passed August 11th, 1783; and all subsequent meetings have been held at the Dispensary and Casualty Hospital.

In 1843, serious accidents happened to laborers in the Saperton tunnel and elsewhere, on the line of the Great Western Railway; all which were brought for relief to the Casualty Hospital. The treatment of these cases, and of injuries from machinery in the clothing mills, from the fall of earth in quarries, and from various other casualties, which occurred in several following years, fully established the reputation, and attested the great advantages of this charity; and slightly augmented its annual income.

At the Annual meeting of the United Institution, held May 22, 1850, the following legacies were reported, viz. :— £100 to the Dispensary, and £100 to the Hospital, from the will of Mr. Robert Hughes; £100 to the Hospital, from Mr. Wm. Clutterbuck Chambers; and £19 19s. from Mr. Wm. Lee. The resignation of Dr. Gooch, as physician, was also announced; and Dr. James Sandys was chosen in his stead. As a token of the Society's "thanks to Dr. Gooch for his nine years kind and assiduous attention," a sum of £57 was raised by subscription, with which a silver tea and coffee service was purchased and presented to him.

At an adjourned General meeting, held June the 18th, 1851, Dr. Paine was appointed assistant physician; and shortly afterward he became the sole physician, by the retirement of Dr. Sandys.

At the Annual meeting of May the 27th, 1852, the treasurer reported the receipt of a legacy of £100, from the late Mrs. Elizabeth Phillips ; and, at the Annual general meeting, May the 26th, 1853, the sum of £76 6s. 10d. was reported as a donation from Earl Ducie, to the capital fund.

At the Annual meeting, May the 25th, 1854, the medical officers represented the want of several accommodations in the Hospital premises, for themselves and the in-patients. The desirableness of the object proposed was fully admitted, and it was afterwards taken into serious consideration ; together with a proposal for converting the two Institutions into one. A survey of the premises was then made by Mr. Joseph Franklin ; [6] from whose report it appeared practicable to effect all the accommodations required, by a re-arrangement of the interior of the stone portion of the edifice, and by making some small additions to it. For these purposes he kindly furnished the necessary plans, and offered to superintend the works, gratuitously. At a special general meeting of subscribers and friends, held April the 5th, 1855, it was resolved to form the Dispensary and Casualty Hospital into one; and that the funds of both should be amalgamated, and applied without distinction, for the general purposes of the United Institution ; that the Casualty Hospital should be forthwith enlarged, and alterations made in it according to the plans of Mr. Franklin It was further resolved that money should be raised by general subscription, for defraying the expenses of the intended improvements, and for adding to the permanent fund, which should be available for the support of the United Establishment.

In order to promote the last-mentioned object, an address was prepared, dated April 26, 1855, and extensively circulated, wherein it was stated that " in the Hospital department (which was open for all cases of accidental injury) during the previous nineteen years, more than 1000 casualty cases had been admitted ; nearly 100 of which were of such a serious nature as to require amputation, or other capital surgical operations ; that, during the same period, between 7000 and 8000 medical and surgical out-patients had been relieved by means of the Dispensary ; and that, during the last eight years, (for which alone a computation could

6 He was an eminent architect, late of Liverpool, but had retired to Cooper's Hill, which he had purchased in order to be near his native town ; and there he died.   He was a man of great taste, judgment and kindliness.

be made,) the cost of each patient had been very much below the average expenses *per* head in all the other Hospitals of the same character in the kingdom." And, appended to this address, were a few names of persons who headed the list of subscribers.

At the Annual meeting of May 31, 1855, it was announced that the executors of the late Mr. John Ballinger had paid his legacy of £100 to the treasurer of the Hospital ; and the names of seven gentlemen were added to those of the old trustees of the premises.

After this, additions were rapidly made to the list of donations, amounting in the whole to £1028 18s. 5d. : and it is due to the memory of the late Mr. Biddell, of Stratford Abbey, 7 to say that the Charity was greatly indebted for this large sum, to his hearty interest in the object, and his personal application, throughout the borough and neighbourhood, to nearly every one of the donors.   At the same time, and with the like energy, he solicited and obtained several additions to the free annual subscriptions for the Casualty department.

In pursuance of the resolutions of the meeting of April 5, 1855, the contemplated alterations and additions were made, at the cost of £295 8s. 7d. The new wards were furnished, and surgical instruments procured, at the further expense of £48 3s. : and at the General meeting of May 19, 1856, it was reported that the Hospital premises then furnished room for fourteen beds ; and contained the physician's room, a patients waiting room, a kitchen, pantry, washhouse, sleeping room and other accommodations for the nurse ; besides a properly-lighted operating room, a dead room, water closets, &c., &c. It was also reported that £90 had been received as the balance of two legacies of £50 each, given to the Dispensary and Hospital by the late Miss Mary Ann Biddell ; and that the several funds of the united Institution having been found to amount to £2280 6s., the committee had, thereout, purchased a sum of £2400 three per cent, Consols, in the names of William Capel, Joseph Watts Hallewell, Rev. Arthur John Biddell, and Alfred John Stanton, all of the parish of Stroud, as trustees for the establishment.

At the Annual General meeting of the subscribers to the Dispensary and Casualty Hospital, May 27, 1858, which

7 He died April 25, 1863, aged 74 years.

closed its twenty-second year, it appeared that, in the Dispensary department, 283 patients had been relieved at the expense of £70 15s. for medicine and dispensing, being at the rate of 5s. for each patient ; and, in the Hospital department, thirty four in-patients and thirty two out-patients had been admitted,—of whom 60 had been discharged cured, one incurable, one had died, and four were left in charge,—at the cost of £127 0s. 6d., being after the rate of two pounds for each patient. This was the last Annual General meeting, and the last public statement of the accounts, of the United Institution.

As early as May, 1853, the medical officers had requested that each of them should be allowed one bed at the Hospital, for the admission of a poor in-patient : and, at the Annual meeting of May 19, 1856, it was resolved that four beds should be set apart for poor sick persons, to be admitted on the certificates of the medical officers that they were proper objects of the charity ; and further, that each subscriber of one guinea or more to the Casualty Hospital department, should be entitled to recommend and send to it one poor person as an in-patient, on a like medical certificate, for six months, on payment of an additional guinea at the time. At this meeting, sundry rules and regulations were made as to persons eligible and not eligible to admission, and as to linen, &c., to be brought with them ; and those resolutions were confirmed at the meeting of May 27, 1858, before mentioned.

Hitherto the establishment had been well supported, especially by the annual free donations to the Hospital : and this, with the admission of in-patients by the medical officers and subscribers to the Hospital department, led to a direct recommendation of the former, and many of the latter, to convert the Institution into a General Hospital,— to which, indeed those admissions were a kind of experimental approach.

This proposal was well received, and led to various meetings of the committee and subscribers, to consider the subject, and to revise the rules and regulations for conducting such an Institution, that had been laid before them. At length, at a Special General meeting, on the 25th of January, 1859, it was resolved to increase the usefulness of the united Establishment, by giving to it the more enlarged character together with the name, of The Stroud General Hospital.

From that time, the Dispensary, which had existed more than a century, lost its venerable name; but left a history, of which we may be justly proud : and from the same time, the General Hospital began its course of usefulness, and the creation of a history of its own. Of that history the proceedings of its seventh year are the latest we can notice.

From the printed report of the year ending December the 31st, 1867, it appeared that its permanent fund had been augmented by donations and legacies to the sum of £2926 15s. 3d., £3 per cent. Consols ; besides a donation of £100 from G. P. Scrope, Esq., which has since been invested.

The receipts for the year were :—

	£	s.	d.
Subscriptions to the casualty department	232	15	6
Ditto to the general department	193	14	6
Donations and collections	100	5	5
Dividends on £3 per cent. Consols	85	10	7
	£612	6	0

The payments were :—

	£	s.	d.
Due to the treasurer, 31st Dec., 1866	82	7	1
Sundries	505	11	6
Balance in treasurer's hands	24	7	5
	£612	6	0

The patients admitted were :—

In-patients, by tickets ... 26
Ditto, as casualties 53
79

Out-patients, by tickets ... 497
Ditto, as casualties 122
—— 619
Home-patients, by ticket... 151

849

It further appeared that the cost for medicine and dispensing, did not exceed 3s. 9d. for each out-patient ; and that the number of tickets to be allowed for each subscription of £1 1s., was limited to four, "to be in force for one month."

Of the Stroud General Hospital.—The president is the Earl of Ducie ; vice-president, William Capel, Esq.;[8] treasurer, J. C. Hallewell, Esq.; physician, William Henry Paine.[8] M.D., member of the Royal College of Physicians, London ; consulting surgeon, E. A. Uthwatt ;[8] surgeons, Charles Wethered and G. R. Cubitt ; house-surgeon and secretary, Alfred S. Cooke. The attention of the medical officers to the whole of their duties has been worthy of all praise, and has earned the thankful acknowledgments of the community.

The public advantage of a General Hospital for poor persons suffering from sickness, or from accidental or other bodily calamities, is so obvious and so great that it can hardly be over-rated. Indeed, of all benevolent institutions it is one of the most valuable on all accounts, and the least exceptionable on any : thus commending itself to the generous sympathies of mankind. It cannot be doubted, therefore, that ample funds will always be forthcoming from this populous and wealthy neighbourhood, to maintain and even to increase the efficiency and reputation of the STROUD GENERAL HOSPITAL, for a century—aye, for centuries to come.

[8 These three gentlemen have since died.]

CHAPTER XXXV.

UPPER LYPIATT—THE STEPHENSES OF LYPIATT— THE SUCCEEDING
OWNERS OF THE ESTATE.

THERE are four Tithings in the parish of Stroud, viz. :
Upper or Over Lypiatt ; Lower or Nether Lypiatt ;
Steanbridge ; and Pakenhill or Paganhill.

Upper or Over Lypiatt, sometimes called Lypiatt Superior
and Old Lypiatt, occupies a central position in the home
portion of the parish, from its western end upward, to its
junction with the parish of Bisley.

The manor of Lypiatt, was held of the honor of Hereford,
and was anciently in the family of the Mansells. William
Mansell died seized of Over Lupeyate, held of the Earl of
Hereford, by homage, fealty, and suit of Court of the said
Earl, at Gloucester from month to month, as appears by
an Inquisition after his death,—18th Edward II., No. 51
(1315). [1] Philip Mansell died seized thereof,—19th Richard
II (1396).

Sir Robert Atkyns says the Whittingtons were formerly
lords of this manor : and Mr. Fosbrooke says that it was
alienated to them in the fifteenth century. But Mr. Rudder
seems to doubt it ; saying, "they were, indeed, lords of the
manor of Rodborough, in the reign of Henry VI. and Henry
VIII., and they contributed to the building of the south
aisle of the church of Stroud ; but what estate they had, if
any, he had not been able to discover." [2] However, I have
met with notices of the Courts Baron of Thomas Whytington,
held for the manor of Lupeyate, on the 12th of October in
the 36th and in the 37th years of King Henry VI., and on
April 20th, 17th Edward IV. A.D., 1478. [3]

1 Fosbrooke, vol. 1, 338.
2 Rudder, 712.
3 From an old MS. book in the possession of Sir J. E. Dorington, Bart.

According to Mr. Fosbrooke, and the pedigree given by the Rev. Samuel Lysons in his "Model Merchant of the Middle Ages," 4 Maud, the only daughter of Thomas Whitington (in the pedigree called "Of Lypiatt."—his will dated 1490) 5—married William Wye ; and, as her father's heir, took this manor with two others, to the Wyes. It was held by that family for three generations,—Atkyns and the rest say for several. One of the Wyes is mentioned by Leland, as residing at Lypiatt in his time. 6 This was Robert, William's eldest son. " Accordingly Christopher Pyard died seized of a messuage, nine acres, &c., called Little Feris, in Olde Leppiatt, held of Robert Wye as of Olde Leppiatt, service unknown." Esc. 16th Henry VIII (1525) 7 Thomas Wye, son of Robert, was sheriff of the county in 1575, and died seized of this manor, and ten messuages, two hundred acres of land, sixty acres of meadow, one hundred acres of pasture, forty acres of wood, and other particulars, in Over Lypiatt, Stroud, Bisley, and Winston ; as appears by the escheator's inquisition, taken at Cirencester 18th September, 26th Elizabeth (1584) 8 He died in 1581, and was the last Wye of Lypiatt : for, in 1583, his widow Juliana, who was entitled to the estates for her life, re-married with John Throckmorton ; who, in 1591 and 1596, purchased the interests of those in remainder, and thereby ultimately obtained the fee of the manor and estates.

Sir Robert Atkyns says that John Throckmorton "was concerned in the Popish powder plot" : and a room in the mansion-house of Lypiatt has always been pointed out as the identical place where the conspirators met. But this may have arisen from the circumstance that he was a Roman Catholic ; and that several of his relatives, who had probably often been visitors there, were actually implicated in the plot ; 9 and from the remarkable fact that the name of Fawkes, (which was that of the arch-conspirator,) is still

4 8vo London, 1862.

5 Mr. Fosbrooke calls Thomas Whitington the second son of Robert ; Mr. Lysons calls him more correctly, the fourth son of Sir Guy de Whitington.

6 Itin. vol. vi.

7 Fosbrooke.

8 Rudder.

9 Catesby, Tresham, and Winter, were among his relatives.

frequent in the parish of Stroud, and especially in the valleys below Lypiatt Park. Throckmorton's own innocence may, however, be inferred from his having escaped all adverse notice from the Government on that occasion. In connection with this subject, it may be noticed that the Lord Mounteagle, Lord Morley's son, who took a somewhat strange part in the discovery of the Gunpowder-plot, has been himself suspected of complicity with it : and there is a letter extant, written by him to Robert Catesby, one of the conspirators, and addressed to him at this place, which has been interpreted as having connection with the plot. This letter was found by John Bruce, Esq., F.S.A., together with one from Thomas Winter (another conspirator) to Catesby, in a volume of the Cotton manuscripts. Mr. Bruce, being acquainted with Upper Lypiatt, immediately recognized it as the place to which Lord Mounteagle's letter had been directed ; and in February, 1840, communicated both the letters to the Society of Antiquaries, with observations, in which he ventured to fix the date of Lord Mounteagle's letter in September, and Winter's in October, 1605.

Lord Mounteagle's letter is as follows :—

"To my loving kinsman Robert Catesbye; Esquier, geve theise Lipyeat.

"If all creatures borne under the mone's spheare can not endure without the ellimentes of aier and fyre, in what languishment have wee lede owre lyfe, since wee departed from the deare Robine, whose conversation gave us such warmeth as wee neded no other heate to maintayne owre healthes. Since, therefore, yt is proper to all, to desire a reamedy for their disease, I doe by theise, bynde the by the lawes of Charitye to make thy present aparence here at the Bath : and let no watery Nimpes diurt you, who can better lyve with the aier, and better forbeare the fyre of your spirite and vigoure than wee, who accumptes thy person the only Sone that must ripene our harvest. And thus I rest

"Ever fast tyed to your friendshipp,
"W. MOWNTEAGLE."

This letter, which in diction resembles the euphuism of the time of Queen Elizabeth, is so figurative and obscure that it seems designed to cover and convey some secret information or direction ; and if its assumed date were correct, it would go far to justify the imputation against the writer.

In 1840 and 1841 David Jardine, Esq., M.A., communicated two memorials on the letters, to the Society of Antiquaries, in disproval of the supposed date of 1605, and of Lord Mounteagle's guilty knowledge of the Gunpowder treason. But, as Mr. Jardine admitted, it is "one of the most remarkable mysteries in modern History" ;

and there is much to be said in favour of the original suspicion, even if no "fresh evidence" should arise to connect "this letter with the argument."

In the year 1610 John Throckmorton sold the Manor and estates of Upper Lypiatt to Thomas Stephens, Esq., of the Middle Temple, London, Attorney-General to Prince Henry and Prince Charles. [10] He was the third son of Edward Stephens, of Eastington. He married Elizabeth, daughter and co-heir of John Stone of London, by whom he had issue (besides two daughters), three sons, viz. :— Edward, born April 22nd, 1596 ; John, born at Watford in the County of Hertford, September 26th, 1603 ; and Nathaniel, born at Lypiatt July 29th, 1611. He died, April 26th, 1613,[11] leaving all his sons minors. Of these, Edward, the eldest, was ancestor of the Sodbury family of that name ; Nathaniel, the youngest, was progenitor of the Stephenses of Cherington, and John, his second son, became possessed of the manor and estates of Lypiatt, by purchase from his eldest brother, Edward Stephens, in 1624. In the great Civil War, Lypiatt was garrisoned for the Parliament, by Colonel Massey ; and was afterward (A.D., 1642) taken by Sir Jacob Astley, from Cirencester, in the absence of the captain who commanded there. But the garrison "had instructions to draw off, if at any time an enemy fell down"; and the house being unfortified and incapable of defence, it was soon taken, when they lost a lieutenant and fifty private soldiers. [12] John Stephens was one of the knights of the shire returned to the last Commonwealth Parliament, in the year 1658-9.

The following passages in the life of this John Stephens are worthy of notice, both on his own account, and as an interesting page in the early history of Quakerism. I met with them in an old pamphlet ; [13] from which I learn that soon after the year 1665, Robert Silvester, Philip Grey, and Thomas Onyon, three Friends, were bound over to the Quarter Sessions, at Gloucester, for their behaviour during

10 Its value was estimated by Thomas Stephens, the purchaser, at £4400. The price was £5000, but it included the Manor, &c., of Frampton Mansell and Pitchcombe, &c., which he reckoned at £600.

11 Fosbrooke, by mistake, gives this as the date of his *burial*, at Stroud, vol. 1, p. 320

12 "The Military Government of the City of Gloucester," by John Corbet. London, 1645.

13 "Some Memoirs of the Life of John Roberts, written by his son Daniel

worship in the church of Cirencester ; being only (as the
narrator phrases it) " for standing in the Steeple-house with
their hats on, though they said nothing." And then he
proceeds to say—

" My father, at their desire, accompanied them to the Sessions ; and when
they were called, and the Priest had accused them, the Bench, in a rage, without asking them any questions, ordered their mittimusses to be made. These
unjust and illegal proceedings kindled my father's zeal : insomuch that he,
stepping forward, called to the Justices, saying, 'Are not those who sit on the
Bench sworn to do Justice? Is there not a man among you will do the thing
that is right?' Whereupon John Stephens, of Lypeat, (their Chairman), cried
out, 'Who are you, Sirrah? What is your name?' My father telling him
his name, he said, 'I am glad I have you here : I have heard of you : you
deserve a stone doublet: 14 there's many an honester man than you hanged.'
'It may be so,' answered my father ; 'but what dost thou think becomes of
those that hang honest men?' The Justice replied, 'I'll send you to prison ;
and if any insurrection or tumult be in the land, I'll come and cut your throat
first with my own sword : for I fear to sleep in my bed, least such fanatics
should come and cut my throat ;' and snatching up a ball of wax, 15 he violently threw it at my father ; who avoided the blow by stepping aside. Their
mittimusses were then made, and they were all sent to prison. On the morrow
my father went home, having the jailor's leave." (His discharge was effected
by the interference of his uncle Sollis, who was one of the justices.)
" In the night, a concern came upon him with such weight that it made
him tremble till the bed shook under him. My mother asking the reason of
it * * * he said, 'I must go to this John Stephens, who is my great
enemy, and sent me to prison.' * * * He arose and prepared for his
journey, but durst eat or drink nothing. When he mounted his horse, the command of the Lord was to him, 'Remember Lot's wife : look not back.' So
on he rode very cheerfully eight or nine miles, till he came in sight of the
Justice's house. 16 * * * It being pretty early in the morning, and seeing
the stable door open, he went to the groom and desired him to put up his
horse. While this was doing the Justice's son and his clerk came up, who
roughly said, 'I thought you had been in Gloucester Castle.' 17 John Roberts
—'So I was.' Clerk—'And how came you out?' John Roberts—'When
thou hast authority to demand it, I can give thee an answer. But my business is with thy master, if I may speak with him.' Clerk—'You may if you
will promise to be civil.' John Roberts—'If thou seest me uncivil, I desire
thee to tell me of it.' They went in, and my father followed them ; they bid
him take a turn in the hall, and they would acquaint the Justice of his being
there. He was soon called in ; and my father no sooner saw him, but he
believed the Lord had been at work upon him ; for, as he behaved with the
fierceness of a lion to him before, he now appeared like a lamb, meeting him

Roberts, 12mo., pp. 59. London : sold by Luke Hinde, in George Yard,
Lombard Street (price Sixpence)." My copy has no date ; but the Memoirs
are dated Chesham, 4th month, 1725.

14 Meaning a prison-cell.

15 This was, probably, a ball of soft wax, with which seals appended to
official documents were formerly made.

16 Roberts lived at Siddington, somewhat more than nine miles from
Lypiatt.

17 At that time the Old Castle of Gloucester was the County Prison.

with a pleasant countenance, and taking him by the hand, said, 'Friend Hayward, 18 how do you do?' My father answered, 'pretty well'; and then proceeded thus :—'I am come in the fear and dread of Heaven to warn thee to repent of thy wickedness with speed ; * * * and to preach the ever-lasting Gospel to thee.' The Justice replied, 'You are a welcome messenger to me ; that is what I have long desired to hear.' * * * The Justice then caused my father to sit down by him on the couch, and said, 'I believe your message is of God, and I receive it as such. I am sorry that I have done you wrong ; I will never wrong you more. I would pray you to forgive me, and to pray to God to forgive me.' After much more discourse, he offered my father the best entertainment his house afforded, but my father excused himself from eating or drinking with him at that time ; expressing kind acceptance of his love. And so in much love they parted."

John Stephens married four wives ; and by his third wife, a daughter of John Moulson of Hargrave in the county of Chester, he had issue, Thomas, who on his father's death, in August 1679, inherited Lypiatt.

Thomas Stephens married Ann, daughter of ———— Child, of Northwick in the County of Worcester. He served the office of high sheriff of this county in 1693, and was elected one of the knights of the shire in 1713. On his death, in February 1719, Thomas, his son and heir, suc-ceeded to Lypiatt. This Thomas Stephens married Ann, daughter of John Neale, of Deane in the county of Bedford, by whom he had eight children ; and of these, John, his eldest son, inherited Lypiatt.

This John Stephens married Elizabeth, daughter and heiress of Henry Phill, Esq., of London, by whom he had several children ; and died March 19th, 1778, in the eighty-first year of his age.

Of the five generations of the Stephenses who possessed Lypiatt, two only had monumental memorials raised to them in their parish church of Stroud, viz., the first and the last,—the original purchaser, and his great-great-grand-son. The memorial for the former was a large, elaborate, mural erection ; that for the latter, a small, plain, marble tablet, which was not erected until thirty-six years after his burial. He had survived all his children ; and the tablet recorded the touching fact, that "he was the last of the Lypiatt branch of that ancient family." Both these monu-ments stood against the east end wall of the south aisle, above the family vault in the floor below.

In the year 1833, workmen were employed to repair the floor over this vault; and, on taking off one of its large

18 His father's name was John Roberts, *alias* Hayward. The family called themselves Roberts ; but they were commonly known by the name of Hayward, in the place where they lived.

covering stones, they exposed a coffin which had been covered with crimson cloth, and richly ornamented with brass. It much excited the curiosity of the persons present and induced them to attempt the making of further discoveries concerning it. Accordingly, they baled out the water in which the coffin lay, and forced open its lid, which they removed entire. They then cut out the upper half of the lid of an oaken shell within, together with the corresponding portion of an inner lead coffin, to which the shell had been closely fitted.

This done they unfolded a winding-sheet, and disclosed a corpse which had on a cap with radiated points—or "death-crown,"—a crimson neckcloth, and a shroud of fine linen plaited on the breast. [19] The body lay, for two-thirds of its depth, in a darkish antiseptic liquid ; and was so well preserved, (after the lapse of seventy-eight years,) it presented the features of a handsome young man. After a while the workmen became affrighted from any further intermeddling with the corpse. They hastily replaced all the parts of the coffins, except the lead which they had cut from the innermost ; they laid, on the lid of the outer coffin, a loose plate of lead which had been found lying on the inner one, rudely inscribed " Farrington Stephens, aged 20 years " ; [20] and restored the covering stones of the vault. Farrington Stephens was the eldest son of the last John Stephens of Lypiatt, and was buried February 11th, 1775. The face of the corpse was so firm, that the late J. S. Howell, the parish clerk, informed me it was "as hard as iron " ; and that the original plate of the outer coffin (pewter with gilt letters) was taken off and removed to the vestry, where it lay for several years, until it was lost. He also said that close by the coffin already described, were three others, much injured by the water : one of them being suitable for a body about sixteen years old, and the others for infants ; [21] but that they were without lids, and there were no human remains in either of them.

I will not attempt an explanation of these last facts, if they were facts ; but will say that when, in 1793, the low arches which formerly separated the south aisle from the

19 At that time there was a penalty of five pounds for burying a corpse in any other dress than one made of woollen.

20 Mr. Fosbrooke called him Torrington Stephens (vol. 1, 321). But the parish register, as well as the coffin-plate, give it as above.

21 Probably they were the coffins of the three other children of John Stephens, viz. :—John, Elizabeth, and Hester, the two last of whom died infants.

nave, were taken down and replaced by Tuscan columns, the family vault of the Stephenses was broken into, a part of it was appropriated for the foundation of the most easterly of the new pillars, and a very large coffin, (probably that of John Stephens himself,) was displaced to make room for it.

It remains however to be further stated, that when the floor of the new church was being levelled for the purpose of laying down its pavement, the covering stones of this vault were, (on February the 25th, 1868,) again removed, in the presence of the incumbent, Dr. Badcock; and Farrington Stephens' coffin appeared in the state already described as that in which it was left in 1833. But, on lifting off the lead plate, the lid of the outer coffin, and the severed piece of the shell, it was found that the air admitted in 1833 and the intervening thirty-five years had done their work: the head and chest had disappeared, having sunk into the dark liquid that remained in the lead coffin; and this, when examined with a spade yielded fragments of blackened bones. As to the three other coffins mentioned as being in the same vault,—one yet remained there, having a lid, and being, apparently, entire; and an infant's coffin lay crushed in the water of the vault.

On the death of the last John Stephens, the manor and estates of Lypiatt came to Thomas Baghott De la Bere, Esq., of Southam in this county, his nephew and devisee; and he, after disposing of several of its outlying portions by auction, sold the residue, (consisting of the mansion, park, &c.,) to Mr. Paul Wathen, of Woodchester, in February, 1802. In the year 1810, Mr. Wathen was nominated high sheriff of the county: and, when Lord Strangford, (then absent as Ambassador at Lisbon,) was created a Knight Grand Cross of the Order of the Bath, Mr. Wathen was knighted by the Prince Regent, that he might stand proxy for his lordship, whom he represented on that occasion: and, on May 15th, 1812, he— (then Sir Paul Wathen)— obtained the Royal License to take the surname of Baghott. He left a memorial of his being proxy for Lord Strangford in a life-size full-length portrait of himself, standing in the dress of a G.C.B.; except the mantle of the Order, which by way of distinction, is borne on his left arm. This portrait is now in the hall at Lypiatt. From Sir Paul Baghott, Lypiatt became the property of Mr. William Lewis of Brimscomb, who resided there from 1825 to 1842.

On January the 8th, 1842, it passed by sale from Mr. Lewis to Samuel Baker, Esq., who on the 25th February, 1847, sold it to John Edward Dorington, Esq., [22] its present possessor.

It may be thought an interesting coincidence respecting these two latest owners of Lypiatt, that the wife of Sir John Edward Dorington, is the sister of the late Captain Speke, the African traveller, who in 1861, was with Captain Grant, the first European who visited the Lake Victoria Nyanza, (as they named it,) in central Africa, and which they regarded as the chief source of the Nile : and that Mr. Samuel Baker's son, Sir Samuel White Baker, who resided at Lypiatt in his youth, was, on the 14th of March, 1864, the first European who saw and navigated the great Lake Albert Nyanza, (as he named it,) into which the Victoria Nyanza and the other equatorial waters fall, and from which they issue as the entire White Nile. Mr. Baker was knighted for his achievements : and it will not be forgotten that he was accompanied throughout his travels by his stout-hearted wife, who shared all his labors, and often overcame his difficulties and dangers by her tact and courage.

[22 Father of Sir John Edward Dorington, Bart.]

CHAPTER XXXVI.

LYPIATT PARK — OTHER ESTATES IN UPPER LYPIATT TITHING —
MURDER IN BISMORE BOTTOM.

LYPIATT Park is situated on the Cotteswold range, about two miles from Stroud, a mile and a half from Bisley, and nine from Gloucester.

The mansion stands at the edge of a plateau, with its eastern front overlooking the beautiful valley of Stancomb, winding down to Bismore and Toadsmore Bottoms. In a terrier of the estate, made on its purchase by John Stephens in 1624, it is called "a fair house of stone, with brewhouse, malthouse, stable, barns, gardens," &c.; and I have not met with any other description of its architectural features : but, in Sir Robert Atkyns' History of Gloucestershire, there is a print giving a bird's-eye view of it with the detached buildings ; drawn and engraved for that work by J. Kip some short time before 1712. [1]

The chief building, which includes the great hall in its longitudinal direction, has a northerly aspect, and is entered by an embattled porch. The hall forms the entire centre, having the other portions of the edifice at either end, and thus dividing them from one another. It is as lofty as the main walls, and has attics in the roof : the other parts of the house are of two stories, chiefly with attics.

In the front, (and nearly parallel with it, at the distance of about twenty yards,) was "the gatehouse," with a long range of stables, and also the chapel with its tower-steeple, at a somewhat less distance. These were a great protection from the cold winds of that high region, by partly inclosing the court, across which (from the gatehouse) was the general approach to the mansion. In these and other respects,

[1] This is one of the sixty-one views of the seats of the nobility and gentry then residing in the county, which it contains.

LYPIATT PARK.

The Seat of Sir John E. Dorington, Bart. M.P.

Lypiatt House and buildings were, in the year 1803, (as I well remember,) in full accordance with Mr. Kip's print; [2] except that, in the room adjoining the upper end of the hall, sashed windows had superseded two of the mullioned and labelled windows which appear in the print.

The chapel was not specified in the terrier before referred to. The first mention I find of it is in the marriage register of Stroud, where under the date of June 5th, 1688, is entered " Edward Fust Esq., son of Sir John Fust, of Hill in this county, married Ann Mary, daughter of Thomas Stephens of Lypiatt, in the chappell atte Over Lippiatt. " The marriage must have been solemnized there by special license, probably by the minister of Stroud who made the entry: and perhaps the chapel was fitted up for that occasion. Sir Robert Atkyns, in 1712, mentions it as "a handsome chapel, decently kept in repair"; but in 1740, it was a receptacle for lumber. [3]

The hall is twenty-one feet high ; and was, originally, thirty-eight feet six inches long, by twenty-six feet wide ; having along its south wall an open gallery on wooden pillars, with an open passage under it ; and these supplied the means of communication between the several upper and lower parts of the house, which were separated from each other by the intervention of the hall.

Formerly the entrance porch opened directly into the side of the hall, at its lowest end ; as did also the small room over the porch.

From the gallery spectators could look down upon the feasts and other gatherings in the hall ; and in the room over the porch musicians could he placed as was wont, to entertain the guests or lead the dancers. The access to this room was through a trap-door in the floor, by means of a step-ladder from the porch ; as is indicated by marks yet remaining in the plaister of the ceiling. At some later period the passage from the porch across the lower end of the hall was inclosed, by a partition of its whole height. This reduced the length of the hall to thirty feet six inches, and rendered it more comfortable as a banqueting room ; the gallery and passage, however, remained open to it as

2 It is not meant, however, that the several parts were drawn by him on an exact scale, or in exactly relative proportions.

3 It appears from an "inventory of the effects of John Stephens, in and about his house, &c., at Over Lupiat in 1740, " that the chapel contained "one cider press, one grind-stone, three hen-coops, and two pairs of steps."

before. It was lighted by a lofty embattled bay window, near its upper end ; and by two square transom labelled windows lower down : and I remember it in that state.

On Mr. Wathen's becoming the owner of Lypiatt Park he proceeded to make alterations in and about the mansion. He removed the gatehouse and the whole range of stables from before the front, with many of the domestic and other buildings in its rear. He took down part of the front wall of the hall, and rebuilt it with only one window, but that a larger bay window, in the centre, four feet deep, and reaching from the floor to the ceiling. He altered both the sashed and old windows in the apartments at the west end of the house ; and added an advanced square embattled tower, with other buildings in that quarter ; which, in the character of a gothic cloister, he extended at a right angle to the chapel. He also added considerably to the length of the east front, and made the passage from the old porch continuous with it, which he finished with a handsome gothic porch, as the garden entrance, bearing the inscription "NISI DOMINUS." Among other alterations within the mansion he partitioned off the open gallery and passage in the hall, which reduced its width to twenty feet six inches ; thereby restoring its old relative dimensions, and making it still more comfortable as a dining room. He decorated its ceiling with a fine copy of Guido's Aurora, which nearly covered it ; 4 and adorned its south side with two large pieces of exquisite Gobelins tapestry, one representing Queen Esther being attired for her interview with King Ahasuerus, and the other his kind reception of her,—the figures being life-size.

When Mr. Lewis came into possession, he made several other improvements, as did Mr. Baker ; and Sir John Dorington and his father have very much enlarged and embellished the whole house at various times. They have, moreover, very much increased the extent of the surrounding estate, by various and important additions, comprising some of the most beautiful scenery in the neighbourhood.

Amongst the Estates in Upper Lypiatt tithing, are those which formerly belonged to the ancient family of Arundel of the Field. The mansion called "The Field" is pleasantly situated on the south side of the highway from Lower-street, Stroud to Bowbridge. It stands on the site of "a

4 Its place is now supplied by a representation of the story of Mutius and Porsenna.

certain ancient messuage called Huckvale-place, of which Richard Arundel died seized with the lands thereto belonging, together with Prowle Grove in Lypiate Superior," as appears by the Escheator's Inquisition, 42nd Elizabeth, about 1598. 5 Huckvale-place stood nearly in the centre of the estate, when it extended—as it once did—over almost the whole southern side of the hill, from its spine or ridge above, down to the River Froom in the valley below ; including the ground on which all the town above Nelson- street was built, together with what has been previously described as its early enlargement.

The connection of this family with the Freams of Lower Lypiatt—from whom they inherited part of their old estate —appears by their children sometimes bearing the baptismal name of Fream before their patronymic of Arundel. Fream Arundel, who died in 1805 aged nineteen years, was the last lineal descendant of this old family ; and his father James Arundel, who survived him, was the last of the name who possessed the Field and its remaining estates. These now belong to the Rev. J. C. C. B. P. Hawkins, (who married Elizabeth the daughter of the Rev. John Gregory of Hordley,) and his issue in tail. The Arundel's portion of Prowle—or rather Prowd—Grove has been converted into pasture ground. It is situated on the hill, beyond the uppermost part of the town ; and the road now called Middle Hill is the present, as it was the ancient, way into it.

At some small distance from this Prowd Grove, is the Prowd Grove of William Capel, Esq. ; the largest portion of the woodland ground originally of that name.

Beyond this in a narrow ravine or comb in the hill-side, is the dwelling-house and homestead of Abbey Farm, the property of Mr. John Phipps : and here are the remains of a Wych Elm that had been long noticed for its great age and size. This tree was thus mentioned in an Address read at Gloucester, February 15th, 1859, by T. B. Ll. Baker, Esq., to the Cotteswold Naturalists' Field Club, of which he was the president.

" It is hardly to be matched in England. Alas ! we were unprovided with measures. We decided, however, that it was about sixty feet in circumference ; and though only a thin shell of wood was attached to the bark, yet the latter

---

5 So says Mr. Rudder's History, p. 713. Probably, however, Prowle is a mis-print or mistake ; for, in all the title deeds I have seen, it is called, and is now universally known, by the name of Prowd Grove.

was entire with the exception of a gap some three feet wide, by which we entered, and a hole cut in the opposite side through which a handle had worked, when the hollow had been used as a shed for a cider-press. The shell, I think, was from fifteen to twenty feet high ; and from thence rose a very vigorous growth of young wood, which is frequently topped to prevent its weight from breaking its thin shell of trunk. The manner in which the bark has rounded the edges of some of the small holes in the tree, and formed a complete rose in the hollow is very curious."

A measurement of the trunk of this old tree was made in 1852, when its circumference at the base was found to be fifty-one feet, and its height sixteen feet ; and, besides having once contained "a cider press," cows have been milked, calves fattened, and pigs kept in it by various tenants of the farm.

The years through which this tree has lived, have been very eventful years : but their whole story may be briefly told in the fact that, while its leaves have periodically fallen and been renewed, sixteen successive generations of men have been passing away, and working out their portion of the world's history. [5a]

We must now turn back to notice the pleasant valley of Horns. The way to it from the town is through "The Fields," entering them near Trinity Church.

It is well known to the young, for with them it is a favourite walk ; and many of the aged remember it with quiet pleasure as the scene of their early enjoyment. But the spoiler, in the shape of the builder of a whole town of small houses and shops, has been there, and it has long since lost its former rural beauty and interest. Its bosky banks and sheltering trees have been cut down, to widen and straighten the roads through it ; and with them have disappeared the choice places where children gathered wild flowers, and collected the pretty spiral snail shells that lurked in the grass. Here, too, the lover [5b] has loitered to indulge his dreams of fancy ; and here, in my youth, I met with the following lines, delicately carved in small capital letters, on the smooth bark of a secluded beech tree :—

Love was always kind to me,
'Till he fix'd my soul on THEE ;
And, if thou unkind remain,
He'll unfix my soul again.

[5a This tree has now in its turn passed away.]

[5b The old Author himself.]

This place was, however, visited by someone who had no sympathy with the young dreamer; for, within a few days, the verses were scored through, and nearly destroyed: and perhaps the dream itself had passed away as soon.

In the summer of the year 1868, I went through the public part of the valley to take a last look, and to compare its then present, with its former condition—so well, and so fondly remembered: but the picture of it in my mind's eye was rudely effaced by what I saw; and it did not return until I had been sometime removed from the effect of the (comparatively) unlovely reality. But, even then I espied among the wild luxuriance, some such flowers as had bloomed there of old. At the same time, I regretted to see that Holliwell (Holywell) Thicket had been cut down, and the well dried up, for want of the abundant foliage that formerly surrounded it.

Another estate in this division of the parish is Hill House, belonging to Richard Wyatt, Esq., J.P. It was formerly part of the possessions of the Ridlers of Edgeworth. From them it passed by conveyance of Samuel Ridler, in 1754, to Thomas Crozier, Esq., of London. From him it came to his nephew Thomas Crozier Arundel, then to James Arundel his brother and heir; and, on his death, to his widow Ann Arundel. She gave it to her nephew, Thomas Handy Bishop; and he sold it, together with Hill Farm, to Mr. Wyatt, in the year 1853. It is situated about a mile above Stroud, on the road to Bisley, just below the ridge of the high level of the Cotteswold range at that place; and has a grand view of the vales of Stroud and Stonehouse, the river Severn, and the Forest of Dean beyond. Prior to the abolition of military tenures, this estate, (as part of the Honor of Hereford,) was holden in Chivalry or by knight's service;—the tenant *in capite* being, in the reign of Charles the First, Henry Lord Stafford: and the title discloses the remarkable circumstance that both Lord Stafford the mesne Lord, and Nathaniel Ridler, his sub-tenant in fee, were minors at the same time,—and each of them purchasing from his immediate lord the seignorial right of wardship and marriage, to which tenure in chivalry was subject. The king, accordingly, as lord paramount, granted or released such his right to the Earl of Arundel and Surrey, as trustee for Lord Stafford; and the earl, as such trustee, made a similar concession to Ridler, by virtue of which he became entitled to choose a wife for himself with impunity, and further was exonerated from other feudal exactions incidental to that honorable, but oppressive, tenure.

Here too is Kilminster's Farm, the property of W. H. Paine, Esq., M.D.; having a charming prospect of the whole Slade valley.

Beyond this is Fennels, originally a part of Upper Lypiatt estate. It passed from Sir Paul Baghott to Mr. Lewis, from him to Henry Wyatt, Esq., of Farm Hill, by sale, in 1842, and now belongs to his three daughters.

The mills in the tithing of Upper Lypiatt are :—Bad-brook mill belonging to Mr. Daniel Wood, and Wallbridge grist-mill, of which Mr. Sidney Biddell is the owner, [6] both being on the river Slade; Capel's mill, with the Brick House and Mansell's Mead, belonging to Mr. Arthur Capel; Arundel's mill, dyehouses, &c., late the property of Mr. Edwin Gyde, and now of Mr. John T. Woolwright; and Bowbridge mill, belonging to Mr. James Robinson, all on the river Froom; and Newcombe's mill, the property of Mr. J. Y. Sandys, situated on the small stream that flows down the pretty valley of Horns into the Froom at Bowbridge, where it divides the tithings of Upper and Lower Lypiatt from each other.

The mention of Bismore Bottom in the early part of this chapter, brings to mind the following circumstances. Bismore Bottom is a lonely, narrow, and thickly wooded valley. On its side there were formerly three or four scattered cottages called Cuthams. Two of them belonged to William Wicks, in one of which he lived alone; and the other was inhabited by Hannah Warren, a widow, with two sons—Edmund Thomas Warren, aged eighteen, and John Warren, aged nearly sixteen years. Thomas Cox a poor weaver aged sixty-seven, cohabited with this woman and visited her once a week, but he lodged at the Thrupp.

About six o'clock in the evening of Thursday, January 28, 1830, Cox came to Hannah Warren; and shortly passed on in the direction of Wicks' house, saying he was going to meet somebody, but would be back soon. In about half-an-hour he returned; and in the presence of the boys eagerly asked for water and washed his hands, which he said he "had made in a mess" before he came away. He wiped his hands and face with "some rags" that were

[6 The largest part of this mill was consumed by fire on the 26th of April, 1872.]

in the window, "and rubbed both sides of his clothes down before." He afterward requested a clean pair of stockings, which Mrs. Warren brought and helped him to put on, and threw the dirty ones among some linen she had to mend and wash. He put on his shoes, which had been dried at the fire, and between eight and nine o'clock p.m., departed for his lodgings, where his son, William Cox, was sitting up late awaiting his return. On the following Saturday morning, and again in the evening, Thomas Cox came to Hannah Warren's cottage and both of them sat up all night: he dozing sometimes in the window seat, and she drying and ironing linen, including one of Wicks' shirts that she had washed for him. About ten o'clock on the following morning, Sunday the 31st, after some significant hesitation, Hannah Warren went up to Wicks' cottage with his shirt, and on entering it, she saw him lying across the threshold of an inner room. On this she gave an alarm to John Ridler, who was in his garden at a short distance off; and on going in, it was discovered that Wicks had been murdered by several blows on his forehead, temple and neck, with a hatchet which lay by his side covered with blood. It appeared that he had been dead several days. Other persons were called in, and the horrid fact soon became known.

Suspicion of the crime soon fell on Thomas Cox, who had been heard to speak mysteriously of a hoard of money he supposed might be found in Wicks' house; and who had tried, in vain, to get cashed two bills of the Gloucester Bank of Evans and Jelf, who had been bankrupts in 1815. Those bills—the worthless semblance of money—had belonged to Wicks, and were all that was believed to have been stolen from his house or person on the murder. Thomas Cox was apprehended, and arraigned at the next Gloucestershire Assizes, found guilty, and hanged.

It was generally thought that both William Cox the son, and Hannah Warren, were privy to the murder; indeed, the jury at the Coroner's inquest delivered their verdict against William Cox, as an accessory before the fact. The evidence against Thomas Cox being wholly circumstantial, it was at first thought necessary on the part of the prosecution, to bring forward both of them as witnesses. Accordingly Hannah Warren and her two sons were examined at the trial and gave their testimony; but, finally, William Cox's evidence was dispensed with.

At the Coroner's inquest, one Charles Davis testified that on the third night after the dead body of Wicks was found, he slept with William Cox at Chalford Lynch. That, on the following morning he asked Cox, (who had a restless night,) whether he had dreamed of the murdered man, to which he replied—" No I did not :" but soon after he said, " I told you a lie, I did dream of him ; I dreamed that I lay in bed with my arm round the murdered man ; and that I asked him,—' Poor man, do you know who murdered you?'" So appalling are the forms into which conscience can shape the troubled fancies of sleeping men ! His waking realities were not less painful. He was unable to obtain employment at the mills, because other men refused to work with him. He then became the tall, thin, melancholy man who wandered for some time about Stroud as a costermonger, with a basket upon his arm. At length he committed theft, and died a convict on his passage to a penal settlement abroad.

CHAPTER XXXVII.

LOWER LYPIATT—LYPIATT HALL—THRUPP—ESTATES AND MILLS
IN THE TITHING—SAMUEL WEBB OF DOLEMAN'S HAM—
BRIMSCOMB—MIDDLE LYPIATT.

THE tithing of Lower Lypiatt—sometimes called
Nether Lypiatt and Lypiatt Inferior—forms another
division of the parish.

The manor was held of the honor of Hereford, and
belonged to the ancient family of the Freames, who had a
seat there called Lypiatt Hall. By an inquisition (24th
February, 41st Elizabeth) it was found that Robert Freame
died seized in fee-tail of the manor of Nether Lypiatt,
with the Way House in Over and Nether Lypiatt, at
money rents ; and of The Throppe, held of Lord Stafford,
by the yearly rent of a pound of cummin.

About the year 1689, the estates of Freame were divided
between three co-heiresses by a decree in Chancery and
deeds pursuant thereto ; and subsequently Charles Coxe,
Esq., married an heiress of this family, who carried with
her the manor. He was one of the judges of Wales, and
served in several Parliaments for the borough of Cirencester. His son John Coxe who succeeded him, was also
in 1748 elected a representative in Parliament for the
same borough. From him the estates descended to Miss
Coxe, who was married to Robert Gordon, Esq., and subsequently to their only daughter. Charles Coxe rebuilt
the mansion, which is a large edifice situated near the edge
of a steep rocky valley, and there he resided : but for
many years past, it has been occupied by the tenant farmer
of the land belonging to it. It still contains a few dilapidated articles of antique furniture, with other tokens of
his residence : and, near to a part of its once ornamental
grounds, is a noticeable monument which he erected to the
memory of a favorite horse. It is approached by numerous

rude steps, leading down to the wooded ravine known as Lower Lypiatt Wood, on the upper slope of which it stands. The monument consists of an obelisk of the height of twelve feet, raised on a pedestal three feet square and four feet six inches high ; which formerly contained an inscription on a tablet in its eastern side. The tablet has been cut out, and is now lost ; but the traditions of the farm, (as preserved by Mrs. Ridler, a former tenant's wife,) give the inscription as follows :—

> "My name was Wag, that rolled the green,
> The oldest horse that ever was seen.
> My years—they numbered forty-two—
> I served my master just and true."

This tithing lies on the south side of Stroud hill ; and extends from Bowbridge to the extremity of the parish on the east, and from Upper Lypiatt division down to the river Froom. It includes Thrupp, and part of the hamlet of Brimscomb, which are the most picturesque portions of the Stroud valley. [1]

The Thrupp, (as it is named in old documents, and as it was generally called until a few years since,) is now called Thrupp, only. The village consists of two distinct clusters of houses, which stand a considerable distance apart, and are designated Near Thrupp and Far Thrupp, in reference to their respective distances from Stroud.

Its name is said to be probably derived from the Icelandic, in which language "Throp, Thrup and Trop, mean a hill or elevated spot"; or, yet more probably, from the Danish, in which it is said to mean "an aggregation of men or houses,—a village":[2] and with both these representations it corresponds. Its population is considerable ; and to it belongs that scrap of sound sententious philosophy—

> "Nothing put down, nothing take up,
> Say the boys of The Thrupp."

Here is an estate called Thrupp Farm, which, including Way House, formerly belonged to the Freames. In the year 1779 it was the property of James Clutterbuck, from whom it came to William Clutterbuck Chambers ; and

---

1 The chief part of Brimscomb is in the parish of Minchinhampton, on the south side of the river Froom.

2 Vide, *Quarterly Review* of Isaac Taylor's "Words and Places," &c., July, 1864, vol. xiii., No. 231, p. 20.

on his death, March 6th, 1850, it passed by devise to his brother Francis Chambers, whose devisees are its present owners.

The late William Stanton, Esq., had a good house and small estate here, including Stafford's Mill, &c. The house, (which is called The Thrupp, to distinguish it from the *village* of Thrupp,) was built by him ; and, with the estate, belonged to his eldest son William Henry Stanton, Esq., J.P., who was elected a representative in Parliament for the borough of Stroud in June, 1841, and again in July, 1847,—but retired on the dissolution of parliament in July, 1852. The Mill and its appurtenances belong in common, to him, and to the Rev. Joseph John Stanton, and Walter John Stanton, two of his nephews. 3 (Mr. W. H. Stanton is since dead.)

Above Stafford's Mill is Gryffin's Mill ; so called from the name of the family who owned and occupied it from before the year 1600 to September 1788, when Thomas Gryffin the last possessor died, aged eighty years. He was that same " Justice Thomas Gryffin " who has been already specially mentioned in connection with Captain Hawker and old Justice Wyatt; 4 and was the last of his family and name in the neighbourhood. On his decease, the estates were disposed of in lots by auction ; and the mill now belongs to Mr. Charles Hooper.

Beyond this place—following the upward course of the river,—is " Ham Mill." Its ancient name was Doleman's Ham ; and in a deed of January 30th, 43rd Elizabeth, William Webb released it by that name to Nicholas Webb and Thomas Webb. It was enfeoffed to Samuel Webb, the 18th July, 1634 ; and was, by his grandson, Samuel Webb, settled on the issue of his marriage with Elizabeth Smart his intended wife, in 1685. On his death it descended to his only son Robert Webb, who died without issue, May 13th, 1735. Doleman's Ham included a considerable landed estate, situated on both sides of the Froom : and, by a deed dated May 20th, 1685, there was granted, among its appurtenances, "the liberty of fishing from Chalford to Dudbridge, in the river Stroudwater." At present no one claims this extensive privilege ; and probably it could not have been practically exercised

3 This large clothing manufactory is included within the boundary line of one mile, as defined by the Stroud Improvement Act.

4 See pp. 68, 69.

at any former time. The mill was partially destroyed by
fire in 1841, and again in 1866 ; but it has been rebuilt, and
is now the property of Mr. Ritchie.

In the Civil War, the opulent clothiers of the large manufacturing district in which this mill lies, having frequent
intercourse with the woolstaplers of Cirencester and the
merchants of Bristol, had special need of protection against
the military holding those places, or passing through the
neighbourhood. Among those clothiers was the first above
named Samuel Webb, of Doleman's Ham Mill ; and to him,
both Prince Maurice and Prince Rupert granted protections
or safeguards. The Protection of Prince Maurice runs
thus : —

" Prince Maurice Count Palatine of ye Ryne
Duke of Bavaria and Collonell of Horse

To Samuel Webb of Stroude water Clothyer.

Forasmuch as ample satisfaction hath beene given of your allegiance to his
Majesty's and your readyness in his Majesty's service and comands. By vertue
of the power & authority given me.   These are to signify — that noe Officer
or Souldyer or other person whatsoever, whom it doth or may concern do
hence forwards presume to plunder any your houses or take or carry away
any your goods horses Sheep Oxen Beasts or other Cattle upon any pretence
whatsoever, As they shall answer the contrary, att their uttmost perill.   Given
under my hand and seale att armes att my Quarter att Cirencester, the tenth
day of February Anno dni 1642.

To his Ma^{ty} Commanders   Provided that you give no
Officers & Souldyers whom   contribution or assistance to
it doth or may concern   the Rebbels
                           MAURICE."

The Safeguard of Prince Rupert is as follows : —

" By virtue of the Authoritie and power given to mee from our Sovereigne
Lord King Charles under the Great Seale of England as Generall under his
Matie of all his Maties force of horse whatsoever I do hereby straightway charge
and command you & every of you whom it may concerne that ymediatelie
upon sight or knowledge herreof you doe no manner of harme, violence,
Iniurie or detryment by unlawfull plunderinge to Samuel Webb of Nether
Lippiat Cloathyer in ye County of Gloster in his person ffamilie, house Goode
and Chattles whatsoever directlie or indirectlie by your selves or others As
you will answere ye contrairie at your utmost perrills.   Given at Bristol under
my hande and Seale at Armes this sixt day of August 1643.

                           RUPERT." [5]

To all Commanders Officers and
Souldyers whatsoever of or any
way belonging to his Ma^{tis} Army

[5] Both the original safeguards are in the possession of Sir John E.
Dorington Bart.

Prince Maurice's Protection bears date at Cirencester on the eighth day after that town was assaulted and taken by the King's forces under Prince Rupert, who left his brother Maurice in command of it. But, in the mean while, —on the Saturday before its date,—" they," the Royalists, " took away cloth, wool, and yarn, besides other goods from the clothiers about Stroudwater, to the utter undoing of them and theirs "; as part of the great plunder they made by the capture of Cirencester. 6

New House, (to which we now proceed,) stands at the extremity of Far Thrupp. It formerly belonged to the much respected family of Wathen, who resided there, and carried on a large clothing business for many years at Thrupp Mill which is now the property of the trustees of the will of the late Mr. John Ferrabee. Major Samuel Wathen, J. P., who commanded the Severn Volunteer Rifle Corps, of which mention has already been made, died here January 6th, 1817, aged fifty years. His widow and daughters were very zealous patrons and supporters of the Charity Schools in that part of the parish ; but they, and every member of their family have long since left the neighbourhood. New House now belongs to Mr. Philip Evans.

Brimscomb lies at the upper end of this tithing, where is an ancient house formerly called Biggs's Place, with extensive clothing mills adjoining. It was the property of William Dallaway, Esq., who served the office of high sheriff of the county in 1766 ; and was an eminent clothier until his death in 1776. It afterward belonged to Mr. William Lewis ; but its present owner is Mr. Evans.

Of the family of Dallaway there is not any individual now living in this neighbourhood. The last of them resident here was Mr. Joseph James Dallaway of Rowcroft ; whence he retired to Cheltenham in 1834. He was the youngest son of the high sheriff ; and died at Bath in 1859, aged eighty-five years. His representative is his son Mr. Joseph Dallaway of that city.

There was another of this family, who demands a more especial notice, on account of his literary reputation — the Rev. James Dallaway, M.B. and F.S.A. He was the son

6 See "A Relation of the taking of Cirencester, on Thursday, Feb. 2, 1642." Printed in London, 1642. (Feb. 20th) This, however, is the parliamentarian account of the transaction.

of Mr. James Dallaway, a brother of the high sheriff, and, (as before mentioned,) an early banker of Stroud.

The Rev. James Dallaway, was born in 1763, and officiated as curate of Rodborough from 1787 to 1793. During the early part of this period, he resided at the Fort on Rodborough hill, and afterward at Gloucester,—journeying thence to perform his Sunday clerical duties. Then it was that he wrote his "Journey from Rodborough to Gloucester, with a description of the country and an account of the Cathedral." 7 He soon after accompanied Lord Bute to Constantinople, as chaplain and physician of the Embassy to the Porte. He was librarian and secretary to Charles Howard, eleventh Duke of Norfolk ; and died at his vicarage of Leatherhead, in Surrey, June 6, 1834. He had great abilities ; but was pedantic and satirical. The following are among his publications : — " Inquiries into the Origin and Progress of Heraldry in England," &c., Royal 4to. 1793 ; "Constantinople, Ancient and Modern," &c. 4to London, 1797 ; " Lady Mary Wortley Montague's Letters," 5 vols., 1803 ; "Anecdotes of the Arts in England," London, 8vo., 1800; "Horace Walpole's Anecdotes of Painting in England, enlarged," &c.; "A Series of Discourses on Architecture— Military, Ecclesiastical, and Civil," 8vo., 1806 ; and "Antiquities of Bristol in the Middle Centuries," 8vo.

The remaining mills on the Froom in this tithing, are Bourne mill, late the property of Mr N. S. Marling, but now of Messrs. Grist and Co. ; and Dark mill, belonging to the Rev. William George. To these may be added the following, as being in the same tithing : — Lewiston mill, lately erected and named by Messrs. Grist, Son, and Co. ; Gussage mill, Iles's mill, and Todsmore mill, but all these four lie on the small Todsmore stream, which falls into the Froom near this place.

Besides the two Lypiatts already mentioned, there is another, called Middle Lypiatt ; but it is not any recognized division of the parish. It was a possession of the Knights Hospitallers of St. John of Jerusalem ; and was granted to John Pope, 36 Henry VIII. He sold it to Henry Fowler, who died seized, leaving William Fowler, his brother and heir, who sold it 33rd Elizabeth, by licence of alienation,

7 A MS. copy of this "Journey" was in the possession of Mr. Delafield Phelps, of Chavenage House. See his "Collectanea Gloucestriensis." London : Nichols, Pall Mall, 1842.

under the name of *one half of the manor of Nether Lipiat*, to Richard Stephens, [8] who died seized. From hence this estate came by purchase to the Leversages ; and in 1799, it belonged to Mr. Peter Leversage, who resided there with great hospitality for many years. It was sold in 1845 by his grandson, Peter Leversage, Esq., barrister-at-law, to the late Henry Wyatt, Esq., of Farm-Hill. The mansion and a part of the estate lie in the tithing of Upper Lypiatt ; but the remainder, (which is its largest portion,) is in Lower Lypiatt : and probably it obtained its name from being locally situated between the two several estates of Upper Lypiatt and Lower Lypiatt. It now consists of two farms ; one of which retains its original name of Middle Lypiatt, and the other is called Ferris Court : and both of them, together with Fennel's already mentioned, belong to the three surviving daughters of Mr. Wyatt.

8 See Fosbrooke, i. 340.

CHAPTER XXXVIII.

STEANBRIDGE TITHING—ITS MILLS, ETC.—ROUTE OF KING
CHARLES'S ARMY TO BESIEGE GLOUCESTER.

THE tithing of Steanbridge lies on the lower slope of
the north side of Stroud-Hill, between the tithing of
Upper Lypiatt and the river Slade; and extends from Badbrook on the west, to its extremity, in the rural hamlet of
Elcombe, on the east.

The lowest mill on the stream in this division is "Little
Mill" already mentioned, which lately belonged to Mr
Ockford.

The next above, is "New Mills": and here, in the year
1766, a large dwelling-house was erected by Mr. Thomas
Baylis, the owner of the mills and a considerable adjoining
estate. The edifice, when completed, consisted of a central
line one hundred and twenty feet long, and of a wing sixty-
eight feet long, proceeding from each end at a right angle
with it — the north end including the mill. It formed three
sides of a large rectangle, though not an equilateral one;
and, being built on one plan, and in a uniform style of
architecture throughout, it was a handsome structure of
imposing appearance. It stands, with the lawn before it, on
an artificially raised foundation that fills the bottom of the
narrow valley from side to side; and has a pleasant western
aspect. It is well represented in the print of it given in
Mr. Rudder's "History of Gloucestershire."

A large octagonal hall, of the whole height of the building,
formed the centre of the middle line, which is judiciously
broken by the projecting forward of three sides of the
octagon. This hall was fitted up with an organ: and the
house being elegantly furnished, it was opened by Mr.
Baylis to his numerous friends, with a great entertainment
that was long remembered. On that occasion, however, it

New Mills Court & Mills.

very unfortunately happened that a young gentleman, one of the dancers, walking out in the cool evening air, fell into a deep unprotected area, and was killed. One of the sitting-rooms had been retained from the older building that formerly stood there. It opened upon a pleasant garden retreat, and was called "The summer parlour"; and there Mr Baylis' visitors were frequently received. [1]

The whole of this gentleman's property came to his son Daniel Baylis, who disposed of it by public auction about the year 1810; and not one of his immediate descendants remains in the neighbourhood. The dwelling-house, with the mills and some of the land, belonged for several years after to Messrs. William and Mashiter Helme, who made additions to the house, and resided there; but it is now the property and residence of Mr. Libby, and is called "New Mills Court." — Slade House and farm, other part of Mr. Baylis' property, belong to Mr. J. Y. Sandys; and, another part of it, to the Rev. F. C. Fisher. Beyond these is Stroud-Slad farm, the property, of William Capel, Esq.: and higher up the stream, are The Vatch Mills.

Beyond them is the house called "The Knapp," which, with its appertaining estate, formerly belonged to Mr. John Allaway, who resided there for many years. He was a kind, good old gentleman, who duly came to the parish church on Sunday mornings, riding on a double horse, — i.e. a horse carrying two persons, — bringing his wife on a pillion behind him. The house obtained its name from being situated on the ridge of the narrow ravine that breaks laterally into the valley at this place. [2]

The three tithings already described compose the largest portion of the parish; and, at their upper extremity, they also form its widest part, — where they share in the interest that belongs to the following event.

1 A summer parlour was a favorite room in many of our large old dwelling-houses. It had an outer door opening into a garden, with walks between plashed trees, and clipped edges of yew and hornbeam: and was probably the original of the "trim gardens" of Milton's "Il Penseroso." The writer remembers just such another summer parlour at Bridge-end, in the parish of Stonehouse: and their former prevalence is evidenced by the translator of the Book of Judges in our authorised version of the Bible, who called the chamber in which Eglon, king of Moab, was slain by Ehud, "a summer parlour."— Judges iii. v. 20.

2 This ravine is mentioned in chapter xxxvi., with the aged wych elm then standing in it. (See p. 204.)

When, in the Civil war, King Charles moved his army from Bristol to undertake the siege of Gloucester, he chose the route over the Cotteswolds, in order to avoid the dangers of the open country that lay more directly between those places. Accordingly, on the 8th day of August, 1643, they marched from Bristol to Tetbury, a distance of twenty miles ; where his Majesty dined, and then proceeded to Cirencester to Sir William Master's " to supper and bed." On the next day, the army proceeded to Hampton Road, (as Minchinhampton was sometimes called, 3) and descended into the Stroud valley at Brimscomb. Here they crossed the river Froom ; and, ascending the steep south side of Stroud hill by way of Quar-house, passed directly in front of Lypiatt Hall. In traversing the summit of this hill, — (from whence stragglers might look down on the town of Stroud on its lower slope,) they left Middle Lypiatt and Lypiatt House on the right, and then, descending obliquely down the north side of the hill, crossed the river Slade at Steanbridge.

From this place they mounted up Wickeridge Hill in the parish of Painswick, and passed over its narrow ridge, at Bull's cross (between The Frith, and Longridge wood ;) where is a fine view of the town of Painswick in its full length and breadth, upon the lower slope of the opposite eminence. Then, descending its north side by way of Greenhouse lane, they passed the brook at the bottom, and entered Painswick by the steep ascent of Tibby-well 4 Lane, after a march of eleven miles. The next day, the 10th, the army crossed over Painswick Hill, and appeared before Gloucester ; when the King, who had arrived at Matson house, Mr. Selwyn's, summoned the city to surrender. — September the 5th, which was only twenty-six days later, saw the royal army again on Painswick Hill, but this time in retreat ; for on that day the King raised the siege of Gloucester, and many thousands of his troops marched in the rain up the hill, on the summit of which they encamped for the night, in the ancient entrenchment of the part called

3 It was so called because there the great high roads from Bath to Gloucester, and from Cirencester to the passage of the Severn at Newnham, met and crossed each other.

4 Tibby-well—is a corruption of St. Tabitha's well.

Spoonbed-hill. 5   There is a tradition that as King Charles
was sitting on a stone near the camp, one of the young
princes asked him — "When shall we go home?"   To
which he returned the mournful reply, " I have no home to
go to."6   He went on to Painswick, and passed the night
there, probably at the Court House.

5 See " Historical introduction to Bibliotheca Gloucestriensis, " p. 73. 4to.
Gloucester, 1825.

6 Rudder's " History, " 592.

CHAPTER XXXIX.

PAKENHILL TITHING — FARM HILL — FIELD PLACE — STRATFORD
WHITESHILL AND RUSCOMB — REV. JOSEPH WHITE, D.D.

THE tithing of Pakenhill, now frequently called Paganhill, is the outlying portion of the parish, separated
from the west side of its other part in the manner already
described.[1] It contains the considerable village of Pakenhill, situated about a mile from Stroud.

It can still boast of a May-pole, as it has done from time
immemorial : and, probably, it is the only one in the
county or for many miles round it. Whit-Monday was the
annual festival on which the inhabitants erected their may-
pole, or embellished it with fresh paint, and hung it with
fresh garlands for the occasion ; and then they danced on
the Green, which now forms part of the lawn and garden of
Upfield. But, in setting up one, on the 20th of May, 1804,
it fell down by the breaking of a stay-rope, and killed two
children. This sad accident prevented all the further proceedings intended for the day, as also the erection of any
other may-pole for several years : and it gave Charles
Offley, Esq., of Upfield, an opportunity of providing a Well
and Pump of water, much needed for the village. This he
did, at his own expense, on the place where the may-pole
had stood ; and in the hope that it would be regarded as a
preferable substitute for the *Pagan*-like may-pole, in future.
But, so great was the attachment of the people to a may-
pole that, after Mr Offley's decease, they set up another as
near the site of the old one as it might be ; and suffered

[1] See page 6.

the Pump to fall into decay and disuse for many years, until it was recently restored by the Board of Health. At present, the may-pole, (eighty-four feet high,) and the pump stand side by side ; but the aged Blacksmith and Nestor of the village, lamented to me the decay of old institutions and rural recreations, — predicting that this will be the last may-pole erected in Pakenhill.

The manor, like the manors of Upper and Lower Lypiatt, was formerly held of the honour of Hereford. Thomas Warner, died seized of Pakenhill, 17th Charles I. ; and was followed by his son William. To him succeeded Thomas Warner, whose son Thomas died in April 1736 ; and, under his will, Henry Wyatt, Esq., his sister's son, became possessed of the estates of the Warners. He was "old justice Wyatt" the father of John Hyde's pupil, and one of the noted Triumvirate of *bon vivants* previously mentioned. 2 He died in 1784 and his estates were purchased by Mr. Richard Cook of Lodgemore, who erected the handsome mansion called Farm Hill, near the site of the house wherein the old Justice resided.

Farm Hill is situated above the village of Pakenhill, on the lower ascent of Whiteshill, and commands a very interesting semi-circular view, which takes in Stroud, the entrance to Woodchester valley, and the opposite side of the vale of Stonehouse. Mr. Cook did not live to occupy the mansion he had built ; 3 but dying, left Richard Cook, his eldest son and heir, his successor. Elizabeth Anne, the daughter and only child of Richard Cook the son, was married to Mr. Joseph Cripps of Cirencester ; and by them, Farm Hill with a contiguous portion of the estate was sold to Henry Wyatt, Esq., of Stroud, in the year 1833.

Mr. Wyatt made improvements at Farm Hill, among which was a new carriage-drive to the mansion through the grounds, from a point near the village. He had been a warm friend to the abolition of negro-slavery ; and, on its being at length accomplished, 4 he erected a handsome stone arch, as a memorial of the event.

2 See page 68.

3 It was said that just before its completion, he dreamed that he was going into it, when the figure of Death met him, and prevented his entrance.

4 By Act 3rd and 4th William IV., c. 73, 28th August, 1833 which took effect from August 1st, 1834.

It bears the following inscription on a tablet over the front : —

" ERECTED TO COMMEMORATE THE ABOLITION
OF SLAVERY IN THE BRITISH COLONIES,
THE FIRST OF AUGUST, A.D. MDCCCXXXIV,"

and on another tablet over the inner side : —

" DEDIT DEUS LIBERTATEM,
DETUR DEO GLORIA."

This arch forms the gateway of the new approach. Mr. Wyatt lived there in great esteem and usefulness, until his death, January the 24th, 1847.[5] His three surviving daughters are the present owners of Farm Hill estate.

The remainder of the Warner estates and other estates, which had belonged to Mr. Richard Cook the son, are now the property of his grand-daughter, Anne, the wife of Joseph Watts Hallewell, Esq., J.P.

The family of the Fields was long resident in this division of the parish. Thomas Field, Esq., died in 1510 ; and was buried on the south side of the old parish church, where an effigy of him was placed, but long since disappeared. From him, Field Place descended through Richard Field, Gentleman, who died in 1693, Edward Field, Esq., J.P., who died in 1736, and Thomas Field, who held it in 1779, — (all in lineal succession,) — to the descendants of his nephew, John de la Field Phelps, Esq., of Dursley. From them it passed, by sale, to Charles Stanton, Esq., in 1840 ; and is now the property of his eldest son, Charles Holbrow Stanton, Esq., Barrister, of Lincoln's Inn.

Stratford is another estate in this tithing. It stands near the entrance of the high road from Badbrook to the village of Pakenhill, after crossing the intervening part of the parish of Painswick. It formerly belonged to Giles Gardner, Esq., J.P., who resided there for several years, possessing considerable influence in the parish, and there he died. In the year 1779, his widow, commonly called Madam Gardner, was in possession ; and she also died there. On

---

5 There was not any kind of relationship between the two Henry Wyatts, —both of whom were J.P.'s, and both owned, and lived and died at Farm Hill.

Field Place, Pakenhill.

the Sunday morning after her decease, while the coffined remains were lying in her chamber, the female servants in charge of the house, were startled by the ringing of the bell that communicated with their mistress's room. Terror prevented their attempting to ascertain its cause, until other servants returned from church ; when they summoned courage to visit the apartment of the dead, and discovered that an owl had made its way down the chimney ; and, in flying about, had entangled its claws in the bellwire, and caused the alarm. Stratford now belongs to J. W. Hallewell, Esq.

On the ascent above Farm Hill is a large tract of nearly level ground, called The Plain. There stands the village of Whiteshill, partly at the head, and partly on the south-east edge, of the lateral valley which runs out from Whiteshill itself, into the inlet already described as the vale of Stonehouse. And, on the north-west side of the same lateral valley, lies the village of Ruscomb, which is, indeed, the proper name of the whole comb or valley itself.

Both these villages are in the parish of Stroud ; and are united by the various cottages on the high road between them, as it runs from the former village on its way to Randwick. The views on this road and from the heights of Whiteshill, Randwick, and the district in general, are such as can hardly be excelled for picturesque beauty and variety in any part of the kingdom.

For many years, and even generations, the population of Whiteshill, Ruscomb, and the immediate neighbourhood, exhibited a very low type and a very degraded state, of social and moral life. It had the evil reputation of supplying all the beggars. [6] This deplorable condition was caused chiefly by its distance from the parish church and town of Stroud, with their civilizing influences ; and thus it continued, notwithstanding the zealous application of many and long-continued individual efforts to ameliorate it. But at length, by the actual residence of a clergyman at Randwick

---

[6] Their begging circuits were not very confined. Upon one occasion, the writer, when travelling in Somersetshire, passed on the turnpike road a Ruscomb beggar-woman with a child in her arms, whose ragged and dirty person was well known to him. And it was a beggar-man of Whiteshill, who, when the writer said to him — "You have been a beggar for five-and-twenty years," — replied, (after consideration,) — "Why, no Sir, not quite so long as that ; I don't think it is above twenty."

from the year 1819; by the erection of a church and schools at Whiteshill, with a resident clergyman there; by a chapel of Congregational dissenters at Ruscomb; and by the other religious and educational processes in operation— the character of the population has been greatly improved, its old opprobrium has well nigh passed away; and the houses, with the habits of their occupants, now wear the usual appearances of comfort and respectability.

This remote part of the parish is specially distinguished as the birth-place of the Rev. Joseph White, D.D., Regius Professor of Hebrew, and Laudian Professor of Arabic, in the University of Oxford. He was born at Ruscomb about the year 1745;[7] but in his infancy his parents removed with him to a cottage in the parish of Randwick.[8] Thomas White, his father, was a broad-weaver; and his son, when a lad, worked with him in his loom for several years. The father was a respectable Latin scholar, with a little knowledge of Greek; and, having a few Latin books, he often read passages from them to his son, rendering them into English as he proceeded; and thus he inspired his young auditor with an early passion for literature. Joseph soon acquired a considerable acquaintance with the Latin language, — although his father discountenanced his close attention to it, when he found it interfered with the operations of the loom. In the prosecution of his studies, Joseph kept his book "pegged to the wall behind the loom": and while his father was uniting the ends of the yarn broken in the process of weaving, the persevering boy snatched a look at the book.

His maternal uncle, George Harmer, frequently called upon him to inquire what progress he made in his learning; and seldom failed to advise his perseverance, — assuring him that God would provide him with friends, and that he would ultimately become a great man: he likewise supplied him with a little money and some books. Thus encouraged, Joseph proceeded with pleasure and alacrity; and such was his ardour, that he frequently sat up three or four nights in a week, studying by the light of a small

7 Some of his biographers say 1746.

8 In 1822, this cottage belonged to Mr. Edward Hogg; and though in a very ruinous condition, he had it rebuilt, from respect for the memory of Dr White.

candle, without a fire even in the depth of winter. At such times he was often wholly deprived of his night's rest, as his father generally called him to the loom at four o'clock in the morning, and frequently kept him there until nine or ten at night. His constitution could not long endure such incessant labour of body and mind, without injury; and some of his sinews became contracted by the peculiar position in which he constantly sat at the loom, so as materially to inconvenience him in his work.

The first circumstance that brought him into notice by the gentlemen who afterward became his patrons and benefactors, was the composition of a theme, for which he took as a motto,—(probably propounded in his own words):—

> " 'Tis kingly to assist a studious youth
> Whose parents can't him due support afford."

In arguing this proposition, he expatiated on " the loathsomeness of vice, the shamefulness of avoidable ignorance, and the folly of suffering the fair garden of the soul to be over-run with the noxious weeds which render human nature odious"; and then he "urged those who were blessed with the means, to assist such as wish to emerge from ignorance, poverty, and vice." This essay he entrusted to his uncle for perusal; but with a request to keep it secret, for that even his father had not seen it. Mr. Harmer soon brought it back,—regretting the injunction to secrecy, because he wished to show it to Joseph Ellis, Esq., of Ebley, who was well known as the ever-ready friend of young men who aspired to distinction in letters or arts. He resided in the house belonging to, and lately occupied by, Mr. Warman, in that village. A few evenings after this, Joseph consented that the theme should be shown to Mr. Ellis, and to him it was taken accordingly on the following morning. He perused it, and requested Mr. Harmer to bring his nephew to Ebley House on an appointed day; when they were kindly received by Mr. Ellis, and introduced to his brothers-in-law—Mr. Lane, a solicitor of Gloucester, and Samuel Jones, M.D., of Stroud. These three gentlemen conversed with young White, and examined him for nearly three hours, when he answered every question proposed to him, except one. They were so much pleased with him and his acquirements, that they gave him a present of money; and soon after made his case known among their friends, to some of whom they introduced him.   This they did so effectually, that, through their influence and example, a subscription was raised, and he was sent to the College School at Gloucester.   While there, he was both clothed and educated at the expense of his patrons ; and medical aid and exercise were resorted to, with a view to remove the contraction of his sinews, and to improve his general health.   When he was sufficiently qualified by his preparatory studies, the same munificent friends sent him to the University of Oxford, where he was entered of Wadham College ; and all his expenses there were defrayed by them.   Soon after his ordination, he visited the place of his nativity; and preached in the parish church of Stroud to a very crowded congregation.—among whom was Mr. Ellis, his chief patron.   In his sermon, being led away by the ardour of his gratitude, he gave public thanks to all his friends, by whose liberality he was enabled to take upon himself the sacred office ; and, fixing his eyes on Mr. Ellis, he addressed to him, personally his most grateful acknowledgments.

On the 19th of February, 1773, he took his degree of M.A., and in 1774 was chosen a Fellow of his college.   He had, by the advice of Dr. John Moore, afterward Archbishop of Canterbury, 9 directed the main bent of his studies to the oriental languages ; having previously acquired a considerable acquaintance with Hebrew learning.   He made such proficiency in this department of literature, that in 1775 he was elected Laudian Professor of Arabic ; on which occasion he delivered a masterly oration, which he printed under the title of " De utilitate Ling. Arab, in Studiis Theologicis, Oratio habita Oxoniis in Scholia Linguarum," vii. Aprilis, 1775, 4to.   In this the professor urged the great importance and utility of the Arabic language, especially in elucidating the Sacred writings ; and enforced with great energy a more general attention to this branch of learning.   It was well received, and many were induced by it to study the Arabic, who had previously deemed it a barren and unprofitable language.

On the recommendation of Bishop Lowth, he was appointed editor of the Philexenian Syriac version of the four gospels, which he published in 1778, from the manuscript which Dr. Gloucester Ridley had given to New

---

9 A native of Gloucester, the son of a butcher, and educated at the Gloucester Grammar School.

College. About this time he was appointed one of the King's preachers at Whitehall ; and, in a sermon delivered before the University of Oxford, he recommended a revisal of the English translation of the Old Testament. In 1780 he published a " Specimen of the Civil and Military Institutes of Timour" or Tamerlane, translated from a Persian version of the Mogul original, written by the conqueror himself. He also added a specimen of Persian poetry. These Institutes having been translated entire by Major Davy, were printed at the Clarendon press in 1783, under the inspection of Professor White, who annexed a preface, indexes, and geographical notes.

In Easter term, 1783, being then a Bachelor of Divinity, he was appointed to preach the Bampton lectures ; and in 1784 he delivered them to the University in a course of nine sermons, which were greatly applauded. They were printed in the same year, and were welcomed by the public with high and very deserved admiration for their learning and eloquence. Their general design was to exhibit the superior excellence of the Christian religion, in a comparison with that of Mahomet. A second edition was published in 1785, with the addition of a tenth sermon, which the author had preached to the University on the duty of propagating the Christian religion, particularly in the East Indies. He graduated Doctor of Divinity, and was presented to the Rectory of Melford, in Suffolk, in 1787 ; and Lord Chancellor Thurlow, without solicitation, presented him with a prebend in the Cathedral of Gloucester, into which he was installed June 21st, 1788. This at once placed him in easy and independent circumstances ; previously to which he had been in great pecuniary difficulties, occasioned by his liberal and too facile disposition, in entertaining scholars who resorted to him for assistance in their Oriental studies, or for temporary support ; but from these difficulties he had been relieved by some of his University friends, who generously discharged the greater portion of his debts.

Dr. White's reputation was now fully established ; and he was looked up to as one of the chief ornaments of the University. But, to his great annoyance, about the latter end of 1788, it was discovered, and became publicly known, that in the composition of his celebrated Bampton lectures, he had been assisted by the masterly pen of the Rev. Mr. Badcock, of South Molton, Devon, and also by Dr. Parr. Mr. Badcock had been a Dissenting minister, but afterward conformed to the Church of England. The fact of his assistance was disclosed soon after his decease in May, 1788 ; and was substantiated by the Professor's letters to him, which fell into the hands of Dr. Gabriel. Dr. Parr's assistance was authenticated by his own admission, "extorted" from him, as he said, "upon hearing the unjust and provoking reports by which the whole of the Bampton lectures were then assigned to Mr. Badcock." Besides the letters, there was found among Mr. Badcock's papers, the Doctor's promissory note for £500, which he at first refused to pay, but afterward liquidated. Nevertheless, in 1789, Dr. Gabriel printed and published the letters, in order, as he professed, to vindicate the character of the deceased, as well as his own, for the part he had taken in the matter.

In consequence of this proceeding, the Professor published at Oxford, in 1790, "A statement of Dr. White's literary obligations to the late Rev. Samuel Badcock, and the Rev. Samuel Parr, LL.D.," in an octavo pamphlet of 109 pages. This statement contained a detailed account of his connection with Mr. Badcock ; and shewed that, though the latter's contributions to the lectures were many and important, they were by no means to the extent, or in the proportion, that had been represented. It was also shown that Dr. Parr's share, which was specified, consisted chiefly of corrections. Thus ended this unhappy case, which at the time caused great contention in the University. The Doctor's apology, (for such his statement must be considered,) gave sufficient satisfaction not only to his fellow academicians, but to the literary world at large. He had early "discovered that, to complete the lectures on the plan he had formed, it was expedient to avail himself of the best help he could procure." But, after all, he is fully entitled to the great celebrity which his Bampton lectures obtained. He was blamable only for not acknowledging his obligations to those elegant scholars, in a preface to the volume when first published.

In March, 1791, he preached the annual Charity sermon in the church of Stroud ; in which, (as the writer, who was then a little boy, well remembers,) he made a graceful allusion to himself, as illustrating the value of education to the poor.

About the year 1790 Dr. White married Miss Turner, of Gloucester, an amiable and accomplished lady ; and thereby vacated his Fellowship of Wadham College. In his rectory-house in Suffolk he prosecuted his studies, and carried on his literary labours; and having set up a printing press, and furnished himself with Oriental types, he and his wife performed the business of compositors, and a man and maid servant that of the press. Here he printed his "Egyptiaca," relating to the antiquities of Egypt, in a handsome folio volume ; and his long promised edition and version of Abdolatif's History of Egypt. In 1799 he published, from the Clarendon press, his "Diatessaron, or Harmony of the four Gospels," in Greek, which he dedicated to the Archbishop of Canterbury ; and was a work of great use to biblical students. In 1802 he was made a canon of Christ Church, Oxford ; on which he resigned his prebend of Gloucester.

From the year 1800 he generally resided on his Living, in comparative retirement ; and there both he and the literary world sustained a great loss, by a fire which consumed the dwelling-house, with his furniture, books, manuscripts, printing press, &c. ; and the whole family narrowly escaped with their lives. His mother died of the small-pox the 26th of August, 1772, aged forty-nine years ; his father, whom he maintained for more than twenty years, died October 12th, 1804, in the eightieth year of his age ; and he himself departed this life May 22nd, 1814, aged sixty-eight years, without issue. He appointed his friend, the Bishop of Peterborough, his executor and trustee ; and was buried in Christ Church, Oxford.

In person Dr. White was short and heavy ; and shewed in his gait that he never wholly overcame the defect acquired in his early years. His natural temper was reserved and taciturn, but not unsocial. He was kind and liberal to the poor, especially when he came to his native village ; and he subscribed £5 5s. toward the erection of the Charity School-rooms at Whiteshill in 1814.

Late in life he was subject to the abstractedness of thought called absence of mind, of which the following is an instance. Being once on a visit to a friend, the family was assembled round the breakfast table waiting for their guest. At length he appeared, as usual, in his morning gown ; but, on leaning over to reach something from the table, his gown fell partly open, and disclosed that he had forgotten to put on a certain indispensable article of dress. This incident created some confusion among the ladies, and considerable laughter among the gentlemen. But the former retiring with all decorum, and the cause of the merriment being explained to the good man, (who had previously been unconscious of his *sans cullottism*,) he soon resumed the forgotten garment, and afterward greatly enjoyed the occurrence.

It was reported, too, that occasionally he could make a pun, and that having once, by an awkward movement, overturned a small table whereon was a dish of cold lamb, he lifted up his hands and exclaimed, "What a lamentable [lamb-and-table] accident!"

When in residence as a prebendary of Gloucester, he sometimes took a walk in "The Grove," as the play-ground belonging to his old school was called. On one of these occasions, the writer saw him carrying a favourite green parrot on his arm. On another, he accosted a little boy, the writer's youngest brother, and asked him to conjugate the Latin irregular verb *Fero*. This the boy proceeded to do; and when, on coming to the preter-perfect tense, he pronounced it thus,—"tu-li, tu-listi, tu-lit," &c., the Doctor gently corrected him, and said, "The 'u' is not long, it is short; and it ought to be pronounced 'tul-i, tul-isti, tul-it,' &c." The lad remembered the corrector, and the correction, as long as he lived.

The following anecdote is a proof that his elevation in life had not made him ashamed of the humble occupation of his juvenile days. As he was passing through a street in Stroud, after he had attained academical honours and worldly renown, his attention was arrested by the sound of a weaver's loom at work. He entered the house from which it came, and requested the weaver to let him try his hand. The man left the loom, the Doctor seated himself in it, and, after moving the treadles and plying the shuttle for a few minutes, he gave the workman a shilling, and departed.

Such was Joseph White, the weaver-boy. And well may he be regarded as an honor to the place of his nativity, and to the whole county of Gloucester; while we point him out as an example to all young men of humble condition, who are moved by the aspiration of genius, or the desire of honorable distinction.

To return.—With respect to Upper Lypiatt, Lower Lypiatt, and Pakenhill,—whose ancient existence as three several manors, has been intimated,—I have not met with any notice of the holding a Court Baron, or the exercising manorial rights, as belonging to either of them, except the former under the name of "Lypiatt Superior." Sir Robert Atkyns says that the manor of Stroud was, in his time, divided among many considerable proprietors : and Mr. Rudder, when writing his History, refers to this, and says, "but I am informed that it [Lypiatt] belongs at present to John Stephens, Esq., who is also lord of the manor of Bisley : " at the time of its publication, however, the manor, &c., had become the property of Mr. De la Bere, on the death of Mr. Stephens.

The mills in this tithing are : 1st.—A part of Stratford mill, the other part being in the parish of Painswick. This mill is situated on Painswick stream, and belongs [10] to the trustees of the will of the late Mr. John Biddell. 2nd.— Phelps' mill, on the upper course of Cuckhold's brook, and lately belonging to Mr. Phelps, with the residue of the Warner estates. 3rd.—One part of Pucks-hole mill, the residue being in the parish of Randwick. This mill is the uppermost on the brook, and belonged to Richard Barton.

Pucks-hole is a deep and narrow ravine, (at the bottom of the lateral valley of Ruscomb,) through which falls the small stream which is supplied by the watershed of the valley, and afterward becomes Cuckhold's brook. Its name and situation carry the imagination back to the remote time when fairy Puck was believed to be a veritable person, and to have haunted that locality : playing his merry pranks, and misleading night-wanders—

> " Over hill, over dale,
>   Thorough bush, thorough briar,
> Over park, over pale,
>   Thorough flood, thorough fire." [11]

by the light of his goblin lantern. [12]

[10 Or did belong.]

11 Midsummer Night's Dream.

[12 The *Ignis fatuus*—A luminous gas, occasionally seen in motion in the night over marshy places, and supposed to beguile and betray benighted travellers and wanderers there.]

CHAPTER XL.

STROUD was a member of the parish of Bisley until the year 1360, when it became a separate parish.

The ancient Impropriation of Bisley comprises both that parish and Stroud : and the appropriate vicarage of Bisley is, in relation to the tithes, co-extensive with it. The rectory was formerly in the hands of two lay persons ; and was afterward part of the possessions of the college of Stoke Clare, in Suffolk. It came to the Crown on the dissolution of Stoke Clare, among the religious houses suppressed in the 26th year of King Henry VIII. ; and, in the reign of Queen Elizabeth, a lease of it was held by one — Shewell, in which, besides the rent reserved to the Crown, there was a sum of £10 per annum made payable thereout to the curate or chaplain of Stroud.

King James, by letters patent, in the third year of his reign, (1606,) granted the inheritance of the rectory or prebend of Bisley, otherwise called the first and second prebend or portion of the tithes of Bisley, to Lawrence Baskervile and Wm. Blake ; reserving, from and out of the aforesaid rectory of Bisley and the other premises belonging to the same, a fee-farm rent of £33 10s. And the grantees agreed that they, "from time to time for ever, at their own proper cost and expenses, would find and provide a sufficient curate or minister at Stroudwater, in the county of Gloucester, and two deans, viz. : one at Stroudwater aforesaid, and the other at Bisley, in the aforesaid county of Gloucester ; there to celebrate divine service, and whatsoever else belonged to divine worship there to be done." [1] But there is not, in the grant, any reservation of, or any

---

[1] For a copy of this Patent, see Appendix A.

agreement, by the grantees to pay, the annual sum of £10, before payable to the curate or minister of the chapel of Stroud. The Parsonage afterward came to one Willis, who sold it to the Lord Keeper Coventry; and on the contract for sale the £10 was expressly reserved, and has been paid by his successors to this day, with the exception of an interval of six years, which will be noticed hereafter. In the year 1712, and for many years after, the Impropriation belonged to Lord Coventry; and in 1808 to the Honourable Thomas Coventry Bulkley. It was then purchased by Yarnton Mills, Esq., and is now the property of his grandson, Thomas Mills Goodlake, Esq., [2] by whom the sum of £10 is annually paid to the incumbent of Stroud, as in former time by the other rectors. On the Commutation of the tithes of the two parishes of Bisley and Stroud in 1841, [3] it was arranged that,—in order to save the several landholders the trouble of paying one rent-charge to the rector, and another to the vicar of Bisley,—there should be only one rent-charge made on each part of the tithable property; and that such charge should include, or be in respect of, both the rectorial and vicarial tithes. Accordingly, the vicar's portion of the tithes having been estimated at £750 per annum, the payment of that sum was secured, by allotting to him all the annual rent-charges made payable from the tithing of Pakenhill, with those fixed on certain specified parts of the tithings of Upper and Lower Lypiatt, in Stroud, and on certain specified portions of the parish of Bisley,—amounting in the aggregate to £750: and all the rent-charges on Steanbridge tithing, and on the residue of Upper and Lower Lypiatt, in Stroud, together with the remainder of Bisley, were made payable to the Rector; and these amounted altogether to the sum of £1,200, at which the rectorial tithes had been valued.

Anciently, Stroud was a chapelry of Bisley, the mother church, at which the rites of marriage and baptism were celebrated: but, in 1304, a deed of Endowment or Composition was made, of which the following is a translation:—

"Be it known to all men, that whereas, between the Masters Henry Avery and Robert called le Eyre, Rectors of the first and second portion of the church of Bysseleye, and William, Vicar of the same place, of the one part,—and Thomas of Rodeborowe, William Proute, Henry of Monemuwe, Nicholas le Seymour, Henry le Fremer, and the other Inhabitants of the chapel of Strode, appearing by William Benet and Richard the son of Richard, jointly

[2 Or his devisees.]

3 Under the Act 6 & 7 Will. IV., c. 71, s. 63.

and severally, according to law appointed their proctors, and afterward appearing personally ratifying the deed of the proctors themselves, of the other part ;—Concerning the restoration and repair of the chancel of the chapel of Strode and certain other matters, subjects of strife and disagreement had arisen ; which at length, in the presence of us W. Burdon, Archdeacon of Gloucester,[4] hath been set at rest after this manner, that is to say : That whereas, there is no manner of doubt, that between the chapel itself of Strode, and its mother church of Bysselye, so great and so dangerous a distance exists that, in the baptizing of young children, and the administration of the other sacraments of the church, it is not unlikely that grievous peril of souls may happen ; and inasmuch as the Rectors and Vicar aforesaid are bound of their own free will to remedy this evil as far as in them lies,—They will and consent that in the Chapel of Strode itself, at the expense of the inhabitants of the same, henceforth shall be made a place for baptizing, and in it shall be administered the Sacrament of Baptism : the minister of the chapel also, by the aforesaid rectors equally chosen and admitted, in order that he may administer day by day the sacraments of the church, in the chapel itself, shall for the future continually be resident ; with this understanding, however,—that the open piece of ground or tenement in la Strode, which piece of ground or tenement John of Pridie hath hitherto held of the aforesaid rectors at a certain rent, may be appointed by them for the residence of the same priest, but shall have a competent building erected on it by the above-mentioned inhabitants of la Strode themselves, since it is for their own benefit that this piece of ground is so assigned. And as often as, or whensoever this building shall need repair or improvement of any sort, the whole shall be done at the expense of the same inhabitants. The same inhabitants shall also pay there yearly, for it, eighteen pence to the Rectors themselves, as they have hitherto been accustomed to do. But toward the stipend of the aforesaid Minister of the chapel, the inhabitants themselves shall contribute yearly fifteen shillings, at three periods of the year, to wit : at the Feast of Saint Michael, the Birthday of our Lord, and on the Feast of the Purification of the Blessed Virgin. If, however, wilfully, and to the detriment of the Minister of the chapel, they shall cease to give satisfaction in the same, which Heaven forbid ! the aforesaid parties will and consent that the before ordained Chantry,[5] as it was formerly accustomed to be held, shall entirely cease, although had and obtained there. Also the aforesaid tenement shall revert to the same Rectors freely, and without any hindrance whatsoever. Also the same Minister of the Chapel shall administer all and singular the Sacraments in the villages of both Lepeyates, Strode, and of Pagunhull, together with the whole vill of Bourne, from the house or tenement which formerly was commonly called Seredhous, as far as the afore-mentioned Chapel of Strode. And the clerk who is continually to wait on the minister of the Chapel, (himself admitted at the good pleasure of the rectors and to be removed by them whenever they think fit,) shall receive for the future for his stipend what he has been accustomed to, together with that which the beneficed Clerk in the chapel of Pagunhull used to have from the inhabitants themselves for their services. With regard, however, to the repairing and restoring of the Chancel of the Chapel of Strode, the parties have unanimously agreed in this manner, that is to say : That the rectors themselves shall repair the front of the chancel now in a ruinous condition, (if necessary building it up from the very foundations,) and shall make in a competent manner in the same, the window which has before been

4 At that time the Archdeaconry of Gloucester was a division of the Diocese of Worcester.

5 " A Chantry was a foundation or endowment for a priest to say mass for the soul of the founder, without having, necessarily, any parochial duty."

ordered, at their own and proper charge, for this one time only : but, for the future, the before-mentioned inhabitants shall repair and make good all and singular the other defects of the aforesaid place, taking upon themselves and their successors for ever, the burden of repairing, rebuilding, and roofing in, as well the front and the window, as the whole of the aforesaid chancel as often as need shall require.

In all oblations, however, obventions, tithes, payments, collected as well for the maintaining the bells, as the body of the church, or in all other contributions and rights of what sort soever they may be, in what way soever from of old due and accustomed, the before-mentioned chapel of Strode and its inhabitants for ever, as hitherto they have been, shall remain obedient and subject to the aforesaid Church of Bysseleye, as to their mother. For the observance of all these things and each of them, the above-named parties have mutually bound themselves, having taken their corporal oath upon the holy Gospels of God. In witness and assurance whereof, we, W. Burdon, Archdeacon aforesaid, to this present writing made after the manner of a Chirograph 6 between the two said parties at their procurement and instance, have thought fit to have our seal affixed. Written at Gloucester, on the fourth day before the Calends of August, 7 in the year of our Lord One Thousand three hundred and four."

The above English version of this old document was made from the copy of the Exemplification preserved in the Feoffee's chest ; 8 and a copy of the original Composition itself, in words at length, will be found in appendix B. At present we shall make only the following observations upon it.

It might naturally be conjectured that the four parties to the Composition, named as acting on the part of the inhabitants of Stroud, were some of their most influential neighbours, or members of the best families. Accordingly, we find that Thomas de Rodeborowe was lord of the manor of Rodborough, and high sheriff of Gloucestershire, in the 1st and 4th of Edward III.—(A.D. 1332-4 ; 9) and that John Monemuthe, John Seymour, John Fremer, and others, held a fee in Paganhull of Humphrey de Bohun, Earl of Essex, &c., at his death, about 1375. 10

6 Chirograph,—Anciently a writing which, requiring a counterpart, was engrossed twice on the same piece of parchment counterwise, with a space between, on which was written *chirographum* or other letters, through which the parchment was cut, and one part given to each party. It answered to what is now called a *Charter-party.*

[7 29th July.]

8 This English version is from a translation made by Charles Holbrow Stanton, Esq., in 1860, accompanied with a transcript of the original text and explanatory notes ; which he kindly allowed the writer to use.

9 See Rudder, 629.

10 See Fosbrook, i. 340.

We also find that the names Avery and Eyre, (the latter now spelled Ayre and Ayers,) still exist in the vicinity: and that "in nearly all the places where the word chapel is used, it seems to mean a district rather than a building—a Chapelry rather than a Chapel. The meaning of 'the inhabitants of the Chapel of Strode' is sufficiently obvious."

We have not found any tradition of the locality of "the house formerly called Seredhouse," at Bourne; and, indeed, in the lapse of more than 560 years, it might have disappeared long ago, and been forgotten. But a small cluster of houses called Blackness lies there, on the old highway from Stroud to Chalford, partly in the parish of Stroud, and partly in that of Bisley. It might have been, comparatively, an important place in the most remote time: and even now, one of its houses stands at the extremity of the parish of Stroud, and is its first house at that place. Here then, perhaps, we have found the site of Seredhouse; and, in its advantageous situation on a public road, the reason why "the whole vill of Bourne," (of which Blackness is a part,) was, by the Composition, comprised in the chapelry of Stroud. [11]

Neither have we found the remains of "the chapel of Pagunhull," nor any tradition of its locality; nor any other mention of "the beneficed clerk" who is said to have officiated there. But it has been suggested that the Composition "opens a new past for Pakenhill"; and indicates that it "seems to have been a great place in early times, seeing it had a chapel and a beneficiary clerk all to itself, before the year 1304"; even before a provision was made for maintaining a resident priest at Stroud. [12]

Lastly, the swearing to observe the terms of this Composition by the parties to it, seems to show how very weak the obligation of contracts was considered in those days, unless they had been confirmed by an oath: indeed, the history of the olden time shows that engagements were but lightly regarded, when there was the power to break them with impunity, even when assured by that most solemn sanction.

11 See also page 6, note 1.

[12 Undoubtedly the place derived its name amongst its Saxon inhabitants from its having been used by the piratical invading Danish hosts, constantly coming up the Severn. They are always called Pagans in the Saxon chronicle, and such these robbers and sea-kings really were, being literally heathens and worshippers of Odin and Thor.]

The Composition of the Chapel of Stroud was exemplified and confirmed in the year 1493 ; and again in 1598.

The Feoffees' copy of the first of these deeds of Exemplification is to the following effect :—

To all sons of Our Holy Mother the Church to whom these present letters shall come, John Thour, Doctor of Laws, Chancellor and Commissary General, of the Rev. Father and Lord in Christ, the Lord Robert, by divine permission, Bishop of Worcester, sends greeting. We make known, that in the year of our Lord 1493, in the eleventh Indiction, 13 in the first year of the Pontificate of Our Most Holy Father and Lord in Christ, the Lord Alexander the Sixth, 14 on the eighteenth day of the month of July, in the Great Cloister of the Monastery of the Blessed Peter at Gloucester, 15 in the diocese of Worcester, before us sitting in the place of Judgment, [*pro tribunali sedentibus,*] appeared, as well the Wardens as the greater and the more discreet part of the parishioners of Bysseleye, [*tam Gardiani quam major et sanior pars parochianorum de Bysseleye,*] and produced the real 16 and original Composition between the former rectors and the vicar of Bysseleye of the one part, and the inhabitants of the Chapel of Strode of the other part,—not decayed, not cancelled, not erased, nor in any part altered,—though in some degree impaired by age and the obscurity of the writing, as it appeared to us : 17 [*non abolitam, non cancellatam, non abrasam, nec in aliqua parte vitiatam,—licet quodammodo vetustate ac cæcitate scripturæ debilitatam*] : and humbly prayed that, whereas the said wardens as well as the parishioners, present and to come, might have need to use the said Composition—which they have not in duplicate, nor among writings of modern date—in different parts of the country far distant from each other,—and that they might be able to exhibit it for establishing their rights ; [*necesse haberent hujusmodi Compositionem,—quam non habent duplicatam nec in scriptis recentiorum—in diversis partibus, non modicum distantibus uti, eandemque pro jure suo presentare, ostendere et exhibere possent*] ; and that, because this Composition might probably be lost by the risks of travelling, or by other mishaps,—We would take care that it should be copied, exemplified, signed, and brought by the undersigned Public Notary, (taken to be our scribe, for this very purpose,) into a public form. [*transumi, exemplari, subscribi, et in publicam formam redigi*] : so that, to the copy so made, credit may attach equally with the original Composition ; of which the true tenor follows in these words : " *Universis pateat,*" &c. Here follow the words of the original Composition, for which see Appendix B.

13 Indiction, in *Chronology*, was a mode of reckoning by cycles of fifteen years, which commenced about the year 313 ; and was used in charters and public writings, to confirm their dates by an additional reference. It was obtained by adding 3 to the year of our Lord, and dividing the total by 15 ;— the product was the number of the Indiction, and the remainder the year of that Indiction.

14 This " Most Holy Father and Lord in Christ, the Lord Alexander the 6th," was the notoriously wicked Roderigo Borgia, the father of the infamous Cæsar Borgia.

15 The monastery has been destroyed ; but " the great cloister " remains. It is a square, each side of which is 148 feet ; and it adjoins the nave of the cathedral church on the north. It was completed by Abbot Frowster, in 1390 ; and is the most elegant and perfect structure of the kind in England.

16 It was called a real, in distinction from a personal, Composition ; the latter being a payment in money, in lieu of tithes.

17 The original Composition was at that time 189 years old.

Wherefore we John Thour, Chancellor, &c., having examined the said real and original Composition, and found it not erased, nor decayed, not cancelled, nor in any part of it open to suspicion ; [*nec in aliqua ipsius parte suspectam*] : that the means of proof may not hereafter be taken away from the aforesaid Wardens and the other parishioners, present and to come, owing to the age, decay, or faintness of the writing : [*per hujusmodi vetustatem, caducitatem, sive debilitatem scripturæ*] ; therefore, sitting in our place of Judgment, we have published by our authority and decree the Composition, [*Compositionem * * * * * auctoritate et decreto publicavimus*], and have caused the same to be copied by the undersigned public notary, and reduced into public form, and to be signed with his accustomed signature, and to be exemplified. To which copy, so brought into public form, we decree by these presents full credit shall hereafter be attached, as to the said real and original Composition. [*Cui transumpto sic in publicam formam redacto, sicuti dictæ Compositioni * * * plenam fidem in posterum adhibendam fore decrevimus per presentes*]. In witness and assurance of all and singular the above, to this present instrument or copy we have considered that the seal of the aforesaid Bishop of Worcester, which we have at hand, should be affixed. [*In quorum omnium et singulorum fidem et testimonium, huic instrumento presenti sive transumpto sigillum præfati Reverendi Patris Episcopi Wigorniensis quod ad manus habemus, duximus apponendum*]. These things were given and done as above written and recited, in the year of our Lord, Indiction, Pontificate, month, day and place in the beginning of this instrument or copy described. [*Data et acta sunt hæc prout supra scribuntur et recitantur, sub anno Domini, Indictionis, Pontificatûs, mense, die, et loco, in principio hujus Instrumenti sive Transumpti descriptis.*]—Then follows the attestation of James Botiller, clerk of the Diocese of Dublin, Public Notary and Chief Registrar of the Reverend Father and Lord in Christ, Robert, Bishop of Worcester, that, at the time and place aforesaid, and at the command of the aforesaid Chancellor, he had copied and exemplified, [18] the said Composition, and published the copy, and reduced it into that public form ; and with his accustomed signature and name, together with the appendage of the seal of the aforesaid Reverend Bishop as aforesaid, he had signed,—in assurance and witness of all and singular the premises.

It will not fail to be observed that, although the original Composition was granted for the express convenience and advantage of the inhabitants of the Chapelry of Stroud, yet the Exemplification of it was obtained at the instance of the wardens and parishioners of Bisley, for the maintenance of *their* rights, by enabling them to produce an authoritative copy of it. And if, at this distance of time, there may not exist evidence of any occasion on which it had been exhibited in proof of their rights, or even of what their rights consisted, which its production would have established,—the Exemplification has, at least, preserved the original text of the Composition itself.

A copy of this Exemplification "was produced to" the Charity Commissioners, when they visited Stroud under the authority of the Act of Parliament, "for appointing

18 Exemplified :—he made an official recognition of it. Enrolled it among the archives.

Commissioners to inquire concerning Charities in England for the Education of the Poor." [19]   And, in their Report dated July 2nd, 1825, they give an account of the houses, &c., then being within "the bounds of what was called Pridie's Acre," and traditionally known as "the open piece of ground or tenement in La Stroud, which John of Pridie had (formerly) held."

It may be noticed that the Commissioners give "the 4th of August, 1304," as the date of the Composition ; which date they seem to have copied from one somewhat recently endorsed on the copy of the Exemplification so "produced to" them ; whereas, the date of the Composition itself is the fourth day before the calends of August, and that must have been the 29th of July, 1304.

[19] 58 George III., c. 91 ; amended by 59 George III., c. 81, and 5 George IV., c. 58.

CHAPTER XLI.

IN the days of old, to which our subject has led us, there
was great jealousy between the secular and the
regular clergy, and frequent contentions between the parochial ministers and the owners of tithes, occasioned by the
small salaries and emoluments of the former of those
classes, in contrast with the large estates monopolized by
the later.

In the year 1360 a controversy was existing, respecting
the emoluments of the vicar and vicarage of Bisley. It
was brought before Reginald Bryan, Bishop of Worcester, [1]
who decided it by an Instrument which, in the index to the
register of his diocese, was called a Declaration,—or The
Ordinance, of the Vicarage of the Church of Bysseleye.
By Sir Robert Atkyns it is called a Decree ; and by Mr.
Rudder, "an Endowment by the Bishop." It was to the
following effect :—

"To all the children of the Holy mother the Church to whom these presents
shall come,—Reginald, by Divine permission Bishop of Worcester, sendeth
greeting. Amongst other desirable things of our heart, we have earnestly
wished to take away all hurtful doubts of law, and contention, between our
subjects, and establish peace among them ; especially long since between our
beloved sons in Christ, Peter de Lacie, portionary of the first portion of the

---

1 This Prelate was translated from St. David's to Worcester in 1352. In
1356 he was advanced to the See of Ely by Pope Innocent VI. ; but he died
of the plague at Alvechurch, in December of that year, before he could take
possession ; and was buried in the Cathedral of Worcester. He was honoured
with the personal friendship and regard of Edward the Black Prince ; and was
one of the persons to whom he dispatched the first account of the battle of
Poictiers, September 19th, 1356, in a letter dated at Bordeaux, October 20th,
1356 ; and addressed to him at Alvechurch, where it was delivered on the 1st
of December, a few days before his death. The bearer of it was "our most
dear Knight, Roger de Cottesford." . It is now in the archives of the Dean
and Chapter of Worcester.

Church of Bisley, on the one part; and Robert Burgess, perpetual Vicar of the said portion in the Church of Bisley, on the other part. A question being raised concerning the sufficiency of the allowance of the Vicar himself and his Vicarage, and of the profits and revenue allowed to the Vicar who shall be there for the time being, We, well weighing and, as belonging to our inspection, considering,—and the parties aforesaid sufficiently appearing 2 before us,— after deliberation, and by the counsel of the learned, and also with the express consent of the aforesaid parties, both portionary and the vicar and vicarage aforesaid, we have judged and ordained in form following, that is to say; We will and ordain that the Vicar of the aforesaid portion, who is now or hereafter shall be for the time being, shall have and receive for his portion, and the portion of the vicarage of the aforesaid Church, these plain things under written, viz. : the Mansion house which the said Robert Burgess the vicar doth now dwell in, 3 together with three curtilages adjoining, which were late in the tenure and occupation of Simon Tailo, portionary of the said portion; also the oblations to be made in the said Church and parish; all obventions and duties at the altar, or otherwise within the limits of the parish aforesaid; and also whatsoever heriots which pertained to the aforesaid portionary or his predecessors till this time, and ought to appertain. Also the tithes of flax, milk, hemp, butter, cheese, calves, cocks, hens, swans, geese, ducks, pigs, eggs, wax, honey, apples, pears, gardens, grist mills, fulling mills, or soever like, dove-houses, fish-ponds, fowling, rabbits, hunting, merchandising, herbage, firewood, and the small tithes of the whole parish; and also the entire tithes of all hay of lands and meadows, in the tenure of the said portionary, commonly called Worlands, and the herbage of the churchyard of the said church; also the entire tithes of wool and lambs, sheep, pigs, pigeons, geese, ducks, eggs, apples, pears, and of all fruits tithable of the portionary of the aforesaid portion, as well in his demesne lands called Worlands, as which is in his own possession. Also all the tithes of hay, wool and lambs, as well of the tenants of the said portionary, besides Worlands, as also of the whole parish aforesaid. And the same Vicar and his successors may receive all tithes and re-decimations, as is allowed and granted to him and his vicarage, in the mansion of the said portionary of the church aforesaid. Also that the said Vicar who shall be for the time being, shall claim of the portionary of the portion aforesaid for the solid or entire portion of his vicarage nothing besides the premises aforesaid,—but shall hold himself contented with those fruits, tenths, oblations, and obventions, which exceed the clear value of ten marks of silver; unless the said portionary of the portion aforesaid shall of his special favour provide more plentifully for the said Vicar. But the said Vicar and his successors shall bear these burdens under written :—that is to say, that he and whosoever is Vicar shall, either by himself or some other sufficient Chaplain, perform Divine Service as is fitting in the said Church, and undertake the cure of souls, bind the books, wash the surplices when it shall be necessary, and as the said portionary is obliged. And that all the wax to be burned in the chancels of Bysseleye and Strode, on what account soever it shall happen, the same Vicar and his successors shall provide for the same. And also whosoever shall be Vicar for the time being in the first portion of the said Church, shall pay the synodals and procurations to the Archdeacon, and provide Wine for the people to communicate, at his own charge; all other burdens being excluded. Always reserving to ourself and our successors, Bishops of Worcester, the Special Power of adding to or withdrawing from the aforesaid premises,

2 They were probably represented by their Proctors.

3 The present Vicarage house, a modern structure, stands on the site of this old mansion house.

and changing the same, and also of declaring, interpreting, correcting, and supplying, if any thing in the same shall be obscure or doubtful. In witness whereof we have caused our seal to be set to these presents. Dated at Alvechurch, 4 the eighth day of July, in the year of our Lord 1360, and of our translation the eighth.

"This agrees with the Register, compared by me JOHN PENNELL, public notary."

"This is a true copy of the Composition between the Rector and Vicar of Bisley, now in the Diocese of Gloucester, by John Pennell, public notary;—made by me, GILBERT JONES, public notary."

The foregoing translation of the original Instrument is from a copy in the handwriting of the Rev. Stephen Philips, Vicar of Bisley; at the head of which is a notice, (bearing his signature) that it was transcribed by him "from a copy of Thomas Stephens of Lipiat, November 16, 1716." It were to be wished that dates had been affixed to the memoranda of John Pennel and Gilbert Jones: but, from what the latter wrote, it appears that the original instrument was then in the Diocese of Gloucester; and therefore was in existence after the year 1541, when that diocese was created by Henry VIII. In the year 1403 an Act of Parliament was passed by which vicarages and their endowments were made perpetual.

It may be learned from history, that if, in the fourteenth century, the hand of power, both civil and ecclesiastical, was always heavy on the weak and defenceless,—yet that it was, now and then, beneficially laid on some other heavy and oppressive, (but weaker,) hand of power—to the relief of those who suffered under it. And thus it was that Reginald Bryan, in 1360, decreed to Robert Burgess, the poor vicar of Bisley, and his successors, an addition to their income out of the revenues of the Portionary Peter de Lacie. It is said that the latter gave his consent, though, probably, it was a reluctant one, to this settlement of the "long since" contention; but then, the Bishop claimed them both as his "subjects" and, moreover, he provided for the continuance of his, and his successors', authority over them, by reserving "the special power of adding to, withdrawing from, changing, declaring, interpreting, correcting and supplying, if anything in the same should be obscure or doubtful."

---

4 Alvechurch is a village near Bewdley, in Worcestershire; where many of the Bishops resided in old times.

It is well for the present generation, that few of them
have had any practical experience of the old Tithe system.
The law of Tithes, and of Tithing, was a very great
grievance, as well to those who rendered, as to those who
received, tithes. It obstructed improvements in agricul-
ture, hindered the influence of the clergy in their sacred
office, and thus was detrimental to the best interests of
the community. Sir Robert Atkins says that "the profits
of the Vicar were settled " by the foregoing Decree ;
probably referring to the part of it which directed that
the Vicar should hold himself contented with those fruits,
tenths, oblations and obventions which exceeded the clear
value of ten marks of silver, unless, &c. But we have
not seen a copy of the original document, though there
is one among the muniments of the parish of Bisley :—
and the translation seems, occasionally to be somewhat
obscure.

Sir Robert Atkyns says further, that "the re-tithing of
all the tithe-corn and hay belonging to the Impropriation,
and all privy tithes were allotted to the vicar ; most of
which tithes were " (in 1712) "rented at £45 a year by
the Impropriator ; " and that "the rectorial tithes were
then worth £300 a year." Mr. Rudder says (in 1779)
"the Vicarage is worth £150 a year, and the Tithes belonging to the Impropriator about £400 a year." It is, doubtless, owing to the increased population, the larger quantity
of cultivated land, and the great material prosperity, (since
that time,) of the parishes of Bisley and Stroud,—over both
of which the rectorial and vicarial tithes extended,—that
the former tithes were commuted at the annual sum of
£1200, and the latter at £750, under the act for the Commutation of tithes passed in 1836.

It appears from the foregoing document that, in 1360,
the withholding the Cup from the laity in the Lord's
Supper had not been adopted in this part of England :
nor was it general until after the Council of Trent. We
also learn from it that the Vicar of Bisley was bound
to provide wax candles for the chapels of Bisley and
Stroud.

It appears moreover that a former Portionary, or holder
of the great tithes, was one Simon Tailo. He was probably
an ancestor of the family of that name (now spelled Tayloe),
which resided in the parish for many generations. They
were eminent clothiers at Chalford ; and their Residence

R2

was the house now belonging to Mr. Dangerfield, situated on the east side of the old steep highway called the Dark Lane, where, (after being crossed by the Stroud and Chalford turnpike road,) it proceeds on its way up to Chalford Hill.

CHAPTER XLII.

IT is not known how long the Vicars of Bisley supplied the wax candles burned in the chancel of the chapel of Stroud, under the provision of the Endowment of Bisley, made A.D. 1360; nor how long the inhabitants of the Chapelry paid the 1s. 6d. per annum, reserved to the rectors of Bisley, under the Composition-deed of 1304. But, from time out of mind, the inhabitants or the feoffees of the charity-property of Stroud, have repaired and maintained the chapel, with the gable and window of its chancel, according to the stipulations of the last-mentioned instrument,—as likewise the church itself, of which the chapel and chancel were a part. Further, they continued to pay the 15s. per annum to the Curates for the time being, as stipulated by the same document, until the year 1653; when it was raised to £15, at the request of the inhabitants, and was paid by the feoffees to the ministers in possession, (with occasional interruptions,) until 1733: and in 1741 it was fixed, permanently, at £20 per annum by the Decree of the Lord Chancellor Hardwicke, in the Cause—Henry Bond the curate, against Giles Gardner and others, feoffees; of which an account will be given.

It cannot be doubted that, by the Composition of 1304, the Rectors of Bisley were entitled to choose and admit the Minister of the Chapel of Stroud, and his Clerk; nor that, by virtue of the grant in the Patent of 3 James I, to Messrs. Baskervile and Blake, they and their successors were bound to find and provide, at their own cost and charges, a curate or minister for the same chapel. It is not known, however, that the Rectors ever nominated any one to the chaplaincy; but, on the contrary, down to the middle of the eighteenth century, the Inhabitants of the chapelry generally made the appointment. This may have arisen from the neglect of the Rectors to nominate, on account of the small value of the Curacy ; or because they wished to be relieved from the burden of their duty ; and then, the Inhabitants,—perhaps in ignorance of the terms of King James' grant in that respect, or on account of the great desirableness of an acceptable minister, (who was chiefly dependant on their contributions for his maintenance,) —proceeded to elect one, and presented him to the Bishop for a license to officiate.

The following is a list of the Chaplains, Curates, or Ministers of Stroud, from the earliest period to which our researches have been successfully directed :—

1623	Mr. Day.	1757	John Warren.
1630	James Crumpe.	1774	James Webster.
1645	Mr. Stephenson.	1804	John Seagram.
1646	Robert Pleydell.	1833	William Frederick Powell.
1679	Thomas Phipps.	1839	Mathew Blagden Hale.
1686	Francis Owen.	1845	George Proctor.
1688	William Johns.	1858	Thomas Henry Tarlton.
1722	Henry Bond.	1865	John Badcock.

1885   Henry D'Ombrain.

We are indebted for the discovery of the first name on the list of ministers, to his successor, or the person who acted for him, but who himself remains unascertained.

This *un-named* successor found no entry of christenings in the parish register, for one whole year after 8th September, 1628 ; and thereupon he wrote the following notice between that last, and his own first entry of 6th September, 1629 :— "Anno dni 1629. Mᵈ That frome the 8th daie of September above saide Mr. Day late minister tooke the record untoe September laste and soe dyed and the same was lost." It is probable that Mr. Day, who seems to have begun this register, had taken loose notes of the baptisms as they occurred, intending to enter them altogether at the end of the year, or some other future time ; but which his death prevented. The previous entries seem to have been made in the same manner ; as do nearly all those in the succeeding registers, down to the time when the present forms of registration were introduced, about the year 1813. We observe that in only a few instances do the ministers' names appear in this early register, or indeed, in any subsequent one : but Mr. Crumpe made his entries very carefully, and subscribed his name to them at certain intervals, thus :—"Ita testor Ja : Crumpe Curatus de Stroud " ; or " Curatus "—or " Ibidem."

We have not been able to learn the name of any chaplain or curate before Mr. Day, in 1623 ; but in the feoffment of February 12, 1636, one of the charity "tenements" conveyed thereby to new trustees, is said to have been formerly in the tenure of William Woodwall, clerk, and another in the tenure of Walter Sweeper, who in a subsequent feoffment is called clerk. We also find, by the same deed, that Mr. Crumpe, the then curate, occupied one of the feoffees' houses; and by a feoffment of March 22nd, 1677, that Mr. Pleydell, the then curate, occupied the house formerly of Walter Sweeper. Walter Sweeper was buried here June 9, 1636, and William Woodwall on March 3, 1636-7. It appears, therefore, probable that Walter Sweeper and William Woodwall had once filled the office of chaplain ; and that one of them had been the immediate predecessor or successor of Mr. Day.

Further, we have been enabled to place Mr. Stephenson, (though without his christian name,) among the ministers of Stroud, by means of the following extract we possess, " taken out of the Churchwarden's Book " that was produced on the examination of witnesses in the suit of Bond against Gardner and others ;—" From 1645 to 1647, pd. Mr. Stephenson, Minister, his stipend £0 15s. 0d. "

Mr. Phipps, like his predecessors, was nominated by the Parishioners, and licensed by the Bishop. But Mr. Owen, his successor, obtained a license from Dr. Frampton, the then bishop, without having been so nominated : and the first mention of Stroud or its Curates, found in the register of the diocese of Gloucester, occurs on that occasion. It is contained in the following entry in " A book of oaths and declarations in ordinations and preferments":—'November 16, 1686. *Ego Franciscus Owen, A.M., nunc licentiandus et admittendus ad inserviendum curiæ ecclesiæ parochialis de Strowd, in diocesi Gloucesteriensi, omnibus Articulis subscribo.*' ' *Fiat licentia.*'

At that time, however, the minister's salary was very small, independently of the voluntary contributions of the inhabitants ; and these last being withheld from him, probably because of the manner in which he obtained his license, Mr. Owen resigned the curacy before the expiration of two years.

His successor was Mr. Johns, who, with his charitable bequests, has been already mentioned. [1] He was nominated by the parishioners, and was licensed by the same

1 See pp. 16, 17, 18.

bishop. Mr. Johns died in 1721; and Mr. Bond was
appointed by "some" of the parishioners, in February, 1722.
and was licensed by Bishop Wilcox. But, at the same
time, there was another candidate for the office, "one Mr.
Bedford," in whose favour a petition signed by upwards of
200, (alleged to be a majority,) of the parishioners and
landowners, was presented to the Bishop by the Honourable Henry Berkeley, Kinaird De la Bere, Esq., and others;
to whom the bishop replied that he had given a license to
Mr. Bond, and could not retract it. It appears that Mr.
Bond had advanced a sum of £320 for the purpose of procuring an augmentation of the curacy; and this with £200
raised by several of the inhabitants, and some other money
from Queen Anne's Bounty, [2] was laid out in the purchase
of a small estate called Rodway, (Roadway,) in the parish
of Randwick, for that purpose.

Upon this augmentation, Stroud became (by stat. 2 Geo.
I., c. 10,) a Perpetual Curacy, and subject to the nomination
of the bishop by lapse,—*i.e.* on the neglect of the true
patron to present a clerk in six months after an avoidance;
and further, by Act 36 Geo. III., c. 83, it became, as a perpetual curacy augmented, a benefice presentative.

Subsequently about the year 1750, Dr. Martin Benson,
Bishop of Gloucester, compiled a manuscript book which
purports to be an account of his Diocese, and of its several
benefices; wherein it is stated that the Bishop is the undoubted patron of the Perpetual Curacy of Stroud. Since
that time, the Rectors not having presented any one to the
benefice, all the curates since Mr. Bond have been appointed
by the Bishops of the diocese. In the case of Mr. Warren,
the admission is recorded in the diocesan register as being
on the donation of the Lord Bishop (of Gloucester), the
true and undoubted patron of the said perpetual curacy (in
full right); in the cases of Mr. Webster and Mr. Seagram,
as on the collation, and in all the other cases as being on
the donation, of the Lord Bishop.

But this claim of being "the true and undoubted"
patron is not borne out by King Henry the Eight's
Endowment of the Bishopric, when he created it in 1541;
inasmuch as his Grant enumerates, by name, all the benefices,
&c., with which he endowed it,—and the Chapel of Stroud
is not one of them. [3]

2 Statute 2 Anne, c. 11.

3 For an English version of this Grant of Endowment, see Rudder's
"Gloucestershire," Appendix viii., p. 15.

On the vacating of the curacy by Mr. Seagram in 1831, a Case was stated and laid before Stephen Lushington, LL.D., for his opinion on this subject ; and he, in his reply, dated March 21, 1833, says :—" I think the Patronage of this Curacy belongs to the Rector ; and most probably there will be found in the Rolls Office an enrollment of the original Grant from the Crown of this Rectory, and in that, some reference to this Curacy ; and most likely it will throw some light upon the Rector's title. If the Rector could show a *prima facie* title, I think the Bishop could not maintain any right to the Patronage : I entertain very little doubt that the Bishop's claim is founded solely on usurpation." In order to elucidate this subject, the writer procured an extract of the Grant of the Curacy of Stroud contained in the Patent of 3 James I., and has given the substance of it in chapter xl., and a copy of the original in Appendix A. ; and it confirms Dr. Lushington's opinion.

CHAPTER XLIII.

THE earliest parish register now remaining here is headed—" Register book of the Christenings Burialls and Marriages performed in the Chapple of Stroud and entered from the latter end of the year of our Lord God Anno dni 1624 : as followeth etc." It commences with a baptismal entry of February the 27th, which day was " at the latter end of that year," according to the civil reckoning adopted here and in other parts of the kingdom at that time ; for the year was considered to have begun on the previous twenty-fifth day of March : and the years continued to be divided in like manner throughout the whole register, which closed in 1683. [1]

Mr. Stephenson's and Mr. Pleydell's curacies comprehended the period of the great struggle for the establishment of civil liberty, and the maintenance of Protestantism, which is termed by Clarendon The Rebellion. They included also the Commonwealth and the Restoration ; and it might be expected that the old parish register already mentioned would contain some signs or intimations of the effects of that period on the civil and ecclesiastical affairs of that parish. Accordingly, we find that, from the last entry made in it by the methodical Mr. Crumpe on March 13th, 1641-2, down to 1652, there are such noticeable blank intervals and breaks in the continuity of the entries ; so many various and bad hand-writings, such bad spelling, such scribblings and careless treatment of several of its

---

[1] This custom gave rise to the mode of dating, for the period between the first of January and the 25th of March, both ways,—as 1748-9, or 174-8/9 ; which is sometimes met with in old documents. But by the Act for altering the style in 1751, the civil year now commences with January 1.

pages, as indicate some considerable disturbances and changes in the governmental and officiating departments of Church matters during that period: but the register does not supply any explanation of their nature, or their causes. We noticed, moreover, the great paucity of marriage entries between October, 1647, (with which Mr. Pleydell's registration seems to have begun,) and 1660 ; the number in those thirteen years being only twenty-three, while the baptisms are 811. This may be attributable, in part, to the general rule that times of civil war and commotion are always unfavourable to marriage ; but it may have been caused also by a dislike to the Ordinance of the Long Parliament (chapter vi., passed August 24, 1653,) concerning marriages. [2]

Among the entries (headed "Weded") are the two following, standing together though separated by nearly a year in point of time, and attracting attention by their peculiarity :—

"John Brownen and Mary Bennat proclaimed to be mared the nomannaten was the 16 day of november 1655 the 2 day was the 23 november the 3 proclaimen was the 30 of november 1655."—"Thomas Harcut and Margary Dunn being published 3 marcut (market) daies in the town of Painswicke ware mared by Mr. John Lygon, Justes of the pease the 7 day of August 1656 according to the late Ackte." (Act.)

The explanation of these entries may be found in the Ordinance above mentioned, whereby it was enacted that

"Whoever shall agree to be married in the Commonwealth of England, the Register shall publish the names, &c., of the parties three Lord's days in the publique meeting, commonly called the church or chapel, or (if the parties so to be married shall desire it) in the marketplace next to the said church or chapel, three market days in three several weeks next following, between the hours of eleven and two. * * * And all such persons so intended to be married shall come before some Justice of Peace within and of the county, &c., * * * * and the marriage shall proceed in this manner :—The man to be married, taking the woman by the hand, shall plainly and distinctly pronounce these words 'I, A. B., here in the presence of God the searcher of all hearts, take thee C. D., for my wedded wife ; and do also in the presence of God, and before these witnesses, promise to be unto thee a loving and faithful husband.' Then the woman, taking the man by the hand, shall plainly and distinctly pronounce the sewords : 'I, C. D., do here, in the presence of God, the searcher of all hearts, take thee, A. B., for my wedded husband ; and do also in the presence of God, and before these witnesses, promise to be unto thee a loving, faithful, and obedient wife.' [3] And then the Justice of Peace

2 Scobell's Collection of Acts and Ordinances. Fo. London, 1658.

3 A similar simple form of marriage is still observed by the Society of Friends, called Quakers ; but the notice preceding it is given only in the Meeting-house at which the ceremony is to take place—not in the Market-place as formerly.

shall declare the man and woman to be from henceforth husband and wife; and the same shall be good and effectual in law. And no other marriage, whatsoever, within the Commonwealth of England after the 29th September, 1653, shall be held or accounted a marriage according to the law of England."

It seems probable that John Browning and Mary Bennet were "proclaimed" at the church of Stroud; but that Thomas Harcourt and Margery Dunn, or one of them, lived at Painswick, and desired to be "published" in the market-place of their own town; though they were married at Stroud because, probably, the nearest Justice of Peace resided there.

The above are the only marriage entries in that form,— all others containing merely the names of the parties, and the dates of the marriages: and, as there is no appearance in the register of several other matters enacted and required to be done in it by the Ordinance, we may infer that very small regard was paid to the Ordinance, at Stroud. Indeed, its last and most stringent clause was annulled by an Ordinance (A.D. 1656, chap. 10) passed by the Parliament, which has been called the Little Parliament and the Barebone's Parliament; so that, thereafter, and especially from 1660, the time of the Restoration, until the end of the register, all the entries were made with greater regularity; though still in the bad hand-writing of inferior scholars.

During the period first specified, the Long Parliament had passed the Ordinance for removing ignorant and scandalous ministers; and others for taking away the Book of Common Prayer, for establishing and putting into execution "the Directory" for the public worship of God as therein set forth according to the Presbyterian mode, [4] for abolishing bishops, [5] and for substituting presbyters in the government of the church. [6] And though we have not ascertained the precise effect of either of those Ordinances, in regard to Stroud, we find that William Aston, (who is called Ackson by Atkyns,) vicar of Painswick, was, on a second accusation by his parishioners, ejected in February, 1639-40; as was his successor, Thomas Wild, afterwards.

4 Scobell, 1645, c. 51.

5 *Ibid*, 1646, c. 64.

6 *Ibid*, 1648, c. 118.

It is supposed that Mr. Aston was the second parochial clergyman sequestered. 7

We likewise find that Thomas Potter, the incumbent of Nympsfield, in the deanery of Stonehouse, was ejected from his benefice in 1644; and William Hart, clerk, was appointed in his stead, by the Gloucestershire, Hereford, &c., Committee for Scandalous Ministers. The original instrument by which this was effected has come into the writer's hands. It is written on a foolscap sheep of paper; and, from the rarity of such a document, and as a historical curiosity, a copy of it is given in Appendix C. It belonged to Mr. John Heart, who was for many years an inhabitant of Stroud; and whose monument was erected against the east wall of the north aisle of the church. A tradition has come down in his family, together with this writing, that Willlam Hart had an elastic conscience; and could be either an Episcopalian or Presbyterian, as best suited his worldly interest.

But the Restoration had its victims, as well as the Rebellion. Of these we are reminded, by finding the following entry in the old register:—" 1679. Daniel Capel, buried September 24." Daniel Capel was born at Gloucester, and had been rector of Shipton Moigne, in the deanery of Stonehouse, but was ejected from his Living in 1662, for his non-conformity: 8 on which he settled at Stroud, and practised physic there, chiefly for the benefit of the poor, as long as he lived. To this may be added the fact that, on the third line below the entry of his burial, is recorded the burial of Mr. Pleydell, the curate of the parish, in the following words:—" 1679. Robert Pleydwell, minister, buried November 8th": so near each other did these two good men live and die.

Here it may not be inappropriate to state that Daniel Capel was the son of the learned and eminent Richard Capel, who was for twenty years rector of Eastington, in Stonehouse deanery; which benefice he resigned in 1633, because he could not consent to read in his church "the

7 Walker's Sufferings of the Clergy, part i., p. 52; part ii., p. 182. He seems to have been in doubt whether Mr. Aston and Mr. Wild were vicars of the *same* Painswick. But both their names appear in Atkyns' list, *in loco*.

8 Under the Act of Uniformity, 13 & 14 Charles II., c. 4.

Book of Sports." 9   He retired to his living at Pitchcomb, where he was in great repute; preaching gratis to his congregation, and acting as a physician, (having studied physic at Oxford,) for the most part gratuitously.   He died there in the night of Sunday, September 21, 1656, aged 75, after preaching twice in the day, and recapitulating his discourses to his family in the evening; and was buried in the churchyard, where his monument, with a memorial of him yet stands; restored by some kind hand about the year 1850.   Among other valuable works, he published "Of Tentations; their nature, danger, and cure," which was dedicated to Sir William Guise, knight, and attained a fifth edition, with the addition of a fourth part in 1655, the year before his death.   His "Remains," with a quaintly written preface containing an abridgement of his life, was published by his friend Valentine Marshall, minister of Elmore, May 20, 1658.

Among the Ministers of Gloucestershire who were said to have been silenced and ejected by the Act of Uniformity, the name of Mr. Butt, of Stroud, appears in Calamy's list and in all others based on it; but we have not met with any local account of his officiating here as a Presbyterian minister, or otherwise.

The following particulars remain to be related, as belonging to the history of Mr. Pleydell's curacy, and of the rectory.   When Mr. Pleydell had been the minister for about fourteen years, George Lord Coventry, the owner of the Impropriation, suddenly withheld from him the £10 which he, his father and grandfather had previously paid to the incumbent; and continued to withhold it for about six years.   In consequence of this, Mr. Pleydell, about the year 1668, presented to him a petition, supported by a certificate from John Stephens, Esq., of Over Lypiatt, and another from the inhabitants of Stroud, requesting his Lordship to resume the accustomed payment.   Mr. Pleydell urged his claim on the ground of "having very little more profit besides, for the supply of the place, save what arose out of the charitable contributions of the parishioners, for the maintenance and support of his wife and family."   To

9 The Book of Sports was originally put forth by King James I., in 1618; and contained a list of games declared by him to be lawful for his subjects to practice on Sundays after evening service.   It was ordered to be read in churches.   In 1633 it was republished by King Charles I., and ordered to be so read.

this Mr. Stephens' certificate added, by way of personal recommendation of Mr. Pleydell, that he was "an honest man, an able, peaceable, orthodox minister, and no Presbyterian, as that term is used in opposition to Episcopal government." And he alleged that the Lord Keeper Coventry, when he purchased the Rectory, had an allowance made in his bargain, for continuing the old payment, [10] "as Thomas Tayloe of Bisley, an ancient grandjury-man, who says he was present at the contract between Mr. Willis, Clerk of the Crown, and Mr. Dashfield, secretary to your Lordship's grandfather, the Lord Keeper, saith he will depose." [11] Perhaps George Lord Coventry withheld the payment, because he had discovered that the grant of King James had not laid the grantees, his predecessors Baskervile and Blake, under any obligation to make the annual payment: and probably he became ready to accede to the petition, when he found that Mr. Pleydell, Mr. Stephens and the other inhabitants of Stroud, asked no more. But we have not any knowledge of what was the result of the application, further than that the £10 per annum has been regularly paid from that time to the present, by the successive Impropriators.

The name of another member of the family of Pleydell is spelled Pladwell in this register. In other writings we have seen it spelled—(and it was probably pronounced as spelled)—Pledwell, Plaidwell, Playdwell, Pleydell. "Josias Pleydell, the minister's son of Stroud, in Glo. (as Anthony Wood calls him) was entered a student of Brasen Nose Coll. 9th July, 1659, aged fifteen years. * * * Afterward he became minister of St. Peter's Church in Bristol, and Archdeacon of Chichester. He is the author of several sermons, &c." (Athenæ, Oxon.) We have also met with the name of Edward Pleydell as a witness to an attested copy of a

10 Probably because the old Lease, under which the £10 was payable, had not then expired.

11 Here, in 1668, we catch a sight of "Thomas Tayloe, an ancient grandjury-man of Bisley," as he flits across the long vista of 500 years: at the farther end of which we saw "Simon Tailo, the former portionary of a portion of the tithes" of that parish, in the Bisley Endowment of 1360. And these, with the good Hester Tayloe of 1788, and the prior and subsequent eminent clothiers of that name at Chalford, down to a few years since, furnish us with glimpses of a family which few others can rival in antiquity, and in such a continued residence in their original parish. Copies of the petition and certificate above referred to were kindly supplied us by the Rev. Thomas Keble, vicar of Bisley.

deed of Conveyance, in 1717; from which it may be conjectured that he was an attorney in Stroud, or its neighbourhood.

The name of Mr. Phipps, who succeeded Mr. Pleydell in the curacy, occurs only once in the old register, namely, in his signature with those of the two churchwardens, in the following entry:—"Collected for the breife of East Dereham, in the county of Norfolk, the sume of £01 01s. 11d., upon ye 21 day of March, an: 1679. Thomas Phipps, William Cole, Richard Fletcher."

This was the form required by law to be entered in the parish register; and also to be endorsed on the Brief itself, as the return of the persons to whom it had been addressed. The calamity, on occasion of which this Brief was granted, was a great fire which had almost destroyed the town of East Dereham in that year:[12] and, as the date of the entry is prior to the burial of Mr. Pleydell, it may be inferred that Mr. Phipps had been his assistant-curate in his life time.

12 A Church Brief was the King's open letter under the privy seal to the Archbishops, &c., licensing the petitioners for the brief to collect money for charitable purposes therein specified. Briefs appear to have been always subject to great abuses: and the statute 4th Anne, c. 14, enacted several regulations concerning them; especially as to the practice of farming briefs, or selling, upon a kind of speculation, the amount to be collected. They were read in churches, &c., and the alms were afterwards collected from the congregation, or from house to house. According to Burn's Ecclesiastical Law, title "brief," the charges of the brief and collecting £614 12s. 9d., for repairing a church in Westmoreland, amounted to £330 16s. 6d.; thus leaving only a clear sum of £283 16s. 3d., for its object. This expensive and objectionable machinery was abolished by statute 9, Geo. IV., c. 42. Briefs were common in my youth. The last I remember was in 1834; and soon after the issuing of them was discontinued. P.H.F.

CHAPTER XLIV.

IN the year 1635, that part of the charity property of the
parish which is now vested in the Trustees consisted
of—First : a piece of ground or tenement in Stroud, which
is supposed to be the same as was called "John of Pridie's"
in the Composition of 1304, with the several houses erected
thereon : which property was subject to the uses and purposes therein mentioned concerning it. Secondly : sundry
lands and tenements, the site of which was for £3 11s. 8d.
enfeoffed and released by Robert Bigg to Thomas Shewell,
Walter Shewell, and others, in the 15th year of Henry
VIII. (1524) by the description of "one tenement and one
garden in Stroud, *tenendum de Roberto Wye armigero ut de
manerio suo de Over Lippiat, pro redditu annuatim 4d., et
alia servitia inde primo debita*" : but of which no uses or
trusts were declared in the feoffment. Thirdly : a house or
capital messuage in Stroud, formerly in the tenure of
Thomas Weather, and a close of land called Church Furlong, containing four acres, in Nether Lypiatt, which had
been acquired by purchase from Giles Payne, in the 10th
year of Queen Elizabeth ; of which also no trusts had been
declared.

These three several properties were, by a feoffment of
February 12, 1636, made by Giles Davis and Edmund
Warner, (though signed by Giles Davis only,) granted and
enfeoffed to Thomas Freame, Esq., and others, upon trust
to expend all the rents and profits thereof, "to the uses,
intents, and purposes for which the same were at first given
and bestowed, that is to say, for and toward the reparations and amendments of the church of Stroud, so oft as
the same shall require ; and for and towards the relief,

maintenance, and support of the poor inhabitants within the said parish": and that, when the feoffees should be reduced by death to three, the survivors should, at the request of the whole or greater part of the parish, make a new deed of feoffment to twelve or more of the chief and most substantial inhabitants, on the same trusts.

The whole property so conveyed is described in that deed, as being eight several dwelling-houses within the town, together with "the Market-house lying near the churchyard there, and all the shops or rooms thereto belonging or adjoining"; and also the close of ground called the Church Furlong. This deed of feoffment is the first that declares these specific trusts of the property; but it states them to be the same trusts for which it was first given; although those trusts were, (as to the land supposed to be Pridie's,) very different from the purposes originally specified concerning it, in the Composition.

Besides the above premises, Samuel Watts, by his will dated 28th January, 1631, gave £200,—half of the profits of which were to be applied yearly toward the maintenance of the Lecturer in the chapel of Stroud, if it shall be continued; and the other half for the use of the poor of the parish: and, in case the lecture should not be continued, then the whole £200 to be employed for the use of the poor, and the profits thereof distributed unto them at four several times of the year, if conveniently it might be done; which £200 was, by Mr. Watts' executors, with the consent of the parish, laid out in the purchase of a messuage and about thirteen acres of land, called Warner's, in Colthrope, in the parish of Standish; and the same was, in 1634, in consideration of £189, conveyed by Giles and Walter Theyer to Daniel Watts and others, upon trusts similar to those mentioned in the will.

By a feoffment, dated November 11th, 1728, the whole of the before-mentioned charity premises was, by the direction of the four then surviving feoffees, conveyed to, and became vested in, John Stephens, John Cox, Edward Field, Thomas Warner, Henry Window, Thomas Stephens, Giles Gardner, Robert Webbe, Richard Plummer, George Bubb, Thomas Arundell, Thomas Bond, Brice Seed, and William Capel, their heirs and assigns, to the following uses and purposes, namely—as to the messuages, &c., in the town of Stroud and the Church Furlong, the same as are stated in the feoffment of 1636; and, as to one half of the rents of the land in Colthrope, for the maintenance of a Lecturer in the chapel or church of Stroud, to be chosen by the parishioners ; [1] and, as to the other half, for the benefit and maintenance of the poor inhabitants of the town and parish of Stroud : and, in case the lecture should cease, then all the profits should be to the maintenance and relief of the said poor : with a trust for renewing the number of feoffees, when reduced by death to four.

It has been already stated that the 15s. directed by the Composition of 1304 to be paid by the inhabitants toward the stipend of the curate, was raised to £15 ; which was paid by the feoffees out of the trust property. It was paid, though not uniformly, first to Mr. Pleydell, and then to Mr. Phipps, and Mr. Johns in succession : and, as to Mr. Johns, he sometimes received rents to the extent of £13 10s. in part, and was charged the remaining £1 10s. as a rent for the house he himself occupied for many years, which thereby acquired the name of the Minister's house. [2]

But, when Mr. Bond became the minister, not only was that sum withheld from him, but the party who had opposed him, immediately laid a Case before Mr. Serjeant John Cheshire, for his opinion as to the possibility of setting asside Mr. Bond's license to officiate, on the ground that the major part of the parishioners had the nomination of the minister, and that he had not been duly elected ;—but the Counsel's opinion dated Dec. 11, 1722, did not encourage any attempt to dispossess him.

In 1726, however, when Mr. Bond had been the minister for four years, some doubts arose as to his right to the £15 per annum ; and the majority of the then existing feoffees met, on the 6th of August, to consider the subject ; when, being of opinion that he ought to have the payment made to him, they signed an order for it, which order was "subscribed by almost all the substantial inhabitants of the parish"—who had then become generally reconciled to

1 Lectures first began to be established in the reign of Elizabeth. Archbishop Laud was for suppressing them, because they did not come by Presentation, but by the choice of the inhabitants : and probably, that was the reason why Mr. Samuel Watts made provision against their possible discontinuance at Stroud.

2 "The minister's house" is supposed to have been one of the feoffees houses, situated near the Cross. In the year 1689, £22 10s. 3d. was laid out in repairing and fitting it up for Mr. Johns. It was rebuilt about 1824, having its frontage in Nelson-street.

S2

him—"testifying their consent." Still, however, the £15 was not regularly paid until after the feoffment of 1728 had been made ; and then, on the 15th December, 1729, the major part of the new feoffees made an order "that it should be augmented to £20, until the arrears of £45 due to Mr. Bond should be satisfied ; and that the collector of the rents should pay it accordingly."

Among the opponents to the licensing of Mr. Bond to the curacy, and perhaps the most hostile of them, were Giles Gardner, Esq., of Stratford House, and Mr. William Capel, for several years churchwardens, and very influential persons in the parish : both of whom signed the last-mentioned order.

The augmented *beneficium* was duly paid for three years, and then it was discontinued : for Mr. Gardner having, as he said, discovered that the trusts of the feoffments did not warrant the payment of it—and Mr. Capel having concurred—"they acquainted the collector of the rents that he should not pay any more money to Mr. Bond with their consent" : and then, at a meeting of the feoffees on the subject, Mr. John Heart was appointed to receive and retain the rents of the premises in question, "to answer the true intention of the trusts, when determined."

Under these circumstances, Mr. Bond prepared to appeal to the law, for redress. And, on November 17th, 1737, an Information was filed in the Court of Chancery by the Attorney-General,[3] at the relation of Henry Bond, clerk, against Giles Gardner, William Capel, and the other feoffees ; in which, (after setting forth his election and license as minister of Stroud, the Endowment or Composition of 1304, the new trusts of the feoffments of 1636 and 1728, and the feoffees' order of 1726, with divers other matters and things,) he claimed that, by virtue of the ancient Composition, the said Henry Bond was entitled to the rents and profits of the several messuages and buildings erected on the piece ef ground called John of Pridie's, which buildings he described as "The Market-house, and the butchers' shops and other shambles and stalls thereto adjoining ; and all those messuages in the several possessions of Samuel Colborne, James Winchcombe, Ann Bubb,

3. Dudley Ryder, afterward Sir Dudley Ryder, Chief Justice of the King's Bench in 1754, and father of the first Lord Harrowby ; he himself having died just prior to the completion of a patent creating him a peer.

widow, and John Elby, all in the town of Stroud ": 4 or at
least that he was entitled unto the full and clear sum of
£15 a-year, to be issuing out of the same, and chargeable
thereon, as his predecessors had received the same for
eighty years and upward, which he was willing and thereby
offered to accept. And that he ought also to hold and
enjoy the house called the Minister's house, which was
therein stated to have been purchased out of the rents and
profits of the other buildings; and also a moiety of the
rents of the land at Colthrope.

The complaints laid in the Information were directed
chiefly against Messrs. Gardner and Capel, who it alleged
had "taken on themselves without the concurrence of either
of the other trustees, to hinder the plaintiff from receiving
any benefit from the said premises."

To this Information all the defendants put in their
Answers, admitting that there was some such ancient
Composition or agreement as set forth in the Information.
Messrs. Gardner and Capel, in two joint and several answers,
said, among other things, they had heard there was some
Land lying in or about the town of Stroud, called Pridie
Hay, or Pridie Hay Acre; but in what part of the town or
where the same exactly lay, they did not know; they did
not believe that the Market-house, messuages, &c., mentioned in the Information, or any of them, had been erected
or did stand upon the void piece of ground, in the Composition said to have been held by John of Pridie; and they
denied that the Relator had been chosen to be the Lecturer.
Messrs. John and Thomas Stephens, in their joint answer,
admitted that there was in Stroud a piece of ground which
might formerly have been in the tenure of John de Pridie,
and they believed some of the buildings and messuages
mentioned (if not all) had been esteemed to stand on such
ground or some part thereof; and that they were not for
hindering the Relator from receiving the £15 per annum,
and the moiety of the rents of the land at Colthrope.
But, both Messrs. Gardner and Capel and Messrs. John
and Thomas Stephens denied that the Relator was nominated to the curacy by the major part of the parishioners,
or that he had a right to the rents, &c., of the property in
Stroud, or to the "Minister's house"; and they maintained

4 Those four "messuages" occupied the sites of the five houses described
in page 59.

that the trusts named in the feoffments ought to be confirmed. The other defendants, Messrs. John Cox, Henry Window, Richard Plummer, Thomas Arundell, Thomas Bond, and Brice Seed, (the six other feoffees,) admitted, in their joint answer, that the Relator was well nominated to the curacy, and entitled to such dues as belonged to it; and they were willing that he should have the £15 per annum out of the premises; as also one moiety of the land at Colthrope, and the minister's house; and they admitted the feoffees' order for the £15 per annum.

At length, on the 4th May, 1741, after evidence given and counsel heard on both sides, the Lord Chancellor, Philip Lord Hardwicke, gave his Judgment to the following effect :—It would have been happy if the case had rested upon the agreement in 1726, but the Court must determine upon the mere right. I am of opinion that the Composition, of which the exhibition appeared, was the ancient one; and that, under the ancient Composition, the Curate of Stroud was entitled to the whole area or void piece of ground formerly held by John of Pridie, for his maintenance, and a house built for him thereon by the inhabitants; for *mansus* does not signify only a house for habitation, but takes in a curtilage, a garden or orchard. That, if the inhabitants had built other houses upon the area, yet the chaplain priest was entitled to the rents and profits of them, after the inhabitants had been reimbursed what they had expended; which, it might be presumed, they had long since been paid out of the profits. That it was manifest that in the deed of trust of 1636, Pridie's area, tenement, or acre, with the buildings thereon, were comprised; but were not the whole estate,—purchases made subsequent to the ancient endowment appearing. That the declaration of trust must follow the nature of the right; and therefore the uses of that and the subsequent feoffments, after the words —"To such uses as they were first given," ought to be rejected as contrary thereto. That the old rent of 1s. 6d. was to be continued to the Rectors; that the *Stipendum* of fifteen shillings per annum was to be paid to the Chaplain, though not to be considered as a rent, but as a personal contribution among the inhabitants. Then, as to the usage,—I consider that, from 1653, the fifteen pounds had been paid; and sometimes Mr. Johns had been allowed to receive certain of the rents as part of it. And, though there was no uniform payment, I think the order of 1726 a reasonable one, and it seems to me well settled. I am of opinion that the Curate is entitled to the rents of all the tenements built upon the land comprised in the Composition, if it can be distinguished ; otherwise it may be better to submit to the payment of £15 per annum ; which, if the parties do, the Court may by consent decree it ; but if they do not, I must direct an Enquiry, as to what tenements were built upon the land formerly held by John of Pridie. The minister is also entitled to a house, and he ought to enjoy it. As to Watts' (the Colthrope) land, the Friday Lecturer is entitled to half the rents of it, and not the Curate of Stroud ; but if he does preach the lecture, he might then be entitled to it, provided he be chosen."

The Chancellor also said of the Composition, " it is one of the clearest penned Instruments to be seen, considering its antiquity." [5]

The Lord Chancellor put off his final Judgment for seven days, in order that the feoffees might come to an agreement with Mr. Bond : and this was effected by the apprehended difficulty of ascertaining what was John of Pridie's land, by the delay and expenses that would be caused in the Inquiry, by the fear that the cost of the Suit would be decreed against the party failing in it, and by Mr. Bond's agreeing to accept £20 per annum in lieu of his claim of the estate, and of the house he claimed as the minister's. This was communicated to the Court ; and then, on May 15, 1741, the Lord Chancellor made his Decree by consent ; whereby it was ordered—" that the Trustees of the Charity in question should for ever thereafter pay to the Relator and his Successors, Curates or Chaplains of Stroud, £20 per annum by half-yearly payments at Lady-day and Michaelmas, clear of all deductions, taxes, &c., out of the rents and profits of the houses, land, and premises in Stroud, mentioned in the Information, to commence from the time when the annual £15 ceased to be paid ; and that the annual sum of £20 should be accepted and taken in full satisfaction of any claim or demand which the Relator, or his Successors, Curates or Chaplains of Stroud, might have or claim out of any of those lands or houses, and also in lieu of a dwelling-house

5 The writer has given the foregoing account of the Judgment, from letters (in his possession,) written by Mr. John Turner and Mr. Thomas Stephens, from London the day after its delivery, at which they were present. See also Barnardiston's Report.

for the Relator and his successors.   His Lordship further
declared that one moiety of the clear rents and profits of
the land and premises in Colthrope, called Watts' Lands,
ought to be applied towards the maintenance of the Friday's
Lecturer of Stroud aforesaid ; and that all parties should
be paid their costs out of the surplus rents and profits of
the said premises, over and above the £20 per annum.

In this suit Mr. Richard Plummer, of The Thrupp, one
of the feoffees, was attorney for the plaintiff ; and Mr. John
Turner, of Ebley, for the defendants.   Mr. Coxe was counsel
for the plaintiff, and Mr. Murray [6] for the defendants.

It will be seen that the Decree did not settle what was
the proper application of the surplus rents of the houses,
&c., on Pridie's land, which the Chancellor had said was
included in the feoffments, because by the compromise
between the parties, that question had ceased to be a
subject for adjudication.   But, from the Judgment delivered
we learn his opinion, that the expressed trusts of the feoffments concerning them were void, as being contrary to the
rights of the case.

6 William Murray, afterward successively Solicitor and Attorney-General,
and in 1756 Chief Justice of the King's Bench, and the first Earl of Mansfield.

CHAPTER XLV.

COPIES OF THE COMPOSITION — THE EXEMPLIFICATION OF 1493
— COPIES OF AN OLD TRANSLATION OF IT.

IN the year 1724 there were extant in this neighbourhood
several manuscript copies of the original text of the
Composition of the Chapel of Stroud, either singly or comprised in copies of the Exemplification of it ; but we know
of only two of them as being in existence at present.

Of these, one is contained in the copy—the only known
copy—of the Exemplification before mentioned as being
in the feoffees' chest. It is in an old handwriting, upon
foolscap paper somewhat damaged by much use ; and is in
words of which many are abbreviations, as was usual, and a
few are illegible, or imitations of illegible words.

In the text of this copy, the words which designate the
land held by John of Pridie and set apart by the rectors,
are "*Area*" (an open or void space) "*seu tenementum in la
Strode*" ; and those used to express the object or purpose
for which it was to be set aside, are "*ad mansum*," (from
mansus a dwelling-house,) for the residence of the chaplain
priest.

The other copy of the original text is contained in the
Case laid before Sergeant Cheshire, as before mentioned :[1]
and is in the possession of the writer with other papers of
the attorney for the defendants in the Chancery suit. This
copy is in words at full length, and was evidently made
from a text differing from that first above mentioned—
having many verbal variations from it ; among which the
words used to designate Pridie's land, are "*Acra*"—(an
acre in quantity)—"*seu tenementum*" ; and those that express its purpose or object, are "*Ad mensam*," (from *mensa*
a table to eat on, and)—by metonymy a meal, or a maintenance for the priest. Here the term "*acra*" corresponds
with the name "Pridie's Hay Acre,"[2] by which some land

[1 p. 259.]

[2 It is remarkable that Haie is Hedge in French, and that there still is a
place in the upper part of the town of Stroud called Acre Hedge !]

"in or about Stroud" was traditionally spoken of; as was admitted by Messrs. Gardner and Capel in their joint Answer filed in Bond's suit.

There was yet another copy "in a parchment writing" in the hands of Mr. John Stephens, of Lypiatt, which he and his son, in their answer filed in the suit, called "the Exemplification, or a copy of the Exemplification, before John Thour, Chancellor of the Bishop of Worcester in 1493; in which parchment," they say, "the land is called *Area seu tenementum in la Strode, quam vel quod Johannes de Pridie pro certo redditu hactenus tenuit de rectoribus ante dictis*, which then piece of void ground has since, as these defendants believe, by corruption been called Pridie acre, or Pridehay acre." But they do not say by what words the object of appointing it was expressed. This "parchment writing" they offered to produce to the court, and probably it was so produced, but it is not known what has become of it.

Besides the copy of the entire Exemplification, and the copy of the Composition (alone) above mentioned as still existing in their original text, there is an ancient English version of the whole Exemplification, of which two copies are yet extant.

One of them is in the handwriting of the Rev. Stephen Philips, vicar of Bisley, and is marked by him as having been "copyed out of a copy of the original" which he "had from Mr. Tho. Stephens of Lypiatt ye 16 of November 1716." In the Composition which it comprises the appointment of John of Pridie's land is stated thus;—" So that the place of void ground or tenement should be by them "—the rectors—"applied for the maintenance of the same priest:" and if in this respect its original was faithfully rendered, it must have been different from both of those before mentioned. It is now preserved in the feoffees' chest along with their copy of the original Exemplification.

The other copy is in the writer's possession. It is on a sheet of foolscap paper, the fly-leaf of which is damaged by much using: and probably it is the copy formerly belonging to Mr. Stephens, from which Mr. Philips made his transcript. This may be inferred from their exact accordance with one another in all their verbal and other peculiarities.

Among these peculiarities is the following strange mis-translation in the Composition. In stating the great and dangerous distance between the chapel of Stroud and the mother church at Bisley, the original text reads, "*tantam et tam periculosam distantiam existere nullatenus ambigatur*"; and the translator has rendered the two last words, which in English mean "no manner of doubt," by "that men can't well pass betwixt" those places. Another peculiarity is in the substance of the Exemplification which, although it was made from the same original as the feoffees' copy—the first Exemplification—and carries the date of 1493 in the body of it,—yet, in its beginning (and no where else) it has the name of John Chews instead of John Thour; and ends with the date of the second Exemplification—(41 Elizabeth, January 10, 1598)—copied from its original Latin text. Mr. Philips did not make any comment on this strange confounding of the names or of the dates.

It is probable that, in preparing the Information filed in his suit, Mr. Bond's solicitor made use of a translation similar to Mr. Philip's copy, in stating the contents of the Composition; for they are accompanied with the mistranslation—"that men can't well pass betwixt," as appears in that copy. [3] The Information also states that, in the year 1493, the Composition was exemplified by John Chews, Doctor of Laws, Chancellor, &c., of the then Bishop of Worcester; and again by John Thour, Chancellor, &c., in 1598: but it does not appear that this allegation raised any question, or had any bearing on the matters at issue, nor have we met with any copy of the latter Exemplification.

Further,—it may be presumed from what the Lord Chancellor said when he delivered his Judgment in the Cause, that the ancient Composition referred to by him, "whereof the exhibition appeared," was in the original text; [4] and that he well knew how the different copies of the Composition contained different words to designate John of Pridie's land, and different words to express the purpose for which it was appointed.

3 Mr. Rudder saw both the original text of the Exemplification, and its English version in the handwriting of Mr. Philips; for he has introduced this singular mis-translation into the article, "Stroud," in his History of Gloucestershire.

4 It might be thought that the feoffees' copy was the one exhibited; but it is not marked with the usual evidence of an exhibit.

CHAPTER XLVI.

IT may now be inquired,—where in Stroud is John of
of Pridie's land? This is a question of local curiosity
even now; and it may become of so much greater importance hereafter, as to justify an attempt to answer it.

At this distance of time we cannot expect to find any
precise account of the early dealings of the inhabitants, or
the parish authorities who represented them, with the place
referred to: but they must have been acquainted with the
terms and conditions on which it was given to them; and
it may be safely presumed that they erected on it a house,
as directed by the Composition; though it cannot be
known whether it was occupied as a residence for the
chaplain priest. It may also be presumed that, in course
of time, other houses were built upon it; and that, at
length, a market-place was set out, and a Market-house
erected on this convenient piece of open ground, to meet
the wants of an increased population: and that the inhabitants received and applied the rents of it, together with those
of the other charity property subsequently obtained by gift
from Robert Bigg, and by purchase from Giles Payne.

We have likewise seen that all the charity property,
passed by the feoffments of February 12th, 1636, and
November 11th, 1728, by the descriptions therein contained
of its several parts; that it came to the feoffees, against
whom Mr. Bond brought his suit in 1737; and is now
vested in their successors the present trustees.

It also appears, according to the Lord Chancellor's Judgment, "that in the feoffments Pridie's Area Tenement or
Acre was comprised."

Moreover, in "some ancient Court rolls of the manor of
Over Lypiatt, (which includes Stroud,) one Giles Davis
was entered as a free-tenant for Pridehay:"[1] and it is

---

[1] This was stated in the Answer of Messrs. John and Thomas Stephens,
filed in Bond's suit. The Court Rolls were 2, 10, and 20 of Elizabeth.

noticeable that Giles Davis is one of the two surviving feoffees, who are named as grantors of all the charity property to the succeeding feoffees, in the deed of 1636.

If, therefore, we can ascertain the particulars of the respective premises obtained from Bigg and Payne, and can determine their present situations in the town, so as to eliminate them from the residue of the parish property, we shall not fail to have discovered, in that residue, the required John of Pridie's land.

Now, though Bigg granted his property in 1524 to Thomas and Walter Shewell and others, by the description of "one tenement and one garden in Stroud," it was conveyed by their survivors to the new feoffees in 1570, as "all their lands and tenements in Stroud which they held of the feoffment of Robert Bigg;" from which it may be inferred that it was of considerable dimensions, and had been then further built upon. We also find from an old account-book of the feoffees, that, in 1607, "a plot of ground in length from north to south ten yards, and from east to west nine yards or thereabouts, with certain inches," (on which one Edward Pritchard had then lately built a house,) was demised by the feoffees to him and William and Jane, his son and daughter, for their lives, at the rent of 6s. 8d. per annum, which plot must have been part of Bigg's gift; and we find, from the same old account-book, that in 1723 the feoffees paid Mr. Stephens, the then Lord of the Manor, £2 for waste land, which was probably added to it. From this we conclude that the property of the trustees, which now forms the east or upper end of the Cross, and extends forty-three yards up the north side of Nelson-street, is the present representative, and occupies the site, of what was conveyed by Mr. Bigg.

Further, it cannot be doubted that the "house or capital messuage in Stroud," bought of Giles Payne, is now represented by the single large dwelling-house and shop situated nearly in the centre of the south side of High-street, with the garden behind it, lately rented by Mr. James Butt. This house was, some few years since, rebuilt by the feoffees, on the site of the old house in which Miss Jenner formerly lived and kept the Post Office. [2]

The residue of the charity property in Stroud lies in a quadrangular group, between Church-street on the east,

2 For which see p. 42.

Mr. Withey's house and other premises on the west, the churchyard on the north, and High-street on the south : and there, I apprehend, we have found John of Pridie's land—the "Area" of the Composition.

It contains the six houses, the Corn Hall, the Shambles, and Market-house, mentioned in pages 59 and 60 ; comprising all, (except "the minister's house,") that was claimed by Mr. Bond in his suit ; and has always been traditionally regarded as the site of John of Pridie's land.

It must not be forgotten, however, that it has been called Pridie's Acre. Sir Robert Atkyns says, when mentioning the benefactions of Stroud, "There is an acre of land called Priddy, lying at the end of the town, which has been improved by building, to £17 yearly." 3 And though the quadrangular area in question is only one rood and twenty-two perches in extent, it may be the remainder of a full acre, reduced to its present size by some rectors having in times long past sold, or otherwise disposed of, the other parts of it for building ground.

There are many instances of land having retained its original name long after it had ceased to be of the quantity indicated by the original name ; and the "Area" called Pridie's Acre is one of them. Accordingly, if we take the length of the quadrangle as the base of a somewhat irregular triangle, extended westward toward the bottom of High-street, the area inclosed is an almost exact acre in extent, and will represent the original "Acre"—Pridy-Hay acre—situated at the end of the town.

In confirmation of this, Giles Davis, by a deed of January 20, 1619, covenanted with Wm. Rogers and Wm. Gough to levy to them a Fine of, (among other things,) "Those messuages and cottages in Stroud, in the lower end of the town, in the tenure of Wm. Cook and John Street, which were erected on a parcel of ground there called Pridy-hay, and of several little messuages or cottages in Stroud aforesaid, in the lower end of town, then in the tenure of Giles Gosling and Robert Wathen, but also upon parcel of the ground called Pridy-hay, to the use of Giles for life, with remainder to Anne, his wife, for her life, and after her decease,—the first messuage to the use of John Davis his son in tail ; and, of the seven latter, to the use of Wm. Davis his son in tail."

3 History, p. 368, 2nd edition.

The addition of the following particulars concerning the Market-house, Market-place, houses, &c., on this quadrangular area, may be interesting.

On May 15, 1650, John Bond took a lease for lives of "All those standings, pantices, [pent-houses], shambles and stalls, in a place called the Pitching, all pickage [pitchage] and stallage there, all benefit of stalls and standings in the said place called the Pitching; except the standings adjoining the house of Nathaniel Gardner and under the Market-house," (which had been previously let,) "at the rent of £6 10s. per annum."

The west and south sides of the Market-place which forms the interior of the group, were anciently fitted up with massive oak stalls, having heavy stone-tiled roofs, for the market butchers; and these were yet standing in my boyhood. But, about the year 1845, the stalls against the south wall were removed to make room for an enlargement of the two houses, against the backs of which they stood; and those on the west side were replaced by others, the tables of which were raised up and let down on hinges, having a light stationary roof supported on iron pillars: and, when the stalls were not in use, the roof was, and still is, a continuous covered way of sixty-five yards, from High-street to the main entrance-gate of the churchyard.

In 1726, £3 was received for shops and ware-room "in the Market-house and Blind-house"; £1 10s. was paid by Joane Derrett for three-quarters of a year's rent "for the butter women's stools," on the lower floor; and John Bond rented the collecting of the tolls for the stalls, &c., at £6 12s. for one year. The amount collected depended, perhaps, on the vigilance of the collector; for, in November, 1728, the sum received of Richard Bond "for two days he collected before Michaelmas was 19s. 2d.; and of George Bubb for the two days he collected 18s. 4d.," as the total accounted for in that year.

In 1727, Thomas Bubb paid £1 for a year's rent of a room in the Market-house; and Wm. Adey £2 12s. 6d. for three-quarter's of a year's rent of the Blind-house and lower floor of the Market-house. And a lease for twenty-one years was granted to Wm. Adey, of "the Pitching, the Market-house under the Hall, the Blind-house, the two tenements, &c., with all the standings thereof," at the rent of £38 10s. per annum, from Michaelmas, 1727; but the rent was irregularly paid, and soon ceased altogether.

Originally the Lectures before mentioned were preached by clergymen of the neighbourhood, chosen by the parishioners and paid by their contributions. But, from the year 1742, the Incumbents of Stroud, having been chosen to preach the Lectures, have received one-half of the yearly income of Watts' Charity, and the other half ought to have been distributed among the poor of the parish, according to the trusts of it. 4

These lectures, formerly called The Friday Lectures, were delivered on the mornings of twenty successive market-days after Good Friday in each year, being chiefly intended for the benefit of persons who came to the market : and I knew an old lady who, in her early days, had seen butter women come into the south aisle of the church, and place their baskets beside them during the service.

In 1826, at the expiration of nearly 100 years, the Charity Commissioners of Enquiry reported that "the bounds of what is called Priddie's Acre, are traditionally known ; that it lies contiguous to the churchyard ; and has four tenements, with the Market-house and shops, Shambles, and three stables upon it ; also a garden, and a lock-up house, or temporary place of confinement. That the four houses are severally let to four distinct tenants, but one of the tenants holds, together with his tenement, the Market-house and garden." And further, that one of the houses near the Cross, which was formerly occupied by the clergyman, had been rebuilt by the feoffees out of the savings of the income, at the cost of £700. In noticing the rest of the feoffees' property, however, they confounded the separate acquisitions made by the gift from Bigg to Shewell, and by the purchase from Payne,—attributing both to Bigg. But they stated the rent of the whole as follows : the four houses, Market-house, Market-place, &c., £169 ; the other house in High-street, and the three houses at the Cross and Nelson-street, £115 ; the Church furlong, £9 ; and the land at Colthrope, £15 ; making a total of £308 per annum.

Since that report was made, the stables and lock-up house, which stood at the north end of the Market-house,

---

4 For which see Chap. xliv. Upon only two occasions was any such distribution made, from 1742 to 1814.

have been taken down ; and a covered butchers' market erected on the site. This was done in 1848, though it is not now used for that purpose : and, since that time, some rooms have been built on part of it, for the use of the Judge and officers of the County Court. The large room or Hall, formerly the school-room, in the Market-house, is now rented for the sittings of the County Court, the local Magistrates, the Local Board of Health, and other purposes ; but it is to be regretted that the Pitching, Shambles, or Market-place, (as it has been indifferently called,) and the room under the Hall, have not lately been so much frequented, as formerly, by butchers and other marketfolks.

For many years prior to Mr. Bond's suit, the annual income of the Feoffees' Charity Property was expended on the fabric of the church, and in payments made to the churchwardens for purposes connected with the maintenance of Divine worship in it ; and then, what remained was given to the poor. That remainder was for the year 1715, £5 15s. ; for 1716 and each of the six following years, £4 10s. ; and for 1736, £9 13s. 6d. ; which sums were distributed, at Christmas time, among the poor of the four tythings of the parish, by respectable persons residing there.

But, when the feoffees had discharged the costs of Mr. Bond's suit, and the arrears of his old salary, they thenceforward disposed of the whole of their net income in the payment of £20 per annum to the Minister according to the Lord Chancellor's decree, in the repairing, improving, and rebuilding their various house property, and in those other matters which, otherwise, must have been done and provided at the expense of the churchwardens ;—such as, the enlargement, and walls of the churchyard ; cleaning, warming, and lighting the church ; visitation fees ; salaries of clerks, sextons, and organists ; chiming the bells ; clock and chimes ; surplices, and wine for the communicants ; and whatever else was necessary for the due celebration of Divine worship therein :—so that no church-rate was levied on the parish from that time.

This was done by repayments to the churchwardens for the expenses they had incurred ; and was continued until the year 1859, when a question was raised as to the lawfulness of the feoffees' expenditure for those purposes. This was referred to the Charity Commissioners of England and

Wales,[5] and they ordered the discontinuance of all such payments in future.

The number of the feoffees was now reduced by death to four;[6] and the Commissioners, by an order of June 20, 1862, "discharged them, at their own desire, from being trustees of the Charity ; and appointed the Incumbent and Churchwardens for the time being of the parish of Stroud —Sebastian Stewart Dickinson, William Henry Paine, James Charles Hallewell, George Holloway, George William Saunders, Sidney Biddell, Richard Grist, William Lane, William Henry Withey, John Dutton Hunt, and William Holmes, to be new trustees for the managing of the same Charity."

The following is a statement of the gross income of the Charity property for the year 1869 :—

1st.—*Pridie's " Area," comprising:*

		£	s.	d.
The Town Hall—Judge's and officers' rooms—				
Use of by the Stroud County Court		40	0	0
Ditto „ Magistrates in Petty Sessions ...		10	0	0
„ „ Local Board of Health		2	10	0
„ „ Highway Board		2	0	0
„ „ Occasional Meetings		8	12	3
Tolls of Shambles and Market-place		7	19	9
The Corn Hall Hotel, and Corn Hall		60	0	0
The three houses fronting High-street		135	0	0
		266	2	0

2nd.—*Robert Bigg's:*

					£	s.	d.
The three houses above the Cross, and in Nelson-street	80	16	0				
Land, Church Furlong, at the Thrupp ...	9	0	0				
					89	16	0

3rd.—*Giles Payne's:*

	£	s.	d.
The house on the south side of High-street	55	0	0
	£410	18	0

Watts' Charity, held on its own separate trusts, as before mentioned:

	£	s.	d.
House and land at Colthrope	15	0	0
£177 7s. 6d., 3 per cent. Consols, (the produce of timber felled in 1806,) now vested in the Charity Commissioners	5	6	4
	£20	6	4

[5] Acting under Stat. 18 & 19 Victoria, c. 124; and the other powers vested in them.

[6 viz. : W. H. Stanton, W. Capel, Robert Gordon, and C. H. Fisher.]

CHAPTER XLVII.

REV. HENRY BOND — HIS CHARITY SCHOOLS — REV. JOHN WARREN — REV. JAMES WEBSTER — REV. WILLIAM ELLIS, HIS OFFICIATING CURATE — MR. ELLIS' SUNDAY SCHOOLS.

AFTER the decision of the Lord Chancellor in Mr Bond's suit, the relation between Mr. Bond and his parishioners became more friendly during the remainder of his incumbency. He took a great interest in the conduct and improvement of the several charity schools established by the Rev. William Johns in the year 1700. And, with this object, certain "Orders" were agreed upon by the "Society for the better management of the Charity schools, October 12th, 1732," under the signatures of "Henry Bond, Minister—Joshua Thorpe, (a resident physician,) Treasurer, and

Richard Arundell	John Dallaway	John Hearte
J. Stephens	Richard Cole	Robert Browne
Thos. Stephens	Joseph Colborne	Jas. Winchcombe
J. Hearte, junr.	Samuel Colborne	Anth. Pettat
Jona Wathen	Thomas Bond	Richard Aldridge : "
Robert Webbe	Richard Plummer	

All of whose names are worthy of being honourably recorded "as real friends of the poor."

A treasurer of the society was annually chosen, and fifteen several persons filled that office in the next twenty-six years. Mr. Bond was the author of a sermon entitled —"A Legacy for a Careless World; or, the Christian's Task, set forth in a discourse upon the funeral occasion of Samuel Packer, from Ecclesiastes ix. 10; by Henry Bond, L.L.B., Curate of Stroud; with a preface on the Evils of Idleness. Gloucester, printed for the author, 1739." S. Packer was a poor man, of whom the preacher said—"His thatched cottage and low condition of life hindered not the influence of his shining virtues from falling down upon the minds and hearts of the neighbourhood round about him."

But I have not found his name in the parish register of burials. An anonymous pamphlet entitled—"A New Year's Gift for the parishioners of the parish of Stroud," printed at Gloucester in 1749, is also attributed to Mr. Bond. It consists of sundry books of "Observations and Instructions"—being a collection of proverbs, wise sayings, &c.

Very early in the curacy of Dr. John Warren, who succeeded Mr. Bond, he, with Mr. Samuel Arundell and several other parishioners, became dissatisfied with the small stipend of £20 per annum for the Minister; and were desirous that the whole of the Feoffees' Fund should be appropriated according to the original intention of the Composition of 1304. With this view, money was raised by subscription to enable them to commence legal proceedings; and Dr. Warren obtained the opinion of the Solicitor-General on the case, who advised that the decree made by the Lord Chancellor in 1741 would be considered as binding upon the charity, the trustees, and the curate or chaplain of Stroud: to which he added that—considering the antiquity of the original endowment, and the expense, inconvenience, and difficulty of making strict enquiries, and restoring matters according to the precise original right, at that distance of time, he by no means thought it advisable for Dr. Warren, or any succeeding curate, to attempt unravelling the grounds and merits of that decree:[1] and, thereupon, the attempt was relinquished.

It has been already stated that Mr. Webster succeeded to the curacy in 1774; which date was given on the authority of the diocesan register. But, in reality, he had become the Minister of Stroud, and had entered upon his clerical duties and the receipt of the income in 1772,—two years before that time. We learned this fact from two letters of Mr. John Colborne, of Stroud, to Mr. Webster; the first dated September 26, 1772, wherein he says: "Mr. Coulson"—(the previous officiating Curate)—"has left us; and Mr. Ellis has entered on the Cure, much to the satisfaction of your parishioners";—the second dated February 27, 1773, saying he had received rent from one of the tenants of the parsonage land. An explanation of the discrepancy in those dates may probably be found in a

---

[1] This appears from a letter addressed by Dr. Warren to "Mr. Samuel Arundell, at Stroud," dated November 28, 1760, in my possession.—P.H.F.

letter of July 19, 1773, (of which we made a note,) from
Dr. Warburton, Bishop of Gloucester, to Mr. Webster,—
relating to the exchange of the curacy of Stroud for Much
Cowerne, in Herefordshire, which it seems had been pro-
posed ; and on this account, perhaps, the entry of Mr.
Webster's license in the episcopal register was delayed
until the question of the exchange had been settled. Mr.
Webster married a niece of Dr. Warburton ; and from him,
Mr. Webster obtained the curacy of Stroud, the vicarage of
Much Cowerne, the archdeaconry of Gloucester, and the
rectory of Dursley, which last was annexed to that dignity.

In consequence of the non-residence of Mr. Webster at
Stroud, the Rev. William Ellis, his officiating Curate, had
the sole clerical charge of the parish for thirty-two years,—
terminating only at his death.

Mr. Ellis had a taste for music and drawing ; but he was
a subject of colour-blindness, so that if his colours were
accidentally disarranged, he sometimes used one instead of
another ; and I have seen a lady's portrait, drawn and
coloured by him, in which the cheeks were tinted green
instead of flesh colour. His sight was also weak ; and
when the chancel of the church was rebuilt in 1789, its
semi-circular headed window was made so large as nearly
to fill the east end, in order to supply him with sufficient
light in the reading desk and pulpit. He was somewhat of
a humourist and punster ; and it has been said that at a
clerical meeting, where he was called on after dinner for a
toast, he proposed, in the comprehensive words of the old
hundredth psalm, " All people that on earth do dwell ! "

It must be recorded to the honour of Mr. Ellis that,
besides the great interest he took in the daily schools
established by Mr. Johns, which were supported by subscriptions and by collections at an annual sermon,—he,
with the help of a few members of his congregation, introduced the important institution of Sunday schools into this
parish ; and opened four of such schools in May and June
1784, viz., at the Market-house, Whiteshill, Stroud's-hill, (as
its place in Parliament-street was then called,) and Thrupp.
Thomas Aldridge, the sexton of the parish, was the first
master or teacher of the Sunday school at the Market-
house.

On the 29th of July in the same year, being the thanksgiving day for the Peace that followed the American war,
Mr. Ellis preached a sermon " On the method of keeping

the Sabbath day, and its rewards," from Isaiah lviii., 13, 14; which was printed and published for the benefit of those Sunday schools. To the printed sermon was appended "Rules for the management of the Sunday schools in the parish of Stroud," of which the first directed that—

"The master or dame, appointed by the subscribers, shall attend at his or her house every Sunday morning during the summer, from eight till half-past ten; and every Sunday evening during the summer, from half an hour after five till eight o'clock, to teach reading, the church catechism, and some short prayers from a little collection by Dr. Stonehouse; and also to read (or to have read by some of those who attend, if they can do so sufficiently) three or four chapters of the Bible in succession, that people may have connected ideas of the history and consistency of the Scriptures."

The second rule states that—

"The persons to be taught are chiefly the young men who are past the usual age of admission to the weekly schools, and by being obliged to labour for their maintenance cannot find time to attend them. But grown persons that cannot read, who are desirous of hearing God's word, and to learn the church catechism, are desired to attend and endeavour to learn, by hearing the younger taught and instructed."

In explanation of the first rule, it must be noticed that then, and for many years after, there was not any public building in the parish adapted for a Sunday school, except the Market-house; and, in explanation of the second rule, that children were admitted to the day-school when about five years old, and were removed from them by their parents, and sent to work at the mills or elsewhere, at the early age of seven.

Other rules stated that some of the subscribers would in turn visit these schools; and that—

"All that attend these schools should, as much as might be, attend the public worship both morning and afternoon on Sunday." To these rules Mr. Ellis added "an account or explanation" of them, "for the benefit of those who might be disposed to establish schools of the like nature in other places"; and therein he stated that "as soon as he was apprised of the beneficial effects of Sunday schools as conducted at Gloucester, he perceived they would at once lessen his Sunday evening's labour of teaching, examining, and instructing the poor children of the parish in the church catechism, and render it more effectual." That "some of the children who were brought up to other communions, are enjoined to attend their respective places of worship devoutly, and required to give an account of the preacher's text." "The youngest are taught first, Dr. Watts' short prayers, pages 42 and 43; and when they are perfect in them they learn the additions to them." The minister and some of the subscribers attend one of these schools every Sunday evening, and make such familiar observations on the Scriptures and catechism as they think adapted to such young minds. The teachers are sober, serious persons, whose indigent circumstances make the moderate pay of one shilling per Sunday an adequate recompense."

Thus simple and unpretending were the origin and the plan of the important institution of Sunday schools in Stroud. These schools, which were at once attended by 140 persons, are said to have been the first established after the introduction of Sunday schools into Gloucester in 1783. Mr. Bond's "orders" contained much of the principle of a Sunday school, which was being acted upon at the time the Rev. Mr. Stock preached a sermon at Stroud on behalf of our weekly schools, in 1782 ; and as Mr. Stock was the friend and coadjutor of Mr. Robert Raikes, it has been suggested [2] that what had fallen under his notice there, probably furnished some idea for the management of the (supposed) original Sunday school, on its first establishment in Gloucester.

In the year 1760 Mr. Thomas Baylis, of New Mills, was chosen treasurer of the charity schools ; which office, with that of an attending subscriber, he filled with great zeal for nearly forty years, viz., until 1799, when he was succeeded as treasurer by Messrs. Benjamin and Joseph Grazebrook, bankers ; and someone connected with their successors in the Bank has held that office up to the present time.

On May 7, 1799, it was resolved that an annual steward should be chosen at the meeting to be held on the evening of the day on which the charity sermon or sermons should be preached ; who should, among other things, "audit the accounts of the treasurers for the payments of moneys, and solicit the assistance of a clergyman to preach the charity sermon for that year." From this time until 1833 the steward was nominated in the vestry, after the evening service of the day on which the annual charity sermons were preached, and the contributions collected were handed to the treasurer ; and he provided and entertained the preacher of the next annual sermons ; but since that year the preacher has been selected by the Incumbent. The amount of the sums collected on those occasions has varied from year to year according to circumstances, of which the chief seems to have been the popularity of the preacher for the day.

---

2 By the Rev. John Williams, in his interesting "Account of the Sunday and Weekly Charity Schools, established in the parish of Stroud, for the religious instruction of the children of the poor," &c., and his report of the schools for 1814-15.

The Sunday schools were originally supported by a fund distinct from that of the daily schools ; and Mr. Ellis, being appointed treasurer to them, discharged the office until his death ; when the Charity was indebted to him in the sum of £51 10s., which was kindly remitted by his executors.

On the 20th of November, 1804, it was resolved that "the subscriptions raised in support of the Sunday and weekly schools should be united into one fund ; with the proviso that the dividend accruing from £150 vested in the Three per Cent. Consols, 3 and the bequest of one pound per annum from the Rev. Wm. Johns, be applied solely toward the support of the weekly schools."

Mr. Ellis lived in the ancient house on Beeches Green already mentioned ; 4 where he died August 2nd, 1804, aged 59 years. There, too, his relict, Ann Maria Ellis, resided ; and there she died, November 21st, 1842, in the 39th year of her second widowhood, 5 aged 84 ; having been the vigilant superintendent of the Girls' Sunday school at the Market-house for many years.

3 This sum was purchased in the year 1799 with the following legacies, viz. :—Mrs. Anne Colborne's £20, paid November 1, 1780 ; the Rev. John Copson's £21, paid October 26, 1785 ; Mr. William Wathen's £5, paid March 26, 1790 ; and Mr. Robert Hughes' £10, paid July 2nd, 1795 ; with other money accumulated in the hands of the treasurer.

4 See p 95.

5 She was the widow of Mr. Robert Hughes mentioned in the note above, and in pp. 58 and 60, when she was married to Mr. Ellis, himself a widower.

CHAPTER XLVIII.

Mr. Webster died at Dursley, June 7, 1804, in the 72nd
year of his age.

On his death, the Rev. John Seagram was licensed by
Bishop Huntingford to the perpetual curacy of Stroud;
and Mr. Seagram appointed the Rev. John Williams to be
his curate in charge.

Mr. Williams was a native of Sidmouth, Devonshire;
but, in his early years, his parents removed to Plymouth,
where he was educated at Dr. Bidlake's seminary. Becoming a constant attendant on the ministry of Dr. Robert
Hawker, vicar of Charles, in that town, he frequently
accompanied him on his visits to, and his prayer meetings
at, the houses of his poor parishioners. At length encouraged by Dr. Hawker to enter the Christian ministry, he
received preparatory instruction from the Rev. T. Drewett,
incumbent of Cheddar; and, after studying at St. Edmond's
Hall, Oxford, was ordained from thence.

He commenced his clerical duties at Stroud, April 18,
1805 ; and Mr. Seagram being non-resident during the
whole of his incumbency, Mr. Williams had the care of
the parish for twenty-eight years. He preached his first
sermon on the following Sunday, April 21, from the words
of St. Paul (1 Corinthians ii. 2)—"I determined to know
nothing among you, save Jesus Christ, and him crucified."
And, following up the theme of Jesus as the Christ—even
the crucified one,—he made justification by grace through
faith, and good works as the fruit and evidence of faith,—
(those cardinal doctrines of the Reformation) the chief
subjects of his teaching as long as he lived. His youthful
enthusiasm, the spirituality of his views, and his earnestness of purpose, at once aroused attention. He was

welcomed by thoughtful persons ; and his general accept-
ableness was shewn by a considerable increase in the
number of his hearers,—many of whom, being moved to
anxious inquiry after scriptural knowledge, made a more
decided profession of religion, and manifested a marked
improvement in their outward conduct.

Imitating the example of Dr. Hawker, he soon commenced a series of weekly evening meetings for prayer and
exposition of the Scriptures, which he held in succession,
at Pakenhill, Limekilns, (near Heavens,) Thrupp, and
Stroud's-hill,—chiefly for the benefit of the poor and aged
in those localities ;—and similar evening meetings at his
own house, when the Friday lectures were not in the course
of delivery.

With the assistance of the Rev. Edward Mansfield, vicar
of Bisley, and the Rev. John Burder, minister of the Old
Meeting, Stroud, he established the Stroud branch of the
British and Foreign Bible Society, June 1, 1812, which was
the first in the county. The second was the County and
City Auxiliary, founded at Gloucester, September 7, in the
same year, Mr. Mansfield and Mr. Williams being two of
the only three clergymen of the county who were present
on that occasion.[1] Mr. Williams also originated at Stroud
an Auxiliary Church Missionary Society, and a Society for
the Promotion of Christianity among the Jews.

He employed himself diligently in improving the various
daily and Sunday charity schools of the parish ; and
endeavoured, by oral instruction, to teach the children
religious truths, at the same time that he taught them to
read the words in which those truths were conveyed. He
gradually reared up among them, and preserved to the
last, a goodly number of active and religious teachers, whose
intelligence and conscientious punctuality greatly assisted
him in his pious work.

On May 8, 1813, it was, under his advice, resolved that
the "new system of education," originated by Dr. Bell, at
Madras, should "be introduced into the parish schools for
the education of the poor"; and a portion of the workhouse
in Parliament-street was, with the consent of the Churchwardens, repaired and fitted up as the Stroud's-hill school,
at the cost of £18 12s. 5d.

[1] The other clergyman was the Rev. Richard Raikes ; who was appointed
one of its secretaries.

In the same year he laid the foundation-stone of a school-room at Whiteshill, which was opened July 26, 1814, for the accommodation of the Whiteshill and Ruscomb school children. Its cost of £325 17s. was raised by voluntary subscriptions, in addition to gratuitous contributions in labour, hauling stones, &c., amounting to £28 11s. 6d.

In pursuance of the resolution of May 8, 1813—and after preparatory instruction in "the new system of education"—Mr. Thomas Rowles was appointed master of the Stroud's-hill, and Mr. Joseph Knight of the Whiteshill, schools.

On March 24, 1818, Mr. Williams laid the foundation-stone of a new school at Thrupp. The site was given by Mr. Neale, of the Knap, Minchinhampton; and the building was soon erected, and in use. It was vested in thirteen trustees, who were the first subscribers of five guineas each. The cost was £206 13s. 6d. ; and, in 1826, a further sum of £73 14s. was expended in enlarging it.

On June 21, 1812, Mr. Williams introduced into the service of the church a collection of Psalms and Hymns, compiled with the view of making psalmody a more interesting portion of divine worship, and raising the devotion of the people higher than the psalms of Sternhold and Hopkins, or Tate and Brady, previously in use, had done. This collection was entitled, "Portions of the Psalms of David ; together with a supplement of Hymns for Fasts and Festivals and other solemn occasions, adapted to the service of the Church of England, selected and arranged by the Rev. John Williams, curate of Stroud, Gloucestershire, and Sunday afternoon and Friday lecturer" ;[2] and it was preceded by a preface, in which he says (of the psalms), " I have ventured here and there, though with a sparing hand, to introduce the holy and venerable name of Jesus, where the subjects evidently and forcibly demanded it." [3] These Psalms and Hymns continued in use, and amply fulfilled the compiler's object, so long as he retained the curacy of the parish.

2 Mr. Williams did not consider himself legally bound to give two full services on the Sunday ; but regarded the Easter offerings as his remuneration for the "Sunday afternoon" sermon.

3 A new edition, in 24 mo., was published in 1830. But its title page omitted the compiler's name ; saying only that it was selected and arranged by a " Professor of Sacred Theology in the University of Oxford, and Presbyter of the Church of England."

Mr. Williams opened a classical boarding school, which he conducted for several years. He took his B.D. degree, January 20, 1815, and proceeded to his degree of Doctor of Divinity, December 3, 1819.

In order to lighten his various labours, about the year 1820, he resigned his school into the hands of the Rev. John Elliott, Incumbent of Randwick; retaining only a small number of students, to prepare them for the Universities, at his own house. Mr. Elliott had been his pupil and assistant; and continued to be regarded by him as his valued friend.

He published a few sermons, and small pieces of sacred poetry : but his chief printed work was " Memoirs of the Life and Writings of the Reverend Robert Hawker, D.D., vicar of Charles, Plymouth. Printed by Ebenezer Palmer, 18 Paternoster Row, London, 1831."

Among Dr. Williams' valuable services to the cause of religion and humanity, was his giving several young men gratuitous education, preparatory to their entering the Church Missionary Institution at Islington, and being ordained to the work of the Christian ministry among the heathen, in connection with that society. All of them had been scholars, and teachers, in one or other of his Sunday schools, and had given satisfactory proofs of their aptitude for such pious labours.

Four of them were Joseph and Charles Knight, brothers, and Thomas Browning, natives of Whiteshill; and William Morse, of Bread-street; all voluntary instructors in the school there.

Joseph Knight was a highly-gifted man, and after being admitted to holy orders, he sailed for the island of Ceylon in 1817, and took up his missionary station at Nellore, near Jaffna. 4 There he learned to speak, read, and preach in the Tamil language, and carried on his various missionary duties among the native population for twenty-two years, with zeal and efficiency. He was held in great esteem for his talents and virtue ; and had made considerable progress in the compilation of a Tamil Dictionary ; 5 but, at length,

4 In the year 1820 Miss Ann Knight, a valuable teacher in Whiteshill girls' school, embarked for Ceylon ; where she superintended her brother's house, and the native girls' school under his charge.

5 It is understood that the Rev. P. Percival, a Wesleyan missionary in Ceylon, and a learned Tamil scholar, was engaged in completing this dictionary.

his health required a visit to his native country, and on his return voyage to resume his mission, he died when the vessel was within a hundred miles of its Oriental destination.

Charles Knight was ordained and sent on a mission to Gloucester-town, in Sierra Leone, on the west coast of Africa, where he arrived February 5, 1825, and died of the fever of the country, March 25th following.

Thomas Browning made great proficiency in learning ; and, after ordination, in 1819, proceeded to his station at Kandy, in Ceylon.   There he prosecuted his work among the Singhalese for about nineteen years ; when, being obliged to return to England on account of ill-health, he died within a few days' sail of his native land.

William Morse, after studying at the college at Islington, was ordained and sent out as a missionary—first to Calcutta, then to a station in the West Indies, and lastly he settled as a clergyman at Paris, in Canada.

After these four young men, Dr. Williams gratuitously educated three others, with the same object—Thomas Peyton and Nathaniel Denton, (both of whom were natives of Thrupp, and had been teachers in the Sunday school there,) and Robert Burrows, of Amberley.   He devoted Monday evening in every week to their tuition, at his own house.

There, these three fellow-students regularly met, having prepared their prescribed exercises in the intervals of their daily labour—and walking to and fro, considerable distances from their homes.   Their studies were often prolonged to a late hour of the night, and the entire series extended over a period of six years.   On the recommendation of Dr. Williams, they were admitted to the Institution at Islington, as they became severally qualified.

From the college, Mr. Peyton was sent to Sierra Leone as a catechist, to instruct the liberated negro slaves and others.   Returning to England, he was ordained, and again proceeded to his station in Africa, to prosecute his work. There he established a boarding and day school, for the superior education of native merchants' sons, and others from distant parts of the coast.   At the same time, Maria Ridler—who, having been a teacher in the girls' Sunday school at Thrupp, had gone out and become his wife—took charge of the native girls' school at his station, and conducted it until he died, June 14, 1853, aged 42 ; after a missionary life of sixteen years. His school flourished exceedingly ; and, in 1865, it was under the care of a native clergyman who had been one of his pupils.

His father, Thomas Peyton, was an unpaid teacher first at Thrupp, and last at Stroud's-hill Sunday schools, for thirty-two years ; and for the greater part of that time, (until a few months before his death,) this good old man might have been seen, every Sunday morning, conducting his junior class of children from school to church ; and, every afternoon of that day, seated on the lowest form in the school—with his grey head meekly bowed down —as he taught them their A B C. He died from the effect of a fall, September 5, 1860, in the 83rd year of his age.

On Mr. Denton's first going out to Sierra Leone he was employed as a catechist. He then assisted in commencing a new mission at some distance in the interior of the country ; superintended the erection of a dwelling house, school, &c., and learned to speak the language in which he was to address the people.

On his subsequent return to the colony from England, where he had obtained ordination, he was engaged in much weighty missionary business. He had, for some time, the charge of a Christian Institution at Fourah Bay, for the training of native teachers ; he was appointed successor to the late Rev. W. W. (afterward Bishop) Weeks, in the important station of Regent, including the whole mountain district, containing five churches, and two large government schools, which office he held for upwards of ten years ; and for one year he performed the duties of acting-chaplain to the Government. Besides his clerical duties he had, for several years, the management of various schools, native teachers, repairs of houses, &c., and all the secular duties connected therewith ; and lastly, he became the accountant and secretary of the mission, and correspondent with the parent committee.

Under the pressure of these numerous and heavy duties, Mr. Denton's health failed ; and he was obliged to leave the colony and return to England. But here his health returned ; and he became an esteemed clergyman, with the care of two parishes, in the diocese of Oxford.

Mr. Burrows was ordained from the College at Islington, and sent by the Society on his missionary work to New Zealand, where he laboured diligently for twenty years.

In closing this list I must not omit to say that, how great soever was the gratitude of these men for "the uniform kindness, untiring patience, and cordial Christian spirit which" (as Mr. Denton said,) "characterised the whole of Dr. William's intercourse with them," no less gratification had the good doctor himself enjoyed, in all that he did to promote the missionary cause he so much loved.

In the year 1821 Dr. Williams had been inducted to the living of St. Matthews, Liverpool, in the diocese of Chester. But the Honourable Dr. Henry Ryder, Bishop of Gloucester,—who highly esteemed him as a Christian minister, and was unwilling that Stroud should be deprived of his services—immediately interfered, and induced him to tender his resignation; promising to give him the perpetual curacy of Stroud, in case it should become vacant while he held the see. He then, with much difficulty, prevailed on the Bishop of Chester to accept the resignation of St. Matthew's Church. This being effected, Dr. Williams resumed his clerical duties at Stroud, and discharged them with his accustomed zeal and fidelity, until the early part of the year 1833, when Mr. Seagram, by having accepted the rectory of Aldbourne, in the diocese of Salisbury, vacated his incumbency of Stroud. At that time, however, Dr. Ryder was no longer the Bishop of Gloucester, he having been translated to the see of Lichfield and Coventry several years before.

Under these circumstances the inhabitants of Stroud made immediate efforts to retain their old minister. They again raised the question of their right to elect the minister, as their ancient predecessors had done ;⁶ and also sent a deputation to Dr. James Henry Monk, the then Bishop of Gloucester, requesting him to bestow the Benefice on Dr. Williams, in consideration of his long services. But the Bishop replied that it would be contrary to his episcopal duty to yield to the wishes of the parishioners : and, on February 5, 1833, he wrote to Dr. Williams and informed him he had appointed "the Rev. William Frederick Powell to the perpetual curacy of Stroud ; and that Mr. Powell

6 p. 245.

intended to reside as soon after Lady-day as might be."
In this manner, and to their great disappointment, the long
endeared connection between Dr. Williams and his congregation was summarily broken.

Then came Sunday, the 31st of March, the first Sunday
for twenty-eight years on which Dr. Williams was absent
from his accustomed place. For, on the morning of that
day, the new Incumbent entered on his appointed duties ;
and the Doctor remained at home in retirement with his
wife, who was suffering from bodily indisposition and
anxiety.

But—

"Was I deceiv'd, or did a sable cloud
Turn forth her silver lining on the night?

I did not err, there does a sable cloud
Turn forth her silver lining on the night."[7]

In the afternoon of the same day a gentleman, whom
the Doctor did not know, entered his study, and announced
himself as Mr. Moreton,[8] the Earl of Ducie's son, at whose
disposal (as he said) his father had placed the recently
vacated Benefice of Woodchester ;[9] and then, in the most
courteous manner, he added—"I am come to request your
acceptance of it."

The great and sudden change in the Doctor's feelings at
this moment, his surprise and his gratitude, may be better
imagined than described ; and, so soon as the afternoon
service was ended, the church bells told the news to the
people,—the people repeated it to one another with hearty
congratulations,—and happiness returned to the curate's
home. This valuable gift so opportunely bestowed by
Lord Ducie upon Dr. Williams, gave great pleasure to the
inhabitants of Stroud. It was regarded by them as a
graceful expression of his Lordship's sympathy with their
deep interest in the welfare of their late minister. And on
the 10th of April following, the resolutions of a public
meeting, conveying their respectful thanks, were presented
to Lord Ducie and Mr. Moreton, by Mr. Watts and the
writer, a deputation appointed for that purpose. To these

7 Comus—Milton.

8 Henry George Francis Reynolds Moreton. He became second Earl
Ducie, on the death of his father in 1840.

9 The Rectory had become vacant by the decease of the Rev. Peter
Hawker, a few days before.

resolutions Mr. Moreton returned an elegant and warm-hearted reply on the part of Lord Ducie and himself; and, on the 13th of April, Dr. Williams was inducted to the Rectory of Woodchester, on the presentation of the Earl of Ducie.

There he continued to reside for twenty-four years: and, at the end of that time, his Divine Master called him away to his heavenly home, June 30, 1857, in the 78th year of his age. His remains were deposited in the vault at Stroud, where eight of his children had already been laid.

It now only remains for me to say that of the charitable and pious persons, both lay and clerical, who, since 1833, have traversed the parish of Stroud, and visited the cottages of the poor, relieving their temporal and spiritual necessities, —many have heard affectionate mention of Dr. Williams, together with interesting particulars of his life and labours, and evidences of the salutary results of his counsel and religious teaching—all indicating that he sowed good seed in the gospel field, delivered the pure Word of Life, and wrought powerfully on the consciences and characters of many who had been under his pastoral care.

CHAPTER XLIX.

CHURCHWARDENS — NOTICES OF SOME OF THE CLOTHING PRO-
CESSES — SPINNING HOUSES — A DAME'S SCHOOL — PARISH
CLERKS.

THE churchwardens are, by custom, nominated and
appointed by the parishioners assembled in vestry.

Among the curious and interesting facts which are to be
found in the old parish books, we learn that the churchwardens were chosen from among persons of the highest
degree and intelligence. Their duties were also much
more numerous and burdensome than those of their modern
successors, inasmuch as they had to administer the poor-
laws of that day. At that period one of the many
expedients for providing for children, poor, though not
altogether paupers, was the binding them apprentices
under the provisions of the Act of 43 Elizabeth, chap. 2,
and subsequent Acts. The churchwardens and overseers,
with the consent of two Justices, were thereby authorized
to bind children, whose parents they judged not able to
maintain them, as apprentices to any such persons in the
parish as they should see convenient, and all persons to
whom such children were appointed to be bound were
liable to the penalty of £10 for refusing to receive them.
An Act of Queen Anne directed fifty shillings to be paid
to the master for finding clothing and bedding. The
Parish Officers availed themselves of their powers under
these Acts ; and we find that of 131 poor children apprenticed by them from the year 1753 to 1791 inclusive,—104
were apprenticed to learn the trade of broad-weaving ;
eighteen girls were apprenticed to persons who covenanted
to teach them "the art and mystery of housekeeping ;"
two boys to Cardmakers ; one to a Cordwainer ; (viz., a
shoemaker) and some other children were apprenticed to
labourers, and persons of no particular trade, to serve "in
all lawful business" exercised by the master.

The great prevalence of broad-weavers among the artizans in this district, between the years above specified, indicates the time before machinery and steam power had been generally introduced into the operations connected with the manufacture of cloth ; and when its various processes were performed by hand, at the dwelling-houses of the operatives, especially those of carding, spinning, and weaving. At that time each thread of yarn was spun separately by hand ; and not, as now, it may be, by a machine, which produces two hundred threads at once : and weavers had looms of their own, at which they wrought where they resided, or they worked as journeymen for master-weavers in large weaving shops. At present the cloth is woven by power looms in the large factories, and there are few or no persons to be found who are employed to work at home on their own looms.

At the time before-mentioned, the spinning of yarn was conducted in the following manner : the clothiers appointed numerous stations in towns, villages, and farm-houses, at a distance from their mills, even so far off as Cheltenham, to each of which, once a month, they brought wool, already carded and prepared to be spun. These stations were called Spinning-houses ; and here the carded wool was given out to women who attended to receive, and to spin it, on their old-fashioned single-thread spinning-wheels. At the end of a month the clothiers came to receive the yarn that had been spun, and to deliver out a fresh supply of wool to be converted into yarn in like manner. This gave employment to the women of almost every cottage in an agricultural district, within reach of a Spinning-house.

Once, when the writer was on horseback in a retired part of the Cotteswold range, he dismounted at a cottage to inquire his way ; and on opening the door he found it was a dame's school for children. The mistress was walking backward and forward, spinning some clothier's wool into yarn, and performing her scholastic duties at the same time. A boy was in the act of reading his lesson aloud to her, which he did at the highest pitch of his voice, that she might hear him notwithstanding the noise of her whirling wheel. It was then that the writer found out the difference between reading aloud, and loud reading ; together with the probable cause of the high tone in which country children were then accustomed to read.

Various riots occurred in opposition to the use of machinery,—one of them, (attended by the breaking of a spinning machine,) as early as 1776, and others as late as 1817 : and so great a change has been brought about by its introduction into factories since that time, that many of the old processes in cloth-making are wholly disused, and almost unknown.

The parishioners by custom also appointed the Parish Clerks,—of whom William Shatford was the first with whose name we have become acquainted. It occurs in an entry, signed by six feoffees, in one of their old account books, and is in the following words :—" April 30, 1698— Wee the feoffees of the parish of Stroud Do order that Mr. Shatford the parish clarke shall have the rent of the Church furlong [1] for the year ensuing, for his service, *upon his behaviour.*" Daniel Shatford, his son, was the clerk in 1736. He was also the schoolmaster, and rented the lower room in the Market-house for his scholars, at two pounds per annum ; which sum he was allowed by the feoffees " for his services" as parish clerk. John Pegler, a subsequent clerk, was succeeded by his son Samuel, on whose death in 1786, there were three candidates for the office,—Stephen Price, [2] John Miles, [3] and Stephen Howell ; each of whom officiated once in the church service, that a judgment might be formed of their respective qualifications. [4] Stephen Howell was the one elected ; and held the office until his death in 1816. During Howell's last illness the Rev. John Williams, the officiating curate, engaged, and on his own authority attempted to establish, in the clerkship, Benjamin Franklin, the master of the Red boy's school. But on the Sunday (Whit-Sunday) morning after Howell's death, William Clutterbuck Chambers and William Hogg, the churchwardens,—in order to maintain the rights of the parishioners,—appeared with their wands of office before the reading-desk ; and, when the curate had entered, they crossed their wands before it, and prevented Franklin, who was in attendance to act as his clerk, from following him.

---

1 The rent was £1 10s. per annum.
2 Mentioned in page 14.
3 *Ibid* pp. 41-42.
4 The writer, then seven years old, was present on all those occasions.

Upon this, Mr. Williams quitted the desk, and left the church ; whereupon Mr. Chambers gave notice that there would not be any morning service, and the congregation dispersed. The Rev. Charles E. S. Neville, a neighbouring clergyman, officiated at the afternoon service, with the parish clerk of Rodborough. In a few days after, the churchwardens convened a vestry meeting, at which Mr. Howell's son, John Selby Howell, was elected to the office ; and he, having been duly licensed, continued in it for upward of fifty years; and, since his death in 1867, no other clerk has been appointed.

CHAPTER L.

WHEN Dr. Badcock entered on his Incumbency in
1865, the PARISH CHURCH, dedicated to St. Lawrence, consisted of a nave, chancel, and two aisles, with a
spire steeple, about ninety-four feet high, containing ten
bells, at the west end.

The nave stood between the two aisles, from each of
which it was separated by a range of five Doric columns.
The nave and aisles were each seventy-five feet five inches
long. The nave was twenty-two feet wide ; the south aisle
(called the old aisle) was seventeen feet nine inches wide ;
and the north aisle (called the new aisle) nineteen feet six
inches wide. The chancel adjoining the east end of the
nave was nineteen feet eight inches deep, by twenty-one
feet wide.

The church had a gallery along the west ends of the
nave and new aisle, an ancient gallery along the greatest
part of the south aisle, and a gallery at the east end of
each aisle. The east gallery of the old aisle was entered
from the churchyard by a flight of stone steps leading to a
door in the upper window of its south wall ; and had
another access to it by stairs from within. The whole
church and the galleries had closed pews of oak.

The chapel mentioned in the ancient Composition of
1304 was the origin of the church. It was thirty-three feet
long by sixteen feet wide, in the clear. The first addition
made to it was the steeple, and so much of the nave as
served to unite it with what was then the low arched
entrance of the chapel.

The next addition was the south aisle and its porch.
This aisle was separated from what was then the nave and
chapel by a series of low gothic arches, with their superincumbent masonry ; and had, according to Mr. Rudder, a

chancel at its east end. There was a small door leading from the churchyard into it at this place, called the chancel door, on the stone lintel of which was inscribed T.D., S.W., 1683. The initials were those of Thomas Davis and Samuel Webb, churchwardens in that year, by whom some considerable alterations were made ; but the inscription was not, even if the doorway was, coeval with the aisle itself. On the wall at the east end of this aisle was a large piece of ancient sculpture, which had excited much curiosity ; and, at a right angle with it, was an elevated platform that was formerly railed in by massive balusters, which gave it a chancel-like appearance : and there the Rev. William Ellis, the originator of the Sunday schools of this parish, with his friend, Mr. Thomas Baylis, the treasurer, formerly stood and catechised their earliest Sunday scholars, —reading to them and hearing them read, the scriptures.

With respect to the "chancel," which Mr. Rudder said the south aisle had "at its east end," it may be mentioned that he gave no authority or reason for the statement. Probably he conjectured it from the large piece of ancient sculpture which he saw on the wall there ; but see a notice of this sculpture in the next chapter.

The porch in this aisle had a pointed gothic arch leading by a similar one into the nave, and was the chief entrance into the church. The ancient gallery there was formerly entered from the outside, by a little door at the head of a flight of stone steps, close to the east side of the porch. But, about the year 1806, a vestry-room was built over the porch, which necessitated its enlargement, so as to inclose the little door, together with the site of the steps ; and a new approach to the gallery was made from within the porch, by means of the vestry stairs. The alteration was effected at the cost of £197 to the feoffees.

Sir Robert Atkyns says "the south aisle was built by the Whitingtons, formerly lords of the manor." More probably, however, it was built by them with the assistance, as Mr. Rudder suggested, of some other person whose arms, he says, were sculptured (but had been long defaced) in the wall on the right side of the entrance to the porch, as those of the Whitingtons were sculptured on its left side. In making the above-mentioned alterations in the porch, the Whitington arms were transferred from the side to the crown of the entrance arch, but the defaced—the unknown —arms wholly disappeared.

It may be noticed here, that the arms of the Gloucester-shire family of the Whitingtons are stated, generally, to be only a fesse of two lines checky; though sometimes they bear three or four such lines, having an annulet in the right corner of the shield. The arms on the porch, however, had a fesse with two lines checky, between two crescents, without the annulet; but the repetition, in base, of the crescent in chief, as a mark of cadency, is supposed to be an error of the sculptor. If the Whitingtons, of Lypiatt, built, or had any share in building, the porch, it was probably erected about the middle of the fifteenth century.

Sir Robert Atkyns says the church was ninety feet long and forty feet wide,—the chancel thirty-three feet long and sixteen feet broad. This length of ninety feet included the steeple, and the width of forty feet the nave and south porch. In addition to the steeple at the west end, he mentions "another lower spire in the middle."

The old chancel was the site of the original chapel; and the "lower spire" stood on what had been its western gable—the arched entrance into it; and additions. In an old view of the church, taken from the south, about the year 1784, by George, afterward Sir George Nayler, this lower spire appears rising from behind the roof of the south aisle, indicating the position mentioned by Sir Robert. When he saw the church (probably about the year 1707, for he died in 1709, and his History, 1712, was a posthumous publication), the chancel—the original chapel—was separated from the nave by its low gothic arch; and both it and the nave were divided from the south aisle by the original range of gothic arches.

The added portion of the nave was about seven feet wider than the chancel to which it had been attached; and thus gave room for a seat or pew in the angles formed by the uniting wall. This pew, under the description of "a certain seat or gallery on the north side of the church, next and adjoining to the partition wall between the chancel, in length eight feet, and in breadth seven feet," was, by the faculty in 1733, granted "unto Robert Brown, of Stroud, apothecary, and the future owners and tenants of his messuage or Inn, called the White Hart, as their seat or gallery to hear and attend divine service and sermons, exclusive of all other persons."

The third addition made to the original chapel was the erection of about fifty feet in length of the western part of

the north aisle, and a gallery at its upper end.   This, "with
a new desk and pulpit, was completed in the year 1759, at
the expense of William Dallaway, Joseph Wathen, Thomas
Pegler, Fream Arundell, Thomas Baylis, Samuel Baylis,
Robert Ellis, Richard Aldridge, Peter Playne, William
Knight, and Richard Capel"; as was recorded on a stone
tablet against its north wall.   In effecting this, the then
existing north wall of the nave (up to its junction with the
chancel) was taken down; and the roof that had rested on
it was supported by three Doric columns erected in its
stead.   When joined to the north-west end of the chancel,
it formed a short aisle; and the church then exhibited the
incongruity of a nave, between a low range of Gothic
arches on one side, and a series of tall Doric columns on
the other.   This addition was made under a faculty from
the Consistory Court; by which the pews erected thereby
were annexed for ever to the dwelling-houses of the gentlemen who united to build it.   Those pews were twenty-four
in number, two of which (one on either side of the aisle)
were assigned by lot to each of them; and a pew in the
gallery was appropriated to the successor of Mr. Brown, in
lieu of his old one.

The pulpit erected with the first portion of the north
aisle was a hexagonal structure of excellent proportions
and workmanship, executed in oak.   In form it somewhat
resembled a goblet, the body, or cup, having panelled sides,
with a bold base and cornice, and a handsomely modelled
hexagonal stem or shaft.   Over it was a hexagonal sound-
ing board, with varied mouldings diminishing upward to a
point, suspended from the roof by an iron rod.   It had been
an ornament to the church from the period of its erection.

Mr. Rudder, who saw and described the church about
the year 1777, says: "It has two chancels" and "the
original chapel is now the inner chancel, with a small kind
of spire, in whose base hung two little bells, just above the
roof of the chapel."   He called it the inner chancel in con-
tradistinction to that before said by him to be in the south
aisle.   Mr. Rudder's "small kind of spire" was the "lower
spire" of Sir Robert Atkyns; and, in the old View before
mentioned, it appears to have been of a slender and elegant
octagonal form, rising from between four miniature pinnacles or spires, at its base.

For several years after 1759 a general desire had prevailed to enlarge the church, to render it more light,

commodious, and uniform, and to improve its acoustic properties, by removing the low arches. Accordingly, on the 21st of February, 1787, a vestry meeting was held, at which various important plans were agreed on for that purpose; and they were eventually carried out in the following manner:—First, the north aisle was completed by the addition of about twenty-five feet to the east end of the part previously built, which made it equal in length to the south or old aisle; and by the removal and enlargement of its gallery. To effect this, the north wall of the then chancel was taken down, and the roof that rested on it was supported by the fourth and fifth Doric columns erected there. The east end gallery of the south aisle was also erected; and all this was done in "the year 1787, at the joint expense of John Allaway, Nathaniel Peach, William Capel, Thomas Baylis, Benjamin Grazebrook, Henry Burgh, Edward Thornton, and William Ellis, clerk, minister: moreover, £185 3s. was then expended by them for the improvement and ornament of the church, toward which sum the feoffees gave £50"; as appeared on a stone tablet set up against the upper part of the north wall of the new aisle.

About the same time, a new chancel—with its large semi-circular headed window—was erected on churchyard ground, by the churchwardens, John Hollings and Benjamin Grazebrook, at the cost of £250, paid by the feoffees; and then, the "low gothic arch" that formed the western entrance of the original chapel—and had so long separated the old chancel from the nave, and hindered so many of the congregation from hearing—together with what Mr. Ellis called "the little turret upon it," was removed; and the old chancel became part of the nave.

"The little turret" was the campanile of the old chapel, and it had been intended to re-erect it on the proposed new chancel; but, when taken down, the stones that composed it remained beneath the south wall, near the "chancel door," for several years, and ultimately they disappeared. An old architect, lately deceased, who had seen the turret when standing, greatly regretted its destruction.

On fitting up the new chancel, the old communion table was deposited in the end of the south aisle—the outer chancel of Mr. Rudder—until the vestry was built over the porch; when it was enlarged and removed thither, and used as a vestry table.

Instead of this plain old table on its four stout legs, an altar-like table with a bowed front and a massive base—made to resemble a solid structure—was placed against the east wall of the new chancel, within an iron railing.

This altar table was, in fact, a huge wooden box with a lid on hinges. At first it contained the iron chest in which the parish registers were kept; but latterly it had become the depository of the standards and gas lamps for lighting the church, when not in use for that purpose.

Lastly, the wall and the range of gothic arches, with the heavy masses of stone upon them—which, up to that time, had stood between the south aisle and the old nave and chancel—were removed; and a line of Doric columns was substituted for them—corresponding with those already existing on the opposite side. Thereby the church received additional light, and obtained more symmetry and uniformity. All these alterations were completed in the year 1793; and in 1795 the whole roof of the church was newly laid and repaired.

Until the year 1798 there were two galleries at the west end of the nave—one above the other. The upper one was a small whitewashed structure, and was occupied by the singers; but in that year it was taken down to make room for an organ which was erected in the gallery beneath it. The opening of the organ was a great event in the annals of Stroud, and was thus mentioned by the Rev. William Ellis, the officiating curate, in the parish register: "April 18th, 1798. A new organ, built by Mr. John Avery, of London (a native of this parish), and purchased by private subscription, was opened in this church, with a select concert of sacred music—vocal and instrumental. Principal performers: Signora Mara, [1] Mr. Stroud and Mr. Griffiths, [2] Mr. Mutlow, organist, [3] and Mr. Wilton, *violino principale*." In this same year two clerestory windows were put in the roof of the nave, giving additional light to the organ gallery; and the ventilation of the church was much improved by three other such windows.

Until 1814 the steeple contained only eight bells; but, in that year, the tenor bell fell from its supports, while being

[1] Madame Mara was the celebrated Italian singer of that day. She raised my boyish wonder by the great volume of sound she poured out in singing; and by the very large open mouth from which it proceeded.

[2] Two of the lay clerks of Gloucester Cathedral.

[3] Of ditto.

rung in full peal ; and, in falling, it split the eighth bell, and was itself fractured,—but without doing any injury to the ringers.   This necessitated the re-casting of the broken bells, which was accordingly done ; and on that occasion the inhabitants subscribed for the addition to the peal of two other bells.   To this they were probably moved by the old rivalry between them and their neighbours of Painswick, who possessed a fine musical peal of ten bells.   But, immediately thereon, the Painswick bells were increased to twelve,—and their former numerical superiority was restored.

The broken tenor bell bore the following inscription :—

> Come when I call,
> God bless you all ;

but its date and founder's name are not remembered.   Probably, however, they were the same as the bell No. 9.

The new tenor bell is inscribed thus :—

> May all whom I summon to the grave
> The blessings of a well-spent life receive.

> W. C. Chambers, Esq., and Richard Cook, churchwardens.
> 1815.   Thomas Mears, London, Fecit.

The other bells bore the following inscriptions :—

> No. 1, the treble.
> In sweetest sound let each its note reveal—
> Mine shall be first to lead the dulcet peal :

With the churchwardens' and founder's names as before.

> No. 2.
> We come with harmony to cheer the land—
> The public raised us with a liberal hand.

Churchwardens' and founder's names as before.

> No. 3.
> Prosperity to all my benefactors.   1720.

> No. 4.
> Prosperity to all my friends.   1720.

> No. 5.
> Prosperity to this parish.   1771.

> No. 6.
> Prosperity to this place.   1713.

> No. 7.
> William Knight, Esq., and Mr. Richard Aldridge,
> churchwardens.   1771.

> No. 8.
> The same as on the tenor.

> No. 9.
> John Long and Henry Cook, churchwardens.   1721.
> Cast by Abraham Ruddal, of Gloucester.

In the year 1714 the churchwardens caused the summit of the spire to be repaired, and the weathercock set up at the cost of £7 10s.; and in 1828 a part of its summit was taken down and rebuilt, and a new weathercock set up at the cost of £130, which was paid by the feoffees. On that occasion—when it had been carried up to its former height in the direction of its inclined outline,—the masons added to it about three or four feet of perpendicular masonry before it received the finial; and the correctness of its outline was thereby materially injured. When it was finished, and before the workmen's ladders were taken down, several persons of the town mounted to the summit; and among them was a young man named Henry Ayres, who, standing on the finial, played the tune of "God save the King" on his bugle, before he descended.

Originally, the churchyard was small like the chapel itself. In 1693 an addition under the name of the "new churchyard" was made to it, at the cost of the feoffees. In 1754 they purchased a piece of land at its west end, which they added to it: it cost £10, besides the sum of £44 13s. 4d., for professional expenses, building the wall, consecration, &c. Finally, in 1807 the churchwardens, at the cost of the feoffees, obtained and added to the burying-ground all that part of it which lies on the north side of the body of the church. It was a portion of the garden of the house formerly known as "the House behind the Church."

About the year 1836 John Pitt carved and presented to the parish a new font, and then the plain old one which stood in the "place for baptisings" in the original chapel, in 1304, and had been in use from that time downward, was removed and afterwards broken up!!

The lighting of the church by gas was introduced in 1839; and the curious antique chandelier, with its double tier of branches proceeding from a central globe, which had hung from the roof of the nave for many years—was taken down and sold for old brass.

The various alterations of the church had not been always made with good taste, as respected ecclesiastical architecture; nor was it, as a whole, adequate to the wants of the inhabitants, or suitable to the importance of the town. But, with all its faults, it had a two-fold claim on the writer's regard— it was the church of his childhood, and the church of his old age, as it was of his children also.

CHAPTER LI.

AGAINST the centre of the east end wall in the south aisle was the ancient piece of sculpture before alluded to. It had a carved central slab within what may be called, by way of distinction, its framework. It was entirely of the stone of the country, built into the wall, and was six feet four inches wide by eight feet high from the floor to the sill of the window under which it stood. The framework had a massive redented altar-like base, two feet ten inches high, projecting one foot from the wall; on which was a cabled Doric column at each end, engaged on pilasters, three feet seven inches high, supporting an entablature of one foot six inches, with an affluented frieze and bold cornice. The carved slab contained a table or die, within scroll work, having at its dexter end the profile of a grotesque face with a wide retracted mouth and a tongue lolling out of it; and at its sinister end, a similar face with a flowing beard. Above the dexter face was an escutcheon, bearing three griffins *segreant*, executed in high relief, and over the sinister face was an Esquire's helmet with a wivern *sciant* in a plume of ostrich feathers as a crest. It had been painted white, and there was no indication of the tinctures. The framework was a handsome specimen of the early Elizabethan, or of a prior style and date, and of superior design and workmanship : but the central slab was of a later period, a newer stone, and wrought by another and an inferior artist. It has been lately ascertained that this slab was, independently of its carved relief, only three inches thick, and rested against the wall behind it.

The original structure may have been either an altarpiece, or a monument. If the former, perhaps the central space contained sacred emblems, or a scriptural representation ; if the latter, some obituary memorial : but it is evident that the panel which originally filled that space, whatsoever it contained, had, at some subsequent and long past time, been removed, and the sculptured slab substituted for it. The space within the so-called framework was three feet seven inches high, and four feet ten inches wide; the substituted slab was only two feet one inch high and three feet seven inches wide, the extra space being filled up with wall stones, and the edges of the uncarved part bevelled, to make it flush with the plain surface of the back or ground of the work.

Much curiosity has been felt respecting this piece of sculpture, but the structure itself is silent. There is not, nor does it appear that there ever was, any inscription on the die of the slab, which, though two feet one inch long, is only six inches wide : nor is there any inscription on the framework, or any tradition extant, from which to learn its original purpose, or when, by whom, or why it was first erected, or when, by whom, or why it was so strangely altered.

Under these circumstances, and from the inharmonious effect of the alteration, the central slab may be regarded as an intentional substitute for some superstitious device or emblem, previously existing there; or to supply the place of some obituary memorial which it may have been thought desirable to remove. Of each of these supposable cases, there are not wanting examples in old ecclesiastical edifices. It may be added, that, although none of our county historians have noticed this sculpture, (which Sir Robert Atkyns probably saw, and Mr. Rudder must have seen, in the state described,) Sir Robert says, " There was a handsome monument in [this] the south aisle, for the Whitingtons, which has since been taken down. [and] Another monument for the family of the Wyes."

The last Thomas Wye, of Upper Lypiatt, [1] by his will, dated February 20th, 1580, directed his " body to be buried in the Chapple of Stroud, by his ancestors there." But no recognized monument to them was remaining when Mr. Rudder compiled his list of the monuments. However, the arms and crest on the central slab were undoubtedly those of this family. Their arms were *sable, three griffins segreant, Or*, the *wivern* in the crest *sable*. The crest was a play on the name of the bearer, *Wye-vern*.

1 For an account of that family see page 192.

Whether we suppose this sculpture to have been originally an altar-piece, or a part of the monument of the Whitingtons that had been taken down, it would be very difficult to form a reasonable conjecture why and when the uninscribed slab, having only the mere arms and crest of Wye upon it, was substituted for the original panel,—even though we could suppose the slab to have been a fragment of the Wye monument itself.   On this subject we will only add that Thomas, the last Wye, of Lypiatt, died in 1581 ; and in 1583 his widow Juliana, the tenant for life of the Lypiatt estates, was married to John Throckmorton, who purchased the interest of the persons in remainder, and so obtained possession of the fee of those estates.   He was a Roman Catholic.   But, whatsoever the secret of the alteration may have been, it remains, and probably will remain, unknown.

The following monuments and inscriptions, from among others of a more recent date, are noticeable on account of their local and historical associations.

Against the south wall of the chancel was a handsome monument, ornamented (perhaps overcharged) with emblematical figures of Faith, Hope, Charity, Innocence, Cherubs, Mourners, Death's heads, and other monumental devices ; on the table of which is the following inscription :

Thomas Freame Armiger, ex cohorte centurio, obiit 18 Aprilis, an. dni. 1664, ætatis suæ 63.

> Non cecidit Fræmus, licet hic cecidisse videtur,
>   Ad superas abijt, venerat unde, domos :
> Viva fides, charitas, spes, mens sua firma manebant :
>   Cætera deposuit, mors meliora dedit.

Hic etiam Anna Fream Thomæ quondam Uxor post xxx, viduitatis annos interum Viro conjuncta fuit.   Jan. 26°, 1694.

The writer has rendered the above four verses into the same number of English lines, thus :—

> Though here to have died he seem'd, Freame did not die,
>   He went to, (whence he came,) his home on high.
> Hope, living faith, love, his firm mind, remain'd ;
>   The rest laid down, from death he better gain'd.

Beneath, and joined to the above monument, was a tablet :—

In memory of Thomas Clutterbuck, the son of Samuel Clutterbuck, great grandson of Thomas Freame, of Lower Lypiatt, Esq., who died the 14th of March, in the 9th year of his age, 1715.

And near it, on the same wall, was an oval tablet with this memorial, and, methinks, a sweet, pious verse :—

M.S.

Of Freame Clutterbuck (an infant), the son of Freame Clutterbuck, Esq., of this parish, by his wife Anne, the daughter of Francis Sims, of Kempscot, in the county of Oxon, gent., who departed this life the 17th of July, A.D. 1711, aged one year and seven months.

> When Christ commands away
> 'Tis sin to wish to stay
> Tho' soon thy glass be run
> For Heav'n thou'rt not too young
> For all are like thee there
> Go then and be Heaven's Heir.

Another tablet in the chancel recorded that :

Near this place was interred John Gryffin—Gent., and Elizabeth his wife in the year 1627. Also Elizabeth his Granddaughter wife of John Webb, of the Throp clothier was buried the 31st of July 1681. Also Elizabeth the daughter of John Gryffin of this parish gent. wife of Thomas Clissold, clothier, was buried the 18th day of October 1703. John Gryffin, of this parish, gent., died the 28th of March, 1719. Thomas Gryffin, of this parish, Esq., died September 28th, 1788, aged 80 years.

> He was an upright magistrate,
> A sincere friend,
> And an honest man.

This monument was at first erected in the old chancel : and the words " near this place " must be understood as relating to the upper part of the nave which occupied its site.

On the east wall of the south aisle was a handsome monument, containing (within an arched recess) a coifed effigy, in a doctor of law's gown, kneeling before a lectern, on which is an open book,—having his hands folded in the attitude of prayer ; and upon a tablet beneath the figure is the following :

Thomas Stephens Armiger, legum municipalium Regni Angliæ peritissimus, HENRICO et CAROLO, principibus Walliæ Attornatus generalis, obiit 26 Aprilis, An. Dom. 1613. Ætatis suæ 55.

> Lege perit Stephanus ? Væ nobis lege perimus,
> Omnes peccanti lex datur una mori :
> Non periit Stephanus ; Fertur lex altera Christi,
> Quæ Στέφανον Stephano dat prohibetque mori.

The Greek word in the last verse is a play on the name of the deceased : it means a crown. The following is the writer's English version of those lines :

> Died Stephens by the law? The law alas! kills all,—
> That law which doom'd our sinful race to die.
> But Stephens lives : another law, Christ's law withal,
> Gives him a crown and immortality.

This monument originally stood in the recess of the gable window in the east end of the aisle, directly over the piece of mural sculpture before described.

When the east end gallery was erected in 1787, it was removed to the north side of the window on the same wall, and the window was opened to afford more light to the gallery. On the same wall, and near to the last monument, was a small plain marble tablet with this inscription :

Sacred to the memory of John Stephens, Esq., of Over Lypiatt in this parish, the last of the Lypiatt branch of that ancient family. A gentleman universally esteemed for his integrity and benevolent disposition. He died March 19th, 1778, in the 81st year of his age.

On the south wall of this aisle was a monument :

In memory of Richd Field, of Field's Place, Gent, and Elizth his wife, Daughter of Edwd. Hill of Cam in ys county Esq.

| He | } | dyed | } | Oct. 3, 1693 | } | aged | { | 42. |
| She | | | | March 8, 1715 | | | | 78. |

Joana. Field, Edvardi Field Armigeri, de Loco Fieldi. supra dicto, Uxor indulgentissima : Johannis Delaberi, Armigeri, de Southam, in Parochia Episcop. Cliev. in comit. Gloucestr. Filia delectissima, ob 15? Maij, Anno. Æts. 63?, currente Redemptionis, MDCCXXXmo.

Near the above, but on the east wall of the aisle, was a tablet :

In memory of Edward Field, late of Field Place in this parish, Esq., many years one of his Majesty's Justices of the Peace for this county, who died the thirtyeth day of March, 1736, aged 67 years. This monument is erected by Anne his widow and relict who was his second wife, [2] and one of the daughters of Richard Plummer of this parish, gentleman.

On the top of this tablet was a representation, in high relief, of the full front face of Edward Field.

On the west end wall of this aisle was a monument which had formerly stood against the nearest pillar in the old range of Gothic arches, bearing the following inscription :

[2] His first wife was the Joanna Field above mentioned.

H. S. E.

DANIEL CAPEL, A.M.

Coll. Pemb. apud Oxon. Socius et Ornamentum,
Doctrina potius quam annis maturus,
Parentibus, Amicis, Eccles. Anglicanæ, ob pietatem
   ingenium et fidem carus.
Non modo nomine, sed et virtutibus,
Reverendum Avum Proavumque expressit,
Gravis et urbanus, Prudens et facetus ;
Politioribus quibus inclaruit artibus
Phœbeum Medicinæ Studium adjunxit,
In qua tantum profecit Adolescens
Ut alterum Hippocratem sponderet ;
Donec Libitina imperii metuens
Hunc juvenem peremit
Ne de illâ provectior sine modo triumpharet.
Ob. Jul : 30 anno Domini 1709. Ætat. 24.

DANIEL CAPEL dicti pater
Vir pius, probus, gravis ;
Medicus Peritissimus, qui Praxin
Non minus sibi laboriosam,
Quam ægris suis com nodam, sustinuit :
Sed Proh dolor ! dum aliorum saluti
Attente nimis invigilavit,
Amisit suam.
Obijt die Junij 27 Anno Salutis Christianæ 1714, Ætat. 55.

It needs only to be added that the grandfather and great
grandfather *(avum proavumque)* of the above-named Daniel
Capel, the son, were the Rev. Daniel Capel and the Rev.
Richard Capel, mentioned in pp. 253-4, in order to under-
stand the high honour conferred on this gifted young man
by his near relationship to those useful and Godly men.

Against the west end wall of the north aisle stood a
marble tablet :

To the memory of Thos. Arundel gent., and Anne his wife, (daughter
of Thos. Gregory, of Hordley, in Oxfordshire, Esq.) He died the 26th day
of March, 1742, aged 48 years. She the 29th of July in the same year, aged
50. Fream Arundel their son, died in the year 1721, aged one year and six
months. Also in memory of Fream Arundel, Gent., who departed this life
May 28th, 1785, aged 61 years. Likewise of Jane, his wife, she died the
22nd day of January, 1771, aged 43 years. Jno. Gregory Arundel, son of
Fream and Jane Arundel, died July the 5th 1752, aged six months. Fream
Arundel, their son, died April the 30th, 1784, aged 28 years. Arabella, their
daughter, died the third day of January, 1787, aged 33 years. Samuel
Arundel, their son, died June the 3rd, 1789, and was buried at Rodborough.'
Thomas Crozier Arundel, their son, died Dec. 29th, 1789, aged 39 years.
Likewise James Arundel, gent., their son, died the 11th day of June, 1813,
aged 51 years.

Cojoined to it below was a small marble tablet :

Sacred to the memory of Fream, son of James and Ann Arundel, who died the 1st of August, 1805, aged 19 years.

> His cheerful watch some guardian angel keeps,
> Around yon tomb where youth and goodness lie.
> Mourn then no more. His virtues only sleep.
> Such worth, such genuine worth, can never die.

All these were Arundels of the Field, whose connection with the Freams, of Lower Lypiatt, appears by their children often bearing the baptismal name of Fream, before their patronymic of Arundel.

According to Mr. Rudder, the following anecdote is found in Dr. Parsons' M.S. Collections relating to the County of Gloucester.[3] " It is said that some time in the reign of Queen Elizabeth, the Earl of Tyrone's daughter, Florence, fled with her jewels and valuables from her father's house, with a servant, to London, and there lived, having been privately married to him ; but, burying her husband, she came into this country, and married a cloth-worker, concealing her birth and parentage for many years. At last, falling desperately sick, she discovered the whole, and left in money and jewels £1,000 a-piece to her sons, and £500 each to her daughters, and was interred in Stroud churchyard." Sir Robert Atkyns says that Florence, her daughter, was christened 1588 ; but no baptismal register of that date is now to be found.

[3] They are preserved in the Bodleian Library, Oxford.

CHAPTER LII.

THE NEW PARISH CHURCH.

THE church, of which the history has been given in the last two chapters, was that which will henceforth be designated as the Old parish Church.

Sunday, July the 8th, 1866, was the day on which the usual services were held there for the last time ; and, soon after, it was (with the exception of the steeple) taken down, and a new one erected in its place.

The foundation-stone of the present parish church was laid November the 6th, 1866, in the presence of a large concourse of spectators, by Mr. Stanton and the writer, the former using the trowel, and the latter the level and mallett.

It was opened for public worship the 4th day of August, 1868, and dedicated to the service of Almighty God by Dr. Ellicott, Bishop of the Diocese, who likewise preached a sermon on the occasion.

The architects were Messrs. Wilson and Willcox, of Bath, and the builders Messrs. Wall and Hook, of Brimscomb.

The walls are of Bisley Common stone, faced on the inside with Painswick stone, and the dressings are of Bath stone.

The roof is of English oak, covered with Broseley tiles of blue and red, in alternate courses. Its inside covering is oak. It was intended to be made of the timber that had formed the roofs of the old building, which was oak in good preservation and of stout scantlings ; but the timber was unfortunately consumed by accidental fire while being prepared for the purpose.

The floor is laid with Godwin's figured tiles from his manufactory at Lugwardine, Herefordshire.

The church consists of a nave, aisles, transepts, chancel, chancel-aisles, vestry, and porch. Its length is 104 feet, and the width of the nave and aisles is 66, besides the projection of the transepts and porch.

The nave is 74 feet long and 32 wide,—the space between the tower and transepts being divided into four equal bays of 13 feet each; and the arches of the transepts being equal to two more of such bays.

Above the nave arches (which have columns of rubbed blue Pennant stone), is a clerestory, having three-light windows. The height from the floor to the caps of the pillars is 13 feet to the wall-plate of the clerestory is 31. and to the apex of the roof 46 feet.

The chancel is 27 feet long from the inside of its arch, and is of the same width as the nave, from which it is separated by a low stone screen. Its height to the wall-plate is 23 feet, and to the apex of the roof 39. It is raised by three steps of blue Pennant stone, and by three steps of black Devonshire marble, above the rest of the church; and by the addition of a similar step to the Communion table. This elevation was caused by the rise of the ground at that place. The floor is laid with rich encaustic tiles of appropriate design. It has a large window of five lights, and over it on the outside is a finely modeled sculpture of the Agnus Dei.

The aisles are not of equal width, in consequence of their having been erected on the old foundations,—the north aisle being 18 feet, and the south aisle 16 feet wide. The height of the side walls is eighteen feet six inches, and to the apex of the roof is 31 feet. The north aisle is lighted by four, and the south aisle by three two-light windows, besides a three-light window at the west end of each.

These aisles are carried through nearly to the east end of the chancel, thereby forming two chancel arches, each of which has a three-light window. On either side of the chancel are two arches which open into its aisles. Their central supports are clustered shafts, formed of four Devonshire red marble columns round one of Painswick stone; and each of their responds has two Devonshire red and black marble columns round a central one of stone.

A medallion has been placed between each of these arches,—one of them being a sculptured representation of Our Lord washing the disciples' feet, and the other His revealing himself "in breaking of bread" to the disciples at Emmaus, after His resurrection. The carved work on each of the medallions is two feet four inches in diameter.

In the north aisle of the chancel is the organ chamber ; and in both the aisles are seats for the Sunday school children.

The transepts are 22 feet wide, and 19 feet in projection from the side walls of the aisles. The height to the wall-plate is 25 feet, and to the apex of the roof 40 feet. Each of them has a four-light window in the gable, and a three-light window in its west wall. In the east wall of the south transept is the entrance into the vestry, which is lined with the oak panels from the organ gallery of the old church, inscribed with the original list of benefactions.

On the outside of the south transept, over the gable window, is a figure of St. Lawrence, to whom the old church was dedicated. It is the gift of Mr. Joshua Wall, sculptor, of Stroud, by whom it was designed and carved. All the carvings on the inside and outside of the edifice, comprising the Agnus Dei, the rich and varied capitals of the columns, the crosses, corbels, bosses, symbolical figures, and decorative devices, are of his design and workmanship. The pulpit and font were also executed by him.

The pulpit is chiefly of Painswick stone. It is raised on six columns of black Devonshire marble, with a massive central one of red Devonshire marble, all having richly carved capitals ; between which are three polished alabaster panels, with sculptured figures in pure white alabaster, representing St. Peter, St. James, and St. John, in the act of preaching. It is also enriched with delicate inlays of varied designs, composed of polished coloured precious marbles : and the whole (especially the figure of St. John), fully justifies the high reputation as a sculptor which Mr. Wall has obtained. It is placed below the north-west angle of the chancel.

The base of the font is of Painswick stone, carefully moulded and carved, having four red serpentine marble shafts, round a massive central one of filletted black Devonshire marble, supporting the bowl of richly coloured alabaster,—square in form, and highly polished. The bowl is lined with lead. The whole stands on a platform of black Devonshire marble, nearly at the bottom of the nave.

Already seven stained glass windows have been erected. The first of these is the window in the chancel. It was raised

To the Glory of God, and in affectionate memory of William Stanton, late of The Thrupp, in this parish. He died July 18th, 1841, aged 83. Also of Ann his wife, who died November 16th, 1842, aged 79.

It represents the principal events in Our Lord's history, viz. :—the Annunciation, the Nativity, the Adoration of the Magi, the Flight into Egypt, the Crucifixion, the Resurrection, the Charge to the Apostles, the Ascension, and the Descent of the Holy Spirit.

This fine window is seen to advantage from the upper part of the nave, to which it lends the subdued radiance of its coloured light.

The next is the window in the south aisle of the chancel. It is inscribed :

In Dei gloriam et in Memoriam Caroli Stanton de Upfield Pakenhill qui LXVIII ætatis anno die XXVII Martii A.D. MDCCCLXIII hac vita defunctus in Cœmeterio vicino adquiescit, hanc fenestram exornandam curavit uxor mariti heu præmortui superstes.

It contains illustrations of Our Lord's parable of "The Talents:" [1] the south compartment representing the faithful servants trading with their Lord's money ; that on the north, the slothful servant hiding his talent in the earth ; and the middle compartment representing their Lord rewarding the faithful servants, and punishing the slothful one.

The gable window of the north transept was erected

To the Honour and Glory of God, and in memory of John Biddell of Stratford Abbey, who died April 25th, 1863, aged 74 years, and of Hannah his wife, who died February 22nd, 1860, aged 62 years.

It represents the Acts of Mercy, viz. ;—Feeding the hungry, Clothing the naked, Receiving the stranger, Visiting the sick and the prisoner, Giving water to the thirsty, Leading the blind, and Burying the dead. In the tracery is the martyrdom of Stephen.

The window in the gable of the south transept was erected

To the Glory of God, and in memory of Anne wife of James Mander, who died February 11th, 1868, aged 64 years.

It represents the four Evangelists with their emblems, in the chief compartments ; and three events in the history of St. Lawrence in the traceries.

1 See Matthew xxv. 14—30.

In the north aisle, the third window from the west end was erected

In memory of Charles Goddard, who died October 29th, 1864.

Its subject is the "Raising of Jairus's daughter, and the giving sight to the blind man."
One of the windows in the south aisle was raised

To the Glory of God, and in memory of Thomas Daniel Hill of The Thrupp, near Stroud, who died September 3rd, 1866.

It represents our Lord appearing and making himself known to Mary Magdalene in the garden, after his resurrection. [2]

The seventh stained-glass window is over the outer entrance to the tower. It is called The Children's Window, because it was raised from contributions collected by children—those of the schools and others. Its object is—"Christ Blessing little Children."

The Communion table and two chairs of oak finely carved, were presented by Mr. Joseph Wood; and the handsomely embroidered Communion table cover, the work of Mrs. E. C. Little, was her gift. The covers of the cushions, chairs, stools, &c., were worked and presented by other ladies. The beautiful alms dish was the gift of Mrs. and Miss Jones.

The richly ornamented iron screen, between the tower-arch and the nave, is the work of Messrs. Chew and Sons. The apparatus for warming the church was put up by them; and the gas-fittings for lighting it by Mr. Frank Howell.

---

[2] No painter has adequately represented Mary Magdalene in the scene narrated in John xx, 16, when Jesus saith unto her "Mary." She turned herself, and saith unto Him "Rabboni." Only the human countenance itself, accustomed to express emotional feelings, could do this; and it has been done. The late eminent Rev. Robert Hall was once invited to meet Mrs. Siddons, the great tragic actress, at the house of a mutual friend. Mr. Hall availed himself of the opportunity, and requested Mrs. Siddons would do him the favour to pronounce the word "Rabboni," in the character of Mary Magdalene. To this she consented, and having prepared her friends by drawing the conversation to the sublime and affecting incident, she pronounced the word "Rabboni," accompanied with an expression of the intense surprise, joy, adoration and love which doubtless had been evinced by Mary Magdalene. It may be imagined how deeply Mr. Hall was gratified and affected by the visible display of gestures and emotions which he had long, but vainly, endeavoured to realise to his own mind. This circumstance was related to the writer by a friend of Mr. Hall.

The whole of the seats and doors are of English oak. The seats are all open. The church will afford room for 1,200 persons ; and its acoustic properties are good.

It cost between £10,000 and £11,000, raised by subscription ; of which a sum of £600 was contributed by the trustees of the will of the late Dr. Warneford, of Morton-Henmarsh, in this county ;[3] and £1,000 from the funds of the Stroud Charity Trustees.

The porch is in the south aisle,—occupying the second bay from the west, and is 11 feet square. It is the chief entrance into the church. The other entrances are through the east side of the north transept, and the west wall of the tower.

The bells of the steeple are not rung, as formerly, in the old belfry loft, but from the floor of the tower.

The monuments to the memory of the first and the last Stephens, of Lypiatt, that were taken down with the old church, have been re-erected against the east wall of the south transept : and so many of the other monuments taken down as could be accommodated with room, upon the inside walls of the tower, and the outside of the arch which forms the entrance from it into the nave, have been set up there. But the Mural sculpture mentioned in Chapter LI. is not among them : nor is it intended to erect any other monumental memorials, except in the form of obituary windows.

The old organ has been re-erected ; but the edifice is worthy of a better instrument.[4] There is a fund consisting of £500, New Three per Cent. Annuities, standing in the names of C. H. Fisher and W. H. Stanton, as "the organ committee,"—the dividends of which are payable to the organist for the time being, in part of his salary.

The spire steeple, which is the only portion of the old church that has been preserved and incorporated with the new one, exhibited proofs of good fourteenth century work.

---

3 Dr. Warneford was distinguished as a most munificent contributor on similar occasions during his life. At his death, he left by his will two large sums of money to be held in trust, that the interest of one of them should be annually appropriated in donations to the widows and children of deceased clergymen, and to beneficed clergymen and curates of and in the ancient diocese of Gloucester ; and the interest of the other sum in annual donations for promoting the building, re-building, and repairing of churches, chapels, and parsonage houses, of and in districts principally inhabited by the poor of the same district.

4 A fine new organ has long since been provided by public subscription.

But, not being of due proportions therewith, it is hoped (as the Building Committee desired) that the liberality of the people will, at some future time, take it down and erect another of more suitable size and height, together with an additional bay to the length of the nave and side aisles.

The church of Stroud is in the deanery of Stonehouse, having an income of about £300 a-year. It was formerly a perpetual curacy, but became a vicarage under the "District Church Title Act," of 31 and 32 Victoria, c. cxvii., s. 2, July 31, 1868.

CHAPTER LIII.

HOLY TRINITY CHURCH — WHITESHILL CHURCH.

TWO other churches have been erected in the parish, within comparatively recent times.

The first of these is the church of The Holy Trinity, situated in the field beyond Whitehall, near the upper part of the town. Its foundation-stone was laid by the late William Stanton, of The Thrupp, during the incumbency of the Rev. W. F. Powell, under whose superintendence it was completed, and by whom a sermon was preached on its consecration, October 15th, 1839. At that time, however, Mr. Powell was the recently appointed perpetual curate of Cirencester.

A grant of £1,000 toward the building was made by the Church Building Commissioners ; and another grant by the Incorporated Society for Building and Enlarging Churches. on the condition that 700 free sittings should be provided, which was accordingly done. The rest of the expenses was raised by private contribution. The interior area of the church, not including the vestibule, is 70 feet long by 45 wide, with a gallery at the west end. The raised chancel is 26 feet wide by 22 feet deep, having an apse of five sides, in each of which is a small lancet-shaped window ; and is divided from the body of the church by three lofty arches. On the north side of these arches stands the reading desk, and on the south a handsome stone pulpit. A large gilt eagle with wings displayed, presented by Mr. Stephen Clissold, was set up under the central arch, as a lectern from whence the daily lessons are read. [1]

Since the old writer's death in 1873, The Thrupp has been made a separate Ecclesiastical district, with a Vicar ; extensive alterations and improvements have been effected in this Church : a new vicarage provided, and most complete and useful Parish Rooms erected. The present incumbent is the Rev. E. H. Hawkins.

[1] This eagle had belonged to Ebley Chapel, and was in use there as a lectern as long as the religious services were conducted after the Countess of Huntingdon's rules.

All five of the windows in the chancel are filled with stained glass,—one being "The oblation of the masters and children of the schools of the parish 1838." Three others are obituary windows; one of them "In memory of W. J. W[ood], Jany. 17, 1854, aged 57 years, and his son, F. C. W[ood], May 31st, 1848, aged 19 years." Another "In memory of the Rev. George Proctor, for thirteen years pastor of the parish church, who died September 30th, 1858." And another in memory of the writer's brother, T. T. Fisher, who died August 23, 1869, aged 84. One of the twelve large windows in the nave is also fitted up with stained glass. The church of The Holy Trinity is a chapel of ease to the parish church, and is in charge of the incumbent, by whom full services in the morning and evening of Sundays are provided. As yet it has no special endowment, but the pews are let for the benefit of the vicar. [2]

A marble tablet within the church is inscribed:

Sacred to the memory of Frederick Charles Wood, third son of William John and Catherine Wood of the Thrupp, in this parish; who died at Cairo on his journey home from India, on the 31st of May, 1848, in the 20th year of his age.

The following sepulchral inscriptions are in the church-yard:—

William John Wood of the Thrupp in this parish, died Jan. 17th, 1854, aged 57 years. In the hour of death, and in the day of judgment, good Lord deliver us. Will. Jno., eldest son of William & Catherine Wood, died Dec. 28th, 1839, aged 34.

George Proctor xiii years Incumbent of Stroud, died Sept. 30, 1858, born March 18th, 1809. Blessed are the dead which die in the Lord.

Elizabeth Jane, wife of the Rev. T. H. Tarlton, incumbent of Stroud, born Aug. 13th, 1826, fell asleep Nov. 10, 1858.
"Waiting for the coming of our Lord Jesus Christ."

In remembrance of John Aldridge who departed this life July 14th, 1860, aged 67 years. Also of Hester, the beloved wife of the above, who departed this life August 16th, 1868, aged 75 years.
Her end was peace.

Sacred to the memory of Sophia Aldridge who died Novr. 26th, 1861 aged 97 years. Also of William Aldridge son of the above-named, who died Nov. 12th, 1866, aged 68 years. And of Elizabeth his wife who died March 6th, 1867, aged 68 years.
I am a poor sinner and nothing at all:
But Jesus Christ is my all in all.

Sacred to the memory of Harriet Mary, the beloved wife of the Rev. John Badcock, L.L.D., incumbent of this church and parish. She fell asleep in Jesus Jany. 13, 1868 aged 42 years.

[2 This *was* the state of things in this Church in the writer's time, and he himself, his wife, and his youngest son, sleep in its churchyard.—C. H. F.]

The second of our modern churches, with its embattled tower, was erected in the village of Whiteshill, in the populous outlying tithing of Pakenhill, and is called Saint Mary's Church. The first stone was laid April 22nd, 1840, on ground given by Richard Cooke, Esq., and it was consecrated and opened for religious worship on the same day of the same month in the following year, the sermon being preached by the Rev. John Elliott, perpetual curate of Randwick. The cost of this building was about £1,000, raised by subscription, of which Dr. Warneford contributed £500. It contains about 600 sittings, of which 500 are free. This church is now a vicarage, with an assigned district. One of its earliest incumbents was the Rev. William Harris Roach, who was inducted in the year 1844. In 1845 he erected the Vicarage house by subscription, £500 of which was given by Dr. Warneford; and he built new school rooms by a subscription, (toward which Mr. Biddell, of Stratford Abbey, gave £100,) in the stead of those erected by Dr. Williams in 1814. [2] The site of the new schools was given by Joseph Cripps, Esq. The Church is well attended, and about 250 scholars, boys and girls, belong to the School Board and Sunday schools, with twelve or fourteen Sunday teachers. The endowment has, after several years, been augmented to about £124 per annum; including the estimated rental of the Vicarage house, a sum of £12, the interest of money raised by subscription and placed in the hands of the managers of Queen Anne's bounty, and £96 from the Ecclesiastical Commissioners.

2 For which see p. 283.

CHAPTER LIV.

DISSENTING PLACES OF WORSHIP.

BESIDES the places of worship belonging to the Church of England, there are several Dissenting Chapels in the town and parish.

The earliest of these is the Old Meeting, in Chapel-street. The Church there assembling originally was Presbyterian; but, like most of the English Presbyterians who retained their orthodoxy, it subsequently adopted the Independent or Congregational mode of government and worship.

The exact date of its first formation is unknown. But, in the latter part of the seventeenth century, the Nonconformists of Stroud assembled in Dyer's Court, in Silver-street, where, at the upper end of an orchard, a barn stood in 1675. This barn was afterward (probably about 1687) converted into a place of worship by them, and was called the Nonconformists' Meeting-house. It bore the name of the Old Meeting during a considerable part of the eighteenth century, long after it had been converted into dwelling-houses, and their present place of worship had been built, which, in its turn, received the name of the Old Meeting. The orchard alluded to was, undoubtedly, part of the property called The Knapp, long known as the Rev. Wm. Johns' Charity, having its frontage in Nelson-street.

It is not precisely known when the Old Meeting-house in Chapel-street was erected: but, in 1704, the land on which it stands was obtained of Sarah Viner by John Cooke for such a building: and, in 1770, an old man named Pain was living, who remembered having, when a lad, wheeled stones for it while in progress.

It was, probably, completed in 1711; as in that year a sermon was preached at Stroud, "before an assembly of divines," by the Rev. James Forbes, an Independent minister of Gloucester;[1] and on July 28th, 1712, an invitation was addressed by twenty-four men of Stroud, to Mr. Richard Rawlin, of St. Neots, Huntingdonshire, to become their pastor, and, on April 9th, 1713, he was set apart to that office. In 1729 the house in which the ministers afterward resided was purchased: it stands near the chapel, on the opposite side of the street, and has always been called The Parsonage; but has long become unsuitable for the minister's residence.

In the years 1813 and 1823 the chapel was enlarged and a school-room built, at the cost of about £1,500. In 1832 a school-room was erected in Somers-street, by the friends of the Old Meeting, and opened as a week-day infant school, under the direction of Mrs. Parsons, of Granville Cottages. She has had the sole management of it for thirty-seven years. During that time more than two thousand children have received an early training there; and it is still in active operation. In 1844 a new front to the chapel was erected at the expense of £800; and, in 1854, a new school-room, including the site on which it stands, was built for £600. Of these sums more than £900 were the gift of Mr. S. S Marling.[2] In the year 1864, Mr. Marling also erected a commodious new parsonage house, toward the cost of which the late Mr. Benjamin Franklin contributed £700. It is situated on the north side of the new Bisley-road from Whitehall.

The following is a list of the successive pastors:

1713	April 10th, Richard Rawlin. He died 1725, and was followed by William Atky, who retired in	1727
1728	William Williams, removed	1729
1739	Thomas Jenkins, died there	1749
1753	J. Howell, removed to Poole	1757
1758	Samuel Ball, who had been a schoolfellow of the Rev. George Whitefield, at Crypt Grammar School, Gloucester. He died here	1779
1779	William Harris, removed...	1806
1808	John Jefferis Church, removed	1810
1810	John Burder, A.M., was ordained to this charge, Sept. 5, 1811. Removed to Bedford-street chapel ...	1837
1838	May 27th, Henry Griffiths. Appointed Principal of Brecon College	1842

1 John Forbes was, on the whole, fifty-eight years a minister at Gloucester; and died there May 31st, 1712, aged 83. His funeral sermon was preached by Isaac Noble, of Bristol. This sermon was published, prefaced by Mr. Forbes, "Remains," among which was his "Sermon before the Assembly at Stroudwater;" but I have not been able to procure a copy of it.

[2 Afterwards Sir Samuel S. Marling, Bart.]

1842	Sept. 18th, Watson Smith	...	...	...	...	
1847	August 15th, Thomas Nicholas ...	...	...	...	
1852	August 15th, David James Evans	...	...	...	
1857	August 9th, Edwin Davies	...	...	...	...	
1860	Nov. 4th, Joseph Whiting, removed	...	...	...	1868
1869	Thomas Oxley Chapman ...	...	...	...	...	
1890	Allen Redshaw, the present minister.				

The following are a few notices relating to the Old
Meeting :—

It appears from the baptismal registers that, between
the years 1749 and 1756, (in the absence of a resident
minister,) children were baptised by pastors of other dissenting chapels, when they came occasionally to officiate
here : viz., the Revs. Olding, Dickenson, and Tallamay,
of Gloucester ; Morrison, of Chalford ; Vaughan, of Ross ;
Davies, of Billericay, in Essex ; Jervis, of Nailsworth ;
Parry, of Cirencester ; Morley, of Painswick ; and others
whose residences are not stated. And, in the years 1762
and 1773, several children, whose parents resided at Tetbury
and in its neighbourhood, were baptised here by Mr. Ball,
which seems to indicate that there was no Congregational
minister resident in Tetbury at that time.

On January 3rd, 1765, died Henry Okey, aged 67, who
had been the chapel clerk for forty-one years ; and, during
all that time, he was absent from his place only twice, when
the doors were open for Divine worship.

On January 7th, 1798, died Thomas Tugwell, of the
Thrupp, one of the Deacons, whom I remember as a tall,
coarse-visaged, but grave and gentle man, dressed in an
old-fashioned, faded, blue Sunday coat, which he was said
to have worn for forty years. He was impressed on my
young mind as the personification of an ancient patriarch,
perhaps by my associating him and his coat with the
declaration of Moses, in one of his latest addresses to the
Israelites,—" Thy raiment waxed not old upon thee these
forty years." [2]

The Rev. Wm. Harris, the pastor from 1779 to 1806,
was a native of Pembrokeshire. His religious views were
highly Calvinistic. He possessed considerable abilities ;
and took pleasure in quoting, (which he did aptly,) from
his favourite Latin poets, Ovid and Horace. He married
Miss Winnett ; and, after her death, Miss Humpage, sister
of the (even yet remembered) surgeon of that name, both

[2] Deuteronomy viii., 4.

of this town.   On retiring from Stroud he went to reside at Abergavenny, and afterward to Bristol, where he died suddenly in the chapel during Divine service.

On December 30, 1807, died Nathaniel Butler, an aged man, who kept a small huckster's shop at the angle of Acre-edge and Middle-street. 3   He was often engaged as an occasional preacher here, at Rodborough Tabernacle, and elsewhere in the neighbourhood.

The following is the inscription on the oldest monument in the chapel :—

Near this place lyes side by side the bodys of those as follows.   John Viner, died Dec. 19, 1723, aged near 70 years.   Sarah Viner, his sister, died Feb. 2, 1723, aged near 72 years.

There are also monuments to the memories of

Anthony Paine, clothier, who died Feb. 9, 1735, aged 52.   Anthony Paine, mercer, who died May 2, 1776, aged 52 years : also of Sarah, his wife, who died November 8th, 1801, aged 78 years; and of Anthony Rawlin Paine, their son, who died Jan. 31, 1788, aged 29.

To the memory of Sarah wife of Daniel Bloxsome of this town, mercer, daughter of the late Revd. James Morley of Painswick, who died 8th June 1781, aged 40 years.   Also of the above-named Daniel Bloxsome, who died 4th of Decr., 1808, aged 73 years.   Also of Sarah Aldridge, Spinster, daughter of the late James Aldridge of this town, who died 23rd Octr., 1811, aged 65 years.   Also of Ursula, relict of the before-mentioned Daniel Bloxsome, and sister of the said Sarah Aldridge, who died 1st Novr., 1828, aged 85 years.

On the west end wall of the corridor is a handsome monument, erected by the late Henry Wyatt, of Farm Hill. 4   It is divided vertically into two compartments, the first containing memorials of Hannah his wife and five of their children, and the second the following inscription :—

Originally placed by the Husband and Father, in memory of his Wife and Children who have gone before him, this stone now serves as a memorial of him who raised it.   Henry Wyatt, the Father, on the 24th day of January, A.D. 1847, at the age of 64 years and one day, finished a life of energy and usefulness, lamented and honoured as a good husband, father, and brother, a valuable friend and neighbour, a practical philanthropist, an upright magistrate, and an honest man.   The memory of the just is blessed.   Also of Priscilla Wyatt, his widow, who died March 24th, 1865, aged 83 years.

3 His old house has been taken down and a new one built on its site.

4 It was designed and executed by the late Mr. John Thomas, an eminent sculptor and architect of London.   He was a native of Chalford, and served his apprenticeship to John Hamlett, of Stroud.   He died April 9, 1862, aged 49 years.   He was connected by marriage with two of our much respected townsmen : and, being a man of great abilities and reputation, his almost sudden death called forth an expression of much sympathy.

To many persons the Old Meeting is hallowed by the dust of friends and relatives who have been laid to rest in its grave-yard, and by the faithful ministrations of godly men within its walls.

The Wesleyan Chapel is the next in order of time. It is situated in Acre-street, formerly called Acre-edge; and was built in 1763. About the year 1796 it was considerably enlarged: and, subsequently, galleries, school-rooms, and a minister's house were added. The centenary of its erection was held on Sunday, July 5th, 1863. 5

John Wesley, the celebrated founder of Arminian Methodism, was an ordained minister of the Church of England, though early excluded from most of its pulpits: yet, he so arranged the hours of worship in his United Societies that, for many years, no services were held at the same time of the day as those of the Established Church. This enabled many to attend the Sunday and week-day services at both places.

As early as July 27th, 1795, at the 52nd Conference, held at Manchester, "A plan of pacification" was adopted, containing a rule that "Wherever Divine Service is performed in England on the Lord's day in church hours, the officiating preacher shall read either the Service of the [Established] Church, our venerable Father's Abridgment, or at least the lessons appointed by the Calendar. But we recommend either the full Service or the Abridgment."

Until the lapse of several years in the present century, the chief religious services in the Wesleyan Chapel at Stroud were held in the early morning, before the Parish Church was open; and in the evening, when (as yet) no evening service was held there: and, upon those occasions, they were attended by many of the Church congregation. But gradually the Society of Wesleyan Methodists has come to be considered as an entirely distinct Body or Sect; and their Sunday services are held, (both in point of time and form,) without regard to those of the Anglican Church.

The Baptist Chapel, which follows next in order, was the first Public Building erected in the new part, hereinbefore called the fourth enlargement of the town. 6

[5 This was so in the writer's day. A handsome and convenient new Wesleyan Chapel has long been erected in Castle-street, Stroud. The old building mentioned above is now possessed by the Salvation Army.]

6 See page 154.

It stands on the north side of John-street, and comprises 600 square yards of what was formerly garden ground, lying at the east end of Kendrick's Orchard. This land was bought at the rate of seven shillings per square yard. The purchase was made, and the chapel built and fitted up, by the late Rev. Henry Hawkins, at the cost of about £2,000, raised by his own personal exertions. Of this sum £100 was collected in single shillings. The building was opened for public worship in 1824, when Mr. Hawkins became the pastor, and thereby the founder, of the Baptist Society in this place. 7   He died January 17, 1845, aged 76 ; and was succeeded by his son-in-law, the Rev. William Yates, who resigned, from ill-health, at the end of the year 1867 ; and was followed by the Rev. Walter William Laskey. The Rev. Walter T. Soper is the present minister.

There is another place of worship belonging to the Congregational Nonconformists. It lies on the west side of Bedford-street, which separates it from the Subscription Rooms. The formation of this new church was found necessary, in consequence of the Old Meeting in Chapel-street having become insufficient for the accommodation of all the persons who were desirous of attending religious worship there.

The first stone of this new chapel was laid June 8th, 1835. It was completed in 1837, and opened for public worship September 27th in that year. Its cost, including the purchase of the site, &c., was £2,731 ; which was raised by subscription, chiefly among the persons belonging to the church and congregation assembling at the Old Meeting : and, afterward, galleries, an organ, and an Infant school-room were erected, at the further cost of £650.

This edifice was at first called Union Chapel, from a belief that the street in which it stands would take the name of Union-street, on account of its connecting High-street with George-street ; but the street having finally received its present name, the chapel is known as Bedford-street Chapel.

It is an elegant structure, rounded at the west end ; having a front of forty-five feet to the street, and forming part of the handsome western boundary, as Messrs. Libby

7 He had been the minister of the Baptist Chapel at Eastcombs, in the parish of Bisley, for fifteen years.

and Pearce's large warehouse form a similar eastern boundary, of the square in front of the Subscription Rooms. [8] Its basement story consists of large Sunday school-rooms, &c. ; and the interior of the Chapel above it is eighty feet long, forty feet wide, and thirty-four feet high ; and is fitted up with oak galleries all round. It is approached from without by a handsome winding stone stair-case, within a tower which flanks the north-east corner of its front.

At the opening of this chapel, the old community was divided into two, and each became thenceforward a distinct church ; the Rev. John Burder, the then pastor, taking charge of the new chapel, and another minister, the Rev. Henry Griffith, being soon provided for the old one. The separation was amicably made, by the choice of those who gave in their names to form the new church. At the same time it was arranged that the residence of the minister, and all the other endowments and funds held in trust for the Old Meeting, should continue to belong exclusively to the church remaining there.

After a ministration of six years, Mr. Burder deemed it right to leave Stroud and to relinquish the regular duties of a pastoral charge, and was succeeded, July 2nd, 1843, by the Rev. William Wheeler, of Wells, who is the present minister.

The Rev. John Burder, whose pastorate at the Old Meeting and at Bedford-street Chapel, extended over a period of more than thirty-two years, was the second son of the late Rev. George Burder, an eminent Nonconformist minister of London, the writer of the well-known "Village Sermons," and for many years the gratuitous foreign secretary of the London Missionary Society.

The Rev. John Burder's ministerial life at Stroud was distinguished by constant and laborious application, not only to his official duties, but also to the direction, either wholly or partially, of more than forty religious and philanthropic societies ; and to the general interests of the Congregational body.

The character of his mind, and of his ordinary life as its exponent, was that of order, method, and punctuality ; and his moral character was that of justice and generosity.

Originally gifted with a high imaginative faculty, he had, upon principle, chastened and, indeed, well-nigh subdued

[8 All this has been much altered since the writer's death.]

it ; as though he deemed its exercise might be detrimental to the right employment of the understanding.

His pulpit exercises were carefully composed, and as carefully delivered. In them he eschewed all mere declamation and rhetorical display. But the propositions which he extracted from his texts were always first established by a train of reasoning, so clear and logical, yet withal so simple, as could hardly fail to be understood by any of his congregation ; while they were most highly appreciated by hearers of cultivated and disciplined minds : and then the application of the whole was made with such an earnest persuasiveness as to impress his auditory with a deep sense of the Christian duties, privileges, and blessings which the propositions were intended to illustrate, and to which they led.

His religious principles were more Calvinistic than Arminian, but his aim was to ascertain and declare the genuine sense of the Word of God, without paying undue deference to any human system. He always maintained that there was no reason why any one should be finally lost, but his own unwillingness to be saved. The spirituality of his object, and the moderation of his sentiments, secured him the universal esteem and confidence of his friends.

His sermons ranged from the plainness and simplicity of elementary religious instruction, to the deepest and sublimest doctrines of Christianity. Among them was a course of twenty-four lectures on "Religion." The first division of nine lectures treated of the various systems of false religion, and the remaining fifteen of the nature and claims of true religion.

These lectures were delivered every alternate Sunday evening during the year 1824 ; and were published under the title of "Lectures on Religion, by John Burder, M.A." [9]

On his relinquishing the pastorate of Bedford-street Chapel he took up his residence at Clifton, Bristol ; where he continued to give his valuable assistance to many objects of a Christian and philanthropic kind, and to preach occasionally, until within a short period of his death. And there this devoted servant of his Heavenly Master entered into his rest, Friday, May 17th, 1867, aged 82, and was interred at the Bristol Cemetery, Arno's Vale.

9 8vo., pp. 543. London : Taylor : 1826.

The Chapel of the Society called Primitive Methodists
stands near the upper end of Parliament-street. It was
built in the year 1836 ; and a school-room was attached to
it in 1858.

There is a place of worship belonging to the Brethren,
or the Plymouth Brethren, in Acre-street. It was fitted
up and opened in October, 1852. The Society of this
name originated about the year 1829, "in a movement in
the direction of greater simplicity and godliness of life,
greater spirituality of worship, and a higher degree of
personal consecration to Christ." It began chiefly among
members of the Church of England. Their doctrine is
Calvinistic. They have "no ordained or specially consecrated ministry." They meet on the morning of the
Lord's day "for worship of God, and to break bread in
remembrance of the Lord Jesus Christ." The "object of
their meetings on Sunday evenings is to preach *the Gospel
to the unconverted*." And, at their meetings, "there may
be prayer and singing, reading the Scriptures, and exposition of them ; with quiet pauses of silent worship." 10
Although this Society has not any acknowledged minister
over its congregations, there is seldom wanting some
qualified person to lead the worship at every meeting of
the members.

Besides those before-mentioned, there is a building called
the People's Hall, in Silver-street, erected by Mr. Opie
Rodway, at a cost of £443, and opened March 18th, 1864.
It is, as its name suggests, devoted to general objects of a
philanthropic character; including a united religious service
on Sunday afternoons. Here, too, lectures are given, and
meetings held, to promote the progress of useful knowledge
and social improvement, in those classes of society, for the
assembling of which its situation is so well adapted.

To these I must add the Chapel of Independent or Congregational Dissenters at Ruscomb, near the extremity of
Pakenhill tithing.

10 The above passages, within inverted commas, are extracted from an
Answer to the question, "Who are the Plymouth Brethren?" by H. Grattan
Guinness, 18mo., pp. 47. London : William Yapp, 70 Welbeck-street,
Cavendish-square, W. No date.

The original place of worship is now used as a British school and a Sunday school ; and, at a short distance from it, the present chapel was erected in

1828, by William Edwards, who became its minister. In the interval between

1833 and 1838, religious worship was conducted there by — Hyde and others, under the superintendence of the Rev. John Burder of Stroud.

1838 Sept,, Evan Jones became and continued its pastor until his death, June 17th, 1855, and in

1855 Dec., Daniel Francis Close became, and is the present, minister

The usual number of attendants is about 200, besides the Sunday school, amounting to about 100. The scholars on week-days average from 90 to 100.

The cost of maintaining the schools, and paying the salary of the minister, was borne, for several years, by the late Henry Wyatt, until his death, in January, 1847 : and, from that time to 1869, his liberality was followed by a member of his family.

This is the "Chapel of Congregational Dissenters" before alluded to, [11] as having been instrumental, (with "the other religious and educational processes in operation,") in raising and improving the previously low moral and social condition of this remote part of the parish.

[11] See page 224.

CHAPTER LV.

THE UNION WORKHOUSE — THE CEMETERY.

THE Stroud Poor-law Union comprises the fifteen parishes of Avening, Bisley, Cranham, Horsley, Minchinhampton, Miserdine, Painswick, Pitchcomb, Randwick, Rodborough, King's Stanley, Leonard Stanley, Stonehouse, Stroud, and Woodchester; besides Haywardsfield, a small extra-parochial district consisting of a dwelling-house and about two acres of land, which has been deemed a parish for poor-law purposes, since 1857.[1] This last place is bounded on three sides by the parish of Stonehouse, and on the fourth (the south) side by the Stroudwater Navigation, and a narrow strip of the parish of Randwick.

The Union was constituted in the year 1836. It is managed by a Board of thirty-one Guardians, elected by ratepayers of the several parishes, in numbers somewhat relatively proportioned to their respective populations,—except Haywardsfield, which has no vote; and by the Justices of the Peace who reside in those parishes, and are ex-official Guardians.

The Union Workhouse is conspicuously situated upon the southern slope of Stroud-hill, on the upper (or north) side of the new Bisley-road, and is about half-a-mile from the town. It is surrounded by eight acres of appurtenant land, between that road and the old highway to Bisley, which runs up the central ridge of the hill as before-mentioned.[2] The Register-office belonging to the Union is in John-street; and the registers of births, deaths, and marriages are kept there.

[1] Pursuant to Stat. 20 Victoria, c. 19.
[2] See page 10.

The Workhouse and the Register-office were erected in the year 1837. The cost of these buildings, their fitting up and furnishing, together with the purchase-money of the land, was borrowed on security of the poor-rates, payable with interest by annual instalments, all of which have been paid.

The new Workhouse was opened for the admission of paupers in 1837 ; and then the old one was sold.

The officers of the Union are :

A Master and Matron. A Chaplain. A Medical Officer for the Workhouse. Six other Medical Officers for the fifteen parishes. Three Relieving Officers. A School-master and School-mistress. A Nurse, Tailor, Laundress, and Porter. A Clerk of the Union, who is also Superintendent Registrar of the births, deaths, and marriages.

The Guardians assemble in their Board-room at the Register-office for ordinary business on Friday in every week ; and a Visiting Committee meets for Inspection, &c., weekly, at the Workhouse.

The Chaplain performs Divine service there on Sunday and one other day, and attends the sick and aged and catechises the children on another day, in each week. A Scripture-reader likewise visits the House once a week.

The adult paupers are employed in cultivating the land and garden, and in other needful labour. The boys and girls are educated by the School-master and School-mistress ; and are engaged in such suitable work and healthful exercise as can be provided for them. Some of them are disposed of, by being put out to service or apprenticed ; and others, (together with adult paupers,) voluntary remove themselves in search of employment elsewhere. 3

The Cemetery is also situated upon the southern slope of Stroud-hill, nearly opposite to the Union Workhouse, but on the lower side of the new Bisley-road. It lies between that road on the north, and the way leading through the fields from Whitehall to the valley of Horns, 4 on the south.

In the year 1854, the several burial grounds in Stroud having become insufficient in size and dangerous to health, an Order was issued by the Secretary of State in October of that year for closing them, (with certain exceptional

[3 Since the writer's death, the boarding-out system has been largely adopted.]

4 For a notice of this place see pp. 204-5.

regulations,) from the 1st of September, 1855. Thereupon, under the authority of the Act relating to Burials, (16 and 17 Victoria, c. 134,) the parishioners in vestry appointed a Burial Board, consisting of four Episcopalians and four Nonconformists, with a Clerk, to carry out its provisions as to this place.

The Board purchased of Mr. Joseph Watts six acres of land, part of a wood called "The Conygear;" and thereon erected two chapels with a spire, and an entrance lodge.

The price of the land, timber, &c., was	£756 9 6
and the cost of the chapels, lodge, inclosing, levelling, laying-out, planting, architect's charges, and legal expenses	2,790 16 7
	£3,547 6 1

Of this sum, £3,000 was borrowed from the Public Works-Loan Commissioners upon security of the poor-rates in 1856, and £500 in 1859, payable with interest by annual instalments.

In 1867 an agreement was made for the purchase of a cottage and three acres and thirty-three perches of land, another part of the Conygear, at the price of £508 8s.: and on June 22, 1869, a sum of £1,200 was authorized by the Vestry to be raised for completing the purchase of the additional ground and the expenses attending it, and for fencing, laying-out, and rendering the same ready for interments.

The chapel and about three acres of the Cemetery which had been set apart for the use of the Episcopalians of the parish, were consecrated by Dr. Baring, Bishop of Gloucester, September 1st, 1856; and, on the 4th of the same month, William Lewis, a pauper from the Union Workhouse, was the first who was interred therein.

From that time to the end of 1869, a period of thirteen years and four months, the number of burials was 1,500, being an average of 115 per annum. Of this number two-thirds were buried in the consecrated ground, and one-third, (including fifty-four Roman Catholics,) in the unconsecrated ground.

At the same time the Cemetery contained 130 tombs or other monumental memorials, among which are the following:

The first erected there was an upright head-stone:

Sacred to the memory of Samuel Franklin, who fell asleep in Jesus, October 6th 1857, aged 26 years.

"Looking for the Blessed Hope."

A coped tomb, bearing a plain recumbent cross, records that

Anna, wife of A. J. Stanton, the Thrupp, died Octr. 14th, 1858, aged 30 years. Alfred Wilton, son of Alfred J. and Margaret Stanton, died Decr. 13th, 1866, aged 6 weeks.

A polished white flat marble slab has the following inscription :

In memory of Hannah, the beloved wife of John Biddell, of Stratford Abbey, Stroud, who died Feby. 22, 1860, aged 62 years. She was a humble and earnest disciple of her Blessed Lord, whose doctrines she adorned in her life, and whose spiritual presence was her comfort and support in the hour of death ; so that it may truly be said of her—to live was Christ, and to die was gain. Also of John Biddell, of Stratford Abbey, who died April 25th, 1863, aged 74 years.

A similar marble slab beareth :

In memory of Robert Berrie, who died January 10, 1869, aged 77 years.

And on the base of a richly-carved foliated white marble cross, standing erect on the slab, is :

Margaret Ellen Clifford Biddell, born July 29, 1867, died Feby. 13th, 1868.

Near this is a large and handsome monument, having two gothic recesses in each of its north and south sides, and one in each of its east and west ends. The shafts of the columns which support the arches are of grey granite ; and, within one of the arches on the south side, is this inscription :

Sacred to the memory of Susan Dorington, wife of John Edwd. Dorington, Esq., of Lypiatt Park, born June 5, 1794, died Octr. 4, 1866.
"Thy will be done."

A monument consisting of a truncated Obelisk bearing a draped funeral Urn :

Sacred to the memory of Mary Ann, wife of John Hewlett, who died July 8th, 1858, aged 24 years.

A dwarf Altar-tomb :

In memory of William Davis, Currier, late of Stroud, who died Oct. 7, 1860, aged 58 years. Also of William his eldest son, who died and was buried at Richmond, Virginia, United States, July 11th, 1860, aged 26 years. Also of John his third son, who died and was buried at Ludlow, Shropshire, Aug. 8th, 1860, aged 21 years. And also of Mary his second daughter, who died July 28th, 1861, aged 26 years.

A square Altar-tomb, bearing a decorated pinnacle supported by figures of Faith, Hope, Charity, and Truth. A tablet on its north side is inscribed :

Sacred to the memory of Elizabeth, the beloved wife of Henry Marmont of this town, who died June 25th, 1860, aged 52 years.

A raised coped tomb :

Sacred to the memory of Margaret Dorothea Andrewes Uthwatt, who departed this life Novr. 20th, 1860, aged 59 years.

Sacred to the memory of Harriott Mabella Uthwatt, the beloved wife of Edolph Andrewes Uthwatt, Esq., she departed this life March 3rd, 1863, aged 82 years.

A coped tomb, bearing the symbols of Freemasonry, is thus inscribed :

In memory of Edmund Purnell Miles, surgeon of this town, born April 27, 1800, died Decr. 27, 1861. This monument was erected by a few friends in admiration of his general benevolence, and his warm-hearted friendship.

An oblong gothic tomb, having eight arched recesses between pillars whose shafts are polished serpentine marble : and within one of the recesses is the following :

Here rests the body of Charles Stanton, of Upfield, Pakenhill, who died March 27th, 1863, aged 66 years.

A neat coped tomb has this inscription :

In memory of Sarah Jane, youngest child of William Henry and Caroline Withey of this town, who died October 1st, 1864, aged 11 months.

An ornamental truncated Obelisk :

Erected by the inhabitants of Stroud to the memory of John Selby Howell, for upwards of 50 years parish clerk of Stroud. He died June, 1867, aged 82. He was valued in life for his integrity, and he died respected and regretted.

"I am the resurrection and the life saith the Lord."

On the stone border of a vault is inscribed :

Roger Postlethwaite, of Belmont, Stroud, born April 25, 1807, died Octr. 10th, 1864.

In an enclosed vault lie interred the remains of John Paine, of Corbett House, Stroud, who died May 17th, 1862, aged 77 : and Susan Paine, his wife, who died Jany. 1st, 1860, aged 72 ; also John Burder Paine, infant son of William Henry and E. Julia Paine, who died Octr. 30th, 1857.

In another vault is deposited the body of Thomas Daniel Hill, of the Thrupp, who died Sept. 3rd, 1866, aged 51.

Here also is laid all that was mortal of Joshua Wall, who died Decr. 21st, 1869, aged 34. He had designed and executed many works of high art in sculpture ; which, with 100 of the surrounding monuments, attest his genius and his industry.

Among the aged persons interred here is Susan Dancey Face, widow of William Face. She was born at Stroud,

Novr. 5th, 1763. Her maiden name was Morgan. She was a poor, but respected, member of the society of Wesleyans in Acre-street. She died Decr. 22nd, 1863, aged 100 years and 47 days, and was buried Decr. 26th, 1863. She preserved her mental faculties as long as she lived ; and one of her early remembrances was that, in her young days, she had cleaned the shoes of the Rev. John Wesley, when he was on one of his visits to his Society in Stroud.

The Officials of the Burial Board are a Clerk, a Lodge-keeper, and a Grave-digger. Applications for graves, vaults, and interments are made to the Board, at the office of their clerk.

Visitors are much attracted to the Cemetery by its elevated situation and extensive prospects ; and there are many who will remember the attentions of John Isacké, the kind and intelligent Lodge-keeper. He is ever ready to point out the tombs and grave-stones ; and has some-times dropped an interesting word or two concerning those who rest beneath. He is acquainted with entomology, and generally with the other departments of the natural history of the neighbourhood. He knows where the rarest wild-flowers grow, and fossils are found ; and he freely opens his collection of curiosities. He remembers an Echo which, early on the morning of Whit-Monday in 1858, was returned to him four times from Rodborough hill, in reply to the report of a cannon fired from near Heavens on his left-hand. He is the author of "Leisure Hours, a small collection of Poems," which he published in 1846. He willingly describes to the inquiring spectator the various places and objects which lie before him,—whether around or beneath, in the valleys and the sides of the hills that bound them, the river Severn, the Forest of Dean beyond, —and other localities discernible in the extreme distance. Many who have visited the Cemetery will remember John Isacké, who, like the old writer, has long since passed away ; and this large Cemetery is now full of interments and inscriptions, its fine position and the lovely view obtainable from it rendering it attractive.

CHAPTER LVI.

THE BOROUGH OF STROUD.

THE Borough of Stroud was constituted in the year 1832. It was one of the large populous and wealthy towns to which, (with an adjoining district,) the privilege of returning two Members to Parliament was granted by the Reform Act of that year.

Its boundaries, as fixed by the Boundary Act of the same year, included "the several parishes of Stroud, Bisley, Painswick, Pitchcomb, Randwick, Stonehouse, Leonard Stanley, King's Stanley, Rodborough, Minchinhampton, Woodchester, Avening, and Horsley,—except that part of the parish of Leonard Stanley which is called "Lorridge's Farm," and is surrounded by the parish of Berkeley. [1] The small extra-parochial place called "Haywardsfield" has been a part of the borough since 1857, and another extension of it was made in 1868. By the Representation of the People Act of 1867 (sec. 43), Commissioners were appointed to inquire into the boundaries of boroughs; and this borough was accordingly visited by two Assistant Commissioners, the result of whose inquiry was included in the Report of the Boundary Commissioners made on the 5th of February, 1868. The Commissioners, after stating several matters as to the area, population, trade, and other circumstances of the borough, recommended that it should be enlarged, and should consist of "the [then] present borough of Stroud, and such detached portions of the parishes of Standish and Brockthrop as lie between the [then] present borough and the parish of Haresfield." The extension so recommended was confirmed by the Boundary Act of 1868; and, by the operation of the Reform Act of 1867, the number of voters in the borough was increased from 1,399 to 5,642.

[1] In the Reform Act the parish of Eastington was mentioned as one of the parishes, but was omitted from the Boundary Act.

The following is a statement of the several elections which have taken place in the borough.

The first election occurred December 10th and 11th, 1832, when William Henry Hyett, Esq., of Painswick House, Painswick, and David Ricardo, Esq.,[2] of Gatcomb, Minchinhampton, were elected. On that occasion, the candidates, and the number of votes polled for each, were:

Mr. Hyett	985
Mr. Ricardo	585
Mr. Scrope	562

In June, 1833, Mr. Ricardo resigned, and George Poulett Scrope, Esq., of Castle Combe, Wilts, was elected in his place without opposition.

At the general election, January 7th and 8th, 1835, Mr. Scrope was again elected; and Lieut.-Colonel Fox was elected in the place of Mr. Hyett, who had resigned. The candidates, and the number of votes polled for each, were:

Mr. Scrope	866
Lieut.-Colonel Fox	708
Mr. Jelinger Cookson Symonds	187

In May, 1835, Colonel Fox resigned, and Lord John (now Earl) Russell was elected in his stead without opposition.[3]

At the general election, July 25th, 1837, Mr. Scrope and Lord John Russell were elected. The candidates, and the number of votes polled for each, were:

Mr. Scrope	698
Lord John Russell	681
Mr. Sergeant Adams	297

At the general election, June 30th, 1841, Mr. Scrope and William Henry Stanton, Esq., of The Thrupp, Stroud, were elected. The candidates, and the number of votes polled for each, were:

Mr. Stanton	594
Mr. Scrope	529
Sir William Lascelles Wraxall, Bart.	377

At the general election, July 30th, 1847, Mr. Stanton and Mr. Scrope were re-elected. The candidates, and the number of votes polled for each, were:

Mr. Stanton	565
Mr. Scrope	541
Marcus Meryweather Turner, Esq.	177

2 Mr. Ricardo was the eldest son of David Ricardo, Esq., of Gatcomb, the writer of several important works on Political Economy.

3 See p. 78.

At the general election, July 8th, 1852, Mr. Scrope was again elected; and Lord Moreton (afterward the third Earl of Ducie,) was elected in the place of Mr. Stanton, who had resigned. On that occasion, the candidates, and the number of votes polled for them respectively, were:

Mr. Scrope	567
Lord Moreton	529
Samuel Baker, Esq., of Lypiatt Park	488
Mr. John Norton, of Lincoln	315

In June, 1853, Lord Moreton was called to the House of Lords on the death of his father, the Earl Ducie; and Edward Horsman, Esq., was elected without opposition in his stead.

In 1855 Mr. Horsman accepted office as Chief Secretary for Ireland, in Lord Palmerston's Ministry, and was re-elected without opposition.

At the general elections, March 27th, 1857, and April 27th, 1859, Mr. Scrope and Mr. Horsman were re-elected without opposition.

At the general election, July 12th, 1865, Mr. Horsman and Mr. Scrope were again elected, when the candidates, and the number of votes polled for each, were:

Right Hon. E. Horsman	687
Mr. Scrope	685
Hon. Ashley Ponsonby	287

In August, 1867, Mr. Scrope resigned, after having represented the borough nearly thirty-four years; and Henry Selfe Page Winterbotham, Esq., of Lincoln's Inn, was elected to supply his place. He was opposed by John Edward Dorington, junr., Esq., of Lypiatt Park,—the number of votes polled being, for

Mr. Winterbotham	580
Mr. Dorington.......................................	508

At the general election, November 18th, 1868, being the first under the Reform Act of 1867, Sebastian Stewart Dickinson, Esq., of Brownshill House, Painswick, and H. S. P. Winterbotham, Esq., were elected. The candidates, and the number of votes polled for each, were:

Mr. Dickinson	2,907
Mr. Winterbotham	2,805
Mr. Dorington...	2,096

CHAPTER LVII.

AFTER the preceding chapter was sent to press, I had an opportunity of inspecting the churchwardens' book mentioned in page 247. It is a tall, narrow book, in a limp vellum cover ; and was originally tied with leathern thongs, one of which is yet remaining. It begins with "The accounts of Gyles Fylde and Wm. Fletcher, churchwardens of the Chappel of Stroude in the Diocese of Glouc^{r.} Anno Domini 1623," and ends with "The Acc^{t.} of Brice Seed and Richard Bond, churchwardens in the year 1715," including the receipts and payments for all the intermediate years, except those of 1624 and 1675-6-7, which do not appear.

Each separate account, (whether comprising only one year or several years,) is the account of one pair of churchwardens, made out and entered after the expiration of their official term ; and contains an item of 1s., 1s. 6d., or other such sum, "for making out the accounts." Each annual statement appears to extend from Lady-day to Lady-day.

The accounts for the years 1623-1650, and all intermediate years, have been checked, item by item, with the copies "made out" for them ; but those items do not, nor do any others in the book, contain an intimation of their respective dates. Sometimes the accounts are signed by the churchwardens themselves, but oftener by those who were elected for the ensuing year. Five times they are signed, as "seen and allowed," by Jas. Crumpe the minister, and several parishioners ; twice by Robert Pleydell the minister, and others ; and, occasionally, by two or three parishioners alone. Like other documents of a similar kind, the book contains numerous interesting particulars, which illustrate local and national contemporary history; and from these I have collected some additional notes concerning Stroud in the olden time.

The ordinary ancient income of the churchwardens was derived from the rents of the parish property,[1] (which in the year 1623 yielded £15 13s. 4d.,) and from the fees for "breaking up the church" or "the church-ground," for interments, after the rate of 6s. 8d. for each individual; together with a few occasional payments, such as 5s. "for a forfeiture of the Statute"[2] in 1626, and voluntary donations for special purposes. But, at various subsequent periods, their revenue arose from church levies or rates, from money "received for bread and wine at the Sacraments," (by which was meant the offertory-gifts,) and from payments by the overseers of the poor, and the feoffees. Of these, the early church levies were more in the nature of voluntary contributions, than of enforced parish rates.

From entries in the first page of the book, it appears that Mr. Day was the minister here in 1623, but it is not said how long he had been in the office.

In the account for the years 1629 and 1630, there are several sums charged for "work done to Mr. Crumpe's house and garden"; and, in the account for 1632 there is an item of £1 10s. "paid Mr. Crumpe, his stipend for this year and the last." Here, we learn that Mr. Crumpe was the minister in 1631, and that he was Mr. Day's successor. It is to be observed, however, that there was not any entry made in the parish register with his own hand, until the 14th of April, 1631; and that the notice, or memorandum given in page 246, as an extract from the register in 1629, together with the entries to which it refers, (by whomsoever dictated,) were not written by him.

From entries in the account for 1645, we learn that Mr. Stephenson was the minister in that year, and for one entire year only, being three years later than the time previously assigned to him; and that he succeeded Mr. Crumpe. Of him, and his successor Mr. Pleydell, the same account contains the following :—

---

1 For which see page 257.

2 On a conviction of being drunk, by 4th James I.

	£	s.	d.
P^d. Mr. Stephenson for his stipend	00	15	00
P^d. and given to a minister to supply the place on Sabboth when Mr. Stephenson was in London... ...	00	10	00
—for money lay^d. out at newneham for they^r. Dyet passadge 4 & horsemeate that went to Mr. Pleadell the minister	00	05	00
—for Mr. Stephenson's rent one year & ¾	05	05	00
P^d. Tho. Bub for prchment to ingrosse the names of them who did contribut towards Mr. Pledwell for his ministry in Stroud	00	00	10

Here we learn that the inhabitants raised a subscription for Mr. Pleydell, on his becoming their minister ; and, from subsequent entries, that the churchwardens paid the rent of a dwelling-house for him, until they had prepared one of the parish houses as his residence. The following also appears in their account for 1647—"Payde Mr. Pleydell 00 15 00:" and, from this, (being his stipend for a year past,) we infer that he had become the minister in 1646, one year earlier than was assigned to him in the list of ministers. He was buried at Stroud, November 8th, 1679: and an item in that year's account confirms the statement, (hereinbefore made somewhat doubtingly,) that Mr. Phipps became the minister in 1679. It reads thus :—

> Payd att ye Gorge in 5 Strowde for ye Worp^ll 6 ye Chancellors Dynner Mr. Thomas Phipps Minest^r and other ye prishiners... ... ... 00 . 09 . 6

The churchwardens' book was exhibited May 28th, 1740, (marked A.) and put in evidence, in the suit by Bond against Gardner and others before-mentioned, in order to prove the Ministers' original stipend, and its change from 15s. to £15 per annum. This was shown by a reference to various entries contained in it. The first of those entries appears in the year 1632, thus :—

> "Paid Mr. Crumpe for this yeare and the last yeare being due to him by Ancient Composition" ... ... 01 . 10 . 00

This is succeeded by entries of payments to him, to Mr. Stephenson, and to Mr. Pleydell, of 15s. per annum down to, and "for, the year 52" [1652] : and then follow entries of £15, per annum paid to Mr. Pleydell, down to the year 1670. From that year the Minister's stipend ceased to be

4 The fee for being ferried across the Severn, from the parish of Arlingham to the town of Newnham. It is probable that Mr. Pleydell was residing there when appointed minister of Stroud.

5 The George Inn.   6 Worshipful.

paid by the churchwardens; and began to be paid by the feoffees, to whom the parish property had been conveyed by the feoffment of February 12, 1636, as before stated.[7] A reference is made to this deed by the following entries in the account-book, under the date of 1636:—

	£	s.	d.
Paide Mr. Clifford for makeing of the deeds to enfeoff the parish land, and for chardges against us and for Seissin	00	16	00
Paide for 2 quarts of Sack when the deeds were sealled	00	02	00

From hence it may be inferred that the inhabitants approved of the instrument of transfer.

In the account for 1633, which was only three years before, occurs this entry:—

	£	s.	d.
Paide for a Suger loof which was given unto the ladey Bridgman in respect Sir Jo. Bridgman would take noe fee of us for his Councell touchinge the Composission[8]	01	00	00

It is not known what questions were asked of Sir John Bridgman in the case laid before him, nor what counsel he gave. But the fact shows that the inhabitants of Stroud were acquainted with the nature of the Composition; and probably desired that its provisions and objects should be carried into effect.

After the establishment of the doctrines of the Reformation under Queen Elizabeth, the Lord's Supper was more frequently received by the people, than under the former system; and the quantity of wine used was increased accordingly. In the account for the year 1630, the wine amounted to £3 4s. 2½d., in eight items, of which the last two read thus:—

	£	s.	d.
"Paid for 28 quarts of wyne at Easter at 15d. pr. quart...	01	15	00
for bread at Easter	00	00	08

The fourteen several quantities of wine provided for the fourteen Sacraments that occurred between May 8th, 1651, and the Sacrament following Easter, 1653, amounted to "107 quarts of Muskadine," and "seven quarts of Sack, att 20d. per quart." In the year 1625, the churchwardens had

7 See pp. 257-8.

8 Sir John Bridgman resided at his seat, Prinknash, near Upton St. Leonards.

"payde for the exchaing[9] of the comunion cup £02 18s. 00d.,"
whereby they obtained one of larger capacity ; and in 1634
they "P[d.] for two [pewter] flaggons for the Comunion
11s. 8d." The wine was always supplied at the cost of the
parish ; and, from its large increase, the churchwardens
found it expedient to take and place to their general
account "the money received for bread and wine at the
Sacraments," by which they meant the offertory contributions. This they appear to have done for the first time in
1653. The consumption of such large quantities of wine
on the occasions referred to, may probably be accounted
for by the large number of communicants,—the usual
attendance being nearly universal ;—and by the setting
aside a portion of it for the use of the sick and poor of the
parish. It may also be remarked that the churchwardens
were bound to present to the Ordinary those who did not
receive at Easter, or for any considerable time. [10]

In the year 1629, the steeple contained only six bells.
Of these, five were new-cast in that year, at Stroud, in a
house rented for the purpose : and a bell belonging to the
parish of Miserdine was cast there at the same time. The
churchwardens' account contains an item of :—

	£	s.	a.
Paid for p[r]chment and writting of the bonds and articles between the bell-founder and us	00	01	09

Their other payments did not much exceed £12, including the taking down and weighing the bells, "digging and
carriage of earth for to cast the bells, timber," cole,[11] and
"wood to melt the bells, part of the rent, mending the
belfry-floor," &c., &c. Nor were their receipts for that
year more than the usual rent of the parish property,
except 4s. 6d. "for wood and cole and for casting of the
Miserdyne bell," although the account contained an item
of 1s. "paide writing rates for the bells."
On a fly-leaf at the beginning of the book are the following memorandums, apparently written by the same hand
as was the account for the year 1629 :—

9 Exchanging.
10 In the Churchwardens' account for 1681, there is the following entry :—
P[d.] Y[e] Chancellor's fees concerning those persons that did
    not come to receive the Sacrament ... ... £00 . 04 . 00
11 Coal.

The wayte[12] of the five bells wch were new Cast in ye yeare 1629.

	c.	Q.	lb.
The tenor being ye 6th bell wayeth	20	0	24
The 5th bell wayeth...	14	1	24
The 4th bell wayeth...	11	0	18
The 3 bell wayeth	09	0	9
The 2 bell wayeth, wch was not cast nor wayed... ...	08	3	2
The first or treble bell wayeth	08	2	4
Those five new bells are heavier than they weare before they weare cast	5	0	4

Thomas Warner & William Bubb weare churchwardens when the bells weare caste, and Roger Purdue cast them.

There is no item of money paid to the bell-founder for his work, nor for the additional metal supplied by him ; but there were 10s. "paid to Mr. Kirby for tuneing the bells at Mr. Freams [13] appointment." From this, and from the character of the early church levies, it may be conjectured that the bell-founder was remunerated by a voluntary subscription of the inhabitants, raised for the purpose, of which Mr. Fream of Lypiatt Hall may have been the chief promoter.

With respect to the bell that was not recast in 1629, we find the following items in the accounts for 1713 :—

	£	s.	d.
To Mr. Rudhall new-casting the 2d bell, and mending the other bells	10	0	0
To Thos. Okey for taking down the 2d bell, and making a new frame and clock-case	7	15	0
P^{d.} the carriage of the 2nd bell to Glouc^{r.} and back ...	0	10	0

It is the bell, No. 6, in the catalogue of the present bells. [14]

Besides the six bells, the following extracts mention a clock and chimes, with which the belfry was also furnished

		£	s.	d.
1627-8.	Payde William Curr of Cirencester for new makeing the clock...	04	10	0
	Rec^{d.} of the inhabitants of Stroude what they gave towards the making of the clock	01	0	0
1671.	P^{d.} Mr. Giles Reeve of Glouc^{r.} for ye clock & chymes	26	03	00

12 Weight.

[13 The initial letter of Fream is formed by a double f : and at that time [1629] the letters of the alphabet were distinguished not as *capital and small* but as *double and single*. Even now, there are persons who write their names as ffrancis, ffoulkes, or *ffaulconerr*.

14 For which see page 300.

		£	s.	d.
1679.	Payd William Holloway for mending ye church clock	02	10	00
	Received of Thomas Hawker for ye ould church clock	00	12	00
1682.	P^{d.} Henry Elliotts repairing ye chymes & new .Pricking ye Barrell 15 & other necessaries therunto belonging ... ...:	03	00	00
	P^{d.} for a rope for ye chymes...	00	13	00
	P^{d.} for iron work for ye chymes	00	05	00
	Receved by Lead cutt of ye grate wayte belonginge to the chymes	01	05	09
	Received for ye ould roope belonging unto ye chymes sold for	01	00	00

Among the churchwardens' payments, a few fixed sums were due periodically ; and were payable to the Reeve, and to the High constable of the hundred, of Bisley. They appear with the other memorandums in the fly-leaf before-mentioned.

The Reeve was an officer of the lord of the manor, nominated at his court, whose duty was to collect the lord's chief rents. One of them was a yearly sum of 4d. "for rent for the church lands" of Stroud ; which were, without doubt, the "tenement and garden" granted by Robert Bigg.16 Its last payment appears in the account for 1653. The High constable was an officer appointed at the court of the lord of the hundred ; and the sums payable to him were thus stated :

	£	s	d
The Castle money is xvs . iiiid . To be paide at every Assizes...	0	7	8
The maymed souldiers paid is for the whole yeare 21s . 8d . To be payde quarterly at every quarter Sess^{s.}	0	5	5
For the Kings bench & Marshalsies the whole year is xiis . To be payde quartly at every quarter Sess^{s.}	0	3	0

The Castle-money was for the maintenance of the County gaol, into which the old castle of Gloucester, called the Westgate, had been converted. The latest payment made by that description, was in 1662 ; but it seems to have been

15 Pricking a chime-barrel, is inserting the pins or pegs which lift the hammers that strike upon the bells, in a regulated succession both of order and time, and thus is produced the tune to which it is set. It is probable that on the occasion referred to, the barrel was pricked and set to a new tune.

16 For which see page 257.

continued under other names until 1686, when it ceases to
appear. The castle itself was used as the county gaol until
the year 1784. The last payment for maimed soldiers
appears in the account for 1650, and that for the king's
bench and marshalsea, in 1692. Formerly, the office of
High constable comprised many important public duties :
but, after it had existed for nearly a thousand years, these
have been transferred to other hands, by various acts of
parliament, the latest of which was Victoria 32 & 33, c. 47.
The last High constable of this hundred was Mr. Thomas
Davis of Stroud. He was appointed at the court held at
Bisley in the year 1839, and continued to perform the duties
of his office, so long as any such were required of him.

CHAPTER LVIII.

THE OLD BOOK OF CHURCHWARDENS' ACCOUNTS, CONTINUED.

IT has been already ascertained from the will of Samuel Watts, dated 28th January, 1631, that a Lecture had been established, and was then existing at Stroud.[1] But there is not any mention of it in the churchwardens' book, until in their Account of 1646 we read :

	£	s.	d.
P^{d.} Tho. Carter[2] for ringing the bell for the Frydayes lecture for 3 years, 10*s* a yeare which the prish allowed him	01	10	0
P^{d.} Tho. Carter more[3] for ringing the bell, & towards his wages	01	06	08

The Lecturer's name is not there stated, nor is the subject mentioned in it again, for several years : but, in the Account for 1657 there occurs a payment for the lecturer by name, thus :

> For a yeare's ordinary for Mr. Brittan ... 1 . 14 . 8

In the year 1662, we find the following items :

> P^{d.} for Mr. Brittans License to preach frydayes ... ... 00 . 13 . 04
> Paid for Mr. Brittans ordinary ... ... 01 . 14 . 08

There was no payment for the three succeeding years. But in 1666 it began again, and continued, with small variations in the amounts, until 1678, when we read :

> " P^{d.} Mr. Brittans Ordenary ... . 01 . 04 . 08 "

and again in the account for 1679, where it occurs for the last time, thus :

> P^{d.} Thomas Dayle for Mr. Brittans Ordenary 16 days ... . 00 . 10 . 08

1 See p. 258. 2 He was the parish clerk. 3 Meaning an additional sum.

From this entry it may be conjectured that Mr. Brittan's lectureship closed abruptly, probably by illness or death : but there is no reason given, either for the occasional omission of the ordinary, or the variations in its amount, nor for its final cessation. Mr. Brittan had held his office for seventeen, if not for twenty-two years, all during the ministry of Mr. Pleydell. His name was Richard Brittan. He was vicar of Bisley from 1641 to 1679. (See Atkyns 147.)

It will be perceived that the payments made in respect of the Lecturer, were "for his ordinary ;" which meant his dinner 4 when he had preached the lecture-sermon. The sum of £1 14s. 8d. was for a whole year of fifty-two weeks, and was after the rate of 8d. for each lecture-day. This was the only way in which, (as it appears) the inhabitants of Stroud could be said to have paid for his services. He and his successors, however, received from the trustees of Mr. Watts' Charity, a moiety of the produce of the Colthrope property, as their salary, under the trusts of his will.

During the reigns of Elizabeth, James, and Charles, the interferences and innovations of the Ecclesiastical authorities in church-matters were extremely troublesome and expensive, throughout the kingdom. And, in the last two reigns, they became so vexatious, as to form a material portion of the national dissatisfaction which led to the Civil war, the execution of Archbishop Laud, and the beheading of Charles I. "The people were not merely superintended, they were teased and irritated by perpetual visitations and inquiries, often about trifles." The apparitor or summoning officer, (a most obnoxious functionary), "travelled round from parish to parish, taking with him, besides his summons, which he was paid for delivering, a book of articles, or a brief, or a proclamation, or something or other, which was also to be paid for."

Of these proceedings, Stroud experienced a full share. Its churchwardens were cited to attend frequent visitations at Gloucester, Painswick, Minchinhampton, Cirencester, Tetbury and Dursley, which were followed by the payment

4. It appears by this name, in the churchwardens' account for 1656, which reads thus : "Pd. for the minster's diner after the Leckter [Lecture] 01 . 14 . 08."

of fees,—fees on attending, and fees for being excused. On all these occasions they were bound to deliver in a presentment, a return, or a copy of the register of births, deaths, and marriages, which they were obliged to get written out by some paid scribe; and which were not received or filed, without payment of fees to the officers of the court.   They had also to pay the travelling and other expenses of themselves, and all such as represented the parish.   And when the visitations were held at Stroud, they had also to provide for the entertainment of the visitors, the Chancellor, Archdeacon or Bishop; as also of themselves, the minister, and the attending parishioners. These calls on them were very harassing:—and the following cases are taken from among one hundred and fifty entries of a similar kind, found in the churchwardens' accounts for the year 1623, and up to 1639, inclusive. They are examples of the expenses and fees paid, and of the different occasions on which they occurred: illustrating the nature of the grievances alluded to, and justifying the dissatisfaction they had caused.

	£	s.	d.
P^{d.} to Mr. Day [the minister] for making a presentement	00	01	00
P^{d.} Mr. Day for makeing a wrighteing in p^rchement which was delivered into the registers office & for fees	00	01	06
for a briefe to the Channcellor of Thesalonica	00	01	04
To Mr. Suttons man for fees beinge called into the Co^rte.	00	01	04
Gave to two briefs, one a greacian, 5 & the other a barbarian 6	00	02	00
Payde for putt [sic.] in our p^rseatment ...	00	1	4
Payde the Parreter for the viewing of the churche	00	2	0
Layde out at Glou^{r.} when Mr. Jo. Sedgwick* called us thither for fees and expenses ...	00	06	00
Spent at Tetbury to give meeting with Mr. Sedgwick & other ministers	00	00	06
Layde out at vizataeon for fees and o^{r.} 7 dynners	00	10	10
Paide for somons 8 to vizitaeon	0	0	4
Paide Mr. Persur for excusing Mr. Sweeper 9	0	1	0

5 A Greek.   6 One who had been (perhaps a slave) in Barbary.
7 Our.   8 Summons.   9 This was in 1629.
* Vicar of Bisley. [See Atkyns p. 147]

	£	s.	d.
Paide Thomas Wood for 2 books for the fast	0	2	0
Paide him for his paynes for bringing them	0	0	4
Paide Thomas Wood for fees for not appearing at Cirencester	0	1	4
Paide at the Archdeacons Court	oo	02	04
Gave Mr. Sweeper towards his jorney when he went to London being suspended 10 ...	oo	07	06
Paide for making a seate in the church for his ma^{ties} justyces to sit in	oo	oo	08
Paide at Glour att Mr. Chancellors Court, for fees and o^{r.} p^rsentment	oo	03	08
Paide for writting the register	oo	01	04
For excusing Mr. Sweeper 11...	oo	02	06
for passinge the register	oo	01	04
Paid for charges in Bishops Court & for a compossion with Mr. Sedgwick about the pulpitt cloth	oo	17	06
Paide for Mr. Sweepers fees 12	oo	05	06
P^{d.} the paynter for paynting the X Comandem^{ts.} in the church	oo	13	00
Paide for our dynners and horsmeate at the Archbushopps vizitation at Cirencester 13 ...	oo	10	02
Paid for the receipt of o^{r.} p^{r.}sentment... ...	oo	01	06
Paide at vizitation for our dynners, horsmeate, penticost, booke of Articles, and receipt of o^{r.} prsentment	oo	13	02

10 This occurred in 1630. It may be conjectured that Mr. Sweeper was the Walter Sweeper, clerk, who is mentioned in page 247; but that, instead of his having been a chaplain of Stroud (as was there surmised,) he might have been the lecturer, and was suspended from his office because of his attachment to the spiritual views of religion which then began to prevail; and which the ecclesiastical authorities and the government endeavoured to repress. Among the lecturers persecuted about this time was John Workman "a lecturer in the liberty of Gloucester" who was suspended excommunicated and imprisoned for preaching, as it was said against images. The prosecution of Workman was one of the charges against Archbishop Laud on his trial, A.D. 1640—1644. See Howell's "State Trials" IV 477. — Also, Bibliothecæ Gloucestriensis CXXXVI, note 6.

11 This occurred in 1632. 12 This was in 1633.

13 This was in 1635. It was one of Archbishop Laud's Metropolitan visitations, performed by his Vicar General; "wherein, among other things, the churchwardens in every parish were enjoined to remove the Communion table from the middle to the east end of the chancel, altar-wise, the ground being raised for that purpose, and to fence it in with decent rails to avoid profaneness; and the refusers were prosecuted in the High-Commission or Star-chamber courts."—*Historical & General Biographical Dictionary.* London: 1798, V. IXth, 8vo. Art. Laud.

	£	s.	d.
Paide at Glour, being called thither about the Communion table	00	03	04
Paide for the surveys of the church 14... ...	00	04	04
Paide at the Chancellors court for fees & chardges about the surplus 15	00	03	08
Paide For holland for the surplus & makeinge	01	08	06
Paide for bringeing the proclamation from Scotland 16	00	09	04
for a book from the Archdeacon...	00	00	04
Paide at Mr. Chancellors court for the retorne 17 of making the surplus	00	01	00
Paide for a prayer for the King	00	00	04
Paide for a new communion table	00	10	00
„ Mr. Crumpe for a church book... ...	00	08	00
Paide for a certificate at the Chancellors corte for the Kings prclamation and to the Apparieter	00	01	08
Paide at the Archdeocons Corte at Dursley	00	01	02
Paide for a hour-glass for the church 18 ...	00	00	08
Paide for a table of consanguienity and for the retorne of the same into Corte... ...	00	00	10
Paide the 25 Sept. 1639 for wyne & cakes for Mr.Archdeacon when he viewed ye church	00	01	06
Paide Mr. Crumpe expenses laid out at Court	00	03	08
Paide for the hyer19 of a horse to cicester20	00	01	00
Paide at Tetbury for the 2 vizitations for 1638 & 1639	01	03	08

Soon after the year 1639, such entries as the foregoing ceased to appear in the accounts. A great change had come over the spirit of the time. It became an age of earnest men; and was distinguished by thoughts and actions,

14 The consequences of these surveys of the church were, not only the payment of fees, but of money for work done in and about the church and steeple; as is fully shown in the churchwardens' accounts.

15 Surplice.

16 This occurred in 1638. It was, probably, the proclamation that had been issued by Charles I. to the people of Scotland, "in which he exhorted them to submit peaceably to the use of the Liturgy. This proclamation was instantly encountered with a public Protestation."—See Hume's History, c. 53.

17 Return.

18 The use of the hour-glass in churches may be traced back to about the year 1598. It was attached by a frame to the pulpit, or to the wall close to it; and was employed to regulate the length of a sermon. It continued in use until near the Revolution of 1688; but the last hour-glass for the church of Stroud was purchased in 1656.

19 Hire.   20 One of the local names of Cirencester.

such as only earnest men could think and do. The word Puritan, by which they were subsequently designated, was first employed by Spalatro, "who professed himself a Protestant, and used the word to signify the defenders of matters doctrinal in the English church. Formerly the word was only taken to denote such as dissented from the Hierarchy in discipline and church-government, which was extended to brand such as were anti-Arminian in their judgments. As Spalatro first abused the word in that sense, so we could wish he had carried it away with him to Rome. Whereas, leaving the word behind him in this extensive signification thereof, it hath since by others been improved to asperse the most orthodox in doctrine, and religious in conversation ".[21]

William Fletcher and Nathaniel Ridler were elected churchwardens for the year 1640, and continued to serve until the end of 1646. Their accounts were made up and entered after the whole of their official term had expired. In the early part of that period the Market-house underwent considerable repairs and alterations. It is not known what was their precise nature, or extent ; but, from the materials provided and the work and labour done, (so far as can be ascertained from the several items of payment,) it may be inferred that the roof of the building was altered and its tiles relaid, "the pyne-end" (the weak south wall) "was made up," the steps or "stayers" (forming the wide stone staircase) "were put up," the windows and interior were amended, and among other things, the butcher's shops or stalls, with their "pentesses"[22] in the Shambles were repaired and re-tiled. It appears that the sums expended on the Market-house amounted to £80, of which £15 13s. 4d. "were given by some particular men"; and 1s. was pd. for parchment and engrossing theyr names who did contribut [sic] to ye Market-house." From this last item it may be presumed that the public had taken considerable interest in its reparation.

The account of this churchwardenship extends over seven very important years of the Civil war : and, besides the items already extracted from it, we copy four others, for their reference to national affairs :

21 Fuller's Church History, book x. s. 19.
22 Penthouses.

£ s. d.

P^{d.} for o^r dinner, wth the minister & overseers of ye poore, when the Protestation was
given, & for wrighting they names ... ... 00 . 06 . 10

This item is without date ; but, from its local position in
the account, it may be inferred that it was 1642. We are not
told the subject of the protestation : but it may be supposed
to have contained a declaration, by those whose names were
appended to it, of their political opinions ; and that its name
was adopted from the Scottish protestation, mentioned in
note 16. It is well known that, (like merchants and traders
in general,) the people of Stroud sided with the Parliament
in the great struggle that agitated the nation.

Payde for paving the church where a soldier
was buried ... ... 00 . 01 . 00

P^{d.} for Leading & glassing [23] the church
wyndoes being broken by the soldiers and
prisonners ... ... 01 . 10 . 00

Here we have an incidental evidence of active hostilities
having taken place between the royalist and the parliamentary forces, perhaps in the neighbourhood of Stroud ;
and that the captives were secured in the church ; but the
particulars of the encounter are not stated.

Given to John Smyth gent. who lost all his
estates in Ireland ... ... 00 . 02 . 00

Gave two Irishmen ... ... 00 . 01 . 00

Gave to a poore man who had lost his estate
in Ireland by the rebells ... ... 00 . 00 . 06

The distress indicated by these and the many other items
of a similar kind, in this and the several succeeding years,
was referable to the insurrection in Ireland under Sir
Phelim O'Neale, and to the massacre of forty thousand
Protestants there, in the year 1641. Its cruelty has never
been exceeded.[24]

P^{d.} for a new Directory from the Committe
& by theyre warrant the 8th [Oc] tober 1645 00 . 01 . 06

By an ordinance passed the 3rd day of January, 1644,
the Book of Common Prayer had been "taken away ; "
and the Directory " put into execution for the public
worship, " in its stead. And by another ordinance passed
the 23rd of August, 1645, the Parliamentary Committees
were directed to send " printed books " of the Directory,
"fairly bound up in leather," with all speed to the

23 Glazing.
24 See Hume's narrative of it in his History of England, chap. 55.

constables or other officers in every parish, "to be paid for by the inhabitants," and to be delivered to the minister. It seems that no time was lost in the delivery of a copy of it to the churchwardens of Stroud, with a warrant for its being used.

From the end of this churchwardenship, down to and including that of 1660, we do not find an item which refers to any of the great political events of the intervening period. Even the Restoration of the monarchy under Charles II. is not indicated until the year after it occurred ; and then only inferentially, by the following entry in the churchwardens' account for that year :—

		£	s.	d.
1661.	Pd. the Ringers on Coronation day...	00	. 02	. 0

There were, however, other, and very different, evidences of that event in subsequent accounts. With the restoration of monarchy came the restoration of episcopacy ; and, with episcopacy came back our old acquaintance the apparitor, with his summonses, briefs, proclamations, and books ;— visitations, presentments, transcripts of registers, pentecosts, &c, and their accompanying fees and expenses, all augmented in number and pecuniary amount. Items of this kind are found in each of the succeeding churchwardens' accounts.

The return of episcopalian discipline and worship was generally regarded with favour. The church was restored, and resumed its former officials, its goods, and ornaments ; concerning which, and a few other significant subjects, we return to the old book for information.

1661.	Pd. John Lewes for mossing 25 ye church ...	01 . 07 . 6
	Paide Thomas Taylor for fetching the moss	00 . 05 . 0
	Pd. for the communion table	00 . 19 . 0
	Pd. for a communion table cloath	00 . 15 . 0
	Pd. for the cover of the font	00 . 02 . 6
1662.	Pd. for the Prayer booke 26	00 . 07 . 06

25 Mossing a building, is the act of putting moss between the tiles of its roof, to keep out the wind. It still is, or it lately was, practised in some parts of the kingdom.

26 This was the Book of Common Prayer, established by the Act of Uniformity, 14 Charles II., c. 4 ; under which two thousand ministers, who did not conform to it, were deprived of their livings.

		£	s.	d.
1670.	Paide for 13 ells of fine Holland to make a serplus for Mr. Pleydell	05	04	00
	Payde for a communion cup & cover	05	7	6
	Paide for makeing ye serplus	00	10	00
	Paide for washing ye serplus	00	01	00
	Paide a messinger to fetch Mr. Dorwoods 27 serplus to make one by itt	00	00	08
1671.	Pd. for the Kings armes & carridge	05	02	06
	Pd. for setting up the Kings Armes	00	08	00
1674.	Pd. Mr. Medos 28 for bewtefeing ye church...	05	12	00
1678.	Pd. Tho. Travis pointing the grate Steeple	11	03	06
	Pd. pointing ye Litle steepl 29	01	00	00
	Pd. setting upp ye railes and for bords in the chancell	00	06	08
	Pd. the apparitor for a process before the steeple was pointed	00	03	00
	Pd. fees at ye Worpll. ye Chancellors court to satisfie them that the church & steepl and the bounds belonging was repared	00	01	00
1679.	Pd. Mr. Toby Longford for a Service Booke	00	14	06
	Pd. for a booke of Articles	00	01	00
	Pd. Samuel Longdon repairing ye minesters desk and clarks pew	00	13	00
1680.	Pd. for a pewter flaggon	00	10	06
1681.	Pd. mattin ye rayles round the communion table	00	02	01
1682.	Pd. bindinge ye Church Bible with new claspes	00	07	00
1683.	Pd. binding Bishopp Jewell Booke & [for a] desk 30	00	19	00
	Pd. Wm. Pitt for alteringe ye Chancell doore 31	01	00	00
	Pd. Jno. Collins for a new oken doore	01	00	00
	Pd. for a booke of Homyles	00	10	00

27 Mr. [George] Dorwood was vicar of Painswick. Atkyns, 314.

28 Meadows.

29 This was the spire or bell-turret of the old chapel, mentioned in pages 296-7-8.

30 The desk on which it was laid, that the people might read it. This book was The defence of his Apology, &c., and was ordered to be read and chained up in all the parish churches. It had formed a part of the scanty list of "goods belonging to the church or chapel of Stroude, delivered by Mr. Hodges unto Robert Vyner and Thomas Clissold, churchwardens elected," the 19th day of April, 1635.

31 This was the chancel door mentioned in page 295.

		£	s.	d.
1685.	P^d Knowles for an order to kneel 32	oo	. oi .	oo
1686.	P^d. o^r Lord Bishops Ordinary	oo	. o5 .	oo
	P^d. ye ringers 3 several days at o^r Lord Bishops preaching 33	oo	. o7 .	o6
1687.	P^d. Jno. Webb Tho. Rogers & D. Parry to meet ye L^d. Bishop	oo	. 16 .	oo
1688.	P^d. ye ringers on ye day of thanks giving and delivery from Popery 34	oo	. 10 .	oo
1693.	P^d. for a new holland table cloth & napkin	oo	. 18 .	o6
1694.	A new basin for ye font...	oo	. o5 .	oo
1699.	P^d. ye brasier for two plates for to carry ye bread at ye sacrament	oo	. o2 .	o6
1700.	P^d. Rich. Derritt 35 for keeping the boys in order at church	oo	. o5 .	oo
1705.	P^d. for cloth to make R. Derritt a coat &c	o	. 17 .	o6
	P^d. for makeing ye coat & cap	o	. 5 .	o
1706.	P^d. Wm. Shatford clerck, his wages	oi	. 10 .	oo
1707.	P^d. for a rich pulpit cloth of purple in grain plush, and cushon, with gold and silk freing & lineing...	8	. oi .	7
	P^d. for makeing ye pulpit cloth and cushon, and altering ye old cloth to cover ye two reading desks, and new dyeing the freing ...	o	. 10 .	o
	P^d. for ye two tables of ye ten comandem^ts. and ye two tables for ye Lords Prayer and the creed &c	12	. o .	o

32 Probably, until this order, the communicants at the Lord's Supper had received the bread and wine in a sitting posture, according to the Directory.

33 Doctor Robert Frampton was the Bishop of Gloucester at this time; and it seems that he preached here three several days. On February the 1st, 1690, he was deprived for refusing to take the oaths then appointed.

34 This relates either to the acquittal of the Seven Bishops, whom James II. had prosecuted for a seditious libel; or to the Revolution, by the abdication of James, and the nomination of William and Mary to the Throne.

35 R^d. Derritt was the parish beadle. Besides "keeping the boys in order at church," the beadle's office was to drive out the dogs; on which account the beadle, (in my young days,) was called the Dog-whipper.

CHAPTER LIX.

THE OLD BOOK OF CHURCHWARDENS' ACCOUNTS CONCLUDED —
ADDITIONAL OBITUARY AND OTHER NOTICES.

THE ordinary expenditure of the parish comprised
payments for the destruction of vermin. These were
otters, badgers, foxes, hedgehogs, polecats, jays, and bull-
finches; the last of which were called hoops. Accordingly
in the accounts we find:

		£	s.	d.
1623.	Paid unto Tho. Webb & Abel Poole for 5 otters headss killed & landed in our parish	00	05	00
1646.	P^d· a boy for five hedghogs he catched in John Griffins ground, 2d. apiece...	00	00	10
"	P^d· to a boy for five hedghogs taken in Mr. Freame's grounds	00	00	10
1688.	P^d· for hedghogs jays & fox heds...	00	12	00
1700.	P^d· for Bagers, greys [1] & hedghogs	00	02	07
"	P^d· for 6 foxes and a polecatt	0	06	06
1712.	for foxes, hoops & hedghogs...	00	3	0
1713.	for 16 foxes 11s. & 28 hedghogs 5s/9d ...	0	16	9
1714.	for 5 foxes 3 hedghogs & one Auter [an otter]	0	6	4

And all the other accounts abound with items of a
similar kind. The otters, badgers, and foxes were generally rated at one shilling, hedgehogs and polecats at twopence, apiece. But such payments have long since ceased
to burden the parish rates. It has been ascertained that
some of the so-called vermin are more useful than mis-
chievous; and that others are altogether harmless; while a
systematic destruction of one class of them has resulted in
the injurious increase of another.

1 Another term for a badger.

Among the charitable gifts specified in the Old Book, are the following :—

		£	s.	d.
1642.	Gave two women whose husbands were Slaves in Turkey	00	01	00
"	Given to a merchant who had 2 sons in slavery in Turkey	00	01	06

At that time, the Corsairs of Barbary made slaves of the sailors and others whom they took prisoners in their piratical expeditions at sea. The deplorable condition of these unfortunate men excited both the sympathy and indignation of the European states, whose subjects were the victims. And, in the year 1655, Oliver Cromwell, as Lord Macaulay tells us, "avenged the common injuries of Christendom on the pirates of Barbary." [2]

Under the instructions of the Protector, Admiral Blake sailed for Algiers, Tunis, and Tripoli, to demand satisfaction for the piracies committed on the English, and a release of all English captives. The Algerines and the Dey of Tripoli complied with his demands ; but the Dey of Tunis, confiding in the strength of his defences, treated Blake's message with contempt. " Here," said he, " are our castles of Goletta and Porto Ferino, do your worst! Do you think we fear your fleet ? " Blake, curling his whiskers, as he was accustomed to do when in a passion, consulted his officers, and bore into the bay with his heavy ships ; demolished the castle, burnt the shipping in the haven, and forced the haughty and obstinate Dey to humble submission, and an advantageous peace.

The Sallee rovers, however, continued to make slaves of the English whom they took at sea ; and, in the Old Book, is an account of :

Money collected in the Parish of Strowde for the redeemein of Christians out of slavery from the Turks, in the yeare of oᵣ Lord god 1670 : by Mr. Robert Pleydoll minister, and Thomas Ridler and Samuell Bubb Churchwardens.

Then follow the names of 143 contributors, with the several sums given by them. The total amount is £3 14s. 4d., of which thirty-five items are under twopence each; and beneath them is written :—

2 Macaulay's History of England, v. i. The Protectorate of Oliver Cromwell.

Paid this money unto my Lord Bishopp of Gloucester 3 to the hands of Mr. George Evans his secretary, the eight day of Febbruary in the yeare of o^r· Lord god 1670.

SAM BUBB
THOS. RIDLER.

In the same Old Book, is the following item :—

£   s.   d.

1690.	Gave towards ye Redemtion of Thomas Gill and Richard Slater, and to [two ?] other poore people wth lawful passes	00 . 07 . 03

And here it may be noted that, in 1816, (160 years after Blake's expedition,) another English Admiral, Lord Exmouth, bombarded the city of Algiers, delivered 1,200 Christians from captivity, and put an end to the slavery of Christian men in Barbary.

In a blank page, opposite the Churchwarden's accounts for 1666, is the following :—

Collected and gathered upon the fast day, the 10th of October 1666, the sum of Two pounds one shilling towards the relief of them who were sufferers in the Lamentable Fire in the Citty of London. The money was paid the 19th day of October by me, William Bond to Mr. Thomas Pleyen Chamberlayne, as may appear by his receipt pinned on to this book. 4

JAMES LANDER, } Churchwardens.
JOHN BOND.

Besides the parish paupers who were relieved by the Overseers of the Poor, other cases of want and necessity were attended to by the Churchwardens, out of their own special funds. Of these, the most numerous were persons empowered, by parish and other authorities, to beg from place to place ; and the following are examples of the different classes, extracted from their accounts :—

1648.	To Goody Witsone	0 . 1 . 0
"	Paid a maymed Captain	0 . 0 . 6
"	To a poore man	0 . 1 . 0
"	To Goodwife Browne that lost her sight ...	0 . 1 . 6
"	To a poore distressed woman	0 . 1 . 6
1657.	To a man, woman & 9 children that came with a breife	0 . 1 . 0

3 Dr. William Nicholson was the Bishop of Gloucester.

4 The receipt has disappeared,—the pin-marks remain.

		£	s.	d.
1662.	P^{d.} a Captn. that had orders...	oo	. 01	. o
"	P^d to severall travellers that came with breifes and certificates	oo	. 07	. 06
1666.	P^{d.} to poore travelling people that came with orders	oo	. 06	. 4
1667.	P^{d.} to several poor ministers	oo	. 06	. o
1689.	P^{d.} to several poor people that had lawful Passes	oo	. 06	. o
1694.	To travellers seamen and soldiers	oo	. 13	. 6
1700.	Gave to a Letter of request	oo	. 02	. 06
1707.	To Captn. Hamilton loss of his Limbs &c....	o	. 03	. o
1714.	To a man with a Testimonial to New Eng^{d.}	o	. 1	. 6
"	to a woonded Souldier wth an order	o	. 1	. 6
"	to a man wth an ord from ye Secretary of War	o	. 1	. o
1633.	Paid Mr. Draper for apparell for 2 poore boys, Bracie & Ridler	oo	. 19	. oo
1635.	Paide for 17 payre of Indentures...	oo	. 17	. oo
"	Paide, being called to Painswick before the Justices about placing apprentizess	oo	. 02	. 06
1638.	Paide for Cloth & Stocking and other apparell for Vens child at Whellings	oo	. 08	. 09
"	Paid Susan Arundall for keepinge the child	oo	. 04	. oo
1659.	For cloathes at the binding of Wid Collings sonne to Henry Parker	oo	. 04	. 04
"	for 3 paire of Indentures to binde 2 off Rob Paynes children & one of Collings	oo	. 07	. 6
1671.	P^{d.} Binding Solomon Hobsons [son] an apprentize unto Rich : Pitt	o1	. oo	. oo
"	P^{d.} placeing John Gardner sonne an apprentize unto Edward Cowely	o1	. 17	. 6
"	P^{d.} placeing James Rowland an apprentize unto Sam : White	o1	. o1	. oo
1692.	To Robt. Perks 5 to cure the Wid. Lewes ...	oo	. 05	. oo
1694.	To Dr. Capel 6 bleeding a poor man	oo	. oo	. 6

5 Persons of this name are, at present, resident in the neighbourhood.
6 For the monument and epitaphs of Dr. Capel and his son, see p. 307.

		£	s.	d.
1695.	P^d· Perks for cureing John Restells Legg and Nicholls childs broken Legg...	01 . 10 .	0
1704.	P^d· to Robert Perks cureing Russel	1 . 0 .	0
1638.	Paid for a shroude for Richard Arindall that dyed in the hay tallett 7	00 . 01 . 09
1647.	Paid for a Srewde for Boulies child	0 . 2 .	6
"	Payd for a Srewde for ould Leuse	0 . 3 .	6
1670.	Paide for a shirt and shrewde for Blanch his boy, & to Mary Spencer for keeping him and diging ye grave & carrieing to church	00 . 7 . 00
"	A shrewde & diging ye grave laieing out & carrieing to church Stephen Browne of ye Tithing of Packenhill	00 . 7 . 6
"	A Shrewde for Goodman Chew	00 . 4 . 4
"	A Shrewd for homes [Holmes] 8 and diging ye grave	00 . 4 . 4

There are three more items to be noticed :—

1666.	P^d· William Wake which he p^d to the high Constable for repairing the beacon	00 . 07 . 6

At the time here alluded to, England was at war with
Holland and France ; which, perhaps, caused the repairing
of the beacon.   There are the sites of two ancient beacons
in the neighbourhood.   One of them is Beacon-hill, at the
western end of Broad-barrow Green ; 9 and the other is
Beacon-hill, on high ground in a field called Beaconfield, in
the parish of Sapperton. 10   The turnpike-road from Cirencester to Minchinhampton passes close by it, at about six
miles from the former place, and near to an alehouse called
"The White Horse."   We are not told where the repaired
beacon was situated ; but, most probably, it was at one of
those places.

7 Tallet.   A hay-loft over a stable.

8 Persons of this name, (generally pronounced Homes,) have long been,
and still are, resident in Pakenhill.   William Holmes is the name of the aged
Blacksmith and Nestor of the village, mentioned in p. 221.

9 For this beacon see pp. 84 and 86.

10 For which see Rudder, p. 642.

£   s.   d.

1685.   P^{d.} to the ringers at the takeing of ye Duke,
and ye day of Thanksgiving... ... ...   oo . 10 . oo

This item relates to the capture of the Duke of Monmouth,
after the defeat of his army at Sedgemoor, near Bridge-
water, the 5th day of July in that year.   He was taken
prisoner two days after the battle ; and was beheaded the
15th of July, on Tower-Hill.   The people might well
rejoice and give thanks for the overthrow of a causeless
rebellion and invasion, such as that of Monmouth.   Yet,
we must ever lament the excessive cruelties which marked
the military and judicial executions that followed the
victory, at the hands of Lord Feversham, Colonel Kirke,
and chief Justice Jefferies.

1712.   Expended at 3 several Sessions and one
Assizes, to prevent supernum^rye Ale houses
y^t doth advance ye poors book — &c.... ...   2 . o . o

From this we learn that the old Churchwardens were
fully aware of the evil effects of alehouses, and had made
attempts to reduce their number.   They, however, increased ; and intemperance, and its thousand evils, increased with them.   In the year 1804 there were seventeen
such houses in the parish : at present there are thirty-nine
alehouses and forty-five beerhouses.

A final reference has now been made to the contents of
the Old Book of Churchwardens' accounts : and it only
remains to add a few obituary and other notices, required
by recent events and proposed improvements.

Since the list of interments in Holy Trinity churchyard
was sent to press, the remains of Joseph Timbrel Fisher,
of Stroud, were deposited in a vault there.   He departed
this life the 23rd day of August, 1869, aged 84 years.

On the 24th of January, 1870, the body of Elizabeth
Williams, widow of the Rev. John Williams, D.D., was laid
in the grave-yard of the parish church, in the vault where
her husband was buried thirteen years before. [11]   She died
at Bromsgrove, in the county of Worcester, the preceding
18th day of January, in the 82nd year of her age.

11 See p. 289.

On the 31st day of March, 1870, the mortal remains of William Henry Stanton, Esq., of The Thrupp, [12] were deposited in the family vault, in the old parish churchyard. He died March the 24th, 1870, in the 80th year of his age.

In the Cemetery has been placed the last monumental work which the lamented Joshua Wall prepared for that place. It consists of a recumbent slab, which (on a rising base of three steps,) supports an upright cross, bearing a wreath of emblematical flowers,—all of white marble. On the base is inscribed—" FLORENCE MARY STANTON, born August 16, 1866. Died December 18, 1868." The deceased was the eldest daughter of Walter John Stanton, Esq.

Lansdown, (which in 1864 shewed its first signs of 'becoming a street,' in continuation of King-street), [13] has made a rapid progress. Already, on its northern side is the printing establishment of the *Stroud Journal*, with several dwelling-houses and business offices. As a road, its suggested extension into Slad-road, at a point beyond Little Mill, [14] is also in course of formation ; and when completed it will be, indeed, 'a public benefit,' by opening a nearly level communication with the town, to and from the districts in that direction. [15]

The westward side of Gloucester-street is now completed : and, at its lower end may be noted the Baths,—a complete and commodious building, comprising Turkish, swimming, and general baths. It belongs to a large body of local shareholders ; and is a valuable addition to the accommodations of the town. It has given its name to the new street, which enters Gloucester-street at this place, from the middle of old King-street.

The Golden Heart Inn, as well as the Chequers, having been taken down, new houses and shops are built on both their sites ; and the entrance from King-street into Gloucester-street has been improved.

The proprietors of the Great Western Railway have made a road from the eastward end of their Goods Station, into the London-road, nearly opposite to Union-street. [16]

12 See p. 211.

13 See p. 92.

14 Pp. 92 and 143.

[15 This improvement has of course been long since effected, and is much used. A public Cattle Market has also been established on its northern side.]

[16 The old writer did not live to see the introduction of the Midland Railway (so long desired) into Stroud ; nor the great extension of the suburbs of Stroud called " The Uplands " and " Horns-road."

Here the writer lays down his pen toward the close of a serene autumn day, in the ninety-second year of his age : wishing happiness to all who may find pleasure in the past history of Stroud ; or who shall take a worthy part in forming a new one,—to be as lovingly and faithfully chronicled by some future Old Inhabitant.

APPENDIX A.

Page 232.

GRANT OF THE RECTORY OF BISLEY.

An extract,—with the contracted words written in full, from the Letter Patent of 3 James, 17 July, (1606,) whereby the King granted to Lawrence Baskervile and William Blake various lands and rectories ; and among the latter—

Totam illam rectoriam sive prebendam nostram de Bisley, alias dictam primam et secundam prebendam sive portionem decimarum de Bisley prædicta in prædicto comitatu nostro Gloucestriensis, cum suis juribus membris et pertinentiis universis . . . . . Reddendo . . . de et per prædictam rectoriam de Bisley ac cetera premissa eidem rectoriæ pertinentia triginta tres libras decem solidos . . . . . Et prædicti Laurencius Baskervile et Willielmus Blake . . . . . conveniunt . . . quod ipsi de tempore in tempus imperpetuum sumptibus suis propriis expensa invenient et providebunt unum sufficientem curatum seu ministrum apud Stroudwater in comitatu Gloucestriensis, et duos decanos, videlicet, unum apud Stroudwater prædictam, et alterum apud Bisleighe, in prædicto comitatu Gloucestriensis, ad divina servitia ibidem celebranda et tot et quicquid quod ad divinum cultum pertinet ibidem peragenda ac nos . . . inde acquietabunt imperpetuum."

APPENDIX B.

Page 235.

Copy of the original Composition of Stroud. The contractions in the original words are here given at length :—

"Universis pateat quod cum inter dominos Henricum Averey et Robertum dictum le Eyre, Rectores primæ et secundæ portionis ecclesiæ de Bysseleye, et Willelmum, Vicarium loci ejusdem, ex parte unâ, ac Thomam de Rodebarowe, Willelmum Proute, Henricum de Monemuwe, Nicholam le Seymore, Henricum le Fremer et cæteros habitatores Capellæ de Strode, per Willelmum Benet et Ricardum filium Ricardi procuratores conjunctim et divisim, legitimè constitutos, et in posterum personaliter comparent factum ipsum procuratorum ratum habentes ex alterâ. Super refectione Cancelli (cancellæ in copy) capellæ de Strode et quibusdam rebus aliis litium et dissentionis materia fuisset extortâ ; Demum in nostri præsentiâ W. Burdon tunc Archidiaconi Gloucestriensis conquievit in hunc modum videlicet : QUOD CUM inter ipsam Capellam de Strode et suam Matricem ecclesiam de Bysseleye tantam et tam periculosam distantiam existere nullatenus ambigatur propter quam in parvulis baptizandis et aliis ecclesiasticis Sacramentis ministrandis gravia animarum pericula possint verisimiliter evenire ; quibus ut tenentur obviare (opinare in copy) (1) volentes Rectores et Vicarius (vicarii in the copy) antedicti quatenus in iis est volunt et consentiunt quod in ipsâ Capellâ de Strode sumptibus habitatorum ejusdem de cætero fiat Baptisterium et in eodem ministretur Baptismi sacramentum : Capellanus etiam per prædictos Rectores electus pariter et admissus in ipsâ Capellâ ecclesiastica quotidie ministraturus Sacramenta continue resideat in futurum : ita tamen quod area seu tenementum in la Strode, quam vel quod Iohannes de Pridie pro certo redditu hactenus tenuit de Rectoribus antedictis ad mansum ejusdem sacerdotis deputetur per eosdem per ipsos tamen habitatores de Strode supradictos (supredctos in the copy) (cum in eorum commodum area hujusmodi assignetur) edificabitur competenter. Et quotiescunque seu quandocunque ædificium hujusmodi reparatione vel emendatione indiguerit qualicumque, totum fiat sumptibus eorundem. Reddant etiam inde ibidem annuatim iidem habitatores ipsis Rectoribus octodecim denarios sicut hactenus fieri consuerunt, ad stipendium vero præfati Capellani quindecim solidos ad tres anni terminos, scilicet ad festum Sancti Michaelis, Natalis Domini, et in festo Purificationis Beatæ Virginis pro equalibus portionibus exsolvendos ipsi habitatores contribuent annuatim. Qui si malitiose et in dispendium ipsius Capellani satisfacere, (quod absit,) cessaverint in iisdem, volunt et consentiunt partes antedictæ, quod præordinata penitus cesset Cantaria illa tamen inibi habita et obtenta quæ prius fieri consuevit : prædictum etiam tenementum ad eosdem Rectores libere absque contradictione quâlibet revertatur. Idem etiam Capellanus in villatis, (2) utriusque Lepeyate, Strode et de Paganhull cum totâ villatâ de Bourne a domo seu tenemento quæ quondam Seredhous vulgariter nuncupabatur (nuncu patur in the copy) usque ad Capellam de Strode, sæpedictam omnia et singula administrabit Sacramenta. Clericus autem ipsi Capellano in eâdem Capellâ continuè ministraturus juxta Rectorum arbitrium, admissus et cum expedierit amovendus ab iisdem quod consueverat una cum eo quod Clericus beneficiarius in Capellâ de Paganhull pro suis obsequiis ab ipsis habitatoribus solebat, impendi percipiat in futurum. Super vero refectione cancelli Capellæ de Strode partes unanimiter convenerunt in hunc modum, videlicet, Quod ipsi Rectores gablum (3) ipsius cancelli ruinosum funditus si indigeat reparabunt et fenestram præordinatam in eodem sumptibus suis propriis duntaxat ista vice faciant competenter, omnes autem et singulos cæteros defectus loci supra-dicti habitatores reficiant antedicti. Ex nunc onus reparationis reedificationis cooperturæ tam ipsius gabli et fenestræ quam totius cancelli supradicti quoties opus fuerit in se et suos successores in perpetuum assumentes. In omnibus vero oblationibus, obventionibus, decimis, solutionibus, collectis tam ad campanarum quam corporis ecclesiæ refectionem cæterisve contributionibus ac juribus quibuscunque ab antiquo quomodolibet debitis et consuetis prædictæ ecclesiæ de Bysseleye ut suæ matrici prædicta Capella de Strode et epsius habitatores perpetuo ut hactenus subditi et subjecti permaneant in futurum. Ad horum autem omnium et eorum cujuslibet observantiam ad sancta Dei

(1) "The grammatical construction is here very involved, but the meaning seems plain. The involved grammar is preserved here and in the translation."

(2) "Properly speaking, the inhabitants of a village or vill."

(3) "Gablum,—frons ecclesiæ, frontispicium. Du Cange. Here it means the east end."

Evangelia corporali præstito juramento partes antedictæ se invicem obligarunt.
In quorum testimonium et fidem Nos. W. Burdon Archidiaconus antedictus
huic præsenti scripto ad modum chirographi inter dictas partes confecto ad
ipsarum procurationem et instantiam sigillum nostrum duximus apponendum.
Scriptum Gloucestriæ iv^{to} Calendas Augusti Anno Domini millesimo tricen-
tesimo quarto."

APPENDIX C.

Page 253.

XX° Septembris 1644. At the Committee by ordynance
of Parliament for Glouc^r. Hereff &c. sitting at the usuall
place neere the Kinge's Bourd in Gloucester—

Whereas Thomas Potter Clerke late incumbent of the parishe church of
Nimpsfeild in the Countie of Gloucester is by this comittee eiected and put
from the said parishe Church and Service of the Cure there and the Tythes
and proffitts thereunto belonginge, uppon iust cawses fullie and dulye prooved
upon Oath before this Comittee, And forasmuch as the parishiors of the said
parishe have manifested their desire to have Mr. Willm. Hart a Godlie and
faythfull Minister to serve the said Cure, Whereof this Comittee doe approove
and doe this daie order that the said Mr. Hart shalbe and is placed in the said
Parsonage and Parishe Church to serve the said Cure of Nimpsfeild. And to
have receave and take the Tythes revenues and proffitts to the said Parsonage
belonginge to his owne use in as full and Ample manner as any Minister or
person in the said place have formlie used to doe.

Ex per Halford.

Tho : Pury.
Jam : Kyrle.
Will : Shepheard.

INDEX.

The letter " n " after the number of a page stands for note.

Knapp, The, 16, 319.
Knapp Estate, The, 217.
Knight, Charles, a missionary in Sierra Leone, 284, 285.
Knight, Joseph, a missionary to Ceylon, 284, *n, n,* 285.

Lamb Inn, 54, 111, 180.
Lamburn, Matthew, 15.
Lansdown, 92 ; road, 92, *n,* 158, 362.
Laud, Archbishop, 259, *n,* 347 ; his Metropolitan Visitation, 349, note 13.
Leazes, The, 24, 144.
Lecturer, a, Watts' bequest for, 258, 263, 346, 347 ; chosen by inhabitants, 259, 263 ; called Friday Lectures ; Mr. Brittan, 346, 347, was vicar of Bisley,—see Corrections and additions in page 347.
Leversage, Peter, 136, 215.
Leversage, Grazebrook, and Burgh, Brewers, 136.
Leversage and Watts, Brewers, 136.
Lewis, Edith, *alias* Old Idleehous, 24.
Lewis, Joseph, writer of "John, a model," 81.
Lewis, William, of Lypiatt, 198, 199, 202, 213.
Library and reading room, 170, 172, 173, 175.
Little Mill, 57, 58, 94, *n,* 216.
Local Board of Health, 65, 158, 159.
Lodgemore Mill burned down, 133, *n.*
Lodgemore Volunteers, Capt. George Hawker, 82.
London-road, 35, 156.
Long Parliament, ordinances of, 251, 252.
Longtree, Bisley, and Whitstone Volunteer Cavalry, 73, 74, 90, 184.
Lord's Supper, in the, The Cup was not withheld from the Laity in 1360, 241, 243 ; the quantity of wine used was increased after the Reformation, 341, 342.
Loveday, Thomas, of Painswick, 119.
Lower-street, 11, 12, 31.
Lushington, Sir Stephen, his opinion on the patronage of the curacy, 249.
Lynch, Chalford, and France, 146, 147.
Lypiatt, Upper :—Manor and Estate, 191-202, 230, 231 ; Stephenses of Lypiatt, and successive owners of the Estate, 191-199 ; Tithing of, and Estates therein, 200-206.

Lypiatt House, garrisoned for the Parliament in the Civil War, 194 ; its accordance with Kip's print of it, 201 ; the chapel, 200, 201, *n* ; the hall, 201, 202 ; alterations, &c., in, by Mr. Wathen, 202.
Lypiatt, Lower, Manor, Tithing, &c., 209, 210.
Lypiatt Hall, 209 ; other Estates, 209, 215.
Lypiatt, Middle, 214, 215.

"Machine," the London, a stage-coach, 109.
Machinery, riots concerning, 292.
Maggot's Bridge, 127, 131, 132.
Mail coaches, 54, 111, 112.
Maimed soldiers, payments for, 345.
Malvern Hills, 3, 87, 88.
Mansell's Mead, 8.
Map of Stroud, by John Wood, in 1835, 92, 144.
Market - house, the situation and description of, including ornamental front or buttress work, 60, 61, 62, 63, 64 ; its supposed erection and builder, 61 ; repairs and alterations about 1640, 351 ; schoolmasters and schoolroom, 56, 57, 64, 66 ; Justice-room fitted up in 1816 and called "The Townhall," 64 ; public meetings at, 65, 273 ; alterations in 1865, 65 ; Sunday school introduced in 1784, 277.
Market-day, on Fridays, 10.
Market-place, 60, 271, 273.
Marlborough Head Inn, 45, 77, 78.
Marriages, during the Commonwealth, 251, 252.
Martin, Mills, and Wilson, their Bank, 48, 142.
Mason, old Peter, 33.
Masonic Hall, 141.
Masters' coach, 107, 109, 111.
Maurice, Prince, his protection of Samuel Webb against plunder by soldiers, 212, 213.
Maypoles, at the Cross, 20 ; and at Pakenhill, 220.
Mechanics' Institute, 166, 173 ; Reading Society, 173.
Meeting-street, 12, 14.
Merlin, a prophecy of, (satirical poem), 38.
Merry Walks, The, 159.
Middle Hill, 143, 144, 203.
Middle-street, 12, 13, 14, 15.